Homeland Security Law Handbook

Anthony H. Anikeeff

Edwin R. Bethune

Larry S. Gage

Robert F. Housman

Stacey Kalberman

Albert B. Krachman

Glenn B. Manishin

E. Dee Martin

Lara B. Mathews

Nancy Morrison O'Connor

Lisa J. Savitt

Rebecca L. Sigmund

Jonathan K. Waldron

ABS Consulting
Government Institutes
Rockville, Maryland

Government Institutes
4 Research Place, Rockville, Maryland 20850, USA
Phone: (301) 921-2300
Fax: (301) 921-0373
Email: giinfo@govinst.com
Internet: http://www.govinst.com

ISBN: 0-86587-962-1

Printed in the United States of America

Summary Contents

Part I Scope of Homeland Security

Part II Major Issues in Homeland Security

Part III Organizational Structure
of the Department of Homeland Security

Contents

Part I Scope of Homeland Security

Part II Major Issues in Homeland Security

Chapter 7: Public Health and Bioterrorism 167

Chapter 11: Employment and Worksite Issues 283

Part III Organizational Structure of the Department of Homeland Security

Chapter 12: Management Structure and Leadership 313

Chapter 13: Organizations and Functions of the DHS Directorates 327

Preface

The terrorist events of 2001 triggered reactions that reverberated throughout the United States and beyond. Distant concerns became immediate issues. Congress passed new laws and the private sector established new procedures. Understanding this paradigm change is critical to understanding the emerging homeland security legal discipline. It now influences virtually every legal, economic, social, and policy decision in the halls of government. And it now impacts sectors as far-reaching as media and advertising, insurance, banking and investment, technology, and manufacturing.

The great challenge, therefore, is how our legal and political system will allow this new wave of government to fit in, in a workable and acceptable way. We can draw on similarities to the beginning of the environmental law movement. Events caused a regulatory effect. A new agency was born and a substantial body of law developed through the years. Far-reaching sectors felt the impact of new environmental considerations. As history has taught us, new agencies of government do not easily go away, much less new departments. With the Department of Homeland Security now manning the frontlines in the war on terror, it is more likely that the regulatory impulse will become more intense.

The goal of this book is to consolidate and document the various elements of homeland security law into one work that can be used by all sectors as a reference. Scope, major issues, and DHS organizational structure is the focus. The scope of Homeland Security law is first covered by discussing the development, foundations, and priorities. Next, the impacts on major concerns such as air and maritime transportation security, chemical security, public health, and bioterrorism are discussed. Immigration, border security, cybersecurity, and terrorism risk insurance issues are also addressed. The all-important funding considerations are covered in procurements, grants, and appropriations, followed by sensitive matters in worksite issues faced everyday by employers. Finally, the management structure and leadership of the Department is outlined along with the organization and functions of the Directorates.

The authors and publisher of this book hope that our readers will see this book on the emerging body of Homeland Security law as a work in progress. Just as far-reaching segments were impacted through the years with environmental considerations, so it will be with homeland security considerations. We hope this information will help guide you in assessing its impact and making prudent decisions in your organization, whether it be business, government, industry, or academia. The ultimate goal is that the public and the private sectors work together in order to make our country safe in this new world.

The Honorable Edwin R. Bethune
Bracewell & Patterson LLP

About the Authors

Anthony H. Anikeeff is a Partner with Bracewell & Patterson LLP. He counsels and represents entities regarding various aspects of United States international trade regulation laws and government contracting, such as obtaining contracts, teaming, outsourcing and privatization, solicitations, negotiations, protests, regulatory compliance, contract performance, claims and terminations, dispute avoidance, small business issues, classified matters and security clearances, homeland security, and allegations of fraudulent conduct.

Edwin R. Bethune is a Partner with Bracewell & Patterson LLP in Washington, D.C., and is a former member of Congress. He specializes in representing clients on public policy matters before Congress, the Executive Branch, and the courts. Mr. Bethune has extensive experience in business litigation, federal regulatory law, white collar criminal defense, and government relations. A former FBI agent, he has chaired an ad hoc committee that evaluated, at congressional request, the terrorist threat to Washington Reagan National Airport. He also chaired a separate congressional advisory group that was organized after the September 11th tragedy to evaluate the counter-terrorism needs of the FBI.

Larry S. Gage is a Partner with Powell, Goldstein, Frazer & Murphy LLP. He focuses his practice in the areas of federal and state legislation and regulation, health policy, and general representation of public and nonprofit hospitals and other healthcare organizations. Mr. Gage also serves as President of the National Association of Public Hospitals and Health Systems and as Board Chair of the American International Health Alliance.

Robert F. Housman is Counsel to the Government Relations and Strategy section of Bracewell & Patterson LLP. He has served as Assistant Director of Strategic Planning in the White House Office of National Drug Control Policy (ONDCP) and as a consultant to the National Security Council and the Council on Environmental Quality. Mr. Housman has assisted clients with a variety of national security-related matters.

Stacey Kalberman is a Senior Associate with Powell, Goldstein, Frazer & Murphy LLP for insurance regulation and compliance and corporate law insurance matters. Ms. Kalberman's background is in all matters involving the representation of insurance companies before the various insurance regulators, the development and monitoring of company regulatory and compliance programs, and regulatory licensing of companies and agencies. Ms. Kalberman also counsels corporate clients on the purchase and negotiation of commercial insurance contracts, including general commercial property and casualty coverages, reinsurance and financial guaranty policies, as well as agency/broker agreements.

Albert B. Krachman is a Partner with Bracewell & Patterson LLP. Mr. Krachman's practice focuses on Government Contracts, including contract acquisition and negotiation, multiple award and commercial item contracting, Homeland Security contracting, A-76 competitions, privatization and outsourcing, bid protests, size appeals, injunctions against award and other pre-contractual controversies. Another focus of Mr. Krachman's practice is commercial litigation, including litigation and arbitration of contract, employment, real estate, construction, trade secret, and business ownership disputes.

Glenn B. Manishin is a Partner with Kelley Drye & Warren LLP, specializing in telecommunications and technology policy, antitrust, and legislative affairs. Mr. Manishin heads the cybersecurity practice for Kelley Drye's Homeland Security Practice Group. He has participated in virtually all of the most important regulatory, judicial, and legislative proceedings affecting telecommunications and the Internet for the past two decades, from the *AT&T* and *Microsoft* antitrust cases to the Telecommunications Act of 1996 and the dozens of federal appeals implementing that landmark statute. Mr. Manishin has represented clients ranging from Netscape, MCI, Oracle, and Excite@Home to Siebel, Google, Travelocity, and others on such cutting-edge issues as broadband, software antitrust, cybersecurity and Internet regulation, standards, privacy, domain name competition, Internet gaming and taxation, and universal service.

E. Dee Martin is an Associate in the Government Relations and Strategy section at Bracewell & Patterson LLP. Ms. Martin represents clients before Congress as well as executive agencies. She also focuses on issues relating to energy and the environment, as well as counter-terrorism and security laws.

Lara B. Mathews is a Partner with Blank Rome LLP. She focuses on environmental and maritime transportation law and legislation. Ms. Mathews counsels companies on matters arising under federal and state environmental laws, including the Clean Water Act, the Oil Pollution Act of 1990, CERCLA, and the Clean Air Act, in the contexts of audits, real estate transactions, civil enforcement, cost recovery actions, and legislative and regulatory reform.

Nancy Morrison O'Connor is a Partner with Bracewell & Patterson LLP and has represented corporate clients in labor and employment issues since 1976. She has handled matters involving traditional labor, employment discrimination, health, employment benefits, immigration, civil rights, contract negotiations and disputes, arbitrations, general employment, and securities fraud.

Lisa J. Savitt is Of Counsel with Blank Rome LLP and has a commercial and international litigation practice with an emphasis on aviation and product liability. She represents insurers and their insured, including domestic and foreign manufacturers and airlines. Ms. Savitt also handles cases involving international trade, patent infringement, and computer software litigation.

Rebecca L. Sigmund is Of Counsel with Powell, Goldstein, Frazer & Murphy LLP and is practice group leader of the Firm's immigration team. She advises companies on immigration alternatives for prospective employees as well as matters relating to employment eligibility of workers. Her practice largely involves securing appropriate temporary working visas and permanent residency for executives, managers, investors, technical personnel, and other professionals to authorize their employment in the United States. Another area of Ms. Sigmund's immigration practice involves advising domestic employers on compliance procedures to verify the work eligibility of all new employees as required under the "employer sanctions" provisions of federal law. Ms. Sigmund also serves as the immigration authority on the Firm's Homeland Security Task Force.

Jonathan K. Waldron is a Partner with Blank Rome LLP specializing in marine transportation, environmental, and international law. He regularly counsels and represents clients in matters involving legislative and regulatory issues related to vessel and facility operations, security, pollution, coastwise trade, and criminal defense matters.

Part I

Scope of Homeland Security

Chapter 1

Birth and Development of Homeland Security Law

Bracewell & Patterson LLP
Robert F. Housman
The Honorable Ed Bethune

1.0 The Impact of 9/11: The Birth and Development of Homeland Security Law

The Latin maxim "ratio legis est anima legis; cessat rationc, cessat ipsa lex" translates: "reason is the heart and soul of the law; when the reason for the law changes, the law will change."

On September 11, 2001, Al Qaeda terrorists hijacked four airplanes. The hijackers used the jetliners as weapons, slamming two into the towers of the World Trade Center in New York City and one into the Pentagon.[1] Before the eyes of a disbelieving public, the Twin Towers imploded and a gash burned deep into the Pentagon, the heart of American military might. On that day, the reasons for lawmaking changed. And, in keeping with that Latin maxim, in the wake of these devastating attacks the law has changed.

Since 9/11, the Congress and President have responded with a host of new laws aimed at enhancing the security of our nation's critical infrastructure. These laws touch upon everything from ports to dairy producers. In essence, these new laws and regulations form the nucleus of an emerging field of homeland security law.

The creation of a new legal discipline is, in and of itself, a major development. But, the impact of the 9/11 attacks has gone beyond even that. Essentially these acts have created a new paradigm for government. In the days before 9/11, the political headlines were dominated by partisan fighting over a host of

3

relatively mundane issues. Since 9/11, the focus of our national government have been winnowed down to three paramount goals that eclipse all others: protect the American people; safeguard our critical infrastructure; and insulate our economy from harms attendant to the war on terrorism.

Understanding this new paradigm is critical to understanding the emerging homeland security legal discipline. It now influences virtually every legal, policy, and political decision in the halls of government. For example, in March of 2003, the Congress took up President Bush's proposed massive tax cut. However, as the Congress struggled internally with how to handle the president's proposal, the news of the day and the public attentions of Congressional members were focused on the war on terrorism. Even when the president's tax cut did break through, the proposal was discussed in the context of the war on terrorism: could the nation wage a war on terrorism and cut taxes? Could we cut taxes and yet provide first responders with the tools needed to address an attack on the American homeland? These new paradigm concerns were the primary issues raised with respect to an economic policy proposal that at any other time would have singularly dominated the Congress's and the public's attention.

1.1   The Impact of 9/11

The 9/11 attacks made it frighteningly clear that America's homeland is now the front line in the war against international terrorism. Al Qaeda—choosing its targets carefully—sent a series of deadly, terrifying messages that will resonate for centuries to come. The first target was New York City, specifically the World Trade Center, an icon of American capitalism and economic might. Then, by attacking the Pentagon, Al Qaeda hit the American military on its home turf, at its very core, signaling they could and would strike anywhere in the United States. A third attack failed due to the heroic action of passengers on United Airlines Flight 93, but the terrorist-hijackers were apparently headed for the U.S. Capitol, the symbol of our freedom and democracy. In all the attacks the terrorists let it be known that they are willing to indiscriminately kill thousands of innocent men, women, and children to achieve their goal. The totality of their crime sent a chilling, unmistakable and indelible message to the American people: our economy, our military, our political system, and our people—are in the crosshairs. We are the target.

The losses in human terms from the 9/11 attacks were staggering. Just under 3,000 innocent people died that day in the terrorist attacks on the World Trade Center and the Pentagon and in the crash of United Flight 93 in Pennsylvania. Most of these victims were simply going about their day-to-day lives and jobs. They were corporate executives and managers, firemen and police officers, file clerks and secretaries, data entry clerks and accountants, bankers and bond traders, pilots and airplane passengers, waiters and dishwashers, salespeople and shopkeepers. They were average citizens who had no inkling of the tragedy that day held in store.

From an economic perspective, the damage was astounding. The attacks demonstrated the enormous impact that terrorism can have on our lives, industries, markets, and economy. The insured financial losses alone have been estimated at more than $40 billion. More than 1.8 million jobs were lost. With property, income, and jobs factored in, the total loss is estimated by *Money* magazine to exceed $60 billion. This number could ultimately rise into the hundreds of billions of dollars.

The economic effects of the 9/11 attacks rippled across the entire American economy. American gross domestic product, or GDP, for the following quarter fell by approximately 2.5 percentage points. The stock market, the engine of American capitalism, was forced to close for four days, the longest shutdown since the Great Depression. When the market re-opened, the Dow Jones Industrial average plummeted 684 points. An entire industry—commercial aviation—was nearly bankrupted. In the aftermath of 9/11, the airline industry alone lost more than 10,000 jobs. The travel and leisure industry—airlines, hotels, car rental firms, restaurants, amusement parks, and cruise lines—suffered staggering losses. By December 2001, the occupancy rate for U.S. hotels fell 50 percent from pre-9/11 levels. Sectors as far reaching as media and advertising, insurance, banking and investment, technology, and manufacturing, were all battered by the September 11th attacks.

The economic losses were not contained to the area immediately surrounding Ground Zero. Perhaps the most striking example has occurred within the insurance sector. Faced with 9/11 losses exceeding $40 billion dollars, the insurance industry pulled back from insuring against the risks of terrorism. Businesses subsequently discovered that they could not purchase insurance policies that include terrorism risk. Even where terrorism insurance was available, coverage was impractical because the policies were so costly and limited in scope.

A 2002 General Accounting Office report found that the inability to obtain terrorism insurance coverage caused a number of major deals to be cancelled. In one example, a developer was forced to cancel construction of a new apartment building in New York City because it could not find any insurer that would sell it the terrorism insurance coverage required to get financing from the bank. The loss of this deal alone cost New York City and the nation some 500 construction jobs.

Similar problems were felt across the nation. In the Midwest, owners of a major shopping mall could not obtain terrorism insurance. Their lenders subsequently sued them for breaching their loan agreement. Similarly, a real estate company with properties in cities across the East Coast found itself unable to obtain the terrorism insurance required to fulfill the requirements of its lenders. The best terrorism policy the company could find was one year of $75 million coverage, which did not even cover the replacement cost of one of its buildings, for a premium of $1.125 million. Securities firms found that investors refused to buy some securities when the investments were not protected by terrorism insurance. Moody's Risk Management Services told the markets it would downgrade bonds issued to companies on buildings that lack terrorism insurance.[2]

The immense human and economic damage inflicted by the attacks of 9/11 has resulted in a profound shift in our system of law and government. Few singular events in American history have so deeply changed the landscape of U.S. law. Environmentalists trace the origins of today's environmental movement and laws back to Love Canal and Rachel Carson's *Silent Spring*. Our system of bank oversight and deposit insurance can be traced back to the Great Depression and the Black Thursday stock crash of 1929. Our basic principle of judicial review harkens from the "Midnight appointment" by President Adams of William Marbury to the bench. These momentous turning points in American legal and cultural history are fitting comparisons for the sweeping changes driven by the attacks of September 11, 2001.

1.2   Homeland Security Law Prior to 9/11

The attacks of September 11th were not the first terrorist attacks on American interests. In fact, the attacks of September 11th are part of a much larger trend that has been growing since the 1980s. According to the most current publicly available data, from 1980 to 1999, 414 terrorist attacks occurred in the United States. Of this number, 101 attacks struck at the U.S. government. Just 13 attacked the U.S. military. Foreign governments were targeted 61 times, and in 7 cases the FBI characterized the target as "unknown." The majority of the attacks, 232, struck civilian or commercial targets.[3] While many of these inci-

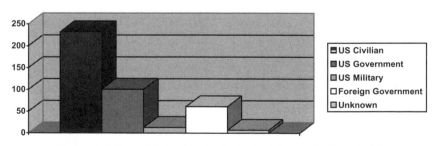

Figure 1.1 Terrorist Attacks in the United States 1980 to 1999
Source: FBI. 1999. Terrorism in the United States. 59.

dents garnered little notice, some made headlines and began to drive the threat of terrorism home to the average American. Two of the most significant pre-9/11 terrorist events were the 1993 Al Qaeda network bombing of the World Trade Center and the 1995 bombing of the Alfred P. Murrah Federal Building in Oklahoma City by anti-government terrorists Timothy McVeigh and Terry Nichols.

Despite the growing terrorist threat, prior to the 9/11 attacks, there was no body of law that could fairly be called a coherent homeland security legal or regulatory discipline. However, as the number of terrorist attacks on the American homeland continued to mount, the American legal system did, to a limited extent, respond to this growing threat. The Congress enacted a handful of laws that mandated actions to reduce the threat of global terrorism. For example, in 1985, the International Security and Development Cooperation Act was passed, which banned assistance to governments designated by the Secretary of State as terrorist supporting nations.[4] Similarly, in 1986 the Congress passed the Omnibus Diplomatic Security and Anti-Terrorism Act, which directed the Federal Bureau of Investigation [FBI] to investigate acts of terrorism directed against Americans overseas.[5] The 1995 National Defense Authorization Act created a joint FBI and Department of Defense program to deter and investigate incidents involving the trafficking of weapons of mass destruction (WMD) and related material. In addition to these pre-9/11 laws, there were a number of important Executive branch actions that were taken with the goal of combating terrorism.[6]

While these pre-9/11 laws clearly touch upon aspects of what we now consider to be homeland security, prior to their incorporation into the new discipline of homeland security law, they were probably best thought of as national security laws, not homeland security laws. At least two factors clearly differentiate these pre-9/11 laws from the emerging, post-9/11 body of homeland security law. The pre-9/11 laws focus on the global threat of terrorism; today's homeland security laws focus on the specific defense of the American homeland. The pre-9/11 laws focus primarily on governmental actions by governmental actors; current homeland security law targets primarily private sector actors. The emerging discipline of homeland security law focuses largely on how to best secure the nation's critical infrastructure, most of which is privately held.[7]

This is not to suggest that during this two-decade-plus period of increasing terrorist activity efforts were not underway to develop the rudiments of a homeland security system. In fact, a large number of public and private initiatives during this timeframe sought to enhance our governmental and legal frameworks for homeland security. For example, in February of 2000, the Environmental Protection Agency issued guidance to chemical plants to increase their security awareness in light of the potential for a terrorist attack. Along these same lines, during the first Gulf War, concerns about potential terrorism attacks on the Trans-Alaska Pipeline caused the federal government to work with the pipeline's owner to review the pipeline's security and take measures to close identified security gaps. However, without the imperative of a 9/11 attacks to drive them, most of these efforts came up short and never reached critical mass.

Efforts to address port security provide an apt example of the pre-9/11 dynamic. Responding to growing concerns about potential terrorist attacks on or via ports, on April 27, 1999, President Clinton, at the urging of Senator Bob Graham of Florida, signed an Executive Memorandum establishing a commission to study security at U.S. ports.[8] In its report issued in the Fall of 2000, the Inter-Agency Commission on Crime and Security in U.S. Seaports found that a terrorist attack on an American seaport could cause "significant damage."[9] The Commission's report also provided that the security at U.S. seaports "generally ranges from poor to fair...."[10] The Commission's findings resulted in proposed legislation intended to ratchet up seaport security. However, the so-called "Graham Port Security Bill" languished in the Congress—that is, until after the attacks of 9/11.

Along these same lines, the idea of a Department of Homeland Security pre-dates the September 11th attacks. For example, in February of 2001, the U.S. Commission on National Security and the 21st Century, also known as the Hart-Rudman Commission for its co-chairs, issued a report that called for the creation of a National Security Agency charged with homeland defense.[11] However, proposals for such a department were not acted upon.

The dynamic surrounding proposals for a Department of Homeland Security and the Graham Port Security Bill are emblematic of the general handling of homeland security legal matters prior to 9/11. The pre-9/11 homeland security legal and regulatory dynamic in essence boiled down to a four-stage process: some public or private actor would raise the specter of a serious threat; the threat was studied; a course of action to address that threat was identified; the proposed action was seldom, if ever, taken.

That said, there were certain notable exceptions to this general pattern, most notably: Presidential Decision Directive 63 (PDD 63)[12] and The Chemical Safety Information, Site Security, and Fuel Regulatory Relief Act of 1999.[13]

President Bill Clinton signed PDD 63 on May 22, 1998. PDD 63 marked the first modern-era, major step toward a specific homeland security policy.[14] PDD 63 initiated a national effort to increase the security of America's privately held critical infrastructure, including, *inter alia*, telecommunications, banking and finance, energy, and transportation. This classified directive required the federal government to undertake risk assessments and planning exercises to reduce the terrorist threat to our critical infrastructure. It also directed the federal government to develop linkages to and information sharing mechanisms with the private sector owners of this infrastructure. PDD 63 also produced a significant interagency review of the security challenges facing America's vital and interconnected critical infrastructure sectors. This review clearly documented that the vast majority of this infrastructure was vulnerable to attack and that such an attack could have catastrophic consequences for the nation.

Under PDD 63, as a matter of policy, the Clinton administration began a series of administrative efforts to work with industry members in these sectors to enhance security. PDD 63 designated an individual officer of government, the national coordinator, charged with infrastructure protection. It created an interagency hierarchy reporting to this national coordinator. It also required agencies to take specific actions to beef up homeland security programs for critical infrastructure. For example, PDD 63 directed the FBI to expand its then-ongoing infrastructure counter-terrorism efforts into a National Infrastructure Protection Center, charged with serving as the national critical infrastructure threat assessment, warning, vulnerability, and law enforcement investigation and response entity. PDD 63 also established the information sharing and analysis center (ISAC) structure, which brings the individual members of industry sectors together to share information and serves as a dissemination tool for the federal government to provide these companies with threat information. While PDD 63 made important steps forward in the development of homeland security policy and programs, it must be emphasized that the charge originated in a national security directive and not in a statutory mandate.

Like PDD 63, the Chemical Safety Information, Site Security, and Fuel Regulatory Relief Act of 1999 (Chemical Safety Act) pre-dates 9/11 and focuses on domestic infrastructure security. While the Chemical Safety Information Act is, perhaps, the nation's first pure homeland security statute, the implementation of the act speaks more to the lack of a compelling body of law before 9/11. The act required the Department of Justice to study and report on the security of the nation's chemical industry with an eye towards the possibility of a terrorist attack on this sector. The act required Justice to submit an interim report containing its preliminary findings by August 5, 2000, and a final report by May 5, 2002. Nearly two years after the requirement to submit a complete report, Justice has still only submitted to Congress a preliminary report. The interim report, which looked at only 11 of the country's thousands of chemical facilities, can best be described as methodological in nature—as opposed to broad-based and analytical.

Apart from PDD 63 and the Chemical Safety Act, to the extent that there was a pre-9/11 body of law pertaining to matters that we now would consider to be related to homeland security, these laws existed to address other concerns.

For example, in the wake of the September 11th terrorism, law enforcement authorities seeking to attack the funding of the Al Qaeda network have relied heavily on anti-money laundering statutory provisions requiring banks to report certain types of transactions. While these anti-money laundering provisions are now being deployed as homeland security measures, they were principally intended by Congress to serve as a counter-narcotics tool aimed at breaking the bank of drug cartels.

For example, the nation's first Maritime Security Act, a Florida state statute,[15] was developed in order to help stem the smuggling of drugs in cargo containers into that state. The original intent of the Florida statute is clear in that the implementation of the act is delegated to the state's drug czar. However, in the wake of the 9/11 attacks, and with serious concerns having been raised about the potential for a terrorist to smuggle a nuclear or biological weapon in via a cargo shipment, this state law has become an important tool in the fight against terrorism. In fact, federal authorities seeking to implement the federal Port and Maritime Security Act have looked to the Florida act and its implementation as a model for nationwide efforts.

Similarly, in response to a recent inquiry by the General Accounting Office (GAO), the Environmental Protection Agency stated that the Clean Air Act could be interpreted to provide the necessary authority for the agency to address site safety concerns at chemical plants.[16] The Clean Air Act provisions the EPA was speaking of in its answer to the GAO pre-date 9/11. These provisions were not passed to serve the goal of homeland security. Rather, they were enacted to increase health and safety, one of the primary mandates of environmental law.

Beyond the paucity of statutory law, before 9/11 there was a smattering of legal cases that applied traditional tort law in response to acts of terrorism. In 1992, Pan American airlines was found liable for the failure to provide adequate security which allowed a Libyan terrorist to blow up flight 103 over Lockerbie, Scotland. This case ultimately resulted in a $500 million settlement by the airline and the families of the victims. In another case, the families of four then Union-Texas Petroleum employees sued the company for the failure to provide adequate security during corporate travel. The four employees had been gunned down in Karachi, Pakistan, while traveling on company business. Based on a, perhaps, unique set of facts and trial circumstances, the jury found the company's security was not negligent.

Similarly, at the time of this writing, a lawsuit brought by victims of the 1993 World Trade Center bombing against the owner/operators of the towers for failure to provide adequate security is underway. Another lawsuit has been brought by victims of the Oklahoma City bombing alleging that the two domestic terrorists who carried out that attack were aided by and acted as agents of the Republic of Iraq. Even given the presence of these isolated lawsuits, before 9/11, few legal experts would have argued that the potential for a catastrophic terrorist attack against the typical company was so great as to be reasonably foreseeable to the point that the reasonable man would have taken exceptional steps to prevent such an attack. For this reason, even in the area of tort law, there was no well-formed, pre-9/11 body of homeland security law.

Before 9/11, it would have been implausible to suggest that these disparate elements—national security laws, laws in other disciplines now deployed for homeland security, and isolated Executive actions—could have been cobbled together to stand as a discernable body of homeland security law. For this reason, the emerging body of homeland security law is rightly seen as the American legal and political system's response to the attacks of September 11th.

This realization is important for more than historical purposes. The origins of the growing body of homeland security law play an important role in understanding the nature and continuing evolution of this body of law.

1.3   Homeland Security Law Post 9/11

In the wake of the heinous attacks of 9/11, Congress wasted little time altering the American legal system to take into account the new, post-9/11 reality. In almost two years since the attacks of 9/11, the Congress and the president have begun to build an entire system of government and laws with the purpose of protecting the nation. While it seems unlikely that anyone set out with the purpose of creating a new legal discipline, the actions taken have had just that effect. When these new laws, reinterpreted laws, and new institutions are considered not as pieces but as a whole, a number of important trends and traits emerge. Understanding these traits provides valuable insights into this body of law as it now stands and where it is likely headed.

1.3.1   Work in Progress

Homeland security law is a new discipline and it is early in its evolutionary process. Despite the broad sweep of its mandates, homeland security law at this stage remains very much a work in progress. There are a host of external and internal factors that will play a role in shaping how this body of law develops. While trends can be spotted, any one of a number of potential events could dramatically alter the glide path of this body of law.

The most significant unknown variable that could drastically skew any such trends here is the potential for a future terrorist attack and its countervailing force, complacency. The United States has enjoyed a period of relative calm on the home front since the 9/11 attacks. Beefed up intelligence and law enforcement efforts have thwarted a number of attacks. As a result, there has not been a significant terrorist attack carried out on our homeland since 9/11. That said, terrorism experts with exceptional unity state that it is not a matter of "if" another attack will occur, but "when."

Should another terrorist attack of some substantial scale be carried out against the American homeland, one can expect that the evolution of homeland security law will be radically altered. In the wake of such an attack, we would expect to see Congress impose a host of new security-oriented mandates. Such mandates would be expected first in the area or sector targeted in the attack. For example, if a terrorist smuggled a dirty bomb into this nation via a trucked-in cargo shipment, early mandates would fall first on the trucking industry. These mandates would then ripple outward to related areas or sectors. In this example, the mandates would likely grow to cover the transportation sector, then trade and shipping broadly, and so on. The expected pace of homeland security law expansion in the wake of a future attack would be exceptionally fast.

On the other hand, if the United States continues to remain relatively unscathed for some period of time—almost ten years passed between the two World Trade Center Attacks—it is natural that some sense of complacency will once again begin to take hold. However, it seems unlikely that even a long period of quiet will cause a rollback of this body of law—the wounds of 9/11 are too deep to allow for that. That said, complacency might shift the form of homeland security law. For example, as discussed below, today's homeland security laws pay little heed to the cost imposed on the private sector by their mandates. If this period of calm continues, it might open the door for efforts to require homeland security laws to balance the costs of new protections against the security benefits of such protections.

1.3.2   Overwhelming Popular and Political Support

In just six weeks following the 9/11 attacks, the Congress passed and the president signed the Uniting and Strengthening America by Providing Appropriate Tools Required to Intercept and Obstruct Terrorism Act of 2001, commonly known as the USA PATRIOT Act.[17] The PATRIOT Act marks the first step in the actual creation of a body of homeland security law. The act itself is a far-reaching statute that covers a wide swath of concerns ranging from international money laundering to border protection to compensation to victims of terrorism and their families. The act's most controversial provisions grant law enforcement agents sweeping powers to tap telephones, conduct unannounced searches, and monitor Internet communications. These provisions have been hotly debated for years between civil libertarians and those who favor tougher law enforcement. However, when these provisions were raised in the context of post-9/11 homeland security, they enjoyed widespread popular and political support. The PATRIOT Act passed the Senate by an astonishing margin of 98 to 1.

Given the significant Constitutional and ministerial ramifications of the PATRIOT Act's provisions, that the act could pass Congress in such a short timeframe, and with so limited debate, demonstrates the political force behind homeland security law. Anchored in the basic responsibility to provide for the common defense and protect the American homeland, the political weight and popular support behind any provision couched in homeland security terms makes such measures difficult to oppose.

In fact, in a variety of instances, industry members have willingly and with little complaint allowed mandates to be imposed under the aegis of homeland security that are far more invasive than many other measures that they have fought vehemently in other settings. For example, the PATRIOT Act expands the reach of "know your customer" financial transaction reporting requirements beyond banks to a host of other "financial institutions," as now defined to include gem dealers, travel agents, and hedge funds. These industries have long fought to keep their members beyond the scope of such reporting requirements.

Parties faced with potentially onerous homeland security requirements find themselves in a difficult position. Consider the circumstances facing universities and other educational institutions. On the one hand, a number of the 9/11 terrorists entered the United States under student visas before they went underground to carry out their plot. Add to this the fact that the Immigration and Naturalization Service has publicly admitted that it lacks the means to adequately track foreign students in the United States and ensure that they are in compliance with our immigration laws. Because of these factors, the American public is increasingly concerned about the apparent ease with which terrorists can enter this nation under the pretense of educational programs. On the other hand, American educational institutions obtain significant revenue from the tuition and other payments made by legitimate foreign students. These educational institutions are highly concerned that ongoing efforts to strengthen immigration enforcement, such as registration requirements for visitors from certain countries, will scare foreign students away and hurt their bottom lines. This dynamic puts these educational institutions in an awkward position of having to either publicly fight against stronger counter-terrorism protections or lose a significant segment of their fee-paying student bodies. And, given the strength of public sentiments, few want to be seen as not being fully in support of the fight against terrorism.

As a result, parties that face potential homeland security mandates must be proactive and seek to shape these provisions before they can harden. They must also shape their messages to avoid the appearance of ignoring their responsibility to the national defense.

1.3.3   Threat-Based and Reactive

The processes that led to the PATRIOT Act and many of these other homeland security statutes also demonstrate another key element of homeland security lawmaking: it is largely threat-based and reactive in nature. For example, the PATRIOT Act includes a provision that subjects truck drivers operating shipments of hazardous materials to background checks as a condition of licensing or license renewal. This provision was a direct response to news reports suggesting that Al Qaeda operatives sought to obtain hazardous materials drivers' licenses so that they could use such shipments as weapons. Along these same lines, early versions of the Port and Maritime Security Act languished in Congress for over a year. The act only began to make headway after a series of news accounts highlighted the potential threat posed by either a terrorist attack on a major port or the possibility for a WMD to be smuggled through a port.

The threat-based nature of homeland security law arguably stands in sharp relief to the risk-based principles that are increasingly becoming ingrained in other areas of the law, such as food and drug law and environmental law. These other areas seek to balance risk and benefits to find a point where the level of risk from a particular bad action is acceptable. In contrast, in its current state, homeland security law is evolving with less focus on weighing risks and more emphasis on eliminating threats. A threat of WMD smuggled in through a port is raised; a law gets passed. Concerns are voiced about hazardous materials shipments; a law gets passed. Security experts regularly talk about the need for risk assessments and the fact that security can never be absolute, so there will always be some level of risk. However, the growing body of law on its face has yet to incorporate that thinking to the extent that other legal disciplines have. For example, none of the post-9/11 homeland security statutes include provisions on risk-based methodologies. In other words, while security in practice may always entail some level of acceptable risk, the body of law now increasingly driving that security is in search of absolutes.

That current homeland security law is reactive is somewhat to be expected. Prior to 9/11 these threats were largely discounted, or at least not well enough understood to form the hue and cry required for attention to them. It took the attacks of 9/11 to drive home the threat of terrorism in a manner so feral as to require action. Before 9/11, there was a significant amount of analysis concerning the threat of terrorism and how the nation should best address this threat. The Hart-Rudman Commission studied the issue and reported out. The FBI studied the issue and reported out. As discussed above, these efforts were strategic and visionary in nature; however, few real or tactical changes resulted from them. Homeland security as we now think of it simply was not a priority. Because we failed to act adequately then, we now find ourselves playing catch up to the ever-evolving threat to our homeland.

The reactive, threat-driven nature of this emerging legal discipline makes this area of law highly fluid and difficult to predict. The direction of homeland security legal efforts are, to a great extent, subject to change on a moment's notice—or, more accurately, in the time required for a nightly news broadcast. This lack of predictability will require potentially affected parties to remain constantly abreast of initiatives underway within the Congress and the Executive branch, as well as wider public opinion.

1.3.4 Singularly Focused without Cost Balance

Because today's homeland security laws are designed to address threats to the security of the nation and the American people, they tend to be far more singularly focused than other areas of the law. Statutory provisions in areas ranging from antitrust to environmental protection often expressly require that a range of interests be balanced in any decision. The most common interest that other legal disciplines require to be considered is cost, by virtue of a cost-benefit test. For example, under federal drinking water regulations, the Environmental Protection Agency must prepare and seek comment on health risk reductions and perform cost-benefit analysis. Similarly, in determining which federal highway programs to fund, federal law requires projects to undergo a comprehensive review of many factors, including cost effectiveness. These far flung examples show the level to which such balancing requirements are now incorporated into our legal schemes.

In contrast, post-9/11 homeland security statutes do not contemplate any interest being weighed against the goal of security. For example, the Port and Maritime Security Act imposes a host of new mandates on regulated parties without even a wink to reducing or minimizing the substantial costs that meeting these new requirements will entail. When the Department of Homeland Security issued the interim final rules under the Maritime Security Act, the regulations included an analysis of the estimated costs of the regulations on the private sector.

This analysis, however, was prepared under, and not through, the underlying, substantive statute. This is more than splitting hairs: an after-the-fact cost review is far different from the mandated balancing of cost in determining the proper regulatory approach.

This discussion is not to suggest that homeland security regulators will not act without some sensitivity to the broader range of interests at play. Rather, it is to highlight the fact that under these new laws there is one, over-riding interest that, for the time being, trumps all others at the end of the day: security.

1.3.5   New Players Speaking a Different Language

In the wake of the 9/11 attacks, federal authorities ordered the closure of Ronal Reagan Washington National Airport. With each passing day, the airport's closure was costing the region millions of dollars each day in lost revenue. The region's business community began a series of lobbying efforts to bring this to the attention of decision-makers to get the airport re-opened. These efforts immediately ran into a major stumbling block. The business community's case for re-opening the airport was based on the economic losses the closure was inflicting. However, advocates for re-opening the airport were not talking to your typical bureaucrat who might have been swayed by such fiscal facts. Rather, they were forced to take their case to the national security establishment, which, charged with safeguarding the essential workings of our Constitutional democracy, was not swayed by mere economic analyses. The leadership of this effort to re-open the airport was told by a senior Congressional member that they had to change their tactics: they had to make the case for resuming airport operations in the terms of national security. As a result the Washington Airport's Task Force engaged Bracewell & Patterson to organize a task force to study whether the airport's closure plan actually increased national security.[18] The task force study found that the closure of Reagan-National provided some added security, but at massive, disproportionate costs; and, that other more effective means were available to further increase security without closing the airport. This study was provided to the key leaders in the Secret Service and the National Security Council, as well as in the Congress. The study's conclusions played a significant role in helping re-open the airport.

This anecdote highlights two important features of homeland security law. First, the players in this new legal discipline are different from the normal cast of characters most private citizens deal with. Apart from the narrow world of defense contractors and their legal advisors, few private parties regularly interact with the national security establishment. However, it is the members of this establishment who are now playing the critical role in setting homeland defense policies that impact huge swathes of the nation's privately held critical infrastructure. The key players who hold sway in homeland security law now include the Department of Homeland Security, the FBI, the CIA, the Department of Defense, the National Guard Bureau, the Coast Guard, the Immigration and Naturalization Service, the Border Patrol, Customs, the Transportation Security Agency, the National Security Council, and state and local law enforcement and first responders. This is not your typical cast of domestic policymakers.

The facts that are compelling in a host of other policy settings—costs, impacts on competitiveness, and the like—are far less compelling when weighed against protecting the American homeland. To be effective in managing home-

land security legal issues, advocates and interested parties need to know these
new players and speak their language.

1.3.6 Rich with Uncertainty

Additionally, a lack of specificity in swiftly crafted homeland security statutes
adds an element of uncertainty to the evolution of this body of law. The hasty
passage of the PATRIOT Act and other homeland security measures has left
inadequately considered many of the nuances of how these mandates will work.
Here again, consider the provision requiring background checks for hazardous
materials drivers licenses. On its face this provision seems like a common sense
reaction to a perceived and possibly substantial threat. However, while the provision had the best of intentions, it was not well thought out. The responsibility
to issue such licenses falls upon the states. Few if any states had a system in place
to work with the FBI to seek and obtain the necessary background checks.
Many, if not most, states lacked the funds necessary to implement such a system. As a result, a number of states simply stopped issuing such licenses until
their state authorities could put a system in place. The unintended impact of
this gap in licensing was substantial because the hiatus fell during the winter
months of 2002—when trucks and drivers were necessary to haul home heat-
ing fuels, many of which were classified as hazardous.[19]

Because many homeland security laws have been passed on fast tracks, the
implementation processes for these statutes are likely to take on considerable
importance. Agencies faced with broad statutory mandates and little specific
legislative guidance have wide latitude in implementing these newly enacted
laws. For example, the recently enacted Port and Maritime Security Act requires
facilities located on or adjacent to the territorial waters of the United States to
have security plans designed to deter and defeat terrorist attacks. The act further requires these plans be approved by the Coast Guard. The failure to have
an approved plan can lead to the closure of any such facility.

Beyond these broad requirements, the Port and Maritime Security Act offers little direction as to what specifically is required of regulated facilities. The
act does not set out in any detail what the required security plans should entail.
The act requires background checks for individuals with access to sensitive port
areas. However, apart from requiring the use of biometrics, the act does not
discuss the process by which background checks and the award of badges should
occur. Nor does the act discuss what sorts of threats these plans are required to
prevent and repulse. For example, must these plans address threats from both
insiders and outsiders? Must they address landside attacks? Seaside attacks? Airborne attacks? Additionally, while the act requires Coast Guard approval of
port security plans, the act does not say what the standard is for determining
what constitutes compliance. None of these important parameters are set out in

the law. In other words, the actual bite of this statute will be determined by the implementing regulations that are now in development by the administration and agencies.

Perhaps the best way to demonstrate the lack of certainty and implementation flexibility in new homeland security legal mandates is by way of a comparison. The entire Port and Maritime Security Act security plan requirements take up fewer words than the definition sections of the Clean Air Act. Another critical uncertainty is how one measures security. In antitrust, market control can be expressed as a percentage of the total market. In trade cases, the origin of a product can be calculated by where its component materials and labor originated. In the environmental area, pollution can be measured down to the parts-per-million. These indicia are objective and calculable through scientific method. However, security success is realized in the absence of a measurable event—an attack. Measuring a negative is all but impossible. As such, any before-the-fact security calculus is necessarily subjective.

1.3.7   Fast Growing

The American system of checks and balances serves as a speed bump on the road to change. Because of this, legal disciplines tend to develop and evolve over long periods of time. For example, our system of environmental laws, one of our most recently developed areas of the law, has taken decades to reach its current breadth and scope.

In contrast, once the attacks of 9/11 broke the logjam, the body of homeland security law grew exponentially and at breakneck pace. In less than two years' time, the Congress has reorganized the federal government to create a Department of Homeland Security; enacted statutory provisions that curtail longstanding interpretations of Constitutional rights with the goal of enhancing security; passed laws that place new homeland security mandates on industries ranging from gem dealers to airlines to agribusiness; and, provided a potentially massive federal terrorism risk backstop to the insurance industry. The speed of change here is even more remarkable when one considers that these changes have come during a period in which neither party enjoyed a substantial majority in the Congress sufficient to ram through new legislation.

1.3.8   Liability Driven

Arguably, the swiftest change in homeland security law occurred immediately with the collapse of the Twin Towers. Before that date, terrorist attacks of such a magnitude were the stuff of Tom Clancy novels. On September 11, 2001, the unthinkable became reality.

In legal terms, the 9/11 attacks arguably raised the standard of care for companies in preventing terrorism.[20] These attacks made almost any form of terrorist attack reasonably foreseeable. If a small band of terrorists could use box cutters to kill thousands by hijacking airplanes, why couldn't they poison milk supplies? Or, blow up a chemical plant? These are the types of questions that now are in the common discourse. The standard of care required under tort law is derived from that which the community deems reasonable. Post-9/11 polling shows that the community of Americans now view virtually any form of terrorist attack as reasonably foreseeable. These polls also show that Americans expect their government and the owners of the nation's infrastructure to protect them from such attacks. In other words, the average American sees terrorism as likely, and believes that there is a duty to prevent such attacks. Along with harm and proximate cause, which are case specific, these post-9/11 views make up the essential elements of a terrorism negligence case.

The greatly enhanced potential for counter-terrorism security liability has already been recognized by the insurance industry. After 9/11, the insurance sector, generally speaking, simply stopped issuing terrorism risk insurance policies—Congress was forced to step in and pass the Terrorism Risk Insurance Act of 2002.

This common law aspect of the law of homeland security arguably is the most important element of this new legal discipline. Post 9/11 homeland security statutes have tended to address specific concerns arising with respect to specific high-risk industrial activities, such as airlines, ports, and pipelines. However, the heightened standard of care and the potential for massive liabilities does not apply to any one industry. The ratcheted-up common law of homeland security is universal in its potential application.

This shift in the common law is particularly vexing to parties that could one day find themselves sued for failing to provide adequate security. Countless companies are now struggling with the difficult question of what is reasonable security. Concerned companies have hired security firms to analyze their risks only to be handed smoking guns for their files: vulnerability assessments that offer long lists of potential risks, large numbers of documented security flaws, and large price tags to close these gaps. Because there presently exists no one standard for security, most companies know the bar has been raised, but they are struggling to determine just how high.

1.3.9 Entrenched

Some commentators have speculated—almost exclusively off the record—that, absent some subsequent earth-shattering event, homeland security concerns will fade from the public's radar screen and this body of law will slowly dissipate. This thinking ignores several important realities.

First, in the American democratic system of law and government, few laws simply vanish:[21] they need to be repealed, requiring an affirmative vote of the

Congress and the president's signature. Having seen the devastation of 9/11, and knowing that there will always be terrorists around the world who seek to do us harm, few political leaders will be willing to take the risk to the American public—let alone the risk to their good names—that a repeal of a homeland security law would entail.

Second, our nation has witnessed only a handful of events of the magnitude of 9/11. While the American people have notoriously short attention spans, events like 9/11 are burned into our collective memory in a manner that other events are not. For example, the United States has not suffered a Great Depression and a run on the banks since the 1920s. However, despite the passage of time, there is little movement afoot today to repeal the system of deposit insurance and bank oversight that resulted from that crash. In fact, it took 66 years for the Glass-Steagall Act, the seminal banking law, to even be amended in any significant form.[22]

Third, the developing body of homeland security law deals with the most essential of our Constitutional rights and our most basic of human fears: the security of our person and families. Providing for the common defense is the most essential responsibility of government. Issues ranging from the scope of antitrust laws to tax policy can be debated. However, there can be no debate that we all want to be protected from a terrorist attack and that we expect our government to provide that protection.

Finally, homeland security law is here to stay because there now exists an entire federal bureaucracy that is charged with its implementation: the Department of Homeland Security. The president's 2003 budget earmarks $38 billion dollars to homeland security. These funds will support a new department of government whose primary purpose is to ensure the safety of America's critical infrastructure, the bulk of which is in private hands. This new department combines 22 existing agencies, with over 170,000 employees. It seems patently obvious to anyone with even a rudimentary understanding of the functions of the federal bureaucracy that a department this large, with a single issue-focused budget of $38 billion, and whose efforts necessarily target the private sector, will not go quietly into the night. The Department will serve as the primary driver of homeland security law.

And, while the large tent that houses the various homeland security agencies is new, the bulk of the agencies that form the action offices of the new department have existed for years. For example, the Coast Guard, which is now part of the Department of Homeland Security, is the nation's longest standing seagoing service—pre-dating even the Navy. These re-organized agencies come into the Department of Homeland Security with their own established bureaucratic momentum. Moreover, unlike the Office of Civilian Defense, which stood down after World War II, the missions of the Homeland Security Department and its various agencies are not fixed to a war that has a defined end state (victory or loss). Terrorism has been around since biblical times and despite our new commitment to stamp it out, it is unlikely to go away any time soon. Moreover, America's role as the lone remaining superpower ensures our nation will remain a target.

Immediately after the 9/11 attacks, President Bush summarized the priorities of the nation as three-fold: protect the American people; safeguard our critical infrastructure; and insulate our economy from the impacts of the war on terrorism. It has been almost two years since the 9/11 attacks. During this period, the nation has faced dour economic prospects, a record projected federal deficit, record high gas prices, the re-entry break up of the space shuttle Columbia, widespread corporate governance scandals, efforts to fundamentally alter existing environmental policies, and countless other serious issues. Despite these other serious challenges and issues, the focus of our government and the public has remained relatively constant on these three goals for nearly two years. In Washington terms, that represents immense staying power.

1.4   The Transition in Government

As noted above, besides beginning to build an entirely new body of homeland security law, the Congress, in response to the 9/11 attacks, has also re-organized the government and created a new bureaucracy to address this threat.

While a variety of agencies, ranging from the National Guard to the FBI, continue to play a role in safeguarding the American homeland, the primary responsibility for directing these efforts is now vested in the newly created Department of Homeland Security.

The Department of Homeland Security was established by Congress on November 25, 2002. The department is comprised of 22 pre-existing federal agencies, which have been placed under the single umbrella of this new Cabinet-level department. The re-organization of these agencies represents the largest single transformation of the federal government since President Harry Truman merged the various individual Armed Services into the Department of Defense. The resulting Department of Homeland Security is the second largest department within the entire federal government.

Although the department is largely a conglomeration of parts of pre-existing agencies, its creation is far more than just a reshuffling of the deck chairs. The shift of these agencies represents a very public re-ordering of their priorities. For example, when the Coast Guard was under the Department of Transportation, its mission orientation served a variety of co-equal goals including commerce, crime prevention, environmental protection, and sea-border integrity. Now the Coast Guard responds solely to the Secretary of Homeland Security. This transfer of authority clearly makes the Coast Guard's main mission homeland security. Now, given a choice between enforcing fisheries treaties and enforcing new security standards for regulated facilities, the Coast Guard will without question focus its efforts and resources on homeland security.

In addition to re-ordering their priorities, many of these re-organized agencies have also been given considerable new powers—and in bureaucratic terms, stature—through the various new homeland security laws.

The Coast Guard has been granted substantial regulatory authorities over vast reaches of maritime-related infrastructure. Clearly, the Coast Guard's tide is rising. Along these same lines, the Immigration and Naturalization Service (INS) has long been viewed by its critics as an agency adrift and incapable of carrying out its basic mission of managing the movement of people into and out of this nation. However, the enforcement side of the INS is now under the Department of Homeland Security and has been given greater powers and more resources. Similarly, the Transportation Security Administration (TSA) is culled, in part, from the Department of Transportation. However, the TSA's powers and responsibilities now extend far beyond those that were vested in the former Department of Transportation programs. For example, the TSA is now charged with the screening of all passengers at all the nation's commercial airports; before 9/11, the various airports were responsible for providing private security to screen passengers.[23]

While the new department represents the cornerstone of the new homeland security bureaucracy, the 9/11 transition of government does not end there. Numerous agencies that have not been shifted into the new department have, nevertheless, taken on new responsibilities. For example, few would classify the Environmental Protection Agency as a security agency. However, the EPA has played a substantial role in ongoing efforts to secure infrastructure components, such as chemical plants.[24] The EPA—apart from the FBI's National Infrastructure Protection Center alerts—has issued warnings of potential terrorist activities to the industry. It has also conducted training programs to assist industry members in preparing vulnerability assessments. The EPA, however, stresses that because these efforts are voluntary in nature, the agency is not monitoring security at these facilities or overseeing their efforts; in fact, a recent GAO Report stresses that no governmental agency is ensuring that security at these potential high-value target is adequate.[25] Additionally, pursuant to the Public Health Security and Bioterrorism Preparedness Act of 2002, the Environmental Protection Agency is now responsible for ensuring that the nation's community water systems conduct vulnerability assessments and prepare security and emergency response plans. This new mandate gave the EPA, which many argue had seen its star dim under the Bush Administration, a new purpose and cause célèbre. Along these same lines, the Congress is presently considering a number of legislative proposals that would dress this once "green agency" still more in the "olive drab" of homeland security.[26]

The Department of Energy has taken on a similar role with respect to energy production facilities. Recognizing the importance of its new homeland security mission, the Department of Energy has formed a new office, the Office of Energy Assurance, staffed by senior-level former military officers, to work with the energy sector to enhance critical energy sector infrastructure security. Similarly, the Department of Transportation has regulatory over the nation's vast array of pipelines. Pursuant to the new Pipeline Safety Improvement Act, the Secretary of Transportation is now required to develop new regulations to increase the counter-terrorism security of critical pipelines.[27] In other words, the re-orientation of government towards the goal of homeland security extends well beyond the walls of the new Department of Homeland Security.

Perhaps the clearest sign of the transition of the Executive branch is the degree to which truces, if not armistices, have been declared in long-fought turf battles. For example, the FBI and the CIA have for ages jealously guarded their roles, their turfs, and even their intelligence, from one in other—and from others including the private sector and state and local law enforcement. In the wake of the 9/11 attacks, the intelligence establishment has worked surprisingly well together and the degree of information sharing between the CIA and the FBI is at unprecedented levels. These agencies are also increasingly sharing information with non-federal law enforcement and even the companies that own and operate the nation's infrastructure. This is not to suggest that the art of bureaucratic infighting has vanished from the Capital landscape. However, the attacks of 9/11 seem to have broken through decades of petty argumentation.

The reorganization of government also extends beyond the Executive Branch. In the Congress, the House has formed the Select Committee on Homeland Security. The Select Committee's task is to study how the House should organize to handle homeland security issues, including the difficult task of deciding what committees should have jurisdiction over homeland security matters. The Select Committee is seen by some as a precursor to a standing committee on homeland security in the 109th Congress.[28]

1.5   The Transition in the Private Sector

The emerging body of homeland security law has not only brought about a significant restructuring of government, it is also beginning to cause elements of the private sector to adapt.

With few notable exceptions, companies have traditionally relegated security concerns to the middle (or lower) ranks of their management hierarchies. Corporate security managers in most instances have had a number of levels of oversight between them and the officers of their companies. And, in many if not most instances, these security managers have reported through the human resources departments. In other words, before 9/11, security did not occupy a prominent place in the corporate suite, nor was the issue high up on upper-level management's agenda.

This is changing. Given the number of emerging statutory and regulatory requirements, and the specter of both penalties and liabilities, many companies have re-organized their security programs. Many companies have hired or plan to hire chief security officers who report directly to upper-most management.

Companies are also dedicating substantial resources to their security and security regulatory compliance. The White House estimates that the private and public (federal, state, and local) sectors now spend roughly $100 billion per year on homeland security. The Council of Economic Advisors estimates that in future years, the private sector may spend up to $110 billion per year on security (up from $55 billion per year, pre-9/11). Similarly, a recent survey by Deloitte Consulting and Aviation Week, estimates that total spending for homeland security in 2003 is projected to range from $93 to $138 billion.[29]

Proactive companies have also begun to manage their security matters through their general counsel offices and with the use of outside law firms, in order to better ascertain and limit their potential liabilities. And, recognizing that security mandates could have large impacts on their bottom lines, potentially impacted companies have begun to beef up their government relations efforts to influence the rules that they will have to live by. In other words, corporate security is shifting from a human relations component to an increasingly legal and regulatory component.

The private bar has also begun to recognize the importance of homeland security law. Firms such as Bracewell & Patterson; Patton Boggs; Venable, McKenna, Long & Aldridge; Powell, Goldstein, Frazer & Murphy; and Preston Gates Ellis have formed homeland security practice groups to offer specific expertise in these dynamic and complex matters.

All this points to the growing importance of homeland security law as a legal discipline.

1.6   The Glide Path of Homeland Security Law

In analyzing the glide path of homeland security law—where the law will be in a decade or two—one analogy is environmental protection. Environmental expenditures add cost to the operations of critical corporate infrastructure but are made necessary as a matter of risk management, regulatory compliance, and disclosure. Security expenditures similarly track critical infrastructure and operations. Both disciplines were met with early resistance from private industry. It took industry decades for the boardrooms of America to fully embrace environmental thinking. Similarly, many industry actors continue to drag their feet on inculcating security planning in their business planning. For example, despite the intervention of the federal government into the marketplace to make terrorism insurance both widely available and less costly, the *New York Times* reports that many companies are now foregoing the option to buy such policies—electing instead to roll the dice that one day they may be directly or indirectly the victim of a terrorist attack.[30] This represents the Ford Pinto school of corporate thinking.

Both environmental and homeland security law are responses to emerging threats to health and safety. Both captured public's attention. Both place the onus on victims and potential victims. For example, the Comprehensive Environmental Response, Compensation and Liability Act, commonly known as Superfund, places the burden on even innocent property owners to pay for the cleanup of pollution damages inflicted by prior owners. In the security setting, companies are being forced to pay when they are not the underlying problem—the terrorists are the real problem. Moreover, the owner of infrastructure that has been attacked not only will have to pay to rebuild[31] but may also be subject to damages for negligent security.

Additionally, both environmental and homeland security law involved the creation of post-New Deal agencies and regulatory schemes. Both focus directly on privately held infrastructure.

Both disciplines respond to public pressure. And, public pressure for the development of each of these areas of the law during their formative periods has been driven by major public events. Pressure for environmental law grew with events like the 1965 New York blackouts and garbage strikes and the burning of the Cuyahoga River. Homeland security law's first impetus was the tragedy of 9/11. Now, homeland security law finds additional momentum with the tangentially connected war with Iraq. From a public opinion perspective, both disciplines begin with a basic, common public understanding of the problem but immense factual misunderstandings.

Given these similarities, environmental law offers a valuable comparative law window into the likely course of homeland security law. To this end, spending on pollution control has been a constantly increasing business cost since the 1970s. Since 1972, business spending on pollution control has risen $105.5 billion—from $16.5 billion in 1972 to $122 billion in 1994. According to the

Survey of Current Business, pollution control cost $122 billion in 1994, or a sum equal to about 1.8 percent of GDP. The government does not have current data on pollution costs, but if it remained at 1.8 percent of GDP spending last year, it would have been about $180 billion.[32] Environmental considerations were once viewed as a mere adjunct to other core functions. Today, the environment is a freestanding and significant law and policy practice. The similarities between these disciplines are adequate enough to indicate that homeland security law will to some extent follow a similar evolutionary process.

There are, however, major differences between these fields that suggest that the developmental process for homeland security law will outpace that of environmental law. Most environmental damages accrue over time and are unintentional and insidious; homeland security damages are intentional and occur from one or more events. Environmental standards rely on scientifically measurable parameters (such as parts per million); homeland security standards are heuristic (safety is the absence of a measurable event). Homeland security matters begin with broad public support and less division than we have come to expect in environmental legal matters. One can argue that at least to some degree that wholesale support is a function of ignorance. Homeland security law begins without a broad public understanding of what true homeland security entails. Once such an understanding develops and the potentially invasive nature of this legal discipline begins to take hold, there is the potential for even greater rancor here. As discussed above, because homeland security law deals with a more immediate threat to life and nation, there has to date been none of the balancing of interests that has slowed efforts to turn certain environmental goals into laws. On balance, these factors suggest that, if anything, we can expect homeland security law to develop more quickly than the several decade long process that led to today's environmental law.

In fact, these differences already seem to be having just such an accelerant effect. In just the first year with both a real homeland security imperative and a department in place, the private sector will spend here roughly two-thirds of what it spends on the fully developed field of environmental protection. It took eight years after the publication of Rachel Carson's seminal book, *Silent Spring*, before the Congress and President Nixon created the Environmental Protection Agency. It took an additional three years before the Endangered Species Act was enacted. In contrast, the Bush Administration created a high-level, Cabinet equivalent homeland security office less than a year after the 9/11 attacks; an actual Cabinet department was enacted just over two years after these attacks.

2.0 Major Issues in the Future of Homeland Security Law

In essence, homeland security law presently exists as a rough sketch of a large edifice. As noted above, over time, that sketch will need to be transformed into a far more detailed construct. Here, by virtue of necessity—the need to secure our nation now—the process of planning and building are occurring on parallel tracks. This raises the potential for miscues and false starts. The following are a number of the important issues that the Executive Branch, legislators, affected parties, and the bar will need to address during this process. Each of the issues discussed below will have a major impact on what homeland security law looks like for the future.

2.1 Acceptable Level of Risk

Ultimately security is an absolute: either you remain secure from attack or you are a victim. However, this absolute is a poor benchmark before the fact in gauging performance and/or compliance. This raises the issue as to how "secure" is "secure?" Security is imperfect. However, what needs better definition in homeland security legal terms are what level of risk is acceptable, and what is the threat basis against which this level of risk should be measured

With respect to what level of risk is acceptable, at present homeland security laws typically require regulated parties to conduct vulnerability assessments and prepare security plans to address the risks. However, these statutes tend to offer little or no guidance as to how secure a facility must actually be. For example, under the Port and Maritime Security Act, facilities are required to have security plans to deter and repulse terrorist attacks. However, the act does not set out what standard that security is to be measured against.

The lack of a risk benchmark is troubling in at least two respects. First, it creates a situation where, because security can be costly, facilities that make themselves more secure could face real and substantial competitive disadvantage vis-à-vis competitors who adopt lesser security programs. This disadvantage would serve as a disincentive for companies to secure their operations and would undermine our national goal of enhanced homeland security. Second, discrepancies between facilities in terms of risk would allow terrorists to "target shop"—seeking the less secure facility in a class. If terrorists can still find a less secure target, we as a nation suffer not only the harm of any such attack, but also the economic drag occasioned by the added costs of security adopted by more forward-thinking actors.

In considering what level of risk is acceptable, homeland security law as a discipline also needs to factor in the nature of the potential harm. A 50 percent failure rate at a facility where an attack could cause minimal harm may be acceptable. However, such a level of risk seems patently unacceptable at nuclear plants where one failure could kill hundreds of thousands of people.

In order to determine a level of acceptable risk, it is necessary to have a threat standard against which security needs to perform. In security terms, this is called the "Design Basis Threat." For example, nuclear plant security requires effective protection against an assault by any of the following: 1) a small number of skilled and well-armed attackers aided by an insider; 2) a lone insider acting alone; or 3) a bomb within a four-wheel drive vehicle. However, despite all their security, in tests involving mock, or "red cell," intruder teams have been able to successfully attack nuclear plants in roughly half the exercises—even with prior notice of the tests.[33]

The design basis threat that is adopted for homeland security regulatory programs will be critical in determining both how secure our nation will be and what is required of regulated parties. For example, a facility could have the best physical security in the world but could remain vulnerable to a cyber-attack that might not kill anyone, but could do millions in damages. Whether such a facility passes muster will depend on what threats the design basis requires that facility's security to address.

2.2 Mandatory Versus Voluntary Versus Market-Driven Programs

Traditionally, private sector security, in all but the most sensitive industries, has been left up to the individual companies. However, the new homeland security statutes tend to create a structure under which the government has the authority to impose mandatory security requirements. For example, under the Maritime Security Act and the Bioterrorism Act the owner/operators of the infrastructure must develop security plans and have them approved by the relevant federal authorities. In some cases, these statutes go even further, venturing into the area of command and control. The Maritime Security Act not only requires facilities to have badge programs to control access, but it requires that these programs incorporate security checks of people and utilize biometric technologies. A facility that fails to meet these requirements can be subject to penalties up to and including closure.

In contrast, other sectors that have not been subjected to new statutory requirements continue to operate on the basis of voluntary security schemes. For example, the chemical industry is not subject to any specific homeland security provisions. The EPA has reported that it believes it has authority under certain Clean Air Act provisions to impose security requirements. However, EPA has not done so for fear of legal challenges to that authority. At the same time, many chemical industry members have begun to upgrade their security, in large part due to voluntary programs being undertaken through their trade associations. Against this landscape the EPA and the Department of Homeland Security have said that they feel that security legislation specific to the chemical industry should be developed. And, there is at least one fairly draconian proposed bill now before the Congress that would mandate extensive security at chemical plants.[34]

There has been a growing criticism from industry and others, that mandatory command and control type schemes, particularly in the field of environmental law, provide inadequate flexibility, impose unnecessary costs and, at times can even frustrate their own goals. However, those who see "voluntary compliance" schemes as oxymoronic counter that without mandates improvements simply do not happen because companies are unwilling to spend money unless forced to. This debate has yet to rage in the area of homeland security. However, as the number of homeland security provisions continues to grow, one can expect to see the mandatory versus voluntary issue come into play.

A third possible approach to homeland security law would rely on market-based mechanisms to drive homeland security. The federal government has already taken a strong step in this direction with the Terrorism Risk Insurance Act (TRIA). The TRIA provides a federal backstop to essentially cap insurance industry losses in the case of future, major terrorist attacks. At the outset, the TRIA also requires insurers to offer terrorism insurance coverage for certified terrorism losses on terms that are not materially different from the terms, amounts, and other limitations applicable to other losses under other property and casualty policies.

By intervening to ensure that a terrorism risk insurance market exists, the federal government has created the condition precedent required for one potential strong market-based homeland security vehicle. It is in the interest of insurers to encourage their insured to reduce the risks of a potential terrorist attack through adequate security and other mechanisms. And, the cost of insurance to the consumer is largely driven by risk. In other words, once the TRIA becomes fully internalized by the market, insurers should begin to require certain basic levels of security from their insured. We should also expect to see insurers offering better terms to those companies that have taken additional steps to further reduce their risks—just as a homeowner gets a better rate for having alarm systems in their home.

Another example of a market-based homeland security mechanism is the now pending Bio-Shield legislation. At present there is little incentive for pharmaceutical companies to make significant investments in developing drugs to respond to threats from weapons of mass destruction. In essence, the current system says to these companies the equivalent of "one day we may need an aircraft carrier, so you in the private sector should use your money to build them, and if we need them, we will call you." Obviously, such an approach would never work. To address this problem, the president has proposed the Bio-Shield legislation, which would provide incentives to help generate market-based impetus for the development of homeland security drugs.

Market-based regulatory schemes are subject to many of the same criticisms as are voluntary programs. That said, profit motive can be an important motivator to encourage companies to embrace a goal.

To what extent homeland security law will evolve as a system of mandatory rules backed by penalties, or market-based programs, or voluntary programs remains to be seen. The body of law to date strongly suggests that the trend favors a mandatory, compliance-oriented scheme. Moreover, there seems to be growing unease among many decisionmakers that significant numbers of companies have not fully embraced their homeland security responsibilities. If this unease grows to the point of frustration, the potential for even more mandates and penalties will only grow. The most likely result is a blend of all three options. However, the proportions of each option in the regulatory mix remain a critical point.

2.3   Public-Private Interplay

The overwhelming majority of our nation's critical infrastructure is privately held and maintained. A critical issue is who should bear the responsibility to secure this infrastructure.

There are examples where at highly critical private facilities the government now takes the responsibility for security. For example, the new Aviation and Transportation Security Act provides that the federal government is now responsible for security and passenger screening at the nation's airports. Along these lines, in the immediate wake of the September 11th attacks, the Governor of Arkansas dispatched state national guard units to provide security at certain munitions manufacturing plants—and sent these facilities the bill shortly thereafter.

There are, however, real issues that arise with the transfer of security responsibilities from the private sector to the public sector. First, security cannot be completely detached from the industrial competitiveness dynamic. If security clearances hold up the availability of workers to perform jobs, those jobs go undone and productivity falls. If security delays the movement of goods and raw materials to a certain degree, just-in-time manufacturing no longer is a viable option and competitiveness suffers. In a capitalist system, competitiveness and profitability are most likely to be obtained where the bulk of factors impacting these variables are controlled by private sector actors. Placing security in the hands of the government would detach it from the economic equation and insulate it from market factors. The ultimate impact would most likely be a serious drain on competitiveness.

However, if our homeland security system is to be built around the private sector as the responsible actor, the importance of public-private coordination grows exponentially. As discussed above, under the Clinton Administration, the federal government began to put in place the infrastructure to allow the federal government to better work with the private companies that own and operate our critical infrastructure. This system remains the principal vehicle for public-private homeland security coordination. In addition, the new Department of Homeland Security has, pursuant to statute, formed a private sector advisory committee to the Secretary. Further, the department has an office dedicated to serving as the liaison to the private sector. Most of the action agencies within the department, such as Customs, have a long history of working in their respective areas with the private sector. Federal agencies, such as the Department of Homeland Security and the Energy Department, have made real efforts to reach out to industry to assist them in becoming better secured. That said, the Bush Administration's first Homeland Security Strategy did not include a chapter, section, or even subsection specifically on working with the private sector.

There are still major challenges in crafting an effective public-private homeland security partnership. Information flow remains inadequate in both directions. While necessary, national security information controls greatly diminish the ability of the government to disseminate information to the private sector frontlines. The existing coordination structures are dominated by, and almost exclusively populated by, major industrial actors. Apart from the major players, most private sector companies remain in the dark about what is required of them. These smaller companies, to which many larger companies are interconnected and dependent upon, are a major weak link in the security chain. Building a better public-private partnership is a real challenge for homeland security law.

2.4   Funded Versus Unfunded Mandates

Related to the issue of who is responsible to provide security is the issue of who should pay for such security. Effective security does not come cheap. By way of example, the American Waterworks Association has called for $2 billion in federal support to help secure just the nation's drinking water supplies. This raises the issue of who should pay the cost of securing America's critical infrastructure.

On the one hand, this infrastructure is largely owned by private companies that profit from this infrastructure. It is in the interest of these companies to safeguard their corporate assets and protect against potential liabilities. In fact, with respect to publicly held companies, these companies have a duty to their shareholders to protect their infrastructure holdings. Couple these facts with the looming, record federal deficit of $304 billion for fiscal year 2004—not including the cost of the war with Iraq—and there is an argument to be made that the private sector should pay for its own security.

On the other hand, the responsibility of providing for "the common defense" is the federal government's, not the private sector's. Moreover, if the private sector is forced to pay the bill for security, the American economy could be the next victim. The Federal Reserve Board of New York estimates that $10 billion in private sector homeland security spending would permanently lower U.S. labor productivity by 1.12 percent, or about $70 billion per year. A study by Deloitte Consulting projects "major private sector companies" will spend between $45.9 billion and $76.5 billion on homeland security in 2003 alone. These economic impacts suggest that the federal government must help defray the costs of homeland security or our economy will suffer.

The indications as to whether homeland security legal mandates will be funded are mixed. The Maritime Security Act includes a provision that authorizes the federal government to give grants to regulated facilities to offset the costs of statutorily mandated security improvements. However, originally no funds were appropriated to that task. The federal government since provided ports $92.3 million in security funding in 2002, and recently announced a second round of grants totaling $170 million. As substantial as this funding seems, these dollars are only a small slice of the approximately $4.4 billion that the industry and Coast Guard believe will be necessary to fully fund the security upgrades called for under the act.[35]

However, the second round of port security grants provides important insights into the funding issue. The majority of the grants provided in the second round went directly from the federal government to private sector companies. For example, the single largest grant in the round was $13,467,015 to CITGO's Lake Charles, Louisiana, operation. Other grantees included Sunoco, Dow Chemical Corporation, BASF Corporation, Shell Chemical LP, CSX Lines, Williams Energy, Partners, and Chevron.

Whether the federal government on a broader scale will fund the cost of private infrastructure security will play a major role in the homeland security law evolutionary process. Regulated parties will be far less likely to fight against homeland security mandates if they do not have to bear the costs of these new requirements. Moreover, if the federal government is willing to pay for added security, any party that opposes a new security provision seriously risks being seen by its consumer public as an unpatriotic corporate actor.

2.5   Liabilities

Another cost issue that looms on the horizon of homeland security law is the issue of liabilities. There are cases in which victims of terrorism have brought suit against companies for their failure to provide adequate security. Potential terrorist attacks against large-scale infrastructure systems in particular raise the possibility of massive losses and, in turn, liabilities. These potential liabilities range from compensation to the families of people who fell victim to such an attack to business interruption claims. By way of example, some experts suggest that business interruption claims arising from the 9/11 attacks could potentially top property loss claims. Lloyd's of London estimates that business interruption claims stemming from the 9/11 attacks will reach $10 billion.[36]

In the wake of the 9/11 attacks, countless terrorist threat scenarios that once seemed implausible now seem very possible. The federal government issues new warnings of possible attacks against infrastructure ranging from cruise ships to chemical plants on an almost daily basis. Things that were once unthinkable seem reasonably foreseeable.

Nevertheless, one can argue whether innocent parties should bear the costs of harms inflicted by third party terrorists.

Proponents of maintaining the tort responsibilities argue that responsible parties owe their employees and customers some measure of reasonable security. Parties who fail to meet that duty are arguably negligent and should be held responsible. Additionally, proponents of allowing liabilities for the failure to secure argue that taking the threat of potential future liabilities off the table would greatly reduce the incentives to companies to encourage them to better secure our critical infrastructure.

Rarely are these issues simple and clear-cut. If we acknowledge that security is by nature inherently imperfect, it is possible for a non-negligent party to become the victim of a terrorist attack—which still could subject them to a lawsuit as well as potential liabilities given the emotive vagaries of the legal system. Additionally, absent a broad, or at least industry, standard for what constitutes reasonable security, companies have no idea to what standard they will be held to after the fact.

For example, in the case of the 9/11 attacks, the terrorist used box cutters as weapons to hijack the planes. At the time, box cutters were not banned by federal rules from being carried aboard a commercial airliner. Many might argue that it is inappropriate to hold an airline negligent for the failure to prevent a lawful instrument from being brought onto a plane. Plaintiffs' advocates would counter that the law sets a bare minimum and, that standard notwithstanding, the reasonable airline should have known better than to allow an instrument that could so easily be used as a weapon on board.

The unease among many to hold companies liable for the malicious acts of third party terrorists factored heavily into the debate over the Terrorism Risk Insurance Act. When the TRIA was debated, a significant number of Congressional members sought to have the measure include broad tort reform provisions that would have substantially limited the liabilities of insurers and companies for damages other than real damages stemming from terrorist attacks. The Republican-controlled House originally passed a version that would have protected property owners from punitive damages. The then-Democratically-controlled Senate's version only banned the use of federal backstop funds to pay punitive damages. The White House favored the House language. After much wrangling between the House, Senate, and the White House, the TRIA as enacted provided only that punitive damages could not be used to calculate an insurer's losses for the purpose of triggering the TRIA backstop. This provision also precludes federal funds from being used to pay for punitive damages.

Tort reform issues were also a major sticking point during the legislative process surrounding the Department of Homeland Security statute. Late—and controversial—additions to the Department of Homeland Security Bill included provisions that would shield vaccine ingredient manufacturers from liability lawsuits and limit the liability of airport security scanning machine manufacturers who made faulty devices. The vaccine provision was touted by advocates as necessary to encourage drug manufacturers to produce the drugs needed to protect the American people from nuclear, chemical, and biological threats. However, the vaccine ingredient provision also barred families of autistic children from suing the makers of a vaccine ingredient that is believed to cause the disease among children vaccinated with drugs containing the compound. This provision caused such political heat that in follow on legislation it was repealed.

In addition to tort liabilities, parties now regulated under new homeland security laws face potential liabilities in the form of penalties for the failure to comply with these statutes. For example, a facility that violates the Maritime Security Act can be subject to a civil penalty of $25,000 per violation. In addition, the Coast Guard can also order a maritime facility in noncompliance to close. These penalty provisions generally mirror those used in other areas of law.[37]

Suffice it to say that these liability issues related to homeland security are not going away. Tort reform issues will continue to be debated in the context of future homeland security legislative developments. The potential liabilities for alleged failures to provide adequate security will be litigated in conjunction with lawsuits resulting from the 9/11 attacks. Any future attacks will also likely bring similar lawsuits. Companies that fail to comply with homeland security laws will face fines. Future homeland security laws will continue to rely on penalties to encourage compliance. This leaves those responsible for securing our critical infrastructure in the lurch. About the only certainties for now are that these companies have a higher burden of security and could face far greater liabilities than prior to 9/11. The prudent course of action would seem to be to proactively manage these risks and potential liabilities—as opposed to adopting a wait and see approach that could end up costing large sums of money down the road.

2.6   Federalism

In most aspects of defense and national security, military units and intelligence agents man the frontlines, or the pointy end of the spear. In contrast, state and local law enforcement, first responders, and agencies largely man the homeland security frontlines. While federal law agencies play a critical role here, their numbers are small in proportion to the numbers of nonfederal assets, from state and local police to firefighters. It is the state and locals who have the closest contacts within their communities and with critical infrastructure companies within their jurisdictions. Similarly, should another terrorist attack occur, the first responders will come from the state and local ranks. For example, Timothy McVeigh, the main Oklahoma City bomber, was captured by an Oklahoma State Trooper who pulled him over during a routine traffic stop that turned up an unregistered firearm. In order to be effective, homeland security will require a coordinated effort between federal, state, and local authorities.

The early relationships between these governmental ranks have been, at times, difficult. State and local officials complain that Washington has handed them significant new counter-terrorism responsibilities without the resources required. A number of governors and police and first responder leaders have called for more federal funding and assistance.

In addition to critiquing performance at the federal level, a number of states have been willing to set their own homeland security agendas. The nation's first port security law was enacted by Florida, not at the federal level. New York State was the first to require public utilities to assess their security and vulnerabilities and report out to the state. The New York legislature is currently considering legislation to require much greater security at chemical plants—even as similar legislation has floundered on Capitol Hill. These developments follow the traditional federalist paradigm.

How these relationships will shake out remains to be seen. The defense and security nature of homeland security, however, suggests that the form of federalism here will be more federally weighted. In other words, we should expect a more hierarchical structure with the federal government playing a greater role in setting priorities and benchmarks. Still, some states will continue to push beyond the federal baselines and serve as test beds for more stringent homeland security mandates.

2.7   Information and the Ostrich Dilemma

Lawyers, particularly litigators, have dreams—in some cases nightmares—about the smoking gun. The proverbial smoking gun in modern day litigation is the one document that proves in one fell swoop that the other side is wrong and is liable. In the aftermath of 9/11, out of fear and/or patriotism, the private sector produced countless potential smoking guns.

The response of many companies after the terrorist attacks of September 11th was to have a vulnerability assessment of their operations prepared. By their nature, such assessments provide laundry lists of potential gaps in a company's security. Unless these processes are tightly managed, such assessments also have the propensity to offer up long lists of options for how such gaps can be closed—options that can be costly prohibitive.

Where a company opts not to address an identified vulnerability without articulating the specific reasons why it did not address the vulnerability, the threat assessment itself can expose the company to greater liabilities—even if the company only declined to do one in a long list of options. In such a case, the assessment becomes the potential smoking gun: a comprehensive summary of everything the company was warned could happen to it, along with how such attacks could have been prevented had the company only done everything recommended. Plaintiffs could use this information to prove key elements in a negligence suit following an attack. Additionally, proof of the intentional decision not to take steps to close a known risk could be used to seek punitive damages, greatly increasing the potential liabilities of the company. Additionally, the impact of making public that a company knew of a risk and did nothing to prevent a deadly attack could cause a company to lose in a trial by media and bring about a major loss of public goodwill.

The risk that a vulnerability assessment could come back to haunt a company is real. In the litigation stemming from the first World Trade Center bombing, plaintiffs have sought access to vulnerability assessment conducted for the New York-New Jersey Port Authority prior to the truck bombing.

The status quo puts companies in a terrible bind. They want to do the right thing to assess and improve their security; however, they don't want such an exercise to potentially increase their liabilities by orders of magnitude. This is the ostrich dilemma: is it riskier to be ignorant or to know? This situation is also a tremendous impediment to improving the security of our nation's critical infrastructure from terrorism.

At present, the only ready means available to help companies protect information developed in a security assessment process is the attorney-client privilege. Generally speaking, the attorney-client privilege protects communications between attorneys and their clients in preparation for litigation. The privilege is extended to communications between attorneys and other consultants, including security consultants, who are assisting in the provision of legal advice to a client. Concerned companies that are contemplating conducting a security assessment to identify and reduce potential legal liabilities should use outside counsel[38] to commission the assessment, oversee the process, produce the final product, and transmit it to the client.[39]

The use of the privilege in any specific case will be determined by specific factual matters and the law of the individual jurisdiction. That said, even in cases where the privilege is claimed in good faith and rejected, the privilege is still of use from the litigant's perspective: plaintiffs may ultimately obtain the document but not without a court's review and supervision. In other words, the privilege may have its limits here, but it remains the best (or only) solution for now.

During the 1990s, environmental law confronted a similar public policy challenge: how to prevent potential liabilities and penalties from serving as a disincentive to companies that want to look at their operations and reduce their environmental impacts. As a result, a number of states passed audit shield laws that limited the exposure of a company that conducted an audit, found a problem, and took steps to address that problem.

While there are differences between the environmental audit shield laws and the security issues discussed here, in general, from a public policy perspective, the audit shield model would seem to be a sound one. A security audit shield law framework could, for example, provide that if a company undertook a vulnerability assessment, and then took reasonable steps to address any major vulnerabilities identified, that assessment could not be used to seek punitive damages.

A parallel informational risk is the risk that arises from the disclosure of security information to governmental agencies. While our nation's critical infrastructure is largely in private hands, threats to this infrastructure are an important national security concern. For this reason, federal, state, and local governments are all actively seeking vulnerability assessment-type information from the owners and operators of infrastructure. It is in our national interest for law enforcement, first responders, and other counter-terrorism authorities to have access to such information. Knowledge is critical to preparation and prevention. However, it does little good for such information to be shared with government agencies if they cannot safeguard that information, in particular preventing its disclosure to our enemies.

Here again, there is the risk of public disclosure. The federal government, as well as the states and many smaller political subdivisions, have freedom of information, or sunshine, laws. If a company provides a governmental agency with information concerning its vulnerabilities, that company risks its information being "FOIA'd" and then seeing its information splashed on the front pages and newscasts.

Certain homeland security information may be protected from disclosure as classified for national security purposes. Broadly speaking, information that is classified cannot lawfully be disclosed and can only be shared on a need to know basis with individuals who are cleared at the level of classification required for access to that specific information. In order for information to be classified, a classifying authority needs to determine that the information is in the possession of the government and must fall within the definitions of the types of information protected by the three levels of classification (i.e., confidential, secret, and top secret).[40]

The use of national security protections in the private sector critical infrastructure context raises a number of challenges. First, the bar for what should be protected as classified is fairly high. For example, the test for confidential, the lowest tier, is that "the unauthorized disclosure of [the information protected] reasonably could be expected to cause damage to the national security."[41] The test here isn't whether the information in question could prove useful to a terrorist or might even lead to an attack; the test is whether the harm would rise to the level of damaging national security. The typical vulnerability assessment might show a terrorist a company's weak spots, however, in most instances even destroying that company is unlikely to damage national security. Second, the limitations on the use of information once it is classified also raise problems for the private sector. If a company's information is classified, that information can only be shared with people who have security clearances. Consider the dilemma a corporate chief security officer might face in requesting a larger budget from a corporate board that likely cannot examine the classified information upon which that request is based. Third, the process for obtaining security clearances can be arduous and expensive. Many private sector employees will find problems with or balk at the intrusiveness of the process required to obtain a clearance.

In addition, there is the substantial risk that information provided to a government agency in the security context could be used against the company in another context. For example, during a recent exchange with a major company, we were informed that a team from one of the homeland security agencies had asked to come onto the company's premises to examine its security and security plans. The company was inclined to open their doors and their books without limitation. But, what if the team had noticed an occupational health and safety violation? Or a violation of the Americans with Disabilities Act related or even unrelated to the security operations? Or, had witnessed some other bad act? The company would have had no protection against these government officials using the information obtained through the voluntary access against the company in some other proceeding.

Recognizing the chilling effect this concern could have on the necessary exchange of information between the private sector and the government, the Congress took a limited step to protect this type of information in the Homeland Security Act. The act provides that if a company voluntarily provides "critical infrastructure information" pertaining to as defined security matters to the Department of Homeland Security, and if that company accompanies this with a statement seeking protection under the act, then that information is exempt from disclosure under the Freedom of Information Act; exempt from statutory and administrative limitations on ex parte communications with decision-making officials; precluded from use by any federal, state, or local agency in any civil proceeding; and protected, absent written consent to the contrary, from any disclosure or use outside the purposes of infrastructure security by any employee of the United States. The statute does provide that the information can be used in a criminal investigation or prosecution; disclosed to Congress and its committees; and disclosed to the Comptroller General for use by the General Accounting Office.

These protections are at once wide sweeping and extremely narrow. Information voluntarily provided to the Department of Homeland Security receives significant insulation. However, information provided to the host of other agencies that now lay claim to some element of homeland security (such as the Department of Energy, the Federal Bureau of Investigations, the Department of Defense, or the Environmental Protection Agency) receives no such protection. Along these same lines, the disclosure protections provide significant insulation to "voluntary" communications. However, the growing number of homeland security statutes increasingly requires regulated companies to provide similar information to governmental agencies. It seems unlikely that information that is provided under a statutory or regulatory mandate could be seen as "voluntarily" provided. In other words, information provided under these new mandates would likely fall outside of the Homeland Security Acts disclosure shield provisions. Thus, this mandatory homeland security information could be subject to Freedom of Information Act disclosure, used in civil proceedings, and the like.

2.8   Security Mission Creep

Another major issue that must be dealt with as homeland security law develops is that of mission creep. The homeland security moniker carries great weight these days. Policies, issues, or projects that can be described as being under the homeland security umbrella can expect greater political and public support, which increases the chances of passage, implementation, and funding. For this reason a host of interests are already trying to spin their parochial concerns into the realm of homeland security. For example, the Natural Resources Defense Council, commonly known as NRDC, is one of the nation's more influential environmental groups. NRDC has long advocated a host of additional restrictions on chemical plants, including the banning of certain chemicals and restrictions on their location. In the wake of 9/11, NRDC has retooled their advocacy on behalf of such restrictions to couch them in the context of homeland security.[42] NRDC's efforts led to Senator Corzine's proposed Chemical Security Act,[43] which calls for many of the environmental protections NRDC has long sought but does so in the name of national security. At the other end of the spectrum, the Bush administration has consistently sought to have the Arctic National Wildlife Refuge opened for oil development as a matter of energy policy. Since 9/11, when the Bush administration discusses opening up the refugee, it routinely focuses on the potential security benefits of greater domestic oil and gas productions.[44]

This is not to suggest that there may not be legitimate security reasons for greater protections at chemical plants. Nor is it to suggest that our national security would not benefit from less reliance on foreign energy. However, these examples clearly show the risk of mission creep, wherein homeland security becomes all things to all people.

The risk of mission creep here is far greater than a loss of conceptual purity. If the mantel of homeland security becomes waylaid to serve only tangentially related interests, the political, public, and fiscal capital needed to address real homeland security needs will be squandered. For example, if the public perception shifts and people begin to believe that they are being asked to make new sacrifices for trumped up security reasons, the American people will be far less willing to forego the day-to-day nuisances that security often requires, such as longer lines and waits, having to provide identification in a host of new settings, and the like. Similarly, the fiscal resources for homeland security are arguably already inadequate to the tasks required; if these finite funds are siphoned off to other purposes, the homeland security-spending shortfall will only worsen.

2.9   Constitutional Issues

It can be argued that modern-day asymmetrical threats, such as terrorism, have created an inherent struggle between the broad promises of the Constitution's preamble—domestic tranquility and common defense—versus the specific guarantees of the other parts of the document and the accompanying Bill of Rights—for example, the right to trial, the equal protection clause, and freedom of speech and assembly. The American legal system has for centuries jealously guarded the rights of the individual. The 9/11 attacks have caused a dramatic re-balancing of these Constitutional protections away from the protections accorded every individual and toward the broader guarantees of society-wide safety and security. The PATRIOT Act gives law enforcement greatly enhanced authority to spy on private American citizens. The rights of the individual who is the subject of such surveillance have without question been eroded; at the same time, the wider right of every American to be secure has arguably been enhanced.

To civil libertarians on both the left and the right, new homeland security laws and rules amount to nothing less than an assault on the most basic American freedoms. Moreover, critics charge that, as Benjamin Franklin said, "They who would give up an essential liberty for temporary security, deserve neither liberty or security."

On the other side, the Bush administration, along with law enforcement and security experts and organizations argue that these new powers are vital to the fight against terrorism. For example, law enforcement authorities point to the case of Zacarias Moussaoui, the alleged twentieth hijacker in the 9/11 attacks. Moussaoui was arrested months prior to the 9/11 attacks in Minnesota for carrying a false passport. Local FBI agents identified him as a possible terrorist threat—he paid cash for flight training lessons; he insisted on training in jumbo jets even though he lacked skills for even small aircraft; and, he wanted instruction on only how to fly, not takeoffs and landings. The FBI field office sought clearance from headquarters to conduct electronic surveillance of Moussaoui, including of his computer hard drive. On August 26, 2001, French intelligence officials told the FBI that Moussaoui had ties to the Al Qaeda Network. Despite all this, the FBI did not believe that the information it had on Moussaoui was sufficient to meet the strict legal test required for domestic counter-terrorism surveillance. The field office's surveillance request was denied. Law enforcement and counter-terrorism experts argue that had the PATRIOT Act's provisions been in place prior to 9/11, the FBI would have been able to better investigate Moussaoui and perhaps even prevent the attacks.

Both sides here make compelling cases. Liberties are of value only to the living. However, security is a Pyhrric victory if it comes at the cost of the basic freedoms that make us a democracy.

The clash between civil liberties and the requirements of security has already resulted in a host of Constitutional litigation. The American Civil Liberties Union has challenged the use of "no fly watch lists" baring certain suspected terrorists from being able to fly on major air carriers.[45] The PATRIOT Act's provisions authorizing the secretive Foreign Intelligence Surveillance Court to issue wiretap and other warrants have been challenged by the defense in the prosecution of five individuals charged with conspiring to help the Al Qaeda network fight U.S. troops in Afghanistan. Library and bookseller organizations, joined by Internet privacy advocates, have brought suit seeking information concerning the implementation of certain controversial provisions of the PATRIOT Act, including those that increase law enforcement's Internet surveillance authorities and allow law enforcement access to records of what books investigation targets read and buy. Towns, cities, and counties across the country have passed resolutions attacking the act and in some cases have instructed municipal employees not to assist federal agents in investigations that they believe violate the Constitution.[46]

To date, the security arguments seem to have prevailed, at least in the legislative arena—witness the sweeping new authorities enacted in the PATRIOT Act. However, these issues are not going away. Each new round of homeland security lawmaking will bring new Constitutional challenges. And, the courts have yet to weigh in on most of these matters. Moreover, history shows that the jurisprudential and legislative back and forth between the powers of the state and the rights of the individual is a struggle as constant as the ebb and flow of the daily tide. As the discipline of homeland security law matures it will be shaped by and will shape these important Constitutional questions.

2.10   Risk of Abuse

One of the biggest challenges facing these charged with implementing the new homeland security laws is preventing their abuse and misuse. Homeland security is emerging as a powerful legal discipline, one that concentrates a great deal of authenticity and responsibility in a few hands. This concentration of power has already raised concerns about the potential for its abuse for political and other motives.

During a recent state political fight in Texas, Democratic state legislators fled the state to prevent a quorum in order to forestall a vote on a Republican-supported Congressional redistricting plan. The federal government is now investigating whether certain homeland security investigative powers and assets were improperly used to assist Republicans in trying to track and force the return of the reclusive Democrats.[47] If it is determined that such abuses occurred, this would play directly into the hands of critics who see new homeland security laws as a long step down an Orwellian path.

The degree to which homeland security law continues to benefit from bipartisan support and public backing will be, in large measure, determined by the ability of those in authority to keep them pure in purpose. With such a great concentration of power, and the accompanying temptation to use it, this may be no small task.

Endnotes:

[1] The fourth plane, United Airlines flight 93, was brought down in a field in Pennsylvania by the courageous actions of the passengers who fought back and prevented the plane from reaching the terrorists' planned target.

[2] Rubock, Daniel, and Tad Phillip. "CMBS: Moody's Approach to Terrorism Insurance for U.S. Commercial Real Estate." 1 March 2002. 14. (Available at https://www.nareit.com/governmentrelations/moodys.pdf)

[3] FBI. *Terrorism in the United States*. 1999, 59.

[4] International Security and Development Cooperation Act of 1985, Pub. L. 99-83, codified at 22 U.S.C. §2371 *et. seq.* (1985).

[5] Omnibus Diplomatic Security and Antiterrorism Act of 1986, Pub. L. 99-399, codified at 22 U.S.C. §4831 *et seq.* (1986).

[6] EO 12938, Nov. 14, 1994; EO 12947, Jan. 1995; PDD 39, U.S. Policy on Counter-Terrorism, 21 June 1995; PDD 62, 22 May 1998.

[7] As with any general statement, there are always exceptions to the broad rule. There are isolated, pre-9/11 statutes that arguably fall within the post-9/11 concept of the law of homeland security. For example, the Chemical Safety Information, Site Security, and Fuel Regulatory Relief Act of 1999 directed the Department of Justice to report to Congress on actions to minimize the risks of information concerning extremely hazardous chemicals from falling into the wrong hands. Similarly, given the nature of the threat they pose, even prior to September 11th, security at nuclear plants was subject to strict federal security standards and oversight.

[8] Inter-Agency Commission on Crime and Security in U.S. Seaports, Report of the Inter-Agency Commission on Crime and Security in U.S. Seaports, Fall 2000, iii.

[9] Inter-Agency Commission on Crime and Security in U.S. Seaports, Report of the Inter-Agency Commission on Crime and Security in U.S. Seaports, Fall 2000, v.

[10] *Ibid.*

[11] U.S. Commission on National Security/21st Century, Phase III Report, 15 February, 2001.

[12] PDD 63, Protecting America's Critical Infrastructure, 28 May 1998.

[13] Chemical Safety Information, Site Security and Fuels Regulatory Act, Pub. L. 106-40, 113 Stat. 207 (1999), codified at 42 U.S.C. § 7401 *et seq.* (1999).

[14] Prior efforts at homeland defense existed under the rubric of civilian defense. For example, during World War II, Franklin Roosevelt created the Office of Civilian Defense within the Office of Emergency Management. This office coordinated all federal, state and local domestic defense efforts during the war. Directives were issued from Washington, and the effort was managed and funded at the federal level. However, implementation occurred primarily at the local, or municipal level. In general, the punishment for failing to comply with a civil defense directive was a fine.

[15] Florida Seaport Transportation and Economic Development Seaport Security Standards, Fl. Code § 311.12 (2002).

[16] GAO. *Homeland Security: Voluntary Initiatives are Underway at Chemical Facilities, but the Extent of Security Preparedness is Unknown*, GAO-03-439, 14 March 2003, 16.

[17] Uniting and Strengthening America by Providing Appropriate Tools Required to Intercept and Obstruct Terrorism (USA PATRIOT Act) Act of 2001. Pub. L. 107-56, 115 Stat. 272 (2001), codified at 18 U.S.C. § 1 (2001). [hereinafter "PATRIOT Act"].

[18] Bracewell & Patterson, "Report of the Ad Hoc Committee, A Regional Airspace Security Response to the Air Terrorism Threat to Our Nation's Capital," 26 September 2001.

[19] By way of full disclosure, Bracewell & Patterson's Homeland Security Practice Group assisted a client whose drivers were covered under this provision in efforts to help licensing resume.

[20] While the attacks may have almost instantly raised the standard of care, what that new standard of care is will not be known for years—until after all the ensuing litigation has been completed.

[21] In a departure from the general rule, some PATRIOT Act provisions sunset after four years unless they are renewed.

[22] Labaton, Stephen. "Congress and the White House Strike Banking Reform Deal," *New York Times*. 22 October 1999.

[23] This authority was only briefly vested in the Department of Transportation during the interregnum between the creation of the TSA and the standing up of the Department of Homeland Security.

[24] Lee, Jennifer. "E.P.A. Said To Be Concentrating on Terror." *New York Times*. 29 April 2003.

[25] Public Health Security and Bioterrorism Preparedness Response Act of 2002, Pub. L. 107-118, 116 Stat. 594 (2002), codified at 42 U.S.C. § 201 *et. seq*. (2002).

[26] Comprehensive Homeland Security Act of 2003, S. 6, 108th Cong., 1st Session, 7 January 2003; Chemical Security Act of 2003, S. 157, 108th Cong. 1st Session, 14 January 2003.

[27] Pipeline Safety Improvement Act of 2002, Pub. L. 107-355, 116 Stat. 2985 (2002), codified at 49 U.S.C. § 60101 *et seq*. (2002).

[28] Willis, Derek. "Jockeying Begins for Chairmanship of Homeland Committee." *Congressional Quarterly*, 6 January 2003. (Available at http://cq.com).

[29] Ante, Spencer, et al., "What Has Changed; Homeland Security." *Business Week*, 16 September 2002, 30.

[30] Teaster, Joseph. "Insurance for Terrorism Still a Rarity." *New York Times*, 8 March 2003, C1.

[31] In truly devastating cases, such as the World Trade Center attacks, some of these costs have been offset by federal assistance.

[32] Blodgett, John. "Environmental Protection: Who Pays, How Much Does it Cost." CRS Report for Congress, Congressional Research Service, 16 April 1997.

[33] From 1991 to 1998, under the Nuclear Regulatory Commission's Operational Safeguards Response Evaluation (OSRE) program, nuclear plant security systems were tested through mock attacks. During this period, 27 of 57 tests found security shortcomings significant enough "that a real attack would have put the nuclear reactor in jeopardy with the potential for core damage and a radiological release." David Orrick, Nuclear Regulatory Commission, *Differing Professional Opinion*, 3 February 1999. After a hiatus, the OSRE program was reinstated in 1998. In 2000 and 2001, 6 of 11 OSRE tests identified major security lapses sufficient to allow terrorists to damage the reactor. Terrance Reis, Nuclear Regulatory Commission, *Physical Security Significance Determination Process,* 30 August 2001; Union of Concerned Scientists, Nuclear Reactor Security, 23 October 2001.

[34] Chemical Security Act of 2003, *supra* note 26.

[35] American Association of Port Authorities. "Ports Praise Security Funding but Need Much More," 14 January 2003.

[36] Widmer, Lori, "Business Interruption—Is Your Solution Strong Enough?" *Risk & Insurance.* (Available at: http://www.riskandinsurance.com/0602choice.asp).

[37] Toxic Substances Control Act, 15 U.S.C. § 2615(a)(1); Solid Waste Disposal Act, 42 U.S.C. § 6928(g).

[38] In-house counsel can also be used to seek to couch a document under the privilege. However, some courts seem less willing to extend the full measure of protection when in-house counsel is substituted for outside counsel.

[39] During the assessment process, counsel should also be charged with ensuring that the client company is in compliance with all relevant laws, rules, and regulations. There are a host of legal requirements that now apply to a company's security status. These requirements range from the application of the Americans with Disabilities Act to a company's evacuation plan to adherence to know your customer or client counter-money laundering requirements.

[40] Executive Order 12356, Fed. Reg., 47, 14874 (6 April 1982).

[41] Executive Order 12356, Fed. Reg., 47, 14874 (6 April 1982), §1.1(a). For example, Department of Defense guidance provides the following examples of the types of information that should be classified as confidential:

> The compromise of information that indicates strength of ground, air, and naval forces in the United States and overseas areas; disclosure of technical information used for training, maintenance, and inspection of classified munitions of war; revelation of performance characteristics, test data, design, and production data on munitions of war.

U.S. Department of Defense, *Information Security Program Regulation*, DOD 5200.1-R, Chap. I, §1-503, June 1986.

[42] NRDC, "The Hole in Our Homeland Security: Why Chemical Security Legislation is Needed Now." *Press Backgrounder*, April 2003.

[43] Chemical Security Act of 2003, *supra* note 26.

[44] AP, "Arctic Oil Gets Tied to Security Debate," 6 November 2001.

[45] American Civil Liberties Union, "ACLU Challenges Government Secrecy on 'No Fly' List at San Francisco Airport," 23 April 2003.

[46] Schabner, Dean. "Conservative Backlash." ABC News, 12 March 2003. (Available at ABCNEWS.com)

[47] Smith, Jeffrey. "In Texas Feud, A Plane of Intrigue." *Washington Post*, 7 June 2003. A1.

Chapter 2

Foundations, Sources, and Priorities of Homeland Security Law[1]

Bracewell & Patterson LLP
The Honorable Ed Bethune and E. Dee Martin

On September 11, 2001, using store-bought box-cutters, 19 terrorists hijacked four commercial airplanes, ultimately demolishing two of the world's largest skyscrapers and severely damaging the Pentagon, a symbol of the United States military. More than 3,000 innocent lives were taken that day, without warning or reason. Borne from the ruins of the devastating attack was the nation's reinvigorated commitment to protecting our people and our homeland. The president and Congress moved quickly to retaliate against our enemy, rebuild our nation's physical infrastructure and economy, and retool our laws to prevent future attacks.

On that September day, our nation experienced what is best described as a paradigm shift. Before September 11th, no one feared visiting a national museum or boarding an airplane. Color code systems described pollen levels. But, as the dust settled that day, our perspective changed. Our national monuments became terrorist targets; many of our commercial industries, potential weapons of mass destruction; our democracy, a double-edged sword; and our people, the subject of pervasive terrorist threat. We sometimes operate under "Code Orange," costing cities and states millions of dollars and undermining the security we feel in our homes.

Terrorism is here to stay, as are the mechanisms that have been and will be implemented to protect our nation from it. Homeland security now reigns supreme as the primary objective of government, achieved in part by sweeping changes in the law. Yet, as the government and private sector make strides toward protecting the homeland, they must balance the requirements of security against the democratic rights of our citizens and the economic realities of our industries and governments.

As described below, homeland security law is complex and far reaching. It is complex because it is driven by the federal government but requires the participation of state and local governments as well as private actors to achieve its goals. For example, the Maritime Transportation Security Act of 2002 (MTSA) requires securing our nation's 361 ports from terrorist attack. The MTSA calls for coordination among the Coast Guard, Customs Service, and local port security entities—private and public—to implement its security measures. The expense is estimated at several billion dollars, a portion of which the private sector and local government will bear. Absent security measures, however, a seaport attack could halt commerce, among other things, resulting in economic devastation. Recall the shut down of some West Coast ports due to labor disputes. Economists estimate that those temporary closures cost the economy $2 billion per day. While it is clear we must strengthen security at United States ports, it is less clear who will pay for this security, a pervasive issue in homeland security law.

Homeland security law is far reaching because it permeates, and could ultimately regulate, every sector of society: water systems, pipelines, technology, food services, financial markets, retailers, employers, truck drivers, teachers, and hospitals, to name a few. For example, the Border Security and Visa Reform Act of 2002 requires schools accepting foreign students to report students who do not show for classes, attempting to halt use of the student visa system for terrorist entry into the United States. Under a final rule published by the Department of Transportation, shippers and carriers of hazardous materials must develop and implement security plans as well as train employees to prevent security threats. This final rule covers 44,000 carriers and shippers. As the federal government passes laws and promulgates regulations, the wise will participate in the political process ensuring their concerns are considered in the furious effort to protect the homeland.

While the goal of curing existing and anticipated security vulnerabilities is broad, resources—government and private—are finite. Thus, to achieve homeland security our government must prioritize some actions over others. This prioritization occurs not only among homeland security issues but also at the expense of important non-homeland security issues. This chapter examines the priorities already established by the government and anticipates homeland security priorities for the near future. Section 1.0 describes the homeland security mission as developed by the current Administration and suggests that this mission is the starting point for the development of homeland security law. Section

2.0 develops the idea that homeland security law, although national in scope, is federally driven. To support this concept, Section 2.0 analyzes presidential directives and the president's budget proposals to tease out a framework for homeland security law. Section 3.0 reviews sources of homeland security law, including Congress, federal agencies, the common law, state and local governments, and the private sector. Section 4.0 analyzes the range of homeland security laws enacted by the 107th Congress, identifying the objective of the law, the communities affected by the law, and the agency or agencies to which authority is delegated.

1.0 Homeland Security Law: A Complex, Still-Evolving System of Law

This section first defines "homeland security" and the concepts that comprise its definition, revealing the breadth and depth of the phrase. Next, this section identifies three bases for the development of homeland security law, as a body of law, in light of the broad "homeland security" definition. We suggest this body of law stems from the need to address fundamental questions that arise from the onslaught of legislation, regulation, organizational governmental change, and new burdens placed upon the private sector. The three bases for homeland security law discussed in this section include the need to 1) address coordination issues, 2) effectuate the homeland security mission, and 3) manage changes in the common law. Viewed together, these cornerstones, or needs, foreshadow the evolution of a large body of law that is still in its infancy.

Homeland security is best described as "a concerted national effort to prevent terrorist attacks within the United States, reduce America's vulnerability to terrorism, and minimize the damage and recover from attacks that do occur."[2] The *National Strategy for Homeland Security*, issued by President George W. Bush in July 2002, set forth this description and further defined each phrase within the "homeland security" definition, discussed below.

"[C]oncerted national effort" places the burden of protecting the United States on the federal, state, and local governments; Congress and federal agencies; and the private sector. "[P]revent" means detecting and eliminating the threat posed by terrorists before harm occurs, in the United States and abroad. "[T]errorist attacks" includes any act that is a "premeditated, unlawful act dangerous to human life or public welfare that is intended to intimidate or coerce civilian populations or governments."[3] "[R]educe America's vulnerability" calls on America's private sector to identify and protect critical infrastructures and key assets, while balancing the cost of mitigating terrorism risk against any economic costs and infringements on individual liberties that the mitigation may entail. "[M]inimize the damage" requires support of local first responders—police officers, firefighters, emergency medical providers, public works personnel, and emergency management officials. Finally, "recover" means establishing and maintaining various financial, legal, and social systems that will aid in the restoration of economic growth and psychological confidence subsequent to an attack. The breadth and depth of this definition makes clear that achieving and maintaining homeland security is an exceedingly complicated mission.

1.1 Bases for Homeland Security Law: Addressing Coordination Issues

The homeland security mission requires coordination, particularly among actors who do not normally work together. State, local, and tribal authorities are adjusting their emergency response systems to comport with the federal government's homeland security plan. For example, the Uniting and Strengthening America by Providing Appropriate Tools Required to Intercept and Obstruct Terrorism Act of 2001 (USA PATRIOT Act, or USAPA)[4] relies in part on information provided to the federal government by local government officials and private citizens, like bookstore owners and librarians. Absent coordination of federal, state, and private efforts, portions of the PATRIOT Act will be rendered less effective.

Similar to environmental law, coordination issues will likely be addressed by the government, making coordination one basis for the development of homeland security law as a body of law. In fact, immediately following September 11th, the president issued an Executive Order establishing the Office of Homeland Security (OHS) and vesting in OHS the broad responsibility for coordinating and implementing a comprehensive national strategy to secure the United States from terrorist attacks. Recognizing the difficulty of coordination, the Executive Order required integration of the full range of homeland security activities into a single plan. The Office of Management and Budget's (OMB) 2002 annual report to Congress underscores the need for coordination and concentrated authority:

> This report illustrates the complexity, the unclear responsibilities, and the confusing legal authorities associated with combating terrorism and homeland security programs, highlighting the need for a single entity with overall responsibility for homeland security.[5]

Congress also acted quickly to aggregate existing homeland security efforts into one entity. On October 11, 2001, Senator Joseph Lieberman (D-Conn.) introduced a bill to establish a Department of Homeland Security (DHS), whose primary mission would be coordinating the activities and employees of a multitude of federal agencies. Following prolonged debate, which in part focused on coordination issues, the president signed a homeland security bill, establishing the new cabinet-level DHS. Immediately, the government charged certain agencies and officials with the task of coordinating this nation's response to terrorism, streamlining responsibilities once spread among 100 agencies and officials.

1.2   Bases for Homeland Security Law: Effectuating the Homeland Security Mission

Coordination is but one cornerstone of the development of homeland security law. The government must also enact laws and regulations to realize the homeland security mission. Following September 11th, the president and Congress quickly began addressing the need for a body of homeland security law. To help those hit hardest by the attacks, on September 18, 2001, Congress passed the $40 billion Emergency Response Fund (ERF).[6] Similarly, Congress acted swiftly to bail out our faltering airlines. The quick and almost unanimous actions taken by Congress and the president underscore the federal government's willingness to tackle existing security vulnerabilities.

Anticipated security vulnerabilities, however, are more difficult to address legislatively. One challenge facing lawmakers is addressing a problem that has not yet surfaced. For instance, before September 11th, airplanes were not used as terrorist weapons. Immediately after September 11th, Congress, faced with the stark reality of aviation security vulnerabilities, enacted the Aviation and Transportation Security Act of 2001 (ATSA),[7] which federalized and strengthened security at United States airports.

Another challenge facing lawmakers is achieving the precarious balance of cracking down on terrorism and protecting individual rights and liberties. Our society is open, yet we face an enemy that uses our democracy against us. Inevitably, a tension emerges: we must battle an enemy that abuses our freedoms, in part, by restricting those freedoms. Concurrently, we must maintain our commitment to openness and democracy. For instance, the PATRIOT Act greatly expands law enforcement agencies' ability to procure and use personal information to combat terrorism. Book borrowing and Internet surfing in libraries, among other things, may now be monitored by the government. Believing it violates the Constitutional rights of individuals, many cities and the state of Hawaii are considering or have passed resolutions condemning the PATRIOT Act. As we create more rules to eliminate an enemy that does not play by rules, we may find ourselves chilling the behavior of members of our open society rather than the behavior of terrorists.

1.3 Bases for Homeland Security Law: Managing Changes in the Common Law

In addition to statutory enactments and regulatory promulgations, changes in the common law provide another cornerstone of homeland security law. Like legislation and regulation, changes in the common law place new burdens on the private sector. To date, many third-party liability cases regarding terrorism have been based on negligence theories against manufacturers, common carriers, or premises owners. Yet, the reality of the post-September 11th world is that terrorism may strike anyone at anytime. To avoid common law liability, all businesses as employers and premises owners will likely take precautionary action, such as employee screening, crisis management plans, regulatory compliance, and information management systems security.

1.4 Conclusion

Although still evolving, the broad homeland security mission requires action from federal, state, and local governments as well as private actors. This action yields coordination issues that will be regulated by law; results in the creation of laws and regulations that protect the homeland; and changes the common law, reallocating fault among actors in the private sector. By identifying these bases for homeland security law, we can begin to shape the morass of guidance, regulation, law, governmental reorganization and private sector precautionary action.

2.0 A Federal Framework for Homeland Security Law

This section describes the framework against which homeland security law operates. The homeland security mission is national in scope, requiring federal, state, and local governments as well as private actors to play important roles. However, we suggest that homeland security law is federally driven. Homeland security law is unique in that it grows out of the nexus of paramilitary and domestic objectives within the homeland security mission. This nexus requires the organizational structure of homeland security to tilt toward an overarching federal system. In fact, as one federal official put it while testifying before Congress, "...there should be one national strategy to combat terrorism with additional planning guidance (*e.g.*, for specific functions) under the one strategy in a clear hierarchy."[8]

This section analyzes the role of the Executive branch in establishing a framework for homeland security law, focusing on the promulgation of presidential directives. These directives articulate national priorities for combating terrorism and protecting the United States. The section concludes with a discussion of the president's budget, which articulates the Administration's homeland security priorities in terms of funding.

2.1 The Role of the Executive Branch in Establishing a Framework for Homeland Security Law

Since 1986, United States presidents have issued directives that delineate national strategies for combating terrorism. In 1998, the Clinton Administration issued the Attorney General's *Five-Year Interagency Counterterrorism and Technology Crime Plan* (the *Plan*). The *Plan*, mandated by Congress, served as the basis for coordination of national policy and operational capabilities to combat terrorism.[9] Progress reports were issued under the *Plan* until 2001, the year of the World Trade Center and Pentagon terrorist attacks.

When President Bush created the OHS, he directed OHS "to develop and coordinate the implementation of a comprehensive national strategy to secure the United States from terrorist threats or attacks."[10] The President ordered that the strategy 1) be comprehensive and integrate the full range of homeland security activities into a single plan, 2) be a national strategy, 3) commit the federal government to a long-term homeland security plan, and 4) set performance measures for evaluating the progress of federal departments and agencies. The Executive Order also required that the strategy provide guidance to state and local governments as well as the private sector.

Following that directive, in July 2002, the Administration developed and published the *National Strategy for Homeland Security*. The *National Strategy for Homeland Security* sets forth the homeland security mission, discussed in Section 1.0, and identifies six critical mission areas: 1) intelligence and warning, 2) border and transportation security, 3) domestic counterterrorism, 4) protection of critical and infrastructure key assets, 5) defense against catastrophic threats, and 6) emergency preparedness response.[11] These critical mission areas provide "a framework to align the resources of the federal budget directly to the task of securing the homeland."[12] It is against this backdrop and according to these priorities that homeland security law will emerge, at least initially.

The *National Strategy for Homeland Security* complements the series of new national strategies that guide United States policy.[13] These *National Strategies* include

- *National Security Strategy of the United States of America*, issued by the president in September 2002
- *National Strategy for Homeland Security*, issued by the president in July 2002
- *National Strategy for Combating Terrorism*, issued by the president in February 2003

- *National Military Strategic Plan for the War on Terrorism*, issued by the Chairman of the Joint Chiefs of Staff, October 2002
- *National Strategy to Combat Weapons of Mass Destruction*, issued by the president in December 2002
- *National Money Laundering Strategy*, issued by the Secretary of the Treasury and the Attorney General in July 2002
- *National Strategy to Secure Cyberspace*, issued by the president in February 2003
- *National Strategy for the Physical Protection of Critical Infrastructures and Key Assets*, issued by the president in February 2003
- *National Drug Control Strategy*, issued by the president in February 2002

Collectively the *National Strategies* serve twin goals. First, they set forth our nation's objectives in preparing for and preventing terrorist attacks in various substantive areas, *i.e.*, cyber-security, critical infrastructure, and money laundering. Second, the *National Strategies* develop a cohesive set of principles and definitions that transcend and link each individual strategy.

Serving the first goal—substance—the *National Security Strategy of the United States of America* and the *National Strategy for Homeland Security* take precedence over all other national strategies. Fulfilling the second goal—cohesion—many of the *National Strategies* cross-reference the others and share common themes, including emphases on increased international cooperation, intelligence gathering, and information sharing. The *National Strategies* also share definitions, such as "terrorism" and "homeland security," helping ensure that organizational, management, and budgetary decisions are made consistently across the entities involved in implementing the homeland security mission. Absent commonly accepted definitions, the potential arises for duplication of effort, gaps in coverage, misallocation of resources, and an overall uncoordinated approach to homeland security.[14]

The *National Strategies* articulate the Administration's priorities for preventing terrorist attacks and establish a cohesive approach to combating terrorism. However, the *National Strategies* do not carry the force of law. Rather, the *National Strategies* provide a framework within which or against which agencies, Congress, state and local governments, and private actors may operate. For instance, the role of Congress in implementing the *National Strategies* is critical. Congress will appropriate funds for the newly established DHS and other federal agencies that combat terrorism and will also oversee implementation of federal programs. Likewise, DHS will promulgate regulations and refine the homeland security mission based on its expertise as an agency tasked with protecting our nation. Similarly, the courts will interpret laws and regulations related to homeland security.

2.2 The Role of the President's Budget in Establishing a Federal Framework for Homeland Security Law

After September 11th, our money reserves did not increase, but our expenses certainly did. Not only do we now require funds prospectively for homeland security measures, but also we require funds for retrospective purposes, such as rebuilding our cities after the attacks. Discussed below are large increases in homeland security funding proposed by the president and debated by Congress. These funding increases illustrate the seismic shift in priority resulting from the September 11th terrorist attacks. Before the attacks, driving political issues included adopting an energy policy and debating Social Security. Following September 11th, the federal government focused on streamlining and strengthening our nation's homeland security apparatus, protecting our people and critical infrastructure from attack, and rebuilding our economy. For state and local governments as well as private actors, these proposed increases in funding represent a shift in priority: paying for homeland security over many other domestic initiatives.

Each year, the president initiates the appropriations process by submitting to Congress an annual budget for the upcoming fiscal year (FY). The president's budget establishes the parameters within which Congress will develop a budget, making the president's budget instrumental in establishing the framework for homeland security law. This section first discusses the president's FY 2003 budget for combating terrorism, then reviews the president's proposed supplemental for FY 2003. This section closes with a discussion of the president's proposed budget for FY 2004.

2.2.1 Homeland Security Priorities: The President's FY 2003 Budget

The FY 2003 budget presented the first real opportunity for the Administration to articulate in funding and policy terms the depth and breadth of homeland security priorities. The areas of emphasis included 1) supporting first responders, 2) defending against bioterrorism, 3) securing the nation's borders, and 4) sharing information and using technology to defend the United States.[15] These funding priorities clearly reflect the priorities set forth in the *National Strategy for Homeland Security* and directly relate to the president's homeland security mission discussed above.

Specifically, the president's FY 2003 budget proposed $3.5 billion for first responders, representing a more than 10-fold increase in federal resources over

FY 2002.[16] Defending against bioterrorism received a proposed $5.9 billion, an increase of 319 percent from the 2002 level.[17] The president proposed almost $11 billion for border security, an increase of $2.2 billion from the 2002 budget.[18] Coordinating information sharing and improving intelligence gathering received $722 million.[19] Other major programmatic funding changes included funds for aviation security ($4.8 billion) and combating terrorism overseas (amount not disclosed).[20] These budgetary shifts in priority effectively require state/local governments and private actors to align their resources and priorities with those of the federal government.

In its annual report to Congress, OMB found that the president's FY 2003 budget proposal requested $44.8 billion for "Combating Terrorism," an increase of 85 percent over the 2002 base level; $3.9 billion to "Critical Infrastructure Protection," a 24 percent increase over 2002; and $412 million for "Continuity of Operations," a 93 percent increase over FY 2002.[21] According to OMB, total federal funding for homeland security is $22.7 billion in FY 2001, $27.5 billion in FY 2002, and $48.7 billion in FY 2003.[22] Using budgetary allocation as an indication of priority, it is clear the protection of the homeland is the top priority for this president.

2.2.2 Homeland Security Priorities: The President's FY 2003 Supplemental Budget

On March 25, 2003, President Bush sent Congress a $74.7 billion FY 2003 supplemental budget request, the majority allocated to fight the war in Iraq. Included in this package was an additional $4.25 billion for homeland security. The president requested $3.5 billion for DHS: $2 billion for the Office of Domestic Preparedness (ODC) and $1.5 billion for the Counterterrorism Fund. The funding for ODC would assist "state and local governments to support federally-coordinated prevention, preparedness, and security enhancements related to the war on terrorism, including the operational costs for protecting critical infrastructure and strengthening environmental detection against biological attack...."[23] The $1.5 billion would support border and port security, enhancements to the strategic national pharmaceutical stockpile, rapid deployment of sensors to detect biological attacks, and support of the Defense Department. The Department of Justice would receive $500 million for the Federal Bureau of Investigation's (FBI) counterterrorism operations and U.S. Marshals Service activities. The final $250 million funds the Executive Office of the President's Emergency Response Fund, supporting immediate terrorism-related prevention and response requirements throughout the federal government.[24]

During Congressional debate on the FY 2003 supplemental budget request, some lawmakers expressed concern that it did not provide enough funds for many items, including funding for states to administer smallpox vaccinations and protect nuclear materials. The president's supplemental proposal also retained for presidential control $59.9 billion of the $62.6 billion the bill contained for Defense, which met resistance from both sides of the Congressional aisle. Both the House and Senate Appropriations Committee chairmen, Representative Bill Young (R-Fla.) and Senator Ted Stevens (R-Alaska), supported curtailing the amount of control President Bush allocated for the Executive branch.[25] Justifying this retention of control, Defense Secretary Donald Rumsfeld testified that the demands of war call for "our budget plan to have flexibility to deal with changing circumstances on the ground."[26]

The debate over the FY 2003 supplemental budget request illustrates the sometimes divergent priorities of Congress and the Executive branch: meeting the needs of states in fighting the war on terrorism and enabling the Executive branch to move quickly against the same threat. Such divergence is inevitable given the combination of finite resources and pervasive threat, particularly when viewed against the far-reaching blueprint for domestic security, the *National Strategy for Homeland Security.*

2.2.3 Homeland Security Priorities: The President's FY 2004 Budget

President Bush's FY 2004 proposed budget calls for $36.2 billion for DHS, a 7.5 percent increase from 2003 and over 64 percent more than the FY 2002 level. The president's request also includes $26.7 billion in discretionary budget authority. Both the House of Representatives[27] and Senate [28] 2004 budget resolutions increase spending on national security and homeland defense but not on most domestic programs.

Against this increased level of funding, it is clear that non-homeland security programs will suffer. For instance, the president's proposed FY 2004 budget cuts $1.2 billion from the "No Child Left Behind" program, which is the equivalent of five percent from last year's enacted level. The president's budget also cuts pediatric hospital funding by 31 percent and eliminates or nearly eliminates funding for empowerment zones, Brownfields redevelopment, and community policing.[29]

2.2.4 Conclusion

At the heart of these budgetary debates looms the issue of allocation, not funding; Congress has indicated its willingness to spend on homeland security. The point is that homeland security funding occupies a prominent position, and the allocation of homeland security funds is an issue with which government will continue to grapple. The dramatic increase in funding not only illustrates the federal government's commitment to protecting the nation but also reveals its knowledge of vulnerabilities within the existing homeland security apparatus.

As the Council on Foreign Relations found, "America remains dangerously unprepared to prevent and respond to a catastrophic attack on U.S. Soil."[30] Identifying and curing United States security vulnerabilities is an enormous and likely perennial task that could dominate the president's budget, and thus subsequent Congressional debate, for years to come.

3.0   Sources of Homeland Security Law

As described in Section 1.0, homeland security law is based largely on the need to address coordination issues, effectuate the homeland security mission, and manage changes in the common law. This section describes possible sources of the laws and regulations that comprise the complex system of homeland security law. Below, we analyze the role of Congress, federal agencies, state and local governments, private actors, and the common law in developing homeland security law.

Similar to the "environmental law system," the homeland security law system is a "way of using all of the laws in our legal system to minimize, prevent, punish or remedy the consequences of actions which"[31] endanger "human life or public welfare [and are] intended to intimidate or coerce civilian populations or governments."[32] Merely listing recent homeland security laws and regulations yields only a partial view of the entirety of homeland security law. Homeland security law is comprised not only of laws enacted to combat terrorism but also those intended to protect the public welfare and this nation's critical infrastructures. Homeland security law will draw upon, *inter alia*, federal immigration laws and customs regulations to protect United States borders and the flow of commerce; the Administrative Procedure Act; state codes to protect public welfare; local, state, and federal criminal codes; the United States Constitution and state constitutions; and treaties.

3.1   The Role of Congress in Developing Homeland Security Law

In the realm of homeland security, Congress exercises its authorization, appropriation, and oversight authorities. New laws will place new burdens on the private sector, delegate authority to agencies for the promulgation of regulations, and spawn changes in the common law. The *National Strategy for Homeland Security* outlined the need for federal legislative action and implored Congress to promote homeland security and safeguard individual liberty. Because homeland security law deals in part with public welfare, the Administration cautioned Congress to "work carefully to ensure that newly crafted federal laws do not preempt state laws or overly federalize counterterrorism efforts."[33]

The *National Strategy for Homeland Security* articulates the following federal legislative priorities:

- Enabling critical infrastructure information sharing
- Streamlining information sharing among intelligence and law enforcement agencies
- Expanding existing extradition authorities
- Reviewing authority for military assistance in domestic security
- Reviving the president's reorganization authority
- Providing substantial management flexibility for the DHS

Congress has acted on some of these Executive recommendations and bypassed or held in abeyance others. Currently, Republicans control both congressional chambers and the White House. However, the homeland security priorities of Congress and the Executive branch diverge at times because homeland security is more than a partisan issue. Identifying homeland security priorities may fall along demographic and geographic lines, notwithstanding party affiliation. For instance, congressional members from border states have a vested interest in coalescing around the issue of border safety, working together to procure funding and identify new technologies. Or, as the debate over the FY 2003 supplemental budget request illustrated, members from both sides of the aisle want funds to fight the war against terrorism at home, while the Administration wants to retain control of funds to prosecute the war against terrorism abroad. At least initially, Congress will act against this background in creating laws to address our homeland security needs. In this section, we analyze 1) legislative actions taken by Congress immediately following the September 11th attacks, 2) the reorganization of Congress to address homeland security, and 3) pending legislative actions of the 108th Congress.

3.1.1 Congressional Action Immediately Following September 11th

In the months immediately following September 11th, Congress aggressively changed the legal landscape as it relates to homeland security. Only three days following the attacks, Congress authorized the use of military force against those responsible for the terrorist attacks.[34] Congress also appropriated $40 billion to pay for recovery and retaliation.[35] Bailing out financially devastated airlines, Congress authorized $15 billion in financial assistance to airlines and limited their liability for damages arising from the attacks.[36] Congress federalized security at the nation's airports by passing the ATSA.[37] By October 2001, the president signed the PATRIOT Act, which substantially expanded the powers of all law enforcement agencies to investigate and prosecute suspected terrorists.[38] The speed with which these laws were enacted speaks volumes about the unanimity of a Congress resolved to allay our nation's vulnerabilities as revealed by the terrorist attacks.

Setting into motion what would become the nation's third-largest government agency, legislation creating the DHS[39] required more time to pass and underwent intense partisan debate. Although Democrats and Republicans agreed on the need to create DHS, the parties could not agree on whether employees of DHS should have civil service protections and collective bargaining rights. The act ultimately passed absent civil service protections or collective bargaining rights during a lame-duck session. President Bush signed the law on November 25, 2002. Although passage of the Homeland Security Act of 2002 (HSA) took more time than some homeland security measures, many say it was not long enough, considering the enormity of the undertaking. Regardless, just over one year following the September 11th attacks, our government agreed to tackle the largest restructuring of federal government since the creation of the Department of Defense over 50 years ago. The DHS is discussed more fully below.

3.1.2 Congressional Reorganization for Homeland Security

DHS is comprised of 22 federal agencies historically overseen by numerous congressional committees of jurisdiction. Overlapping responsibilities could precipitate jurisdictional chaos, raising questions about how Congress could effectively conduct its oversight, authorization, and appropriations roles for DHS. Thus, the HSA instructed the House of Representatives and Senate to review their committee structures. Subsequently, Congress created new homeland security committees, vesting in fewer committees the responsibility for protecting the homeland.

3.1.2.1 Authorization and Oversight

Although other committees in the 108th Congress have ventured into the homeland security fray, the House Select Committee on Homeland Security (HSCHS) anticipates taking a leadership role on the issue. The HSCHS was initially formed in the 107th Congress to write the final House version of the homeland security bill. Unique for a select committee, the HSCHS also exercises oversight authority over homeland security. According to Chairman Christopher Cox (R-Cal.), the HSCHS likely serves as the precursor to a full standing committee in the 109th Congress.

One monumental task faced by the HSCHS is overseeing the merger of 22 agencies into one 170,000-employee department. Once the formation of DHS is complete, HSCHS will monitor the department, determining whether DHS is adequately protecting the nation from terrorism. HSCHS requested and received an operating budget of $11 million for the 108th Congress. HSCHS is comprised of 50 members,[40] many of whom held senior positions on other committees formerly overseeing portions of domestic security. Many speculate that turf wars are imminent, given past leadership positions and jurisdiction control.

The subcommittees of the HSCHS loosely reflect the departmental divisions within DHS, which mirror the president's critical mission areas: 1) Border Security, chaired by Dave Camp (Mich.); 2) Cybersecurity, William M. "Mac" Thornberry (Tex.); 3) Emergency Preparedness, John Shadegg (Ariz.); 4) Intelligence, Jim Gibbons (Nev.); and 4) Rules, Lincoln Diaz-Balart (Fla.). Top Democrats on the subcommittees include Loretta Sanchez (Cal.), Border Security; Zoë Lofgren (Cal.), Cybersecurity; Bennie Thompson (Miss.), Emergency Preparedness; Karen McCarthy (Mo.), Intelligence; and Louise Slaughter (N.Y.), Rules.

Taking a lead role on the Senate side is the Senate Committee on Governmental Affairs. The Senate is not establishing a committee similar to HSCHS, but the Committee on Governmental Affairs continues to exercise authority over homeland security, as in the 107th Congress. Susan Collins (R-Maine) chairs the Governmental Affairs Committee and immediately scheduled a confirmation hearing for Tom Ridge, President Bush's nominee for secretary of DHS. Early in the 108th Congress, the Governmental Affairs Committee held a hearing on port security and intends to take an active role in that area. Also taking a primary role on homeland security issues is the Senate Judiciary Committee, Subcommittee on Technology, Terrorism, and Government Reform. This subcommittee recently held hearings on border security and will continue its work on the issue.

The House Permanent Select Committee on Intelligence and the Senate Select Committee on Intelligence exercise their oversight authorities to ensure that intelligence resources are not misused and that intelligence activities are conducted lawfully. They also draft annual intelligence authorization bills. These committees will continue to exercise authority over the intelligence community, which includes the National Security Agency, the Central Intelligence Agency, the Defense Intelligence Agency, the National Security Agency, the intelligence activities of the Federal Bureau of Investigation, and other components of the federal intelligence community. The House established the Subcommittee on Terrorism and Homeland Security; the Senate Select Committee on Intelligence has no subcommittees. Much of the work of the Intelligence Committees is confidential for national security reasons. They do sometimes hold open hearings, such as the recent *Securing Freedom and the Nation: Collecting Intelligence Under the Law* hearing held by the House on April 9, 2003.[41]

In 2002, the House and Senate Intelligence Committees initiated a joint inquiry into the pre-September 11th intelligence apparatus to determine whether errors were made and the attacks could have been prevented. The joint inquiry also made recommendations for prevention of terrorist attacks. The inquiry's report was completed in December 2002, following a 10-month investigation. All but 28 pages of the report were made public in July 2003. In part, the 858-page report points to failures within the intelligence community to make connections with available information.

Addressing this issue, senior members of the Intelligence Committees recently testified before the National Commission on Terrorist Attacks Upon the United States (the Commission).[42] During this hearing, many suggested merging the intelligence functions of the FBI and the CIA into one intelligence organization, centralizing information. The idea of some type of consolidation has surfaced repeatedly since September 11th. Now that key members of Congress have testified on the matter, the idea will likely gain momentum. Arguments against consolidation exist: removal of counter-terrorism functions yields inefficiency and lost information. As Special Agent Nancy Savage testified before Congress,

> The first rule of intelligence is to know the enemy, and we know this about the terrorists threatening the free world today: they are criminals first and foremost. They associate with criminals and commit criminal acts themselves in furtherance of both their economic existence and their ultimate goal of terrorism against Americans. Terrorists finance their operations through criminal financial transactions, to include the sale of illegal goods, drugs, and weapons. They often travel using forged or fraudulently obtained documents. They purchase illegal weapons, explosives, and other contraband. They launder funds. And terrorists often associate with or receive aid from other criminals. At some point before their ultimate act of terrorism, they will almost certainly have committed a crime that, by itself, would not be defined as terrorism but which, if discovered and prosecuted, might prevent the terrorist act from occurring and uncover other terrorist plots.[43]

Simply put, when federal law enforcement officials gather information, it is not program-specific. Thus, the ability to maintain jurisdiction over a variety of criminal investigations adds to anti-terrorism efficacy. The Commission will continue its independent investigation; recommendations are statutorily required no later that 18 months following the date of enactment, November 22, 2002.[44]

Finally, Representative Curt Weldon (R-Pa.) and Representative Norm Dicks (D-Wash.) are working with Chairman Robert Ney (R-Ohio) and the House Administration Committee to create a new bi-partisan Homeland Security Caucus. The Homeland Security Caucus is open to any member interested in homeland security issues. At the time of writing, the Caucus is in its formative stages.

3.1.2.2 Appropriations

Annually, Congress considers appropriations measures that provide funding for federal government activities. The power to appropriate funds is an exclusively legislative power. The Executive branch may spend only the amount appropriated by Congress and may only use funds for purposes articulated by Congress. Of course, the president has the power to veto or approve the measures. And, as discussed above, the president can influence spending through the annual budget proposal. After the president submits the proposed budget, the House and Senate Appropriations Committees hold subcommittee hearings on the pieces of the budget over which they exercise jurisdiction. The House and Senate Appropriations Committees each have 13 subcommittees. The subcommittees and their jurisdictions are the same in the House and the Senate, to ease confusion during conference.

As Congress responds to the increased need and demand for homeland security legislation, the temptation to authorize expansive and expensive new programs increases. For example, MTSA authorizes a grant program for security risk assessments for ports. Legislators have also worked to authorize new grant programs to meet state and local needs in the war on terrorism. While federal legislation opens these bank accounts, the legislation makes no deposit in them. Only the Congressional appropriations process does that. Given the realities of massive demand, reduced revenue, and risk of increasing deficits, the Appropriations Committee is the critical venue for allocation of funds to the authorized programs.

After September 11th, the House of Representatives and the Senate established homeland security appropriations subcommittees, which is a rare event. Rather than establish a new, fourteenth subcommittee, Congress merged the former Subcommittee on Transportation with the Subcommittee on Treasury, Postal Service, and General Government to form the Subcommittee on Transportation, Treasury, and General Government. Thus, there remain 13 appropriations subcommittees, notwithstanding the addition of the Subcommittee on Homeland Security.

The new homeland security appropriations subcommittees were established in February of 2003. They consolidate many pieces of homeland security formerly dispersed among the other appropriations subcommittees. At the time of writing, the full committees were determining the jurisdiction of the new subcommittees. Members of the House Subcommittee on Appropriations include nine Republicans and six Democrats: Harold Rogers (R-Ky.) chair; C.W. Bill Young (R-Fla.), vice chair; Frank R. Wolf (R-Va.); Zach Wamp (R-Tenn.); Tom Latham (R-Iowa); Jo Ann Emerson (R-Mo.); Kay Granger (R-Tex.); John E. Sweeney (R-N.Y.); Don Sherwood (R-Pa.); Martin Olav Sabo (D-Minn.), ranking member; David E. Price (D-N.C.); Jose E. Serrano (D-N.Y.); Lucille Roybal-Allard (D-Cal.); Marion Berry (D-Ark.); Alan B. Mollohan (D-W.Va.).

Members of the Senate Subcommittee on Appropriations include nine Republicans and eight Democrats: Thad Cochran (R-Miss.) chair; Ted Stevens (R-Alaska); Arlen Specter (R-Pa.); Pete V. Domenici (R-N.Mex.); Mitch McConnell (R-Ky.); Richard C. Shelby (R-Ala.); Judd Gregg (R-N.H.); Ben Nighthorse Campbell (R-Colo.); Larry E. Craig (R-Idaho); Robert C. Byrd (D-W.Va.) ranking member; Daniel K. Inouye (D-Hawaii); Ernest F. Hollings (D-S.C.); Patrick J. Leahy (D-Vt.); Tom Harkin (D-Iowa); Barbara A. Mikulski (D-Md.); Herb Kohl (D-Wisc.); and Patty Murray (D-Wash.).

The demands made upon the homeland security appropriations subcommittees will likely be immense. Private and public entities, and state and local bodies will seek funding to strengthen their unique homeland security efforts.

3.1.3 Pending Homeland Security Legislation in the 108th Congress

By March 2003, members of the 108th Congress introduced over 50 homeland security bills. These bills address a variety of issues, including border security, legal reform, first responders, government reorganization, transportation and infrastructure, and technology. The bills run the gamut from comprehensive overhauls to targeted reforms. For instance, Senators Kay Bailey Hutchison (R-Tex.) and Dianne Feinstein (D-Cal.) introduced air cargo security legislation. Senate Minority Leader Tom Daschle (D-S.D.) introduced a homeland security package authorizing grants for first responders and funding to improve security of water plants, nuclear power facilities, and railroads. Senator Jon Corzine (D-N.J.) reintroduced his chemical security legislation, which failed last year, due, in part, to intense lobbying from the chemical industry. Senator James Inhofe (R-Okla.) recently introduced his version of a chemical security bill as well.

On the House side, Representative Jerrold Nadler (D-N.Y.) introduced legislation requiring security inspections of all United States bound cargo containers from foreign ports. Representative Mark DeWine's (R-Ohio) bill would place the Secretary of Homeland Security in the line of presidential succession, following the attorney general. Representative Jim Leach (R-Iowa) introduced a bill to halt money laundering by terrorists by stopping money flow to offshore Internet casinos. Representative Louise Slaughter (D-N.Y.) is seeking to establish a "northern border coordinator" within DHS.

The range of bills introduced early in the 108th Congress illustrates two important points. First, neither party has cornered the market on homeland security initiatives. Democrats and Republicans alike are attempting to increase cargo inspections, procure funds for first responders, and protect critical infrastructures. Second, almost any issue will benefit from being couched in homeland security terms. For instance, during the Senate debate over the omnibus energy bill, many Senators discussed domestic oil and energy production as a homeland and national security issue. Similarly, members argue that the tax cuts included in the hotly contested tax package would ensure economic security, leading directly to homeland security. Some members argue that strengthening healthcare is necessary to protect our population from bioterrorism. Veracity notwithstanding, the message is clear: for federal, state, local, and private actors, garnering support and attention for an issue will likely require an attachment to homeland security.

3.2 The Role of Federal Agencies in Developing Homeland Security Law

Federal agencies are tasked with combating terrorism and protecting the homeland. Agencies face the challenges of protecting personnel, facilities, and operations as well as prioritizing and expanding existing homeland security activities. Agencies, through statutory delegation or Executive Order, also have the power to promulgate regulations. Rulemaking, the process by which regulations are created, must comply with the federal Administrative Procedure Act (APA). The APA requires the publication of an agency's proposed rule in the *Federal Register*, allowing for public comment on the proposal, in writing or through public hearings. After agency review of the comments, a final rule is published in the *Federal Register*. Once effective, final rules carry the force of law and are annually placed into the *Code of Federal Regulations*. The rulemaking process is an excellent opportunity for those potentially affected by the regulation to shape the development of the rule.

For example, in January 2003, the Food and Drug Administration (FDA) proposed rules on major provisions of the Public Health Security and Bioterrorism Preparedness and Response Act of 2002. These regulations will apply to all facilities for all foods and animal feed products regulated by FDA. These two proposed rules address registration and import notification. According to an FDA official, "This measure will bolster [the FDA's] ability to regulate effectively the more than 400,000 domestic and foreign facilities that deal with food within our country."[45] Given the broad reach of the proposed rule, various sectors within the food industry commented on these rules (*i.e.*, distributors, importers, growers, and retailers), urging FDA to balance security with efficiency and cost. In Section 3.4, we provide more examples of current rulemakings and the private sector's role in the process.

3.2.1 The Establishment of the Department of Homeland Security

Just over a year following the attacks, the president signed legislation creating the DHS.[46] The creation of the new, cabinet-level department marks an historic moment of almost unprecedented action by the federal government.[47] DHS, with a budget of almost $40 billion and over 170,000 employees, represents the third-largest government agency.

The mission of DHS is to effectuate the president's homeland security mission: preventing terrorist attacks within the United States; reducing America's vulnerability to terrorism; minimizing the damage from potential attacks; and recovering. DHS will accomplish this in part by promulgating regulations. For instance, the United States Customs office, which now falls under the auspices of DHS, has promulgated rules concerning import and export of goods. The "24-Hour Rule" requires the submission of a cargo declaration 24 hours before cargo is laden aboard the vessel at a foreign port. If information is not provided to Customs within the time period, then seaports will initiate "do not load" messages to the carriers. Customs is currently working to develop regulations to implement the Trade Act of 2002, which requires Customs to collect electronic cargo information prior to importation into or exportation from the United States. DHS also operates as the primary homeland security contact for state and local officials and manages federal grant programs for enhancing the preparedness of first responders. Finally, DHS sets standards for state and local preparedness activities and equipment and is tasked with minimizing damage from natural disasters.

The federal officials charged with integrating and ultimately running DHS have before them an awesome task. DHS must successfully integrate 22 agencies specializing in disciplines ranging from border and computer security to biomedical research to disaster mitigation. Several of the transferred agencies have their own procurement functions, like Customs and the Coast Guard, that also require management. In addition to successfully creating a cohesive entity, DHS must also maintain strong relationships with other agencies, like the State Department; the Federal Bureau of Investigation; the Central Intelligence Agency; and the Departments of Defense, Transportation, and Health and Human Services, among others. Relations with the private sector, as well as state and local government, are also critical to the success of DHS.

DHS is organized into five major areas, all overseen by the Secretary: 1) Border and Transportation Security, 2) Emergency Preparedness and Response, 3) Information Analysis and Infrastructure Protection, 4) Science and Technology, and 5) Management. Each of the 22 transferred agencies fall into one of the five major divisions identified above, discussed in detail in a later chapter. An additional six agencies play critical roles in the organization of DHS: 1) United States Coast Guard, 2) United States Secret Service, 3) Bureau of Citizenship and Immigration Services, 4) Office of State and Local Government Coordination, 5) Office of Private Sector Liaison, and 6) Office of Inspector General.

The Secretary for DHS is Tom Ridge, former Republican Governor of Pennsylvania and Director of the Office of Homeland Security. Under Secretary for Border and Transportation Security is former Administrator for the Drug Enforcement Administration (DEA) and former Republican Representative from Arkansas, Asa Hutchinson. Michael Brown is Under Secretary of Emergency Preparedness and Response. At the time of writing, President Bush intends to nominate Frank Libutti for Under Secretary for Information Analysis and Infrastructure Protection. Under Secretary for Science and Technology is Dr. Charles E. McQueary. The Under Secretary of Management, Janet Hale, oversees the budget and management of DHS.

The enormity of the task before DHS should not be underestimated. First and foremost, DHS must protect our nation from terrorism. To accomplish this, DHS must operate effectively and efficiently. The effectiveness and efficiency of the agency is based in large part on the ability of its leaders to manage an agency of the size and complexity of DHS. Furthermore, many of the agencies transferred into DHS bring with them pre-existing challenges that must not be left to fester. INS, TSA, the Coast Guard, and FEMA all face problems such as outdated information technology capabilities, human capital issues, and financial vulnerabilities. Finally, DHS must work with private entities, state and local governments, Congress, and the national security and intelligence communities. Failure to accomplish these objectives could undermine the ability of DHS to fulfill its mission, exposing the nation to potentially drastic consequences.[48]

3.2.2   Other Federal Agencies and Homeland Security

The establishment of DHS did not obviate the need for other agencies to accelerate or broaden their homeland security activities. Interagency coordination is critical to an effective homeland security strategy. Through their traditional missions, every agency has developed a unique area of expertise. The homeland security mission requires agencies to bring that expertise to bear as it relates to homeland security. In fact, after September 11th, legislation or emergency supplemental funding directed many agencies to augment their security activities. For instance, the Center for Disease Control (CDC) is now working to prevent or minimize the threat of bioterrorism. The United States Department of Agriculture (USDA) Animal and Plant Health Inspection Service (APHIS) is working at United States points of entry to intercept potential threats to the nation's food supply.

As in the legislative arena, a shift to homeland security among federal agencies represents a shift away from traditional mission areas. Again, finite resources combined with a far-reaching mandate to protect the homeland, yields the downgrading in priority of many domestic objectives. The following synopses illustrate the breadth of homeland security endeavors among federal agencies.

The Department of Commerce is ensuring the security of nationwide telecommunications, banking, transportation, and energy infrastructures. The Army Corps of Engineers is responsible for securing the operation and maintenance of locks and dams and inland waterways as well as hydroelectric power production facilities. The Department of Energy is securing its nuclear weapons complex and stored stockpile materials. The Federal Energy Regulatory Commission has assessed all FERC-jurisdictional dams and developed a security program for hydro projects. The Environmental and Natural Resources Division of the Department of Justice recently announced its top prioritization of homeland security, meaning enforcement actions serving the dual purpose of safeguarding the environment and the homeland.

The Environmental Protection Agency provides water vulnerability assessment assistance to water systems and decontaminates buildings containing anthrax. The General Services Administration manages physical security for federal buildings and property as well as combats cyber-terrorism. The Department of Health and Human Services works to prevent bioterrorism. The Department of the Interior protects the nation's critical infrastructures and national monuments. The Department of Justice is tasked with preventing, investigating, and prosecuting terrorist acts. The Department of Defense and the national security community is responsible for detecting, preventing, deterring, and responding to terrorists and terrorist attacks. And, the Department of State's homeland security activities include preventing terrorists from entering the United States.

Implicit in the above synopses is the necessity of federal agencies to work with private entities and state/local governments. The Department of Health and Human Services (HHS) must work with private and public hospitals to develop strategies for preventing and contending with bioterrorism. HHS also works with the National Association of County and City Health Officials on the bioterrorism preparedness front. The American Chemistry Council, a trade association representing chemical companies, has worked with the Departments of Justice and Energy as well as the EPA and FBI to address the issue of chemical facility vulnerability and to organize security briefings. USDA has worked with representatives of the food industry on issue of biosecurity threats to the food supply. USDA also works with state and local governments through agricultural programs, land grant colleges, and food safety activities. FEMA works extensively with state and local governments, preparing and training first responders. The interrelationship among federal agencies, state and local governments, and private entities are discussed in Section 3.3 and Section 3.4 as well.

3.3 The Role of State and Local Government in Developing Homeland Security Law

State and local governments play an integral role in protecting the homeland. The battle to protect our nation is occurring on our soil, placing our states, counties, and cities on the front line of defense. In the United States there are 87,000 different jurisdictions. Local police, firefighters, public health officers, state legislators, members of the National Guard, governors, and emergency responders are now developing and implementing efforts to secure our cities, municipalities, and critical infrastructures. A successful national homeland security strategy will ensure "vertical coordination between local, state, and federal authorities so actions are mutually supportive and communities receive the assistance they need to develop and execute comprehensive counterterrorism plans."[49] For example, the CDC is working with states to ensure their preparedness for a bioterror attack. In February 2003, the CDC began conducting live distribution drills in various states, delivering up to 50-ton packages of fake antibiotics and other medical supplies. These drills test state distribution plans in the event of a bioterrorism attack.

Governors are developing state-based strategies, addressing the unique needs of their states in the war against terrorism. States are also developing state national security strategies that comport with the federal *National Strategy for Homeland Security*. All 50 states have Cabinet-ranked or high-level offices committed to protecting the state against terrorism. For example, Governor Mark Warner of Virginia established the Office of Commonwealth Preparedness, which serves as the single point of contact in Virginia for DHS. The Office of Commonwealth Preparedness lists as a first priority coordinating its efforts with local and federal efforts as well as private sector initiatives. The Office also works directly with Virginia's active duty military bases. According to the National Governors Association, the primary objectives of states include achieving coordination among all levels of government; sharing intelligence; developing interoperable communications among states; protecting critical infrastructures; enhancing bioterrorism preparedness; procuring federal funding; protecting sensitive information from FOIA requests; securing borders, airports, and seaports; retaining control over National Guard; and demanding that federal agencies integrate with state agencies rather than states adopting federal command systems.[50]

State legislators have also prioritized homeland security in their states, working to increase the readiness of first responders and public health and safety officials. Through budget processes, state legislatures allocate funds to effectuate the homeland security mission. Almost all state legislatures have enacted homeland security legislative measures as well. For example, Indiana passed legislation directing health and emergency officials to bolster the state's bioterrorism response capabilities. Kansas enacted new anti-terror criminal definitions and penalties. The Massachusetts legislature passed a $26 million supplemental anti-terrorism package, providing funds to train and pay 150 new state troopers for one year, among other security measures.

Of course, protecting the homeland costs money, and the federal government will continue pressuring states to assist in homeland security initiatives. Governors want federal grants to help fund state-level homeland security programs. According to Representative Lucille Roybal-Allard (D-Cal.), "Whenever an orange alert is issued, this action creates a huge hardship on localities."[51] Representative Roybal-Allard, who serves on the HSCHS, continued, "In Los Angeles, the last Code Orange alert cost $4.2 million" in additional security.[52] The California Highway Patrol reported spending more than $1 million on extra patrols during a two-week orange alert. To help states prepare for terrorist attacks and offset costs, the FY 2001 Emergency Supplemental Budget provided $212 million for grant assistance through the Office of Domestic Preparedness (ODP). Forty-eight states submitted and received approval of their domestic preparedness plans. The FY 2003 Supplemental bill makes available $2.23 billion for states, also distributed through the ODP. Still, many states face budget deficits, due in part to increased homeland security costs. By FY 2003, 37 states reported revenues failing to meet projections, and FY 2004 budget estimates show 41 states incurring a cumulative budget gap of $78.4 billion.[53] As in the federal arena, states are adopting cost-cutting measures that decrease funding levels for education and many social services. States have also implemented revenue raisers, increasing cigarette taxes or delaying previously enacted tax cuts.

3.4 The Role of Private Actors in Developing Homeland Security Law

Government collaboration with private actors is critical to an effective national, unified homeland security plan. Private actors include individuals comprising the citizenry of our nation and the private sector, our nation's businesses and industries. Of the citizenry, the *National Strategy for Homeland Security* expects volunteerism and support of first responders.[54] Individuals should also take an active role in the rulemaking and legislative processes, either personally or through a consumer interest or citizen's group.

Of the private sector, our businesses and industries, the government expects research and development of innovative technologies to protect the homeland, information sharing,[55] and internalization of security costs.[56] Much of the protection of the nation's critical infrastructures falls squarely on the shoulders of private entities. "Critical infrastructure" is defined as those public or private assets, entities, or functions that if disrupted or incapacitated would have a "serious consequential impact on critical government operations and or society's quality of life."[57] Most people think of protecting an electric power grid or oil pipelines. However, this definition actually reaches the aviation industry, mass transit systems, the maritime industry, nuclear power systems, financial institutions, telecommunications, agribusinesses, chemical plants, ports, hospitals, academic institutions, and water systems, to name a few. In short, all industries have been put on notice that they play a role in protecting our nation's infrastructures, subjecting them to homeland security regulations.

Industry has much to offer by way of collaboration with the government. Businesses have customers and information, technologies and capabilities. Industry drives commerce and trade. Industry provides jobs and often collects industry-specific, valuable information. But, industry also has many reasons not to partner with the government. Protecting customer information, for instance, protects industry's bottom line. Nondisclosure of industry-specific statistics and information regarding security vulnerabilities could curtail government regulation. Recall the earlier discussion about the difficulty of legislating or regulating to prevent a problem that has not yet surfaced. Industry will likely be unwilling to point out problems that could precipitate costly regulations. Thus, government must incentivize desired behavior and strike a balance between mandating security and regulating industry.

In that regard, government has much to offer as well: grants for security enhancements and research and development, protection from civil liability in certain instances, exemptions from sensitive FOIA requests, and training for employees, for example. Government also has a stick: legislation and regulation. In the post-September 11th world, we expect government to regulate more heavily in the interest of public welfare and safety. Thus, now and in the coming years, industry must inject itself into the process, in order to play a critical role in shaping new government mandates. The private sector—corporations or trade associations—can wield great influence over the legislative and regulatory processes. Opportunities abound to testify at congressional hearings, devise and help draft legislation, meet with members of Congress or key staffers, and even write letters expressing concerns. On the regulatory side, the private sector can meet with federal agency officials, comment on proposed rulemakings, and even challenge rulemakings, if necessary.

The hazardous materials rules recently finalized by the Department of Transportation provide an excellent example of the impact industry can have on shaping regulations. DOT published a proposed rulemaking regarding the transportation of hazardous materials that would affect roughly 44,000 shippers and carriers. The proposed rules included, *inter alia*, provisions that would help law enforcement officers trace some shipments and require companies to carry DOT hazardous material registrations in their vehicles. Citing inefficiency and cost, industry responded by generating comments opposing these provisions of the proposed rule. The final rule issued by DOT eliminated the offensive provisions, keeping intact the requirements to develop security plans.

The role of the trade association should not be underestimated in this new climate. Trade associations can often take political positions that a single company would not want to tackle alone. Trade associations also enjoy economies of scale often not available to single entities. For example, in the debate regarding the Terrorism Risk Insurance Act of 2002 (TRIA), the Alliance of American Insurers (AAI) represented over 340 property-casualty insurers nationwide. Due in part to their work, TRIA ultimately passed, providing a federal backstop for the insurance industry in the event of a catastrophic terrorist attack.

The jewelry community recently filed comment on a rulemaking proposed by the Department of Treasury to implement the directives of the PATRIOT Act. The rulemaking would require certain dealers in precious metals, precious stones, and jewels to establish an anti-money laundering program designed to detect money laundering and the financing of terrorism. The broad reach of the rulemaking ignited concern in the jewelry community. In an effort to shape and clarify the regulations, trade associations representing many sectors of the trade filed comment. Representative groups included large and small retail organizations, manufacturers of mass-produced jewelry products, gemstone traders, diamond manufacturers, and precious metal refiners.

As the above examples illustrate, industry's interest in economics and the government's interest in public welfare often compete. Requiring absolute safety, if even possible, would likely bankrupt American businesses or at a minimum, cause flight from the market. The other end of the spectrum, requiring no safety or maintaining the *status quo* would do nothing to allay our nation's security vulnerabilities. The question, then, is how to strike the balance between attaining the objectives of homeland security and sustaining our nation's economy. In light of the high possibility of future terrorist attacks, we suggest the government will acquiesce less and require more of industry. This means industry must be especially aware of and participatory in the rulemaking and legislative processes. Each proposed or finalized rule could impose costly new burdens on industry, which are often passed along to the consumer. Thus, consumers, too, must participate in the process, helping ensure adequate protection for the public while maintaining affordability of the goods and services industry provides.

3.5 The Role of Changes in Common Law in Developing Homeland Security Law

Oliver Wendell Holmes once noted, "The law embodies the story of a nation's development through many centuries...."[58] Along with the myriad of enacted statutes and regulations that shape homeland security law, common law adds a critical chapter to our nation's homeland security law system. As the body of law derived from judicial decisions and opinions, common law constantly evolves. This continual reallocation of fault by federal and state courts guides private sector behavior. The potential imposition of substantial damage awards provides incentive for the private sector to follow the common law mandates.

Influenced by the dictates of common law, commercial entities and individuals will undertake precautionary actions.[59] The escalation of domestic terrorism will spawn civil actions, which will cause the reinterpretation of traditional common law and procedure,[60] especially in actions based on, *inter alia*, negligence, products liability, premises liability, contract breach. Not only will victims of terrorism file suit against terrorists and their networks,[61] but also victims of terrorism could file suit against secondary actors.[62] Now, employers, common carries, building owners, and corporations may be haled into the court. Liability theories and potential defendants are limited only by the creativity of counsel.

Traditionally, Congress shows reluctance in intervening with the judiciary, regardless of the pleas of injured parties. The endless asbestos class action lawsuits and settlements exemplify this trepidation. Yet, in this post-September 11th world, Congress expressed a willingness to tinker with common law procedures and remedies. The Air Transportation Safety and System Stabilization Act of 2001[63] enacted limitations of liability and uniformity in regard to private litigation arising out of September 11th. By creating the Victim Compensation Fund of 2001[64] and granting exclusive jurisdiction for claims to a district court in Manhattan, Congress entered a fray usually reserved for the judiciary. In short, future congressional action may preempt or alter the traditional common law landscape, in light of the threat of domestic terrorism.

Section 3.5.1 and Section 3.5.2 address negligence and contracts. These areas are likely to be encountered in civil actions brought by private plaintiffs seeking redress for injuries arising from terrorist incidents. Negligence and contract theories of liability implicate persons not directly responsible for terrorist acts. Note, though, other causes of actions lie against those responsible for certain occurrences of terrorism;[65] persons or groups that finance such terrorism;[66] and, in narrow instances, against the federal government and its employees.[67]

3.5.1   Civil Actions: Negligence

Simply stated, negligence is careless conduct through an act of either commission or omission. For legal purposes, actionable negligence is defined as the "failure to exercise the standard of care that a reasonably prudent person would have exercised in a similar situation"[68] or as "conduct which falls below the standard established by law for the protection of others against unreasonable risk of harm."[69]

The legal definition may be broad, but "[n]egligence in the air, so to speak, will not do."[70] To be found liable for negligence, a defendant must 1) owe a duty of care to the plaintiff; 2) breach that duty; and 3) cause injury to the plaintiff by the breaching that duty. Although there are additional amorphous subcomponents, underpinning the entirety of the analysis remains basic fairness principles and public policy.

3.5.1.1   Identifying a Duty

The threshold question—whether a duty exists—is a question of law. A duty only arises when the defendant stands in such a relationship that the law will impose upon the defendant an obligation of reasonable conduct for the benefit of the injured party. Absent special circumstances, a party generally has no duty to anticipate and/or prevent the intentional or criminal acts of third parties.[71] Special circumstances, however, may include relationships such as those of landlord and tenant, carrier and passenger, innkeeper and guest, employer and employee. More broadly, special circumstances could include a pre-existing relationship with the victim coupled with the foreseeability of a specific risk of harm.[72] Special circumstances also include situations were the actor's own conduct created or exposed the injured party to a recognizable high degree of risk of harm arising from the intentional or criminal conduct of a third party which a reasonable person would have considered.[73]

In the realm of homeland security law, the existence or nonexistence of a duty is paramount. In terrorist cases prior to September 11th, courts have been reluctant to find a duty to protect victims of terrorist attacks. For example, in cases filed against fertilizer manufacturers arising from the 1993 World Trade Center bombing and the 1995 Oklahoma City bombing, the claims never proceeded past the initial stages; the courts dismissed the actions after finding that manufacturers owed no duty to prevent others from using the fertilizer as a deadly device. In the post-September 11ᵗʰ world, one should not anticipate the same outcome. Where a traditional special relationship is present between parties, courts may be far more willing to find that a defendant owed a duty to protect others from the criminal acts of terrorists.

3.5.1.2 Identifying the Standard: The Post-September 11ᵗʰ Reasonable Person

If a duty exists, the standard of care required by common law is that of a reasonable person under like circumstances.[74] The standard remains constant, but the conduct violating the standard varies. This variance depends upon the magnitude of harm possible and the utility of the harm-causing act itself. The objectively foreseeable standard avoids affixing responsibility for future harmful events that are only theoretically, remotely, or just potentially foreseeable. From a public policy standpoint, certain risk minimizing behavior may be desirable but not if the possibility is too remote and/or the cost to society is too high.

In determining whether conduct is too risky, the court's analysis includes the nature of the hypothetical "reasonable person." The reasonable person is tasked with knowing everything about the risk of harm, which is current common knowledge in the community. In assessing the standard of care, courts may apply a rule regarding specific kinds of conduct, an estimate of how the reasonable person would behave based on a risk-utility formula, evidence of the customary community behavior, or a standard derived from statutes or regulations.

In the wake of September 11ᵗʰ, the new reasonable person emerged, aware that terrorism can strike anywhere at anytime and in any guise. Yet, the road to the courthouse is long[75] and the actual scope of duty imposed on the business community after September 11ᵗʰ may be unknown for years. But, ignorance will be no excuse. Consider the rise of premises liability cases in the last decade that have forced business owners to install outdoor lighting, rip out shrubbery where criminals could lie in wait, and otherwise prevent their land from being an attractive location for criminals. Likewise, the precautionary conduct of businesses will change to accommodate homeland security concerns. The very changes precipitated by terrorist threats may become the new standards for community conduct and custom. Thus, the bar will be raised for all common law actions, not just those arising from terrorist acts.

Courts may also adopt standards of care for common law purposes from criminal or regulatory statute. This requires a showing that the legislatively enacted conduct is appropriate for apportioning civil liability. In situations where the court has adopted statutorily required conduct as the standard for common law, the violation of the statute is called negligence *per se*. Various homeland security statutes, especially those regulating security in the aviation industry, may ultimately be viewed as prescribing the appropriate standard of care under the common law. In one pre-September 11th case arising from terrorist attacks, victims sued a chemical manufacturer and distributor urging the court to find the violation of a state statute as a basis for liability.[76] One may anticipate similar arguments in the future.

3.5.1.3 Identifying Breach of Duty

The second element necessary to claim negligence, the breach of the duty, may be shown through the failure to adhere to usual community behavior, traditional pattern and practice, or industry custom. Under this element, a well-intentioned, safety-conscious defendant's own actions may contribute to liability. A plaintiff may use a defendant's usual behavior to illustrate that a certain practice is feasible, the harm addressed by the practice is foreseeable, and/or that the plaintiff reasonably relied upon a practice by the defendant so that it became negligence for the defendant to omit the practice without warning. For example, in 1997, terrorists in Karachi, Pakistan gunned down employees of then-Union Texas Petroleum. The victims' families sued Union Texas alleging that the company had violated its own security procedures.[77] Here, the defendant's shield became the sword in the plaintiff's hands.

3.5.1.4 Identifying Causation

The third and final element comprising negligence is the causation issue, both actual and proximate causes. Simply put, this is a determination of whether the defendant's conduct was the cause in fact of plaintiff's injury. In regard to actual causation, the question is whether "but-for" the defendant's allegedly wrongful conduct, the plaintiff's injury would have occurred. However, the issue of proximate cause once more requires the difficult assessment of reasonable foreseeability. Proximate cause is the cause that "directly produces an event and without which the event would not have occurred."[78]

Showing negligence in the area of homeland security requires the plaintiff to satisfy the proximate cause prong in light of the supervening cause defense, a difficult but not impossible task. A supervening cause is an independent act that is adequate to cause the injury itself and not reasonably foreseeable.[79] Courts hesitate to find proximate cause where the causal nexus between an allegedly negligent act and the resulting injury has been severed by a supervening cause.

"In determining questions related to foreseeability element of proximate cause, the courts have uniformly applied what might be termed a practical, common sense test, the test of common experience."[80] The common experience test may or may not benefit victims of terrorist attacks.

In a case arising from the 1993 World Trade Center bombing, the Port Authority of New York and New Jersey (then owners of the World Trade Center) sued the manufacturers of the fertilizer products that had been altered and used as explosives in the attack.[81] Negligence and products liability theories were pursued. The lower court dismissed the action, finding that it failed to state a claim for relief; the Third Circuit affirmed. The court found that the manufacturers owed no duty to the World Trade Center owners based on the fact that the product was rendered unsafe through substantial alteration by terrorists and then used "for a violent purpose wholly foreign to their intended purposes."[82] Relying "upon mixed considerations of logic, common sense, justice, policy and precedent,"[83] the court found the intervening acts of the terrorists superceded the manufacturers' negligence. Thus, as a matter of law, the manufacturers of the fertilizer used in the explosive device did not proximately cause the injuries to the World Trade Center and its occupants.

In a similar case, the victims of the Oklahoma City bombing brought an action against the supplier of ammonium nitrate that was sold as fertilizer.[84] Again, the district court found, and the Tenth Circuit affirmed, that the allegations of negligence and products liability should be dismissed based on the suppliers' lack of duty to the victims and the victims' injuries not being proximately caused by the suppliers' actions. Regarding causation, the court found the terrorists actions to be "adequate of themselves to bring about Plaintiffs' injuries as a matter of law" and, thus, a supervening cause. While plaintiffs argued that it was foreseeable that criminals or terrorists may use fertilizer to create and detonate a bomb somewhere in the United States, the court found that it was

> not the level of foreseeability which would permit a finding
> that the acts of the person or persons who bombed the Murrah
> Building were reasonably foreseeable to Defendant and as
> would preclude a conclusion that their acts were the superven-
> ing cause of Plaintiffs' injuries as a matter of law.[85]

In those pre-September 11th bombing cases, federal courts failed to find proximate cause due to the supervening actions of terrorists. But, those cases did not arise in a United States with a color-coded terrorist alert system. Today it is fathomable that a court could find defendants' wrongful conduct was the proximate cause of a terrorist victims' injuries.

3.5.2   Contracts

The fear of civil liability arising from homeland security issues will likely cause a revolution in the drafting, interpreting, and breaching of contracts in corporate America. The formation of contracts and possible defenses are being developed against today's new risks. From supply contracts to leases, drafters must foresee the possibility of terrorist attacks or heightened terrorist alerts. For instance, many standard all-risk insurance policies pre-dating September 11th specifically exclude coverage for acts war, but not for acts of terrorism. In the wake of massive losses on September 11th and President Bush's declaration that the terrorist acts constituted acts of war, many of those insured wondered—needlessly in the end—whether insurance companies would invoke the war risk exclusion. In light of homeland security concerns, the insurance industry is working steadily to delineate terrorism exclusions, separate terrorism policies, revise business interruption policies, and specify *force majeure* clauses.

Generally speaking, a contract is an agreement between two or more parties creating obligations that are enforceable or otherwise recognizable at law.[86] In order to recover for breach of contract 1) a valid and existing contract must exist between parties, 2) the complaining party must have performed or be excused from performing the contract, 3) the defendant must have breached its obligations under the contract, and 4) the plaintiff must have sustained damages as a result of the breach.

Regarding homeland security law, common law actions for breaches of contract will likely involve one party defaulting or seeking to terminate. After September 11th, the number of defaults under transportation agreements, supply contracts, infrastructure contracts, and financing agreements skyrocketed. For instance, when the Federal Aviation Administration closed all United States airports for four days, it rendered the airlines unable to perform their contractual obligations. Or, when attendees refused to travel months after the terrorist attacks, many trade groups terminated contracts for convention space. Direct or tenuous, the result is that terrorism and the rise of homeland security regulation can affect almost every contract.

3.5.2.1   Force Majeure

Notwithstanding the subject of the contract, any breach of contract due to homeland security issues will likely invoke certain standard contractual provisions and time-honored doctrines. Many contracts incorporate a *force majeure*, or impossibility, clause. *Force majeure* is a generic term for provisions allocating the risk if performance becomes impossible or impracticable as a result of an event that the parties could not have anticipated or controlled.[87] Once invoked, a fact-specific analysis ensues. The onus is on the party invoking the clause for non-performance or termination to demonstrate that performance was prevented due to an event beyond the party's control. The same party must also show that no reasonable steps could have been taken to avoid or diminish the event or its consequences.

3.5.2.2 Frustration

Even without a *force majeure* clause, the legal doctrine of frustration may be relied upon to terminate the contract. Frustration is an excuse for non-performance due to some unenforceable and uncontrollable circumstance.[88] It is also applicable when the entire performance of a contract becomes fundamentally changed without any fault by either party.[89] Generally, where a contract is frustrated, all amounts paid under the contract prior to the frustrating event may be recovered, except for amounts retained to cover expenses incurred in performance of the contract. Material adverse change clauses may also be applicable in relation to terrorist events or heightened security status. The right to terminate a contract due to material adverse change depends on the specific circumstances and the relevant contract.

4.0 Homeland Security Laws: Complex and Far-Reaching

After September 11th, every entity in the United States will be touched by terrorism in one of two ways: either as the target of a terrorist attack or as the subject of government regulation regarding homeland security. The entity may be a privately owned corporation, a public school, or a quasi-governmental water system. Each will respond to the threat of terrorism and bear a portion—if not all—of the cost to cure security vulnerabilities. In this section, we analyze the major homeland security laws enacted by the 107th Congress, including the

- Aviation and Transportation Security Act of 2001
- Border Security and Visa Reform Act of 2002
- Homeland Security Act of 2002
- Maritime Transportation and Security Act of 2002
- Public Health Security and Bioterrorism Preparedness and Response Act of 2002
- Terrorism Risk Insurance Coverage Act of 2002
- Terrorist Bombings Convention Implementation Act of 2002
- USA PATRIOT Act of 2002

Subsequent chapters of this book provide detailed analyses of these laws. Here, we summarize the provisions of the law and identify the communities affected by the law and the agency or department to which authority is delegated. Each of these laws are critical to the security of our nation and will spawn regulatory requirements for years to come.

4.1   The Aviation and Transportation Security Act of 2001

The Aviation and Transportation Security Act of 2001 (ATSA) established the new Transportation Security Administration (TSA) within the DOT. The president signed the bill on November 19, 2001.[90] In March of 2003, the federal government merged all TSA operations into DHS. The ATSA is one of the most deadline-driven statutes in legislative history, containing 51 deadlines for aviation security alone. Within one year of enactment, the legislation tasked TSA with hiring and training federal screeners. To meet this deadline, TSA needed to grow from zero to between 40,000 and 60,000 employees. Not without difficulty, TSA met the November 19, 2002, deadline for creating a federal workforce as well as the December 31, 2002, deadline for screening all checked baggage.

ATSA makes TSA responsible for all transportation security, including all passenger and baggage screening at commercial airports in the United States. Congress heatedly debated whether to federalize security or to support the hire of private contractors. The final compromise requires federalization, initially. After two years, ATSA allows airports to have the federal government contract with private firms. Other aviation safeguards established by ATSA include armed air marshals, stronger cockpit doors, anti-hijacking training for flight crews, and background checks on individuals enrolling in flight schools. ATSA also limits the legal liability for certain parties sued after the September 11th terrorist attacks. To date, TSA has focused primarily on aviation security. However, TSA faces challenges beyond aviation, including securing railways, roads, harbors, subways, and bridges. Each of these industries—private, quasi-governmental, and government—comprise the regulated community of the TSA.

Still in its formative stages, TSA keeps finding itself in a maelstrom of bad publicity. For instance, TSA's recent decision disallowing airport screeners to engage in collective bargaining has earned the ire of and a lawsuit from the American Federation of Government Employees.[91] TSA made another controversial decision in March 2003: to award Lockheed Martin Corporation a $12.8 million contract to build a passenger screening system, the efficacy of which is hotly contested.[92] Encroachment of the Federal Air Marshals (FAM), TSA employees tasked primarily with cockpit security, into investigations traditionally handled by the FBI is another basis for criticism of the new agency. Whether the problems identified by critics of TSA evidence systemic flaws within the agency or merely the growing pains of new agency is yet unknown.

4.2   The Border Security and Visa Reform Act of 2002

The Border Security and Visa Reform Act of 2002 (Border Security Act) aimed to strengthen the United States immigration system and cure vulnerabilities exposed by the September 11th terrorist attacks. The president signed the bill on May 14, 2002.[93] The Border Security bill delegates authority to the State Department and the Immigration and Naturalization Service (INS). In March 2003, INS moved to DHS. Border security also falls under the auspices of the Under Secretary for Border Transportation and Security at DHS. Communities affected by the Border Security Act include, *inter alia*, the travel industry, port authorities, bus lines, train and other mass transit authorities, universities and colleges, and the trucking industry.

The Border Security Act strives to strike the precarious balance of enhancing security while maintaining our nation's openness to immigrants, refugees, and those seeking asylum. The Border Security legislation, among other things, authorizes INS to hire more border inspectors and increase their salaries; establishes Chimera, a government-wide, data-sharing system to screen visa applications; and bars temporary business or travel visas for citizens from countries listed as state sponsors of terrorism by the State Department. By October 2004, the State Department must issue visas that contain biometric identifiers and are machine-readable and tamper-resistant. The bill also requires all vessels and aircraft entering or leaving the United States to provide manifests of their crews and passengers. Foreign students will also be more closely monitored, requiring schools accepting foreign students to report students who do not show for classes.

4.3   Homeland Security Act of 2002

President Bush signed the Homeland Security Act of 2002 (HSA) on November 25, 2002.[94] First and foremost, the HSA authorized the creation of DHS and articulated its primary mission areas. Many controversial provisions made their way into the law. On personnel issues, DHS may establish pay and personnel management systems. Citing national security reasons, the HSA also allows the president to exempt DHS employees from collective bargaining. On tort reform measures, the law contains provisions that limit the liability of companies that manufacture anti-terrorism equipment or technology as well as the liability of pharmaceutical companies that make vaccines for smallpox and anthrax. Both the personnel and tort reform provisions underwent heated debate in Congress and split upon party lines. The Administration position, supported by Republicans, ultimately won on both issues, meaning the provisions remained in the bill. The 108th Congress is reviewing the pharmaceutical liability provision, among others.

Other provisions contained in the bill include an extension of the federal Aviation War Risk Insurance program through the end of 2003; the prohibition of certain companies from being awarded federal homeland security contracts; the transference of the Bureau of Alcohol, Tobacco and Firearms to DOJ; the creation of harsh penalties for computer hackers; a statement that Congress would not authorize a national ID system; and the creation of a charitable fund to assist families of personnel who died in the line of duty during the terrorist attack.

Affected communities include, *inter alia*, victims of terrorism, the healthcare industry, port authorities, border patrols, employees of DHS, the trucking industry, and the travel industry.

4.4   Maritime Transportation Security Act of 2002

Port security, even before September 11th, caused concern among federal officials. Ninety-five percent of our nation's imports and exports—excluding trade with Mexico and Canada—flow through ports.[95] Ports are particularly desirable terrorist targets given their proximity to population centers and often combustible and hazardous materials. Numerous terrorism possibilities exist. Terrorists could attack natural gas tanks, petrochemical complexes, oil tanks, or cruise ships. Terrorists could commandeer oil tankers and attack coastal cities. Cargo containers could carry bombs; currently, the government inspects only two percent of the six million cargo containers entering the country annually. In fact, "[m]ost experts believe that a terrorist attack using a container as a weapon or as a means to smuggle a terrorist weapon...is likely."[96]

Attempting to allay these vulnerabilities, Congress passed and the president signed on November 25, 2002, the Maritime Transportation Security Act of 2002 (MTSA).[97] However, Congress failed to agree on funding for the bill, rejecting a proposal to levy a user fee on incoming and outgoing cargo and passengers. Thus, the president and the 108th Congress were left the enormous task of funding the MTSA, helping secure the nation's 361 ports. According to the Coast Guard, the estimated cost of complying with MTSA in the first year is $1.4 billion and $6.5 billion over the next 10 years.

Generally, the burden of maritime security is borne by numerous entities, including tankers, marine terminals, non-maritime facilities located on navigable waters, port facilities, bridges, liners, inland waterways, and cruise ships, to name a few. Communities affected by MTSA include the maritime industry, the import/export industry, and port authorities. MTSA delegates authority to the Secretary of the department in which the United States Coast Guard operates, now DHS, and the DOT. MTSA also allows the Coast Guard to issue regulations without following the APA.

MTSA requires the federal government to perform terrorism vulnerability assessments on United States facilities and vessels as well as develop anti-terrorism plans based on the assessments. Other key provisions of the MTSA address maritime transportation security plans, transportation security incident response, transportation security cards for access to secure areas, grants for enhancing facility security at United States ports for the next six years, cargo security, assessment of antiterrorism measures of foreign ports, maritime intelligence and advisory committees, secure transportation systems, and long-range vessel tracking systems.

4.5   The Public Health Security and Bioterrorism Preparedness and Response Act of 2002

In the fall of 2001, our country experienced an anthrax scare, catapulting bioterrorism to the top of the homeland security priority list. Subsequently, President Bush signed the Public Health Security and Bioterrorism Preparedness and Response Act of 2002 (Bioterrorism Act) on June 12, 2002.[98] The Bioterrorism Act is divided into five titles: 1) National Preparedness, 2) Biological Agents and Toxins, 3) Safety and Security of the Food and Drug Supply, 4) Drinking Water Security and Safety, and 5) Additional Provisions.

The Bioterrorism Act helps ensure the safety of the United States from bioterrorism. The legislation delegates authority to the Secretary of Health and Human Services (HHS), authorizing the Secretary to take action to protect the nation's food supply against the threat of intentional contamination. The Food and Drug Administration (FDA), the food regulatory arm of HHS, is responsible for developing and implementing food safety measures. Communities affected by new regulations include all facilities for all foods and animal feed products regulated by FDA. Businesses that manufacture, process, pack, transport, distribute, receive, hold, or import food will also be subject to many new regulations.

4.6   The Terrorism Risk Insurance Coverage Act of 2002

After the September 11th terrorist attacks, which resulted in an estimated $40 billion in insurance claims, insurance companies claimed they were no longer financially capable of insuring against the risk of terrorism. As government officials and military leaders warned of new attacks, reinsurance companies, those that insure the insurers, ended terrorism coverage in their contracts. To address the problem, the president signed the Terrorism Risk Insurance Coverage Act of 2002 (TRIA) on November 26, 2002.[99] TRIA directly affects insurers, the insured—meaning United States businesses—and victims of terrorism.

Generally, TRIA attempts to ensure the availability of terrorism insurance for United States businesses. TRIA requires insurance companies to offer coverage for acts of terrorism and establishes a federal terrorism insurance backstop for commercial property and casualty insurers. TRIA permits federal money to pay 90 percent of terrorism-related losses of insurance companies once insured losses for the companies exceed certain levels. In some circumstances, the law requires mandatory repayment of the federal assistance. Although hotly debated, TRIA does not prohibit punitive damages. However, TRIA does include provisions that allow the frozen assets of terrorists to be used to pay for court-ordered damages to victims of terrorism. TRIA also grants jurisdiction to federal rather than state courts on all lawsuits involving losses or injuries from terrorist acts.

4.7   Terrorist Bombings Convention Implementation Act of 2002

The president signed the Terrorist Bombings Convention Implementation Act of 2002[100] (Convention Implementation Act) on June 25, 2002. This law helps bring the United States into compliance with two international treaties: the International Convention for the Suppression of Terrorist Bombings and the International Convention for the Suppression of Financing of Terrorism. The Convention Implementation Act federalizes certain crimes, like conspiring, attempting, or actually bombing public, government, or infrastructure facilities. It also criminalizes financial contributions to or fundraising for bombings and other terrorist acts. The Convention Implementation Act imposes harsh criminal penalties: up to life in prison for those convicted of carrying out bombings resulting in bodily injury and the death sentence for those causing death.

4.8   The Uniting and Strengthening America by Providing Appropriate Tools Required to Intercept and Obstruct Terrorism States Act of 2001

The impetus for this legislation lies in Attorney General John Ashcroft's request for expanded police powers to combat terrorism. The President signed the PATRIOT Act[101] on October 26, 2001. The PATRIOT Act grants federal officials greater powers to trace and intercept terrorists' communications both for law enforcement and foreign intelligence purposes. The Secretary of the Treasury is granted enhanced regulatory powers to combat corruption of United States financial institutions for foreign money laundering purposes. The Act strenghtens federal anti-money laundering laws and regulations in an effort to deny terrorists the resources necessary for future attacks. It tightens our immigration laws. Finally, the PATRIOT Act creates new federal crimes, like outlawing terrorists' attacks on mass transit. The Act also increases the statute of limitations for terrorism.

Critics of the PATRIOT Act claim it overreaches, potentially violating the Constitutional rights of individuals. For instance, many librarians and bookstore owners criticize provisions of the PATRIOT Act requiring them to provide information to the government about an individual's reading and Internet habits. To date, 89 cities have passed resolutions condemning the PATRIOT Act and ten more resolutions are pending. Hawaii also has a statewide resolution against the PATRIOT Act. Communities affected by the PATRIOT Act include the banking industry—capturing banks, branches of foreign banks in the United States, thrifts, credit unions, securities brokers and dealers, insurance companies—cities and municipalities, and individual citizens.

Endnotes:

[1] The authors would like to extend a special thanks to our colleague Shelby J. Kelley for her work on Section 3.5. The Role of Changes in the Common Law in Developing Homeland Security Law. The authors would also like to thank Ana C. Reyes and Vijay Shanker for their contributions to this work.

[2] Office of Homeland Security. "National Strategy for Homeland Security," 2 July 2002 [hereinafter "Homeland Security Strategy"].

[3] *Id.* This definition derives from the various definitions of "terrorism" contained in the United States Code and covers, *inter alia*, kidnappings; hijackings; shootings; conventional bombings; attacks involving chemical, biological, radiological, or nuclear weapons; and cyber attacks. *Id.* Terrorists can be "U.S. citizens or foreigners, acting in concert with others, on their own, or on behalf of a hostile state." *Id.*

[4] Uniting and Strengthening America by Providing Appropriate Tools Required to Intercept and Obstruct Terrorism Act (USA PATRIOT Act) of 2001, Pub. L. No. 107-56, 115 Stat 272 (2001), codified at 18 USC § 1 (2001) [hereinafter "USA PATRIOT Act"].

[5] Office of Management and Budget, "Annual Report to Congress on Combating Terrorism," 24 June 2002 (citing the cover letter for the report from Director of OMB Mitchell Daniels to The Honorable J. Dennis Hastert, Speaker of the House of Representatives) [hereinafter "OMB Report"].

[6] 2001 Emergency Supplemental Appropriations Act for Recovery from and Response to Terrorist Attacks on the United States, Pub.L.No. 107-38, 115 Stat 220 (2001) [hereinafter "2001 Emergency Supplemental Appropriations Act"].

[7] Aviation Security Act, Pub. L. No. 107-71,115 Stat 597 (2001), codified at 49 USC § 40101 (2001) [hereinafter "Aviation Security Act"].

[8] United States General Accounting Office, "Combating Terrorism Observations on National Strategies Related to Terrorism," (March 3, 2003) (testimony of Raymond J. Decker, Director, Defense Capabilities and Management) [hereinafter "Combating Terrorism"].

[9] Conference Committee Report (House Report 105-405), 13 November 1997, accompanying the Fiscal Year 1998 Appropriations Act for the Departments of Commerce, Justice, and State; the Judiciary; and related agencies (Pub. L. No. 105-119), 26 November 1997.

[10] Executive Order 13228.

[11] Homeland Security Strategy *supra* note 2, at viii-x.

[12] *Id.* at viii.

[13] Hereinafter, these strategies are referred to collectively as the "*National Strategies.*"

[14] Combating Terrorism, *supra* note 8, at 8-10.

[15] OMB Report, *supra* note 5, at 9.

[16] *Id.*

[17] *Id.*

[18] *Id.*

[19] *Id.* at 10.

[20] *Id.*

[21] *Id.* at 12.

[22] *Id.* Note: Because the OMB categories Combating Terrorism, Critical Infrastructure Protection, and Continuity of Operations overlap, aggregating their funding yields an inaccurate total.

[23] White House, "Supplemental Budget Request for Homeland Security FY 2003," March 2003, 42.

[24] Office of Management and Budget, "Transmission Letter for the Supplemental Budget Request for Homeland Security FY 2003," 25 March 2003, at 4.

[25] Associated Press, "Lawmakers Want Changes to $74.7B War Bill", *New York Times* (online edition at http://www.nytimes.com/aponline/international/AP-War-Budget.html) 28 March 2003 (citing testimony of Defense Secretary Donald Rumsfeld before the Senate Appropriations Committee on 27 March 2003).

[26] *Id.*

[27] *Budget Resolution for Fiscal* 2004, H. Con. Res. 95 (21 March 2003).

[28] *Budget Resolution for Fiscal* 2004, S. Con. Res. 23 (26 March 2003).

[29] Jim VandeHei and Juliet Ellperin, "Bush and Hill in Bidding War Over Homeland Security Funds," *Washington Post*, 26 March 2003 at A06.

[30] Jacob M. Schlesinger and Rob Wells, "After Criticism, Bush Will Seek More Homeland Security Funds," *Wall Street Journal,* 20 March 2003 (quoting Council of Foreign Relations report).

[31] *Environmental Law Handbook*, Sullivan and Oppenfeld. 2.

[32] Homeland Security Strategy, *supra* note 2.

[33] *Id.* at 47.

[34] S.J. Res. 23, Pub.L.No. 107-40.

[35] 2001 Emergency Supplemental Appropriations Act, *supra* note 6.

[36] Air Transportation Safety and System Stabilization Act, Pub. L. No. 107-42, 115 Stat 230 (2001), codified at 49 USC § 40101 (2001) [hereinafter "Air Transportation Safety Act"].

[37] Aviation Security Act, *supra* note 7.

[38] USA PATRIOT Act, *supra* note 4.

[39] Homeland Security Act of 2002, Pub. L. No. 107-296, 116 Stat 2135 (2002), codified at 6 USC § 101 (2002) [hereinafter "Homeland Security Act of 2002"].

[40] **Republican Members:** Appropriations Chairman Young, Rules Chairman Dreier, Transportation and Infrastructure Chairman Young, Armed Services Chairman Hunter, Judiciary Chairman Sensenbrenner, Agriculture Chairman Goodlatte, Science Chairman Boehlert, Energy and Commerce Chairman Tauzin, and Representatives Christopher Shays (Conn.), Curt Weldon (Pa.), Dave Camp (Mich.), Ernest Istook (Okla.), Harold Rogers (Ky.), Jennifer Dunn (Wash.), Jim Gibbons (Nev.), John Linder (Ga.), John Shadegg (Ariz,), John Sweeney (N.Y.), Kay Granger (Tex.), Lamar Smith (Tex.), Lincoln Diaz-Balart (Fla.), Mac Thornberry (Tex.), Mark Souder (Ind.), Pete Sessions (Tex.), Peter King (N.Y.), and Porter Goss (Fla.). **Democrat Members:** Representatives Robert Andrews (N.J.), Benjamin Cardin (Md.), Peter DeFazio (Ore.), Norman Dicks (Wash.), Bob Etheridge (N.C.), Barney Frank (Mass.), Charles Gonzalez (Tex.), Jane Harman (Cal.), Sheila Jackson Lee (Tex.), James Langevin (R.I.), Zoë Lofgren (Cal.), Nita Lowey (N.Y.), Ken Lucas (Ky.), Edward Markey (Mass.), Karen McCarthy (Mo.), Kendrick Meek (Fla.), Fill Pascrell (N.J.), Loretta Sanchez (Cal.), Louise Slaughter (N.Y.), Bennie Thompson (Miss.), and Delegates Donna Christensen (V.I.) and Eleanor Holmes Norton (D.C.).

[41] House Permanent Select Committee on Intelligence, "Securing Freedom and the Nation: Collecting Intelligence Under the Law," 9 April 2003.

[42] The National Commission on Terrorist Attacks Upon the United States is an independent, bipartisan commission created by congressional legislation and signed by President Bush in 2002. The Commission is tasked with preparing a complete account of the circumstances surrounding the September 11th attacks, including preparedness for and the immediate response to the attacks.

[43] FDCH Testimony, FBI Reorganization, Testimony of Nancy L. Savage, President of FBI Agents Association, Before the House Appropriations Committee–Subcommittee on Commerce, Justice, State and Judiciary. 21 June 2002.

[44] Intelligence Authorization Act for Fiscal Year 2003, Pub. L. No. 107-306, 116 Stat 2383 (2002) [hereinafter "Intelligence Authorization Act 2003"].

[45] Natural Products Industry Insider, "Bioterrorism Proposed Rules: How They Will Affect Industry." 1 January 2003 (quoting FDA Commissioner Mark McClellan).

[46] Homeland Security Act of 2002, *supra* note 39.

[47] Over 50 years ago, the federal government undertook a similar endeavor and created the Department of Defense, integrating many agencies whose principal objective was national defense.

[48] United States General Accounting Office, "Major Management Challenges and Program Risks: Department of Homeland Security," January 2003.

[49] United States General Accounting Office, "Homeland Security: Management Challenges Facing Federal Leadership." December 2002. 27.

[50] National Governors Association, *States' Homeland Security Priorities*, 1. (Available at http://www.nga.org/common/issueBriefDetailPrint/1,1434,4303.html).

[51] Martin Kady II, "Lawmakers Intent on More Money, More Demands for Homeland Security," *CQ Weekly,* 22 March 2003, 702.

[52] *Id.*

[53] National Conference of State Legislatures, *Three Years Later, State Budget Gaps Linger.* 24 April 2003 (Available at: http://www.ncsl.org/programs/press/2003/030424.htm).

[54] Homeland Security Strategy, *supra* note 2, at 24.

[55] The formation of Information Sharing and Analysis Centers (ISACs) provide one example of formalized information sharing between the government and the private sector. The National Infrastructure Protection Center (NIPC) reports that ISACs have been established for the chemical industry, surface transportation, electric power, telecommunications, information technology, financial services, water supply, oil and gas, emergency fire services, food, emergency law enforcement, and state and local governments. The NIPC provides security information to private sector ISACs, and the ISACs industries share information with the government.

[56] *Id.* at 24.

[57] OMB Report, *supra* note 5, at 37.

[58] Holmes, O.W. 1881. "The Common Law." New York: Dover Publications (1991). 1.

[59] In the aviation industry, precautionary conduct taken by airlines has spawned its own subset of lawsuits. *See, e.g., Dasrath v. Continental Airlines*, In the United States District Court for the District of New Jersey, Civil Action No. 02-CV-2683 (filed 4 June 2002) (pending discrimination lawsuit filed by traveler).

[60] This phenomenon is already occurring. *See Havlish v. Sheikh Usamah Bin-Mauhammad Bin-Laden, et al.,* In the United States District Court in the District of Columbia, Civil Action No. 1:02cv00305 (authorizing service of process on Osama Bin-Laden, al Qaeda and other alleged terrorists by publication in *The International Herald Tribune* and *Al-Quds Al-Arabi,* and placing the notice on the Internet); *In re September 11th Litigation*, In the United States District Court for the Southern District of New York, Civil Action No. 21 MC 97 (AKH) (consolidating all actions for wrongful death, personal injury, and property damage or business loss against any airline and/or airline security company in the Southern District of New York for pre-trial purposes).

[61] *See, e.g., Burnett v. Baraka Investment and Dev. Corp.*, *et al.,* In the United States District Court for the District of Columbia, Case Number 1:02cv01616 (filed 15 August 2002) (pending case against banks, charity organizations, and companies allegedly supporting terrorism).

[62] Legislation enacted after September 11th has capped the airlines' liability at just over $6 billion, but trial lawyers surely remember that a victim whose husband was killed in the Pan Am Flight 103 attack received a record $17.5 million settlement from the airline. Accordingly, many plaintiffs may be looking for alternate deep pockets, including the Federal Aviation Administration, security companies, the World Trade Center security officials, the City of New York for the security provided by the Port Authority, the architects and designers of the World Trade Center, those who financially supported the terrorist attacks, and the flight schools that trained the attackers. *See, e.g., Mulligan v. The Port Authority of New York and New Jersey*, In the United States District Court for the Southern District of New York, Civil Action No. 02 Civ. 6885 (AKH) (pending class action suit against Port Authority for wrongful death, personal injury, or property damage arising out of September 11th events).

[63] Air Transportation Safety Act, supra note 36, at § 408(b)(3).

[64] As an example of the potential stream of litigation arising from terrorist acts, even when Congress attempted to limit the amount of common law litigation, the implementation of the statute became fodder for litigation. *See Colaio v. Feinberg,* Case No. 03 Civ. 558, In the United States District Court for the Southern District of New York, filed on 24 January 2003 (alleging violations of the Administrative Procedure Act in the implementation and administration of the Victim Compensation Fund).

[65] *See* Foreign States Sovereign Immunities Act, 28 U.S.C. §§ 1330, 1602-11; Antiterrorism Act of 1990, 18 U.S.C. § 2331-2339; USA PATRIOT Act of 2001.

[66] *Id.*

[67] *See* Federal Tort Claims Act, 28 U.S.C. §§ 2671-2680.

[68] *Black's Law Dictionary* 1056 (7th ed. 1999)

[69] Restatement of Torts, Second § 282.

[70] *Bradshaw v. Rawlings,* 612 F.2d 135, 138, *cert. denied* 446 U.S. 909 (1980) (quoting F. Pollack, Law of Torts 468 (13th ed. 1929)).

[71] USA PATRIOT Act.

[72] Restatement of Torts, Second § 302B, Comment e(B).

[73] Restatement of Torts, Second § 302B & Comment d.

[74] Restatement of Torts, Second § 283.

[75] For example, the *In the Matter of World Trade Center Bombing Litigation* pending in the New York state court system has yet to be resolved close to ten years after the terrorist attack.

[76] *Gaines-Tabb, et al. v. ICI Explosives USA, Inc.,* 995 F.Supp 1304 (W.D.Okla. 1996), aff'd 160 F.3d 613 (10th Cir. 1998) (urging the court to find that explosive-grade fertilizer fell within the state statute concerning explosives).

[77] Although the jury ultimately found that, regardless of whether the company's internal security procedures were followed, the specific acts of terrorism were not foreseeable or preventable.

[78] *Black's Law Dictionary,* 2131 (7th ed. 1999).

[79] *Gaines-Tabb,* at 620.

[80] 57A Am.Jur.2d *Negligence* § 489 (1989).

[81] *Port Authority of New York and New Jersey v. Arcadian Corp., et al.,* 991 F.Supp. 390 (D.N.J. 1997), aff'd 189 F.3d 305 (3rd Cir. 1999).

[82] *Id.,* 189 F.3d at 317.

[83] *Id.* (citing *Zaza v. Marquess & Ness, Inc.,* 675 A.2d at 635 (1996)).

[84] *Gaines-Tabb, et al. v. ICI Explosives USA, Inc.,* 995 F.Supp. 1304 (W.D.Okla. 1996), aff'd 160 F.3d 613 (10th Cir).

[85] *Id.,* 995 F.Supp at 1315.

[86] *Black's Law Dictionary,* 318 (7th ed. 1999).

[87] *Id.* at 657.

[88] *Id.* at 679.

[89] *Id.*

[90] Aviation Security Act, *supra* note 7.

[91] ATSA limits rights of collective bargaining. A lawsuit filed by the American Federation of Government Employees seeking a court order to allow the union to represent screeners in collective bargaining is pending in federal court.

[92] Lisagor, Megan. *TSA Awards Passenger Screening Contract*, *Federal Computer Week*, (Available at: http://www.fcw.com/print.asp) 10 March 2003.

[93] Enhanced Border Security and Visa Entry Reform Act of 2002, Pub. L. No. 107-173, 116 Stat 543 (2002), codified at 8 U.S.C. § 1707 (2002) [hereinafter "Enhanced Border Security Act of 2002"].

[94] Homeland Security Act of 2002, *supra* note 39.

[95] Maritime Transportation Security Act of 2002, Pub. L. No. 107-295, 116 Stat 2094 (2002), codified at 46 USC § 2101 (2002) [hereinafter "Maritime Transportation Security Act"].

[96] The Honorable Asa Hutchinson, Under Secretary for Border and Transportation Security, Department of Homeland Security, Testimony before the Senate Governmental Affairs Committee, "Cargo Containers: The Next Terrorist Target?" 20 March 2003.

[97] Maritime Transportation Security Act, *supra* note 94.

[98] Public Health Security and Bioterrorism Preparedness and Response Act of 2002, Pub. L. No. 107-188, 116 Stat 594 (2002), codified at 42 USC § 201 (2002) [hereinafter "Public Health Security Act of 2002"].

[99] Terrorism Risk Insurance Act of 2002, Pub. L. No. 107-297, 116 Stat 2322, codified at 15 USC § 6701 (2002) [hereinafter "Terrorism Risk Insurance Act"].

[100] Terrorist Bombings Convention Implementation Act of 2002, Pub. L. No. 107-197, 116 Stat 721, codified at 18 USC § 2331 (2002) [hereinafter "Terrorist Bombings Convention Implementation Act"].

[101] USA PATRIOT Act, *supra* note 4.

Part II

Major Issues in Homeland Security

Chapter 3

Air Transportation Security

Blank Rome LLP
Lisa J. Savitt

1.0   Overview

The Aviation and Transportation Security Act (the Act)[1] was one of two primary pieces of legislation passed post-September 11, 2001, effecting the aviation industry.[2] The Act established a new Transportation Security Administration (TSA) to oversee transportation security in all sectors of transportation. In particular, the TSA is responsible for replacing security personnel in airports with all federal employees.

2.0   Transportation Security Administration

Born out of the tragic events of September 11th and the need for increased aviation and transportation security and vigilance against terrorism, the TSA was created in order to aid the president's goals of winning the war against terrorism, protecting our homeland, and reviving the economy.[3] The TSA was created in order to implement changes in the transportation industry that would restore the public's confidence in the American transportation system.[4] With the passage of the Act, a comprehensive federal program for airport and airline security was created and consolidated under the authority of the TSA, overseen by the Under Secretary of Transportation. The Act gave the federal government the flexibility to do whatever is necessary to improve aviation security and assist the growth prosperity of the aviation industry.[5]

The passage of the Act and the creation of the TSA was accomplished as part of an overall national strategy to thwart terrorism and adhered to the presidential mandate contained in Executive Order No. 13228 of October 8, 2001, which created the Office of Homeland Security. President Bush identified a "national strategy" behind the creation of various federal programs and identified that strategy as "detecting, preparing for, preventing, protecting against, responding to, and recovering from terrorist threats or attacks within the United States."[6] Moreover, the Executive Order explicitly stated that the Office of Homeland Security "shall coordinate efforts to prevent terrorist attacks within the United States."[7] As part of the coordination efforts, the Office was directed to "work with Federal, State, and local agencies, and private entities, as appropriate, to…coordinate efforts to improve the security of United States borders, territorial waters, and airspace in order to prevent acts of terrorism within the United States.[and to] coordinate efforts to protect transportation systems within the United States, including railways, highways, shipping, ports and waterways, and airports and civilian aircraft, from terrorist attacks."[8]

Section 101 of the Act[9] created the TSA as an administration of the Department of Transportation,[10] with the head of the TSA being the Under Secretary of Transportation for Security, appointed by the president.[11] The Under Secretary is vested with certain responsibilities:

(d) Functions—The Under Secretary shall be responsible for security in all modes of transportation, including—
   (1) Carrying out chapter 449, relating to civil aviation security, and related research and development activities
   (2) Security responsibilities over other modes of transportation that are exercised by the Department of Transportation[12]

The Under Secretary was given a huge mandate to ensure security in all modes of transportation. This included screening operations as follows:

   (1) Be responsible for day-to-day Federal security screening operations for passenger air transportation and intrastate air transportation under sections 44901 and 44935
   (2) Develop standards for the hiring and retention of security screening personnel
   (3) Train and test security screening personnel
   (4) Be responsible for hiring and training personnel to provide security screening at all airports in the United States where screening is required under section 44901, in consultation with the Secretary of Transportation and the heads of other appropriate Federal agencies and departments[13]

The screening of passengers and baggage arriving at and passing through the nation's airports was a prime concern of Congress in passing the Act, and several sections of the Act, discussed *infra*, address airport screening and the methods in which screening programs are to be implemented.[14] Indeed, the detection and prevention of terrorist attacks within the United States was identified in President Bush's Executive Order creating the Office of Homeland Security as being the "national strategy" behind the federal programs in the aftermath of September 11th.[15]

In furtherance of this national strategy, the Act provided the Under Secretary with additional duties and powers:

(f) Additional Duties And Powers—In addition to carrying out the functions specified in subsections (d) and (e), the Under Secretary shall—

 (1) Receive, assess, and distribute intelligence information related to transportation security

 (2) Assess threats to transportation

 (3) Develop policies, strategies, and plans for dealing with threats to transportation security

 (4) Make other plans related to transportation security, including coordinating countermeasures with appropriate departments, agencies, and instrumentalities of the United States Government

 (5) Serve as the primary liaison for transportation security to the intelligence and law enforcement communities

 (6) On a day-to-day basis, manage and provide operational guidance to the field security resources of the Administration, including Federal Security Managers as provided by section 44933

 (7) Enforce security-related regulations and requirements

 (8) Identify and undertake research and development activities necessary to enhance transportation security

 (9) Inspect, maintain, and test security facilities, equipment, and systems

 (10) Ensure the adequacy of security measures for the transportation of cargo

 (11) Oversee the implementation, and ensure the adequacy, of security measures at airports and other transportation facilities

 (12) Require background checks for airport security screening personnel, individuals with access to secure areas of airports, and other transportation security personnel

 (13) Work in conjunction with the Administrator of the Federal Aviation Administration with respect to any actions or activities that may affect aviation safety or air carrier operations

 (14) Work with the International Civil Aviation Organization and appropriate aeronautic authorities of foreign governments under section 44907 to address security concerns on passenger flights by foreign air carriers in foreign air transportation

 (15) Carry out such other duties, and exercise such other powers, relating to transportation security as the Under Secretary considers appropriate, to the extent authorized by law[16]

In addition, the Under Secretary position carries national emergency responsibilities including the power:

(A) To coordinate domestic transportation, including aviation, rail, and other surface transportation, and maritime transportation (including port security)

(B) To coordinate and oversee the transportation-related responsibilities of other departments and agencies of the Federal Government other than the Department of Defense and the military departments

(C) To coordinate and provide notice to other departments and agencies of the Federal Government, and appropriate agencies of State and local governments, including departments and agencies for transportation, law enforcement, and border control, about threats to transportation

(D) To carry out such other duties, and exercise such other powers, relating to transportation during a national emergency as the Secretary shall prescribe[17]

The sections of the Act following section 101 creating the TSA provide details, implementation guidelines, and timelines for execution of the various programs necessary to support the duties and obligations of the TSA and the Under Secretary.

3.0   Transportation Security Oversight Board

The Act in section 102 (49 U.S.C. §115) established the Transportation Security Oversight Board (TSOB) in the Department of Transportation. The Board is composed of seven members—the Secretary of Transportation, the Attorney General, the Secretary of Defense, the Secretary of the Treasury, the Director of the Central Intelligence Agency, one member appointed by the president to represent the National Security Council, and one member appointed by the president to represent the Office of Homeland Security. The chairperson of the Board is the Secretary of Transportation.[18]

Section 102(c) establishes the duties of the Board. These duties include:

(1) Review and ratify or disapprove any regulation or security directive issued by the Under Secretary of Transportation for security under section 114(l)(2) within 30 days after the date of issuance of such regulation or directive

(2) Facilitate the coordination of intelligence, security, and law enforcement activities affecting transportation

(3) Facilitate the sharing of intelligence, security, and law enforcement information affecting transportation among federal agencies and with carriers and other transportation providers as appropriate

(4) Explore the technical feasibility of developing a common database of individuals who may pose a threat to transportation or national security

(5) Review plans for transportation security

(6) Make recommendations to the Under Secretary regarding matters reviewed under paragraph (5)

One of the responsibilities of the TSOB is to assist the Under Secretary in establishing procedures for notifying the Federal Aviation Administration (FAA) about individuals who may pose a threat to airline or passenger safety.[19]

4.0   Airport Security

4.1   Introduction

With the passage of the Act, Congress faced the daunting task of creating a new organizational structure that had to implement dozens of new security measures by the end of 2002. Among the most significant mandates in the Act were increased airport and airline security safeguards. The airport and airline security measures were a manifestation of the Act's "risk-based systems approach to support the identification, analysis, development, and implementation of operational policies, plans, and procedures" to protect the Nation's airports and airlines.[20]

In response to the events of September 11, 2001, which evidenced the security deficiencies in both airports and on airplanes, Congress, with the passage of the Act, sought to improve safety and security around airport perimeters, on airplanes, and in flight decks. Moreover, Congress sought to improve airline crew awareness and to provide a mechanism by which passengers posing potential security risks could be identified. Chief among the measures adopted by Congress, and primarily responsible for the public's outcry over increased aviation security measures, was the adoption of a program that called for the employment of qualified baggage screeners to examine every piece of baggage that passed through various airport security checkpoints. Discussed herein are the various substantive airport and airline security measures adopted by Congress in the Act.

4.2   Baggage Screening

In order to "strengthen and enhance the ability to detect or neutralize nonexplosive weapons, such as biological, chemical, or similar substances; and to evaluate such additional measures as may be appropriate to enhance inspection of passengers, baggage, and cargo,"[21] the Act provided that airport baggage screeners were to become Federal employees under the supervision of the Under Secretary and were to meet certain minimum qualifications, with responsibility for their oversight being transferred from the FAA to the newly created TSA.

Section 110 of the Act[22] established various deadlines for checked baggage screening, including that, within 60 days after the enactment of the Act, all checked baggage be screened.[23] The baggage check mandates contained in Section 110 were essentially stop-gap measures, meant to improve airport security until the baggage screener workforce was placed under Federal control pursuant to Section 111 of the Act.[24] Section 110 provided four methods by which checked baggage could be screened and compliance could be had with the Congressional mandate:

1. A bag-match program that ensures that no checked baggage is placed aboard an aircraft unless the passenger who checked the bag is aboard the aircraft
2. A manual search, which involves opening the bag and searching through it by hand
3. Search by canine explosive detection units, i.e., bomb sniffing dogs
4. Other means or technology approved by the Under Secretary for Transportation Security[25]

Although Transportation Secretary Norman Mineta set off a furor in July 2002 when he stated that he did not believe the 60-day deadline could be met,[26] and despite attempts by the airline industry to extend the 60-day deadline, the TSA met the deadline and, as of February 5, 2002, a system for screening all checked baggage was operational.[27] On January 16, 2002, Secretary Mineta announced guidelines on the methods by which airlines were to implement Section 110 of the Act. According to Secretary Mineta, every available Explosive Detection machine (EDS) would be used to its maximum capacity, and the bags of specifically selected passengers would continue to be screened by EDS. Where sufficient EDS machines were not available, one of the four options outlined in Section 110 were to be used, and every bag was to be screened in accordance with one of them. However, if the bag-match method were to be chosen, it would only be done on originating flights, meaning that the approximately 30 percent of bags making a connecting flight would go unmatched, creating a heightened security risk.[28]

Section 110(c) of the Act required that, not one year after the enactment of the Act, the Under Secretary shall employ at all United States airports "a sufficient number of federal screeners.to conduct the screening of all passengers and property under section 44901 [section 111 of the Act] of such title at such airports." The timeline for implementation of airport baggage screeners pursuant to Section 111 provided for the extensive screening of passengers and baggage consistent with Congress's intent to overhaul aviation security.

4.3   Training of Baggage Screeners

Section 111 of the Act provides guidelines for the training and deployment of aviation security screeners which includes the implementation of a training program. Screeners need to take and pass a Federal examination, be a citizen of the United States, and pass a background investigation.[29] Screeners must also in most instances possess a high school diploma or a general equivalency diploma and pass certain aptitude tests.[30] Screeners will be subject to initial, recurrent, and appropriate specialized training required by the security program.[31]

Although the Act provided minimum requirements for baggage screeners and required them to have a high school diploma, this requirement was relaxed by the TSA to the ire of many United States Senators and lawmakers. In early 2002, the TSA stated that a baggage screener must have a high school diploma or equivalent or, in lieu of a high school diploma, could qualify by having at least one year of full-time work experience in security work, aviation screener work, or x-ray technician work.[32] This relaxation of the qualification for baggage screeners was criticized by Senator Rockefeller, who, in Congressional testimony on Tuesday, February 5, 2002, stated:

> The act requires baggage screeners to have a high school diploma, except for those few who otherwise have sufficient relevant experience to demonstrate that they can do the job. Yet [the Under Secretary] interpreted that as meaning that baggage screeners with just one year of experience as a screener can keep their jobs, even without a high school diploma. This is certainly not what we meant by sufficient experience.[33]

Senator Charles Schumer echoed those same sentiments and, noting the relaxed standards, stated that "not requiring the highest possible standards and qualifications for airline-security workers sends exactly the wrong message.It was not Congress's intent to merely preserve the status quo when we passed the airline-security legislation.how can we expect the public to feel secure when we won't even require the people charged with protecting our airports to meet minimum standards?"[34] Nevertheless, those relaxed standards continue through the present.

The Under Secretary, in Section 111(g)(2), was given 60 days from the passage of the Act to implement a plan for the training of airport screeners including 40 hours of classroom instruction.[35] The Act prohibits screeners from striking.[36]

On January 18, 2002, the Under Secretary met the 60-day deadline for implementing a plan for training screeners. While the actual training plan has not been made public for national security reasons, key elements of the plan included screening of persons, baggage and cargo, stress management and conflict resolution, and professional interaction with passengers.[37] The TSA also sought private-sector help in implementing the mandatory classroom training of screeners, issuing requests for proposals in order to ensure that the screeners were deployed successfully by the one-year deadline.[38] Lockheed Martin was awarded the contract to provide classroom training to screeners and to track their on-the-job progress and training, and in conjunction with the TSA, completed upgrades to passenger checkpoints and installed new screening equipment. Boeing-Siemens was awarded the contract to implement the installation of EDS machines at every United States airport.[39]

The TSA met its deadline to deploy aviation security screeners at every airport in the United States and, as of November 19, 2002, employed more than 44,000 federal screeners at airports around the country.[40] The Federal takeover of aviation security screeners would appear to have been necessary, with, as of July 2002, undercover testers being able to pass fake weapons by screeners approximately 25 percent of the time.[41] Moreover, at certain high-volume airports across the country, the deficiency was even higher, with screeners missing simulated weapons at least 50 percent of the time at Cincinnati, Las Vegas, and Jacksonville Airports.[42] The TSA was to retrain those screeners at airports with high failure rates.[43]

4.4 Explosive Detection Machines

Section 110(d) of the Act required Explosive Detection machines to be implemented in every airport across the country by December 31, 2002. Congress met this deadline, and as of December 31, 2002, all checked baggage was being screened by explosive detection devices.[44]

The criteria for certification of Explosives Trace Detection Systems (ETD) were listed in regulations published in July 2002.[45] The criteria offers definitions for terms used in the regulation pertaining to ETD including explosive trace, baggage, accessible property, and checked baggage. The general requirements of the ETD are that the system must meet the criteria set out by TSA such as having the equipment approved by Underwriter's Laboratory or the equivalent or be licensed by the Nuclear Regulatory Commission. There will be an approved list of vendors who have to provide a general license to allow TSA, air carriers, and airport operators the right to operate the ETD.[46] Further requirements for detection, operation of ETD, and training are set out in the published regulations.

4.5   Airport Perimeter Screening

Section 106 of the Act[47] mandated that airport perimeter screening be conducted in an effort to improve airport security. This was enacted not only because of national security concerns but also to counter the risk of criminal violence, the risk of aircraft piracy at the airport, and the risk to air carrier aircraft operations at the airport. The Act gave the TSA the mandate to deploy personnel to consider the physical security needs of air traffic control facilities, parked aircraft, aircraft servicing equipment, aircraft supplies (including fuel), automobile parking facilities within airport perimeters or adjacent to secured facilities, and access and transition areas at airports served by other means of ground or water transportation.[48] The Act provided for the use of biometric or other technology that positively verifies the identity of each employee and law enforcement officer who enters a secure area of an airport.

While the security mandates of sections 110 and 111 contained specific deadlines for action by the TSA, section 106 contained no such time restrictions and merely stated that the Under Secretary shall require screening of all persons and goods entering an airport "as soon as practicable." Moreover, while the screening of persons or goods entering the airport was mandatory (albeit without a specific deadline), the deployment of security personnel around airport perimeters to counter the risk of criminal violence or aircraft piracy was discretionary.

On May 21, 2002, Norman Mineta stated before the Commerce, Science, and Transportation Committee of the United States Senate that "[w]e are also working hard in the difficult area of perimeter security at airports. We have convened a Perimeter Security TSA Advisory Council that includes TSA and airport personnel and we commissioned a dedicated perimeter security group to assess security gaps and develop recommendations. We are coordinating with other federal agencies in this task."[49] After this May 21, 2002 statement, the next official word on airport perimeter security appeared in a February 7, 2003 Directorate by the White House discussing agency actions in response to the national elevated terrorism threat level. The Border and Transportation Security Directorate listed a vague bulleted point stating that "TSA will increase perimeter security in and around airports."[50] Moreover, "Parking at airports will be impacted. The amount of parking spaces may be reduced and/or there may be increased random inspections of vehicles in and around the airport facility."[51] Unlike the other mandates in the Act containing strict deadlines admirably adhered to by Congress, the discretionary nature of the airport perimeter security provisions may have caused them to fall by the wayside and yield to the urgent mandates requiring the implementation of a working system of baggage screeners and explosive detection devices.

5.0   Airline Security

5.1   Deployment of Federal Air Marshals

The TSA's Federal Air Marshal program is integral to ensuring the safety of the flying public by preventing and thwarting hijackings and terrorist attacks on U.S. civilian aircraft. In the aftermath of the terrorist attacks in which four U.S. airlines were used as weapons of destruction against the World Trade Center and Pentagon on September 11th, the FAA has received funding to greatly expand the Federal Air Marshal program.[52]

The Under Secretary, in section 105(1) of the Act[53] was authorized to "provide for deployment of Federal air marshals on every passenger flight of air carriers in air transportation or interstate air transportation." Moreover, the Under Secretary "shall provide for deployment of Federal air marshals on every such flight determined by the Secretary to present high security risks."[54]

The Federal Air Marshal program has a long history. The Federal Air Marshal program began as the Sky Marshal Program in 1968 and continued through the 1970s as a program designed to stop hijackings to and from Cuba. The current program was created shortly after the hijacking of TWA 847 in June 1985. During that incident, two Lebanese Shiite Moslems hijacked a Boeing 727 departing Athens and diverted it to Beirut where they were joined by additional hijackers.[55] The Federal Air Marshal tactical training facility and operational headquarters is located at the William J. Hughes Technical Center in Atlantic City, New Jersey. The Federal Air Marshals also train at other undisclosed locations throughout the country.[56]

On February 21, 2003, the TSA assumed recruitment responsibilities from the FAA and is now actively recruiting Federal air marshals.[57] The job vacancy announcements are posted on the TSA's employment Web site at <www.tsa.gov>. The site gives information about the job, compensation, qualification requirements, and directions on how to apply.

The extent to which the Under Secretary has implemented section 105 of the Act is unknown. Indeed, only limited information about the Federal Air Marshal program can be made public. The TSA will not reveal the number or identity of the marshals, the details of their training, their budget, nor the routes they fly. What has been said publicly by the FAA and the TSA is that the Federal Air Marshals are continuously deployed throughout the nation and world on all major U.S. carriers, and that Federal Air Marshals fly every day of the year.

5.2   Flight Deck Security

Several additional provisions of the Act, while not as high-profile as the man-dates for the federalization of airport baggage screeners, sought to increase and improve airline security. Section 104(a)(1)(A) of the Act required that, "as soon as possible after the date of enactment of this Act," the Administrator of the FAA issue an order "prohibiting access to the flight deck of aircraft engaged in passenger air transportation or intrastate air transportation that are required to have door between the passenger and pilot compartments."[58] Moreover, the Administrator of the FAA was to issue an order "requiring the strengthening of the flight deck door and locks on any such aircraft.to ensure that the door cannot be forced open from the passenger compartment."[59] At the discretion of the Administrator, development of "video monitors or other devices to alert pilots in the flight deck to activity in the cabin" was permitted. [60]

The Act also discusses the authority of the Secretary, after consultation with the National Institute of Justice, to allow members of the flight deck crew to carry less-than-lethal weapons.[61] The Act also provides a limitation on liabil-ity for acts of those attempting to thwart violence on an aircraft if the person reasonably believed that an act of violence or piracy was occurring or about to occur.[62]

5.3   Computer-Assisted Passenger Prescreening System

Probably one of the more controversial provisions of the Act is the establish-ment of the Computer Assisted Passenger Prescreening System (CAPPS II).[63] CAPPS II is an enhanced version of the existing computer passenger screening system and will aid the TSA in identifying passengers who may be foreign ter-rorists or have terrorist connections before the passengers board U.S. aircraft. Lockheed Martin has been chosen to work with TSA to develop CAPPS II. It will be a passive system activated by a passenger's reservation request. Of utmost concern is balancing national security considerations with individual privacy considerations.[64]

CAPPS II is expected to be tested this spring and will be implemented by the summer of 2004. The TSA has requested Delta Air Lines provide assistance in the development of the system's infrastructure. The system will work by U.S. commercial air carriers providing to TSA the normal information airlines col-lect during the reservation and ticketing process. Thereafter, CAPPS II will receive information from computer databases which will then give an indica-tion as to whether further screening needs to be done of certain passengers. The system will provide the government with more information about each passen-ger who has made a reservation, including the passenger's personal and finan-cial information. It will assign a color code to each passenger that is indicative of a certain threat level: green, yellow, or red. TSA will not have access to the information that is used to generate the information that leads to the additional scrutiny. CAPPS II will be conducted in strict compliance with all privacy act regulations and the TSA will not maintain data that is collected.

The plan for CAPPS II has come under criticism by both civil liberties groups in the United States and the European Union. The European Union is concerned about violation of EU data protection legislation and protecting the personal information of foreigners who fly to the United States.

6.0   Foreign Air Transportation

All foreign air carriers must have a security program which is approved by the Under Secretary.[65] Specifically, Section 115 of the Act[66] requires that air carriers, including foreign air carriers, who operate a passenger flight in foreign transportation to the United States must provide to the Commissioner of Customs a passenger and crew manifest containing certain information. This information must be provided by electronic transmission. The information that must be provided includes the following:

(A) The full name of each passenger and crew member
(B) The date of birth and citizenship of each passenger and crew member
(C) The sex of each passenger and crew member
(D) The passport number and country of issuance of each passenger and crew member, if required for travel
(E) The United States visa number or resident alien card number of each passenger and crew member, as applicable
(F) Such other information as the Under Secretary, in consultation with the Commissioner of Customs, determines is reasonably necessary to ensure aviation safety[67]

6.1   Foreign Security Liaison Officers

Where necessary, the Under Secretary of Transportation will have a Foreign Security Liaison Officer at airports outside the United States. This person will work with foreign security authorities to ensure that United States security requirements are met at that airport.[68] The Under Secretary is required to report to Congress biennially on the foreign air carrier security programs established at airports outside the United States.[69]

7.0   General Aviation

General aviation has been hard hit by the provision of the Act. A number of restrictions on airspace use, particularly around the Washington D.C. area, made it difficult for general aviation pilots to conduct flights after September 11, 2001. It was not until February 2002 that the FAA issued an emergency rule allowing private flying to resume under strict conditions at three airports in Maryland within a 15 mile radius of the Washington Monument.

Section 132 of the Act provides for the Under Secretary of Transportation for Transportation Security to provide a report on airspace or other security measures that should be enacted to improve general aviation security. The Act provides that the Under Secretary may require all pilot licenses to include a photograph and even biometric imprints.[70] The FAA has also issued regulations establishing the procedure by which the TSA will provide notification of individual airmen or those applying for an airman certificate who may pose a threat to transportation security of the method by which those individuals may have an opportunity to be heard.[71]

New airspace control measures have been put in place around Washington, D.C. consistent with National Threat Level Orange.[72] These new measures are available to pilots in the form of Notice to Airmen (NOTAM) and were implemented in February 2003.[73] The NOTAM applied to all persons operating an aircraft to or from the College Park Airport, Potomac Airfield, or Washington Executive/Hyde Field Airport to adhere to certain measures, including filing flight plans with Leesburg Automated Flight Service Station prior to any flight, prohibition on filing flight plans in the air, using confidential pilot codes prior to filing a flight plan, and obtaining an air traffic control clearance from Potomac approach via telephone. Pilots need to monitor for the issuance of NOTAMs pertaining to national security.

8.0   Amendments to Air Transportation Safety and System Stabilization Act

The Act amended the Air Transportation Safety and System Stabilization Act (ATSSA) to allow civil actions against "any person who is a knowing participant in any conspiracy to hijack an aircraft or commit any terrorist act."[74] The Act amended the ATSSSA to allow civil actions against "any person who is a knowing participant in any conspiracy to hijack an aircraft or commit any terrorist act."[75] The Act also amends section 408 of the ATSSSA by limiting the liability of air carriers, aircraft manufacturers, airport sponsors, or persons with a property interest in the World Trade Center to an amount not greater than the limits of liability insurance coverage maintained by these entities. It also limits the liability of New York City to the city's insurance coverage or $350 million.

9.0   Homeland Security

On March 1, 2003, the TSA moved from the U.S. Department of Transportation to the Department of Homeland Security. TSA had gone from a non-existing agency to an agency consisting of more than 60,000 employees and a budget of $5 billion. TSA is one of 22 agencies transferred to the new cabinet-level department.

10.0 Conclusion

After September 11, 2001, Americans woke up to a new world of transportation and, in particular, flying. The aviation industry—from commercial airlines to private pilots, from cargo operators to airports, and from those involved in general aviation to the flying public at large—was forever changed. In a remarkable period of time, Congress enacted the Aviation and Transportation Security Act. Regulations implementing the Act continue to be promulgated, and the Federal government has adapted to deal with these regulations, including the establishment of the TSA and Department of Homeland Security.

Of course, these changes not only affect the United States but they have a global effect. Various aviation organizations, including the International Civil Aviation Organization and the European Union, are working together with the challenges posed in this new world.

Endnotes:

[1] Public Law 107-71, 115 Stat. 597 (19 November 2001).

[2] The other legislation was the Air Transportation Safety and Stabilization Act - Public Law 107-42, 115 Stat. 230 (2001).

[3] Remarks for ADM James M. Loy Acting Under Secretary of Transportation for Security Congressional Economic Leadership Institute; Available at: www.tsa.gov. 18 September 2002.

[4] Statement of U.S. Secretary of Transportation Norman Y. Mineta Concerning Bipartisan Agreement on Aviation Security Bill. 15 November 2001.

[5] *Ibid.*

[6] Executive Order No. 13228 of 8 October 2001, Sec. 3(a).

[7] Executive Order No. 13228 of 8 October 2001, Sec. 3(d).

[8] Executive Order No. 13228 of October 8, 2001, Sec. 3 (d)(iii) and (e)(v).

[9] 49 U.S.C. §114.

[10] 49 U.S.C. §114(a).

[11] 49 U.S.C. §114(b)(1).

[12] 49 U.S.C. §114(d).

[13] 49 U.S.C. §114(e)(1-4).

[14] *See, e.g.,* 49 U.S.C. §114.

[15] *See* Executive Order No. 13228, Section 3(a), 8 October 2001.

[16] 49 U.S.C. § 114(f).

[17] 49 U.S.C. § 114(g).

[18] 49 U.S.C. § 115 (b)(1) and (2).

[19] 49 U.S.C. § 114 (h)(2); *See also* Fed. Reg. 3756 (January 24, 2003) and General Aviation discussion, *infra.*

[20] Remarks for ADM James M. Loy, Acting Under Secretary of Transportation for Security Congressional Economic Leadership Institute. 18 September 2002. *See also* 2/5/02 CONGTMY, 2002 WL 25100039, United States General Accounting Office Testimony of Henry L. Hinton, Jr., entitled "Combating Terrorism." 12 March 2002.

[21] 49 U.S.C. § 44901(6)-(7) (section 110 of the Act).

[22] 49 U.S.C. § 44901.

[23] 49 U.S.C. § 44901(c).

[24] 49 U.S.C. § 44935.

[25] *See generally* 49 U.S.C. § 44901(e).

[26] Jon Hilkevitch "Air Security Deadlines Put on Hold." Chicago Tribune. 24 July 2002. 10. WL 2678419. In a Subcommittee on Aviation Hearing on Implementation of the Aviation & Transportation Security Act with a Focus in the 60-day Deadline for Screening Checked Baggage, several problems with the timely implementation of baggage screening were identified. For example, a bag match program on domestic flights would significantly slow down the aviation transportation system because each time a bag is found without a matching passenger, an airline employee would have to remove the bag from the plane. Moreover, a bag match program would not eliminate terrorist suicide bombings. Manual search was criticized as being too slow, and while search by bomb-sniffing dogs may be effective, it takes along time to train the dogs and each dog can only work for a short time before becoming ineffective. Moreover, the fourth method ("other means or technology approved by the Under Secretary") is criticized as being unclear and may include passenger profiling, a method previously used by the airline industry. Thus, implementation of option number four would merely return to the status quo.

[27] "Results from the Curbside to the Cockpit: Mandates in the Aviation and Transportation Security Act" 5 February 2002. Available at: www.tsa.gov; Statement of Michael Jackson, Deputy Secretary of Transportation and John Magaw, Under Secretary of Transportation for Security Before the Commerce, Science and Transportation Committee United States Senate. Available at: www.tsa.gov/public/display?theme=46&content=266.

[28] Subcommittee on Aviation Hearing on Implementation of the Aviation & Transportation Security Act with a Focus in the 60-day Deadline for Screening Checked Baggage.

[29] 49 U.S.C. § 44935(f)(1)(A) and (B).

[30] *Id.*

[31] 49 U.S.C. § 44935(f)(1)(D).

[32] *See* job description and qualifications for Transportation Security Screener. Available at: www.tsacareers.recruitsoft.com.

[33] 2/5/02 CONGTMY, 2002 WL 25098719. Aviation Security Issues, Comments by Senator Rockefeller at Aviation Security Hearing. February 5, 2002.

[34] Roosevelt Joseph, "Angry Chuck Calls on FAA to Hire Keener Screeners," New York Post, 7 January 2002. WL 4907800.; *See also* Press Release of Senator Bob Barr entitled "Barr Blasts Move to Lower Airport Security Standards, Calls on Transportation Department to Set Minimum Education Requirements." 3 January 2002. WL 7271213.

[35] 49 U.S.C. § 44935(g).

[36] 49 U.S.C. § 44935(i).

[37] www.dot.gov/affairs/dot0702.htm.

[38] RFP's available at www.eps.gov (solicitation numbers DTTS59-02-R-00439 and DTTS59-02-R-00440).

[39] "Transportation Security Administration Progress as of November 19, 2002" TSA Press release, containing list of every United States airport and the date when screeners were deployed.

[40] *Ibid.* As of November 19, 2002, women comprised 35.4 percent of the screener workforce and minorities comprised 41 percent; "Timeline of TSA Accomplishments—A Year of Progress" TSA Press Release.

[41] "Screeners Miss Fake Weapons 25 Percent of the Time." *Airline Indus. Info,* 2 July 2002. WL 5817391.

[42] "Time to Improve Baggage Screeners." South Bend Tribune, 14 July 2002. WL 21488202.

[43] *Ibid.*

[44] "TSA Meeting Deadline for Screening All Checked Baggage" TSA Press Release TSA 147-02, 12/30/02; *See also* www.tsa.gov/public/display?content=487.

[45] 67 Fed. Reg. 48506. (24 July 2002).

[46] *Id.*

[47] 49 U.S.C. § 44903.

[48] 49 U.S.C. § 44903(h)(2).

[49] Statement of Norman Y. Mineta, Secretary of Transportation, before the Commerce, Science and Transportation Committee—United States Senate. 21 May 2002.

[50] Directorate available at www.whitehouse.gov/news/releases/2003/02/20030207-13.html.

[51] *Id.*

[52] http://www1.faa.gov/index.cfm/apa/1279/4322764F-434C-4415-8A54FE6E9493AF9F.

[53] 49 U.S.C. § 44917.

[54] 49 U.S.C. § 44917(a)(2).

[55] http://www1.faa.gov/index.cfm/apa/1279/4322764F-434C-4415-8A54FE6E9493AF9F.

[56] *Id.*

[57] http://jobs.faa.gov/FAMandScreeners.HTM.

[58] 49 U.S.C. § 44903 note.

[59] *Id.*

[60] *Id.*

[61] 49 U.S.C. § 44903(h).

[62] *Id.*

[63] 49 U.S.C. § 44903(i)(2).

[64] Remarks of ADM James M. Loy, Under Secretary of Transportation Security ("TSA has sought to meet the urgent need to heighten security at airports to press the war against terrorists. We will accomplish this without compromising the privacy and civil liberties enjoyed by every American"). Available at: www.tsa.gov. 11 March 2003.

[65] 49 U.S.C. § 44906.

[66] 49 U.S.C. § 44909 (c)(1).

[67] 49 U.S.C. § 44909 (c)(2).

[68] 49 U.S.C. § 44934 (a).

[69] 49 U.S.C. § 44938 (b).

[70] 49 U.S.C. § 114 note (a)(6); *See also* 67 Fed. Reg. 65858 (28 October 2002) providing for Picture Identification Requirements.

[71] 68 Fed. Reg. 3756 (January 24, 2003). *See also* 68 Fed. Reg. 3772 (24 January 2003) which is the final rule expressly making a person ineligible to hold FAA-issued airman certificates if the TSA has notified the FAA in writing that the person poses a security threat.

[72] www.faa.gov.

[73] http://www2.faa.gov/specialnotams/Special_Interest_Notams.htm.

[74] Pub. L. 107-71, §201 (a), 115 stat. 597.

[75] *Id.*

Chapter 4

Maritime Transportation Security

Blank Rome LLP
Jonathan K. Waldron

1.0   Introduction

The terrorist attacks of September 11, 2001, demonstrated the vulnerabilities in America's transportation system. In particular, federal agencies quickly realized that vessels and maritime-related port facilities are vulnerable to large-scale terrorism because of the wide variety of trade and commerce carried out at U.S. ports and by the very open and exposed nature of port operations. U.S. ports were gaping holes in international boundary areas, lacking security infrastructure or federal security funding. Federal personnel and equipment resources were immediately diverted on an ad hoc basis to security-related patrols, boardings, and other measures intended to reduce the threat of terrorism to U.S. ports and vessels operating in U.S. waters.

Accordingly, Congress recognized the need to develop a comprehensive port security framework in the United States. The Maritime Transportation Security Act of 2002 (MTSA or the Act) was signed into law on November 25, 2002. This landmark legislation, the first major maritime legislation in four years, established a series of regulatory requirements including a security infrastructure to protect U.S. ports from terrorist activities. By increasing anti-terrorism security at and on American ports and waterways, the legislation seeks to deter terrorist attacks against vessels and facilities engaged in ocean commerce while at the same time avoiding an adverse impact on the flow of goods through American ports.

The requirements of the Act can be broken down into two broad categories. First, the Act requires government authorities to gather and analyze information on the threats to certain American port facilities and the vessels that use them. These reports will take the form of "vulnerability assessments" of infrastructure and vessels. Second, the data gathered by these assessments will be incorporated into a comprehensive deterrence and response plan to a variety of perceived terrorist attacks. By taking a "tiered approach" to security on the national, regional, and local levels, this framework is designed to significantly minimize the threat and/or consequences of another terrorist attack.

2.0   Overview

This chapter contains a summary of the security related provisions of Title I of the MTSA, which, among other things, contemplates U.S. and foreign port vulnerability assessments; national, area, vessel, and facility security plans; terrorist incident response requirements; security cards, teams, and grants; and automatic electronic identification systems.[1]

Most of the security measures under Title I of the MTSA are contained in section 102, "Port Security," which creates a new Chapter 701 of the United States Code under Title 46 entitled Port Security. This chapter therefore focuses on section 102 of the MTSA, and other pertinent sections of Title I, to the extent that port security matters are addressed.

3.0   Key Definitions

The following definitions, specifically related to maritime and port security, are codified at 46 U.S.C. §70101:

- The term "facility" is defined as any structure or facility of any kind located in, on, under, or adjacent to any waters subject to the jurisdiction of the United States.
- The term "owner or operator" is defined (1) for a vessel, as any person owning or operating the vessel, or chartering the vessel by demise; and (2) for a facility, as any person owning, leasing, or operating the facility. The term "person" includes corporations or other entities, as well as individuals.
- The term "Secretary" is defined as the Secretary of the department in which the Coast Guard is operating. Effective March 1, 2003, the Coast Guard operates in the Department of Homeland Security. In times of war or national emergency, the Secretary of Defense would oversee the Coast Guard.
- The term "transportation security incident" is defined as a security incident resulting in a significant loss of life, environmental damage, transportation system disruption, or economic disruption in a particular area.

4.0   Facility and Vessel Vulnerability Assessments

An essential first step of port security is assessing the vulnerability of facilities and vessels in U.S. waters.[2] These assessments will be the first comprehensive analysis conducted by the federal government of existing security procedures in place at America's ports and onboard the vessels utilizing them. Specifically, these assessments seek to identify those vessel types and facilities that pose a risk of being involved in a transportation security incident. Information gleaned from the assessments will be utilized to craft detailed security plans, allocate funding for necessary security measures (including capital improvements, equipment, and personnel training), and improve inter-governmental communications and procedures in both a pre- and post-incident environment.

The Act requires the Secretary to conduct the assessments in two phases. First, the Secretary will conduct *initial* assessments of vessel types and facilities located on or adjacent to waters under U.S. jurisdiction (*i.e.,* those within the 12 mile limit) and, in so doing, will identify those types of vessels and facilities that pose a high risk of being involved in a transportation security incident.[3] After identifying "risky" vessel types and facilities, the Secretary will then conduct *detailed* vulnerability assessments designed to identify specific vulnerabilities in vessels and facilities.

Detailed vulnerability assessments must cover the following matters:

1. Identification and evaluation of critical assets and infrastructures
2. Identification of the threats posed to those assets and infrastructures
3. Identification of weaknesses in physical security, passenger and cargo security, structural integrity, protection systems, procedural policies, communications systems, transportation infrastructure, utilities, contingency response, and other areas specified by the Secretary

Each detailed vulnerability assessment must be updated at least every five years, and a copy of each assessment must be provided to the owner or operator of the vessel or facility being assessed.[4] It should also be noted that owners or operators may provide the Secretary with their *own* assessment of their vessel or facility, which the Secretary may accept as an alternative to a detailed vulnerability assessment. These alternative assessments, in order to be considered for acceptance, must contain all of the matters required in the detailed vulnerability assessments. Alternative assessments may be conducted by the owner or operator, or by a third party acting on their behalf.

5.0   Security Plans

To promote coordination of efforts in deterring and responding to transportation security incidents, the Act mandates the drafting and implementation of security plans.[5] The Act contemplates three different types of security plans: a National Maritime Transportation Security Plan (National Plan), individual Area Transportation Security Plans (Area Plan) for each area designated by the National Plan, and individual plans for each vessel (vessel plan) and facility (facility plan) that the Secretary believes may be involved in a transportation security incident.

5.1   National Maritime Transportation Security Plan

One of the two main goals of the National Plan is the deterrence of transportation security incidents. To accomplish this, the Act requires the Secretary to delineate planning duties between agencies and/or departments at the federal, state, and local levels.[6] The National Plan also requires the development of procedures, criteria, and techniques for identifying and deterring potential transportation security incidents. While most of the deterrence methodology set forth in the Act is of a general nature, the Act does mandate several specific deterrence procedures. One deterrent specifically required by the Act is the development of "a system of surveillance and notice," the purpose of which is to ensure the earliest possible warning of potential security threats. To accompany the surveillance system, the Act requires the establishment of criteria and procedures to ensure immediate and effective identification of transportation security incidents or "substantial" threats of transportation security incidents. Finally, the Act specifically requires the Secretary to divide the waters under the jurisdiction of the United States into "security zones" and evaluate the risk of potential security breaches in each of them.

The Act also requires that the designation of "areas for which Area Maritime Transportation Security Plans" should be developed and mandates the appointment of a Coast Guard official (called a "Federal Maritime Security Coordinator") to be in charge of Area Plan development. Area Plans, discussed *infra*, will provide comprehensive deterrence and responsive methodology specifically suited to a given geographical area. In addition, the Secretary must inform vessel owners/operators and facility owners/operators of provisions in the National Plan that the Secretary considers necessary for security purposes. Vessel and facility owners and operators would then be able to incorporate that knowledge into their own vessel or facility security plan.

In the event that a transportation security incident *does* occur, the Act sets forth guidelines in the National Plan for use in a coordinated federal, state, and local government response. While the Act mainly speaks in general terms, it does require that the National Plan mandate the development of methodology for efficiently re-establishing the flow of cargo through U.S. ports following a national security incident.

Federal agency action must, to the maximum extent possible, be in accordance with the guidelines set forth in the National Plan. Revisions to, or amendments of, the National Plan shall be made whenever the Secretary deems it necessary.

5.2   Area Transportation Security Plans

This provision requires the appropriate Federal Maritime Security Coordinator (Coordinator) to consult with an Area Security Advisory Committee to develop procedures that, to the maximum extent possible, deter transportation security incidents in a given geographic area. The Coordinator should also consult and coordinate with the Department of Defense on matters relating to Department of Defense vessels, with other Area Plan Coordinators, and with vessel and facility owners or operators. To ensure maximum effectiveness and protection, each Coordinator must ensure that an Area Plan is integrated with other Area Plans and individual vessel and facility plans.

The Area Plans, which should be implemented in conjunction with the National Plan, must describe the area and infrastructure falling under the Area Plan's coverage. Areas of population or of special economic, environmental, or national security importance should be identified in the Area Plan, as well as the potential risks and damages that a transportation security incident would pose to each. The Plan must also include any other information required by the Secretary and must be updated every five years. Upon submittal, the Secretary shall initially review and approve each Area Plan and shall conduct periodic assessments of the plans after approval. If an Area Plan contains a "security zone" (as designated by the Secretary pursuant to the National Plan), the Secretary shall consider certain security alternatives and enhancements.[7]

5.3   Vessel and Facility Security Plans

As noted previously, individual vessel and facility security plans are required for those vessels and facilities that the Secretary believes may be involved in a transportation security incident.[8] These vessel and facility security plans are due six months after the Secretary issues interim final regulations.[9] Beginning 12 months after the interim final regulations are issued, those vessels and facilities identified by the Secretary as posing a risk of being involved in a transportation security incident may *not* operate unless the Secretary approves the plan and the vessel or facility is operating in accordance with the plan. However, the Act does allow the Secretary to permit a vessel or facility to operate without an approved security plan for a period up to one year after the owner or operator has submitted a proposed plan. For such an exemption to apply, the owner or operator must certify that they have "ensured by contract or other means approved by the Secretary to deter to the maximum extent practicable a transportation security incident or a substantial threat of such a security incident." Thus, vessel and facility owners are not required to cease their operations due to the failure of the Secretary to approve their vessel or facility transportation security plans in a reasonable time period. However, until a security plan is approved, the Secretary may implement necessary interim security measurements affecting any vessel or facility located within or adjacent to waters subject to the jurisdiction of the United States.

Much like the National Plan and Area Plans, requirements for individual vessel or facility security plans focus largely on the twin goals of deterrence and containment.[10] An individual vessel or facility security plan must identify a "qualified individual" having full authority to implement security actions. Each individual plan must include methodology for (1) communicating with the appropriate federal official(s) during plan development and implementation; (2) overseeing the establishment and maintenance of the physical security of the vessel or facility as well as its passengers, cargo, and personnel; (3) overseeing the establishment of security procedures for and controlling access to secure areas of the vessel or facility; (4) overseeing the creation of security policies; (5) supervising the development of communication systems; and (6) overseeing the creation of other security systems.[11] Whereas the Area Plans and National Plan identify the risks of types of transportation security incidents and the preferred methodology and procedures for dealing with them, the individual vessel or security plan must identify and implement *specific* security measures. Each individual plan must identify and ensure, by contract or other means approved by the Secretary, the availability of security measures necessary to deter, to the maximum extent practicable, a transportation security incident or a substantial threat of one. In addition, each individual plan must contain the training and methodology to be used by security personnel on the vessel or at the facility.[12]

Upon submittal of an individual vessel or facility security plan, the Secretary must promptly review and either approve or reject each plan. The Secretary may require amendments to any plan not meeting the requirements of the Act. At the very least, each individual vessel or facility security plan must be updated every five years. Major changes that substantially affect the security of the vessel or facility must be promptly submitted to the Secretary for approval. In addition to owner or operator-provided updates, the Secretary must conduct a "periodic review" of the individual plans to ensure continuing compliance with the Act.

5.4   Facility and Vessel Response Plans

The Act requires the Secretary, not the owners or operators, to develop and establish "security incident response plans" for vessels and facilities identified in the Secretary's initial assessments as posing a risk of being involved in a transportation security incident.[13] To promote coordination of a federal, state, and local governmental response to a transportation security incident, the Secretary shall make the security incident response plans available to the Director of the Federal Emergency Response Management Agency (FEMA) for inclusion into FEMA's response plan covering U.S. ports and waterways. The Act requires, as a general principle, that the security incident response plans contain a "comprehensive response" to an emergency, but it specifically requires the inclusion of methods in securing and evacuating a facility or vessel. A security incident response plan may be included in a facility or vessel security plan.

5.5   Maritime Security Advisory Committees

To increase the effectiveness of deterrence and implementation of security techniques, the Act requires the Secretary to establish a "National Maritime Security Advisory Committee" and authorizes the Secretary to establish localized "Area Maritime Security Advisory Committees" to advise the Secretary and/or Congress on general maritime security issues.[14] In addition, the Area Committees may review, upon request by the Secretary, the applicable proposed Area Plan and may make proposed recommendations. All Committees will meet on an annual basis (or more) and will consist of seven members appointed to five-year terms by the Secretary. To qualify for membership, all candidates must have at least five years of "practical experience in maritime security operations." The National Maritime Security Advisory Committee will automatically terminate on September 30, 2008, but there is no set termination date for Area Committees. However, each committee established pursuant to this section must submit to Congress a recommendation regarding whether the Committee should continue to exist.

6.0   Identification Procedures

Given that the Act seeks to deter transportation security incidents, it should come as no surprise that the Act imposes heightened identification requirements for facility and vessel personnel operating in secure areas, for vessel crewmembers, and for the vessels themselves.

6.1   Transportation Security Cards

One of the key aspects of an individual vessel or facility security plan would be procedures to identify and protect "secure areas." The Secretary shall promulgate regulations that prevent unauthorized access to secure areas. Individuals may enter secure areas only if they are authorized by the individual vessel or facility security plan to enter a secure area or are accompanied by such an individual and they either possess a "transportation security card" themselves or are accompanied by someone who does.[15]

Those entitled to receive transportation security cards are (1) those allowed "unescorted" access to a secure area as designated in an approved individual vessel or facility security plan; (2) an individual issued a license, certificate of registry, or merchant mariner's document; (3) a vessel pilot; (4) an individual engaged on a towing vessel assisting a tank vessel; (5) an individual with access to security sensitive information, as determined by the Secretary; (6) other individuals engaged in port security activities (as determined by the Secretary); and (7) individuals licensed to carry hazardous materials pursuant to 46 U.S.C. § 5103a. Biometric transportation security cards *must* be issued to these individuals *unless* the Secretary determines that the individual poses a terrorism security risk.

Individuals who pose a terrorism security risk, and therefore may be denied issuance of a transportation security card by the Secretary, fall into several categories. First are those individuals who have either been convicted of a felony (or were found not guilty by reason of insanity) within the previous seven-year period or have been released from incarceration within the preceding five-year period for commission of a felony. In addition, the Secretary must believe either that the felony could cause the individual to be a terrorism security risk or that the underlying felony was for causing a severe transportation security incident. Second, the Secretary may deny transportation security cards to those individuals who may be denied admission to or be removed from the United States.[16] Finally, the Secretary may deny transportation security cards to an individual who "otherwise poses a terrorism security risk to the United States."

To determine whether an individual poses a terrorism security risk, the Secretary may ask the Attorney General to conduct background checks of transportation security card applicants. The Attorney General may review relevant criminal history databases, a check of databases containing "alien" status, a check of the relevant international databases, or any other national security related information or database identified by the Attorney General. Information in the background checks that serves as grounds for denial of a transportation security card may not be released to the public and may only be used by the Secretary for purposes of making a decision whether to issue a transportation security card.

In other words, the Secretary may only inform the individual's employer about whether the individual has or has not been issued a transportation security card, but information related to the basis for such a denial may not be released. The Secretary may, however, share such background information with other federal law enforcement agencies.

Individuals who would otherwise be ineligible to receive transportation security cards may still be able to petition the Secretary for an exception. To issue a transportation security card to an otherwise unqualified individual, the Secretary must determine that the individual does not pose a terrorism risk warranting denial of the card. Factors to be considered are the individual circumstances of the disqualifying act performed by the individual, restitution and remedial efforts, and other factors that may lead to a determination that the individual does not pose the aforementioned risk. In the alternative, the Secretary does not need to make an individual determination if that individual's employer establishes "alternate security arrangements" relating to the individual that are acceptable to the Secretary. Unqualified individuals who are still denied transportation security cards may initiate a formal appeal with a right to notice and an opportunity for a hearing.

6.2   Crewmember Identification

The Act also requires new procedures for the identification of all crewmembers of a vessel, regardless of whether they have access to a secure area.[17] The Secretary, in consultation with the Attorney General and the Secretary of State, shall require crewmembers on vessels calling at U.S. ports to carry and present on demand any identification that the Secretary decides is necessary. The Secretary, acting in consultation with the Attorney General and the Secretary of State, will establish the requisite forms of identification and documentation.

As an example of heightened crewmember identification requirements, the Department of State published a proposed rule to eliminate crew list visas on December 13, 2002. Comments were due by February 11, 2003.[18] Previously, aliens serving as crew were allowed to use their crew list as a valid nonimmigrant visa. This proposed rule would eliminate the availability of crew list visas. Instead, each crewmember would be required to apply for an individual visa. To obtain an individual visa, each crewmember would be required to complete the nonimmigrant application form, submit a valid passport, be interviewed, and undergo a background check.

6.3   Automatic Identification and Vessel Tracking Systems

In addition to creating new identification requirements for personnel and crewmembers, the Act imposes new identification requirements on vessels. Vessels operating on the navigable waters of the United States must be equipped with an automatic identification system[19] (AIS). The AIS *must* be installed on all self-propelled commercial vessels 65 feet in length or longer and towing vessels of at least 26 feet in length and with 600 horsepower. The Act also calls for the Secretary to require an AIS on passenger vessels that carry a certain number of passengers. The regulations issued on July 1, 2003, set several different AIS carriage thresholds. Any passenger vessel on an international voyage subject to SOLAS or with a capacity of more than 150 passengers is subject to AIS carriage requirements. The Act further allows the Secretary to require *any* other vessel to install and operate an AIS, provided that the Secretary determines that the AIS is necessary for the safe navigation of the vessel. The Secretary retains broad powers to exempt a vessel if the Secretary believes that an AIS is not necessary for the safe navigation of the vessel.

In conjunction with the vessel AIS, the Secretary may, either independently or with the assistance of existing maritime organizations, develop and initiate a long-range automated vessel tracking system. The tracking system would allow authorities to track all vessels operating in U.S. waters utilizing the Global Maritime Distress and Safety System or equivalent satellite tracking technology. The professed goal of such a tracking system would be to allow the Secretary to receive information on a vessel's position for purposes of deterring transportation security incidents.

6.4   Maritime Intelligence

The Secretary shall implement a system to collect, interpret, and analyze information concerning vessels operating on or bound for waters subject to U.S. jurisdiction.[20] Again, the Act gives the Secretary broad powers to collect this information; the Secretary may consult with the Transportation Security Oversight Board, other federal departments and agencies, and any other private and public entities.

7.0   Safety and Security Teams

The Act authorizes the Secretary to create, train, and equip maritime safety and security teams.[21] These teams, acting in coordination with applicable federal, state, and local agencies, shall protect vessels, harbors, ports, facilities, and cargo lying within the jurisdiction of the United States. The teams' primary goal is to deter and respond to threats of maritime terrorism. Specifically, the Act permits these teams to enforce moving or fixed safety or security zones; conduct intercepts of suspects and or their vessels; board, search, and seize contraband presenting a security risk; rapidly deploy to supplement U.S. armed forces at home or abroad; and carry out any other security missions designated by the Secretary. These teams should be assembled immediately, as the Act contemplates their assistance in the facility vulnerability assessments mentioned *supra*.

8.0 Grants

The Secretary, through the Maritime Administration, shall establish a grant program to assist in the implementation of Area Maritime Transportation Security Plans and facility security plans and authorizes the appropriation of such sums as may be necessary to carry out the program for each of the fiscal years 2003 through 2008.[22] The funds are to be allocated among port authorities, facility operators, and state and local agencies required to provide security services. The Secretary will file reports with Congress on an annual basis updating progress in addressing vulnerability and compliance issues and recommending any necessary changes in the grant program. In addition, the Inspector General of the Department of Transportation will make annual assessments of the research and development grant program and report the findings to Congress. In 2002, the Department of Transportation awarded $92.3 million in grant funds to 77 seaports nationwide.[23] That amount increased to $105 million in 2003.[24]

8.1 Implementation Grants

Grants for the implementation of security enhancements required pursuant to Coast Guard-identified port security vulnerabilities, and reimbursement of such enhancements dating back to September 11, 2001, may be partially funded by the federal government. In addition, this section provides partial funding for costs associated with continuing compliance with Area Plans and facility security plans. The kinds of costs that may be funded by these grants (collectively referred to as "implementation grants") are as follows:

1. Salaries, benefits, overtime compensation, retirement contributions, and other costs for security personnel required by the Coast Guard
2. The cost of acquisition, operation, and maintenance of certain security equipment or facilities, including equipment and facilities for security monitoring and recording, security gates and fencing, marine barriers for designated security zones, security-related lighting systems, remote surveillance, concealed video systems, and security vessels

3. The cost of screening equipment, including equipment to detect weapons of mass destruction and conventional explosives and equipment to test and evaluate the detection equipment
4. The cost of conducting vulnerability assessments to evaluate and make recommendations with respect to security

8.2 Research and Development Grants

The Act identifies national laboratories, private nonprofit organizations, institutions of higher learning, and other entities as potential recipients of grants under the research and development grant program for port security technology. The Act authorizes $15 million for each of the fiscal years 2003 through 2008 for the program. The following technologies are singled out as the development objectives of the program:

1. Methods to increase the Coast Guard's ability to inspect, or target for inspection, merchandise carried on vessels that arrive in U.S. ports
2. Equipment to accurately detect explosives or chemical and biological agents that could be used to commit terrorist acts
3. Equipment to accurately detect nuclear materials, including scintillation-based detection equipment capable of being attached to spreaders to signal the presence of nuclear materials during the unloading of shipping containers
4. Improved tags and seals designed for use on shipping containers, including "smart sensors" that can track a container throughout its entire supply chain, detect hazardous and radioactive materials within that container, and transmit that information to the appropriate authorities at a remote location
5. Tools to mitigate the consequences of a terrorist act at a U.S. port, including a network of sensors to predict the dispersion of radiological, chemical, or biological agents that might be intentionally or accidentally released.

8.3 Funding Limitations and Restrictions

The Secretary shall establish a grant program for port security technology research and development. Generally speaking, the federal government will fund up to 75 percent of an eligible project's cost; projects that require a higher level of funding may petition the Secretary, who is permitted to grant more funds to projects that merit support. However, federal matching restrictions do not apply to small projects costing $25,000 or less. To prevent overlapping and duplicative federal funding of projects, the Secretary may require users of ports and port facilities that receive federal funding to enter into cooperative working agreements. Likewise, the Act requires the Secretary to ensure research and development grants are not awarded for research and development projects already under way.

8.4   Grant Administration

For implementation-type grants, applications must include a copy of the applicable Area Plan or facility security plan; a comprehensive description of the type of project, which should include a description of both the project's relevance as well as its relationship to the Area Plan or facility security plan; and documentation from the Coast Guard Captain of the Port certifying that the project meets the funding eligibility requirements as set forth in the Act (*i.e.,* the funds will go toward addressing vulnerabilities or compliance efforts). The Act does not impose a similar requirement on research and development grant applications.

Applications for implementation grants should be approved by the Secretary if the Secretary determines that the project is consistent with vulnerability assessments and/or ensures compliance with Area Plans or vessel security plans, enough funds are available, the project can be completed without unreasonable delay, and the recipient of the grant monies has authority to implement the project proposal. After receiving an award of grant money, regardless of the purpose of the grant, the recipient must keep and make available for review any records that the Secretary deems necessary and must follow proscribed accounting methods.

9.0   Foreign Ports

In addition to protecting port facilities and vessels operating in U.S. territorial waters, the Act also seeks to ensure effective anti-terrorism protections are in place at foreign ports. These protections take three forms. First, the Secretary will conduct an assessment of foreign port security measures. Next, if the Secretary finds foreign port security to be ineffective, the Act requires the Secretary to notify the foreign government of the deficiencies. Finally, the Secretary may impose sanctions and/or restrictions upon those ports or the vessels utilizing them.

9.1   Foreign Port Assessments

The Act mandates assessment of anti-terrorism techniques, equipment, and personnel in place at foreign ports (1) served by vessels documented in the United States; (2) serving as a departure port for foreign vessels transiting to the United States; or (3) believed by the Secretary to "pose a security risk to international maritime commerce."[25] The assessment of foreign ports will be carried out in a manner similar to the assessments of U.S. ports, with particular focus on the screening of containerized and other cargo and baggage; security measures to restrict access to cargo, vessels, and dockside property to authorized personnel only; additional security onboard vessels; licensing or certification of compliance with appropriate security standards; the security management program of the foreign port; and other appropriate measures to deter terrorism against the United States. The Act gives the Secretary a broad mandate to gather and assess intelligence relating to the terrorist threat that exists in foreign countries and the possible risk that those terrorist activities may affect international maritime commerce.[26]

9.2   Notification of Foreign Officials and Sanctions

Should foreign port assessments reveal defects in a foreign port's antiterrorism measures, the Secretary must notify the appropriate governmental authorities in the foreign country.[27] Notification to the foreign country would include the type and severity of the defects and would recommend remedial measures to improve antiterrorism protection. The Act also requires the Secretary, in cooperation with the Secretary of State, to offer a "port security training program" to those ports in foreign countries that lack effective antiterrorism measures.

If a foreign port does not remedy the defects in their port security measures within 90 days after notification by the Secretary, the Act permits the Secretary to impose restrictions upon vessels utilizing these foreign ports that seek access to the United States. If the Secretary believes that "a condition in the foreign port exists that threatens the safety or security of passengers, vessels, or crew traveling to or from the port," the Secretary may impose *immediate* restrictions on such vessel movements without having to wait 90 days. Failure by vessels utilizing these foreign ports to adhere to the restrictions may result in the denial of entry into the United States. These restrictions may apply to any vessel arriving *into* the United States from that foreign port, or any vessel *carrying* cargo or passengers originating from or transshipped through that port. These restrictions may only be lifted if the Secretary determines that the ineffective antiterrorism measures have been remedied. Furthermore, the Secretary must notify the Secretary of State of a finding that a port does not maintain effective antiterrorism measures and passengers shall be given public notice of the ineffectiveness of such measures.[28]

10.0 Secure Systems of Transportation

Cargo shipped in oceangoing containers accounts for approximately 90 percent of the total worldwide cargo shipments.[29] With United States ports handling over 95 percent of U.S. overseas trade, and with total imports and exports volume moving through U.S. ports expected to double within the next 20 years, the Act specifically imposes heightened security on international intermodal transportation. Specifically, the Act requires the Secretary to establish a "program to evaluate and certify secure systems of international intermodal transportation."[30] The program will include the establishing of procedures related to (1) the pre-loading screening and evaluation of cargo; (2) in-transit security of cargo; (3) container security; and (4) any other measures the Secretary deems necessary.

11.0 Other Key Sections of Title I Relating to Port Security

As previously stated, the bulk of the port security measures in the Transportation Security Act may be found in Title I, Section 102. However, the following sections of Title I are also of importance to port security and therefore merit discussion.

11.1 International Seafarer Identification (Section 103 of the Act)

This section encourages the Secretary to negotiate an international agreement that provides for a uniform, comprehensive, international system of identification for seafarers that will enable the United States and another country to establish authoritatively the identity of any seafarer aboard a vessel within the jurisdiction of the United States or the other country. In the alternative, if the Secretary fails to complete a negotiation process to address international seafarer identification within 24 months of enactment of this Act, the Secretary shall transmit draft legislation to the Congress that would establish such a system for seafarer identification.

11.2 Extension of the Territorial Sea for Purposes of the Magnuson Act (Section 104 of the Act)

The Magnuson Act was enacted in 1917 providing for security protection authority in the territorial waters of the United States.[31] Specifically, it provides authority for the Coast Guard to take appropriate actions against subversive terrorist planning and to protect vessels, harbors, and waterfront facilities in territorial waters. An Executive Order implementing the Magnuson Act provides broad discretionary authority to establish security zones and to control access to vessels and waterfront facilities.[32] Section 104 of the MTSA extends the territorial sea of the United States, for purposes of enforcement of the Magnuson Act, to 12 nautical miles to conform to Presidential Proclamation 5928 of December 27, 1988, which extended the territorial sea of the United States for foreign affairs purposes. The Act establishes a civil penalty of up to $25,000 per violation each day for any person violating the port security statutory requirements or regulations established pursuant to the Magnuson Act.

11.3 Extension of Deepwater Port Act to Natural Gas (Section 106 of the Act)

This section provides for the permitting and licensing of natural gas deepwater ports or terminals under the Deepwater Port Act of 1974, which currently only regulates deepwater terminals for the handling and transfer of oil in waters beyond the U.S. territorial sea.

11.4 Assignment of Coast Guard Personnel as Sea Marshals (Section 107 of the Act)

This section amends the Ports and Waterways Safety Act to permit the Secretary to dispatch properly trained and qualified armed Coast Guard personnel (*i.e.*, sea marshals) on vessels and public or commercial structures on or adjacent to waters subject to U.S. jurisdiction to deter or respond to acts of terrorism or transportation security incidents. In addition, this section directs the Secretary to report to Congress on the possibility of using non-Coast Guard personnel to serve as sea marshals.

11.5 Transmittal of Information to the Customs Service (Section 108 of the Act)

This section makes technical amendments to the Tariff Act of 1930 relating to the reporting of undocumented cargo to the Customs Service. This section also amends the Trade Act of 2002, requiring the Secretary to promulgate regulations providing for the transmission to the Customs service, through an electronic data interchange system, of information pertaining to U.S. import or export cargo prior to the arrival or departure of such cargo.

11.6 Maritime Security Professional Training (Section 109 of the Act)

This section requires the Secretary to develop standards and curriculum to allow for the training and certification of maritime security professionals not later than six months after enactment of this Act. The Act specifies minimum standards that include elements related to (1) training and certification standards in accordance with accepted practices; (2) training in all aspects of prevention, detention, investigation and reporting of criminal activities in the international maritime environment; and (3) the provision of off-site training and certification courses for certified personnel to develop and enhance security awareness and practices. The Secretary may make this training available not only to federal, state, and local law enforcement and maritime security personnel but also to private law enforcement and maritime security personnel in the United States and to personnel employed in foreign ports used by vessels with U.S citizen crewmembers or passengers. This section authorizes $5.5 million to be appropriated for each of the fiscal years 2003 through 2008.

11.7   Additional Reports (Section 110 of the Act)

The Act establishes three separate types of reporting requirements regarding the effectiveness of security measures. First, the Act amends the International Maritime and Port Security Act to require the Secretary to report and analyze activities affecting port security against acts of terrorism. Second, the Coast Guard must, in 2005, report on the feasibility of creating a "Center for Coastal and Maritime Security" for purposes of training personnel in the prevention and mitigation of terrorist threats. Finally, the Act requires the Secretary to transmit to Congress a report on the effectiveness of the secure system of transportation program (as required by section 70116, discussed *infra*) within one year of implementation. The report should contain an evaluation of the program and any suggested improvements.

11.8   Performance Standards (Section 111 of the Act)

This section requires that, not later than January 1, 2004, the Secretary is to (1) develop and maintain an antiterrorism cargo identification, tracking, and screening system for containerized cargo shipped to and from the United States either directly or via a foreign port and (2) develop performance standards to enhance the physical security of shipping containers, including standards for seals and locks.

11.9   Report on Foreign-Flag Vessels (Section 112 of the Act)

This section requires the Secretary to report to Congress, within six months after the Act's date of enactment and annually thereafter, the following information related to foreign-flag vessels:

1. A list of all nations whose flag vessels have entered U.S. ports in the previous year
2. Of those nations, a separate list of nations:
   i.   Whose flag vessels appear as Priority III or higher on the Coast Guard's Boarding Priority Matrix

ii. That have presented, or whose flag vessels have presented, false, intentionally incomplete, or fraudulent information to the United States on passenger or cargo manifests, crew identity or qualifications, or registration or classification of their flag vessels

iii. Whose vessel registration or classification procedures have been found by the Secretary to be noncompliant with international classifications or do not exercise adequate control over safety and security concerns

iv. Whose laws or regulations are not sufficient to allow tracking of ownership and registration histories of registered flag vessels

3. U.S. actions to improve transparency and security of vessel registration procedures in the questionable nations listed in section 11.8(b) above

11.10 Revision of Port Security Planning Guide (Section 113 of the Act)

The Secretary shall, after consulting with the National Committee and the Coast Guard, publish a revised, electronic copy of "Port Security: A National Planning Guide" within three years after the date of the enactment of the Act.

12.0 Implications of Actions Taken at the International Level

The Act recognizes that the International Maritime Organization (IMO) was working on new maritime security protocols relating to global maritime security at the time of enactment and encourages U.S. authorities to implement new international systems to complement the new protocols.[33] Many of the port security requirements imposed by the MTSA were coordinated with international efforts at the IMO to facilitate harmonization of domestic and international regimes.

An IMO Conference of Contracting Governments to the International Convention for the Safety of Life at Sea, 1974, (SOLAS) was held in London on December 9–13, 2002. A new, comprehensive security regime for international shipping was adopted and is set to enter into force in July 2004. The Conference was attended by 108 Contracting Governments to the 1974 SOLAS Convention and other observers, United Nations specialized agencies, intergovernmental organizations and non-governmental international organizations. The Conference adopted a number of SOLAS amendments, the most far-reaching of which enshrines the new International Ship and Port Facility Security Code (ISPS Code).

The ISPS Code contains detailed security-related requirements for Governments, port authorities and shipping companies in a mandatory section (Part A), together with a series of guidelines about how to meet these requirements in a second, non-mandatory section (Part B). The Conference also adopted a series of resolutions designed to add weight to the amendments, encourage the application of the measures to ships and port facilities not covered by the ISPS Code and pave the way for future work on the subject. The deadline for implementation of the ISPS Code is July 1, 2004.

13.0 Implementation of the MTSA

On July 1, 2003, the Coast Guard issued a series of six interim rules promulgating new security requirements mandated by the Act. These interim rules went into effect immediately. Comments were due on July 31, 2003. These rules cover the following topics: Implementation of National Maritime Security Initiatives, Area Maritime Security, Vessel Security, Facility Security, Outer Continental Shelf Facility Security, and Automatic Identification System carriage requirements. The Coast Guard intends on publishing a final rule before November 25, 2003, to replace the interim rule.

Facilities and vessels covered by these regulations must submit a vessel or facility plan by December 29, 2003. By July 1, 2004, facilities and vessels required to have a security plan must have available at the facility or onboard the vessel one of the following: (1) an approved security plan (plus a letter of approval), (2) a copy of the security plan submitted for approval (plus an acknowledgement letter from the Coast Guard stating that the security plan is under review for approval), or (3) a copy of an Alternative Security Plan (plus written confirmation by the owner/operator that the facility/vessel is in full compliance).

Facility and vessel owners and operators not in compliance with the new security plan rules must obtain a waiver from the Coast Guard to continue operating. Owners and operators may obtain a waiver of any requirement of this rule only if the waiver will not reduce overall security. Likewise an owner or operator may propose for consideration by the Coast Guard an equivalent security measure in lieu of a particular requirement of the rule.

In addition, the Coast Guard may approve an industry or third-party-developed Alternative Security Program in lieu of the security plan requirements if it provides an equivalent level of security. For a complete summary of these regulations please visit our website at <www.blankrome.com/publications/maritime/update0703_8.asp <http://www.blankrome.com/publications/maritime/update0703_8.asp>.

Endnotes:

[1] Title I is entitled Maritime Transportation Security and includes sections 101-111. The non-security maritime related provisions of the MTSA are found under Title II, Maritime Policy Improvement; Title III, Coast Guard Personnel and Maritime Safety; and Title IV, Omnibus Maritime Improvements.

[2] 46 U.S.C. § 70102.

[3] Note that the initial risk assessment evaluates "vessel types" while the detailed vulnerability assessments focus on "vessels." Subsequent detailed assessments will then be required for *individual vessels* that fit within each category of vessel type.

[4] For security reasons, the Act does not require the Secretary to disclose information gained from port vulnerability assessments.

[5] 46 U.S.C. § 70103.

[6] The Act *specifically* requires the coordination of the Coast Guard maritime security teams and Federal Maritime Security Coordinators created pursuant to the Act.

[7] The Secretary shall consider the use of public/private partnerships to enforce security within the security zone, shoreside protection alternatives (and the environmental, public safety, and relative effectiveness of such alternatives), and technological means of enhancing the security zones of ports, territorial waters, and waterways of the United States.

[8] This determination will be made in accordance with the Secretary's assessments, discussed *supra*. The Act excludes Department of Defense vessels and facilities from the plan requirements.

[9] As of the date of publishing, these regulations had not been issued. The Coast Guard has indicated it plans to publish regulations by mid-2003.

[10] To facilitate coordinated efforts, the Act requires individual vessel or facility security plans to be consistent with the National and Area Plans.

[11] The "qualified individual" mentioned in the Act is responsible for "communications" with the persons providing personnel and equipment of the type listed.

[12] Security-related information developed pursuant to Chapter 701 is not required to be disclosed to the public notwithstanding any other provision of law.

[13] 46 U.S.C. § 70104.

[14] 46 U.S.C. § 70112.

[15] The Transportation Security Administration, the Coast Guard, and the Maritime Administration are developing a Transportation Worker Identification Card (TWIC) program that will most likely fulfill the transportation security card requirement of the MTSA. The TWIC program will create a standardized biometric identification card for workers across the transportation industry. The TWIC program is currently in the technology evaluation phase at two regional pilot facilities.

[16] *See* Immigration and Nationality Act, 8 U.S.C. § 1101 *et seq.*

[17] 46 U.S.C. § 70111.

[18] 67 Fed. Reg. 76711.

[19] 46 U.S.C. § 70114.

[20] 46 U.S.C. § 70113.

[21] 46 U.S.C. § 70106.

[22] 46 U.S.C. § 70107.

[23] The Honorable Norman Y. Mineta, Secretary of Transportation, Port Security Announcement at Battery Park, New York (June 17, 2002). This round of grant money was authorized prior to the enactment of the MTSA. FYO2 Department of Transportation Appropriations, P.L. 107-87 (18 December 2001).

[24] The Honorable Norman Y. Mineta, Secretary of Transportation, Press Book Announcement B03-003 (14 January 2003).

[25] 46 U.S.C. § 70108.

[26] The Secretary may consult with the Secretary of Defense, the Secretary of State, appropriate authorities of foreign governments, and vessel operators to gauge the level of terrorist threats in foreign ports that could pose a risk to international maritime commerce.

[27] 46 U.S.C. § 70109.

[28] 46 U.S.C. § 71110.

[29] U.S. Customs Container Security Initiative to Safeguard U.S., Global Economy Factsheet, U.S. Customs Service (February 2002). Available at: http://www.customs.ustreas.gov/xp/cgov/newsroom/press_releases/22002/02222002.xml

[30] 46 U.S.C. § 70116.

[31] 50 U.S.C. § 191.

[32] Executive Order 10173 (18 October 1950).

[33] *See* Maritime Transportation Security Act of 2002, Title I, Section 101(15).

[34] 67 Fed. Reg. 79742 (30 December 2002).

[35] 67 Fed. Reg. at 79744.

Chapter 5

Chemical Security

Lara B. Mathews
Charles E. Wagner, Jr.
Blank Rome LLP

1.0   Introduction

The terrorist attacks of September 11, 2001, gave rise to immediate increased attention and a sense of urgency with respect to vulnerabilities and critical infrastructure that can be used as weapons. Chief among these are facilities that produce, store, and transport chemicals and hazardous materials and substances. In general, legislative and administrative responses to threats identified in other critical infrastructure areas have included (1) increased inspection and enforcement, (2) new notification and reporting requirements, (3) new vulnerability assessment and planning requirements, and (4) the imposition new civil and criminal penalties. Chemical security is one area in which a comprehensive legislative or regulatory response has not been adopted, although legislative proposals are pending at press time.

In the wake of the September 11th attacks, a number of developments have further increased the scrutiny on chemical facilities, as well as the pressure for a broad response. A report of the General Accounting Office in March 2003 concluded that industry voluntary security efforts were inadequate and recommended that the Department of Homeland Security (DHS) and the Environmental Protection Agency (EPA) jointly develop a comprehensive national security strategy, including vulnerability assessments and required corrective action at "high-risk" facilities. In addition, a review of chemical facilities conducted by the EPA identified 123 facilities in which a chemical release could endanger more than one million people. In public comments in March 2003, Attorney General Ashcroft drew a clear link between environmental compliance and homeland security with a particular focus on pipelines, fuel tanks, chemical plants, and drinking water facilities.

At press time no federal law explicitly requires that chemical facilities take security actions or conduct assessments related to protection against a terrorist attack. Environmental statutes that pre-date the September 11th attacks do impose some physical security, planning, and reporting requirements addressing primarily the risk of accidental releases of chemicals at such facilities. In addition, comprehensive legislative proposals, including one developed by the Bush Administration, are pending in the 108th Congress at press time. These proposals focus on requiring covered chemical facilities to conduct vulnerability assessments and develop security and/or response plans.

2.0 Overview

This chapter contains a brief outline of existing statutory authorities related to safety and security at chemical plants, particularly with respect to accidental releases. These authorities include the Clean Air Act (CAA), the Emergency Planning and Community Right-to-Know Act (EPCRA), and the Resource Conservation and Recovery Act (RCRA). It then provides a more detailed summary of two comprehensive legislative proposals pending in the 108th Congress at press time. S. 994, the Chemical Facilities Security Act of 2003, represents the Bush Administration's chemical security proposal and was introduced by Senate Environment and Public Works Committee Chairman James Inhofe (R-Okla.) and Senator Zell Miller (D-Ga.). The Act gives the Department of Homeland Security (DHS) jurisdiction over chemical security issues and requires certain facilities identified by the DHS to conduct vulnerability assessments and prepare site security plans. S. 157, introduced by Senator John Corzine (D-N.J.), is identical to the version of S. 1602 that was reported out of the Senate Environment and Public Works Committee amid some controversy in July 2002 during the 107th Congress. S. 157 would apply to a broader range of facilities and would require those facilities to conduct vulnerability assessments and to prepare prevention, preparedness, and response plans.

3.0 Pre-9/11/01 Authorities

3.1 Clean Air Act (42 U.S.C. §§ 7401 et seq.)

The primary statutory authority requiring some degree of security measures at chemical facilities is the federal Clean Air Act section 112(r), which provides that the owner or operator of a stationary source that has more than a threshold quantity of a regulated substance must prepare a risk management plan to address potential accidental releases. The Risk Management Program (RMP) regulations, 40 C.F.R. Part 68, implementing that section require facilities to assess chemical *accidental* release risk and develop prevention programs and emergency response plans to address that risk. The RMP regulations apply to facilities with more than a threshold quantity of any of 140 listed chemicals in a process, including ammonia, hydrogen sulfide, nitrogen oxide, sulfur dioxide, and toluene. The accidental release program provides for periodic compliance audits of submitted risk management plans.[1]

These provisions have some additional "teeth," including a General Duty clause in section 112(r) that directs owners and operators to design and maintain safe facilities, identify hazards that might result from releases, and minimize the consequences of releases should they occur. In addition, the Clean Air Act imposes criminal penalties for the knowing violation of section 112(r), including the General Duty clause, and of any regulations promulgated thereunder, including all of the 40 C.F.R. Part 68 RMP requirements.

3.2   Chemical Safety Information, Site Security, and Fuels Regulatory Relief Act (Public Law 106-40)

The Chemical Safety Information, Site Security, and Fuels Regulatory Relief Act was enacted in August 1999. It was intended, in part, to respond to concerns regarding the public availability of Clean Air Act section 112(r) "worst case scenario" data and its potential use as a "road map" for a terrorist attack. This law required the Department of Justice to review the vulnerability of chemical facilities and issue a final report to Congress by August 2002. At press time, a final report has not been issued. The Department of Justice has asserted that Congressional appropriations have been inadequate to carry out the statutory mandate.

3.3   Occupational Safety and Health Act (OSH Act) (29 U.S.C. §§ 651 et seq.) and Emergency Planning and Community Right-to-Know Act (EPCRA) (42 U.S.C. §§ 11001 et seq.)

The OSH Act, which includes a General Duty clause, and EPCRA both impose safety and response requirements that may incidentally reduce the likelihood and mitigate the consequences of an attack on a chemical facility. OSHA regulations impose process safety management (PSM) requirements for preventing or minimizing the consequences of catastrophic releases of toxic, reactive, flammable, or explosive chemicals.[2] These requirements include controls, training programs, and management systems to ensure the safe operation of covered processes. Local Emergency Planning Committees (LEPC), established under EPCRA, are required to prepare emergency plans to address releases of hazardous materials. LEPCs generally work with representatives of chemical facilities to incorporate counter-terrorism measures in their plans.

4.4 Resource Conservation and Recovery Act (RCRA) (42 U.S.C. §§ 6901 *et seq.*)

RCRA, which addresses the treatment, storage, and disposal of solid and hazardous waste, imposes some limited physical security requirements that apply to many chemical facilities. These provisions require that generators of hazardous waste operate in a manner to minimize "unplanned sudden releases" of hazardous wastes and undertake security measures, such as surveillance, fencing and signage.[3]

4.0 The Chemical Facilities Security Act of 2003 (S. 994)

The Chemical Facilities Security Act of 2003, which is the Bush Administration's proposal, was introduced by the Senate Environment and Public Works Committee Chairman James Inhofe (R-Okla.) and Senator Zell Miller (D-Ga.) on May 5, 2003. It was referred to that Committee. There has been no Committee action on the bill.

4.1 Key Definitions

As with many environmental statutes, definitions are a critical element in determining the jurisdictional boundaries and substantive applicability of the statute. The key definitions of the Chemical Facilities Security Act of 2003 include the following.

- The term "chemical source" means a non-Federal stationary source[4] for which (A) the owner or operator is required to complete a risk management plan in accordance with the chemical accident prevention provisions of the Clean Air Act,[5] and (B) the Secretary of Homeland Security is required to promulgate implementing regulations under section 4(a)[6] of the Act.
- The term "owner or operator" means any person who owns, leases, operates, controls, or supervises a stationary source.[7]
- The term "security measure" means an action carried out to ensure or enhance the security of a chemical source. The term "security measure" with respect to a chemical source includes measures such as
  - (i) an employee training and background check
  - (ii) the limitation and prevention of access to controls of the chemical source
  - (iii) the protection of the perimeter of the chemical source
  - (iv) the installation and operation of intrusion detection sensors
  - (v) the implementation of measures to increase computer or computer network security

    (vi) the implementation of other security-related measures to protect against or reduce the threat of

        (I) a terrorist attack on the chemical source

        (II) the theft of a substance of concern for offsite release in furtherance of an act of terrorism

    (vii) conduct of any similar security-related activity, as determined by the Secretary

- The term "substance of concern" means (A) a chemical substance present at a chemical source in quantities equal to or exceeding the threshold quantities for the chemical substance, as defined in or established under the chemical accident prevention provisions of the Clean Air Act[8] and (B) such other chemical substance as the Secretary may designate.
- The term "terrorism" means any activity that (A) involves an act that is dangerous to human life or potentially destructive of critical infrastructure or key resources and is a violation of the criminal laws of the United States or of any State or other subdivision of the United States; and (B) appears to be intended to intimidate or coerce a civilian population; to influence the policy of a government by intimidation or coercion; or to affect the conduct of a government by mass destruction, assassination, or kidnapping.[9]
- The term "terrorist release" means (A) a release[10] from a chemical source into the environment[11] of a substance of concern that is caused by an act of terrorism, and (B) the theft of a substance of concern by a person for off-site release in furtherance of an act of terrorism.

4.2   Vulnerability Assessments and Site Security Plans

The heart of S. 994 is the requirement for owners or operators of chemical sources to conduct a vulnerability assessment and prepare and implement a site security plan.[12] The DHS Secretary is directed to promulgate the regulations requiring vulnerability assessments and site security plans not later than one year after the date of enactment. Vulnerability assessments must determine the exposure of the chemical source to terrorist acts and must identify the hazards that might result from a terrorist release. Thus, the assessments address both the prevention of terrorist-caused releases and the mitigation of such releases should they occur.

    Following the vulnerability assessment, owners or operators are required to prepare and to implement site security plans. At a minimum, the site security plan must include security measures designed to reduce the vulnerability of the chemical source to terrorist attacks and must describe equipment, plans, and procedures that would be implemented in the event of a terrorist release.[13] Security measures include enhancements to physical security, such as perimeter fences, guards, video surveillance, intrusion detection sensors, and access controls. Security measures also include conducting background checks for employees and contractors, training employees to recognize and be alert to suspicious activities, and strengthening computer security.

S. 994 also requires the DHS to provide, to the maximum extent practicable, an owner or operator with threat information that is relevant to the particular chemical source.[14] The intent is that chemical sources can then increase physical security in response to such alerts. The alerts also are intended to allow local law enforcement agencies to increase surveillance of potential targets. One criticism of this approach is that unfortunately, experience thus far suggests that the DHS has not possessed specific information about potential targets during instances of heightened threat levels.

Under S. 994, only chemical sources listed by the DHS require vulnerability assessments and site security plans. The DHS is directed to develop the list not later than 180 days after the date of enactment. The list is to be drawn from the 15,000 facilities that were required to develop risk management plans under the accidental release prevention program in section 112(r) of the Clean Air Act. S. 994 requires the DHS to consider a number of criteria in preparing the list of chemical sources subject to the vulnerability assessment and site security plan requirements. These criteria are

- The likelihood that a chemical source will be the target of terrorism
- The nature and quantity of the substances of concern present at a chemical source
- The potential extent of death, injury, or serious adverse effects to human health or the environment that would result from a terrorist release
- The potential harm to critical infrastructure and national security from a terrorist release
- Cost and technical feasibility
- Scale of operations
- Such other security-related factors as the Secretary determines to be appropriate and necessary to protect the public health and welfare, critical infrastructure, and national security[15]

Not later than three years after issuance of the vulnerability assessment and site security plan regulations, the DHS must update the list to add new facilities that meet the listing criteria and delete facilities that no longer present a sufficient risk to be listed. S. 994 grants the DHS the authority to issue regulations establishing procedures, protocols, and standards for conducting vulnerability assessments and preparing site security plans. Furthermore, the Secretary may establish a "safe harbor" provision identifying security measures that, if implemented, would establish the sufficiency of a vulnerability assessment or site security plan.[16]

The Secretary may also recognize procedures, protocols, or standards that are established by industry; federal, state, or local authorities; or other applicable laws.[17] Security codes adopted by industry trade groups, such as the American Chemistry Council, the Fertilizer Institute, the American Petroleum Institute, the Chlorine Institute, and the Synthetic Organic Chemical Manufacturers Association, may be eligible for recognition and endorsement by the DHS Secretary.

Organizations must petition the Secretary to endorse an existing protocol. The Secretary must then make a determination that (1) the protocol is substantially equivalent to the vulnerability assessment and site security plan requirements under S. 994 and (2) the protocol was in effect on or after the date of enactment. The Secretary must issue a written response to the petition either endorsing the protocol or providing a clear explanation why the endorsement was denied. Even if an industry protocol is recognized and endorsed, the Secretary may require that a chemical source address a particular threat or type of threat in its vulnerability assessment and site security plan.

Any vulnerability assessment or site security plan prepared by a chemical source before, on, or after the date of endorsement of a protocol[18] shall satisfy the requirement for an owner or operator to conduct an assessment and prepare a plan under section 4(a) of S. 994.[19]

The Secretary may, by regulation, designate or exempt certain chemical substances in particular threshold quantities as substances of concern. The Secretary may also adjust the threshold quantities of a chemical substance. In designating or exempting a chemical substance or adjusting its threshold quantity, the Secretary must consider the potential extent of death, injury, or serious adverse effect to human health and the environment that would result from a terrorist release.[20]

Owners and operators must submit a written certification to the DHS that they have completed a vulnerability assessment and have developed and implemented a site security plan by a specific deadline to be established by the Secretary. Upon request, the owner or operator shall provide copies of the vulnerability assessment and site security plan to the Secretary.[21] Not later than five years after the date of this initial certification, the owner or operator shall review the adequacy of the vulnerability assessment and site security plan and certify completion of the review to the Secretary. Thereafter, this review must be completed not less often than every five years or on a schedule established by the Secretary. Upon request by the Secretary, the owner or operator must submit a description of any changes to a vulnerability assessment or site security plan.[22]

4.3   Protection of Information

Because vulnerability assessments and site security plans may be used to provide a "road map" to a terrorist seeking to attack a chemical source, S. 994 includes provisions to protect against disclosure of this security sensitive information. With the exception of the initial and five-year certifications, any information obtained under S. 994 or derived from that information shall be exempt from disclosure under the Freedom of Information Act and any equivalent state or local laws. Furthermore, the Secretary is directed to establish confidentiality protocols for the use of any information obtained from owners or operators of chemical sources. These protocols must require that copies of vulnerability assessments and site security plans be kept in secure locations and that access is limited to persons designated by the Secretary.[23] Those designated persons may disclose information to state and local law enforcement officials and first responders to the extent disclosure is necessary to carry out the provisions of S. 994.

Any designated individual who acquires chemical security information and who knowingly or recklessly discloses that information will be deemed to have committed a class A misdemeanor and shall be imprisoned for not more than one year, fined, or both and shall be removed from federal employment.[24]

4.4   Recordkeeping and Entry

S. 994 requires the owner or operator of a chemical source to maintain current copies of the vulnerability assessment and site security plan. The Secretary (or a designee) shall have right of entry to the chemical source and any premises where the copies of the vulnerability assessment and site security plan are kept and may access and copy those records and any other documentation necessary for review of the assessments and plans.[25]

4.5   Enforcement and Penalties

S. 994 requires the Secretary to issue compliance orders as the first step of an enforcement action. If an owner or operator fails to submit a vulnerability assessment or site security plan, the Secretary may issue an order requiring submission and certification in accordance with section 4(b). In addition, the Secretary may disapprove an inadequate vulnerability assessment or site security plan that does not address the results of the vulnerability assessment or a threat of a terrorist release. The Secretary shall (1) provide a written notification that clearly explains the deficiencies, (2) consult with the owner or operator to identify steps to achieve compliance, and (3) if, following consultation, compliance is not achieved, issue an order requiring the correction of the deficiencies.[26]

If the Secretary determines that an owner or operator of a chemical source is not maintaining or permitting access to records, the Secretary may issue a compliance order.[27]

With the exception of the misdemeanor penalty for federal employees who knowingly or recklessly disclose sensitive security information, S. 994 provides for civil and administrative penalties only. Any owner or operator who violates a compliance order or fails to comply with its site security plan may, in a civil action brought in United States District Court, be subject to injunctive relief and a civil penalty of not more than $50,000 for each day on which a violation occurs.[28]

Furthermore, the Secretary may issue an administrative penalty order of not more than $250,000 for failure to comply with any order issued by the Secretary. Before issuing such an order, the Secretary must issue a written notice of the proposed order and provide the opportunity for the owner or operator to request a hearing.[29]

5.0   The Chemical Security Act of 2003 (S. 157)

The Chemical Facilities Security Act of 2003, S. 157, was introduced by Senator John Corzine (D-NJ) on January 14, 2003, and was referred to the Senate Environment and Public Works Committee. It is identical to legislation introduced by Senator Corzine (S. 1602), as reported out of the Committee in the 107th Congress. There has been no Committee action on the bill this Congress.

5.1   Key Definitions

The key definitions of the Chemical Security Act of 2003 include

- The term "chemical source" means a stationary source as defined in the chemical accident prevention provisions of the Clean Air Act[30] that contains a substance of concern.
- The term "covered substance of concern" means a substance of concern that, in combination with a chemical source and other factors, is designated as a high priority category by the EPA Administrator under section 4(a)(1).
- The term "safer design and maintenance" includes, with respect to a chemical source that is within a high priority category designated under section 4(a)(1), implementation, to the extent practicable, of the practices of

(A) Preventing or reducing the vulnerability of the chemical source to a release of a covered substance of concern through use of inherently safer technology

(B) Reducing any vulnerability of the chemical source to a release of a covered substance of concern through use of well-maintained secondary containment, control, or mitigation equipment

(C) Reducing any vulnerability of the chemical source to a release of a covered substance of concern by implementing security measures

(D) Reducing the potential consequences of any vulnerability of the chemical source to a release of a covered substance of concern through the use of buffer zones between the chemical source and surrounding populations (including buffer zones between the chemical source and residences, schools, hospitals, senior centers, shopping centers and malls, sports and entertainment arenas, public roads and transportation routes, and other population centers)

- The term "security measure" means an action carried out to increase the security of a chemical source and includes
  (A) Employee training and background checks
  (B) The limitation and prevention of access to controls of the chemical source
  (C) Protection of the perimeter of the chemical source
  (D) The installation and operation of an intrusion detection sensor
  (E) A measure to increase computer or computer network security

- The term "substance of concern" means any regulated substance under the chemical accident prevention provisions of the Clean Air Act and any substance designated by the EPA Administrator under section 4(a). The term does not include liquefied petroleum gas that is used as fuel or held for sale as fuel at a retail facility.

- The term "unauthorized release" means (A) a release from a chemical source into the environment of a covered substance of concern that is caused, in whole or in part, by a criminal act; (B) a release into the environment of a covered substance of concern that has been removed from a chemical source, in whole or in part, by a criminal act; and (C) a release or removal from a chemical source of a covered substance of concern that is unauthorized by the owner or operator of the chemical source.

- The term "use of inherently safer technology" with respect to a chemical source means use of a technology, product, raw material, or practice that, as compared with the technologies, products, raw materials, or practices currently in use

(A) Reduces or eliminates the possibility of a release of a substance of concern from the chemical source prior to secondary containment, control, or mitigation

(B) Reduces or eliminates the threats to public health and the environment associated with a release or potential release of a substance of concern from the chemical source.

The term "use of inherently safer technology" includes input substitution, catalyst or carrier substitution, process redesign (including reuse or recycling of a substance of concern), product reformulation, procedure simplification, and technology modification so as to

(A) Use less hazardous substances or benign substances

(B) Use a smaller quantity of covered substances of concern

(C) Reduce hazardous pressures or temperatures

(D) Reduce the possibility and potential consequences of equipment failure and human error

(E) Improve inventory control and chemical use efficiency

(F) Reduce or eliminate storage, transportation, handling, disposal, and discharge of substances of concern

5.2 Vulnerability Assessments; Hazard Assessments; and Prevention, Preparedness, and Response Plans

The core of S. 157 requires owners and operators of "high priority categories" of chemical sources to conduct a vulnerability assessment and a hazard assessment and prepare a prevention, preparedness, and response plan. The EPA Administrator is required to promulgate regulations establishing high priority categories and the requirements for assessments and plans not later than one year after the date of enactment.

The Administrator, in consultation with the DHS Secretary and state and local agencies, must promulgate regulations designating certain combinations of chemical sources and substances of concern as high priority categories. The designation is to be based on the severity of the threat posed by unauthorized releases from the chemical sources. The Administrator also shall consider

(A) The severity of the harm that could be caused by an unauthorized release

(B) The proximity to population centers

(C) The threats to national security

(D) The threats to critical infrastructure

(E) Threshold quantities of substances of concern that pose a serious threat

(F) Such other safety or security factors as the Administrator, in consultation with the Secretary, determines to be appropriate.[31]

The EPA Administrator, in consultation with the DHS Secretary, state and local agencies, and the United States Chemical Safety and Hazard Investigation Board, must promulgate regulations requiring the owner and operator of each chemical source that is in a high priority category to (1) conduct a vulnerability assessment to a terrorist attack or other unauthorized release; (2) conduct a hazard assessment identifying the hazardous of an unauthorized release; and (3) prepare a prevention, preparedness, and response plan.[32] The owners and operators must conduct the assessments and prepare the plans in consultation with local law enforcement, first responders,[33] and employees.[34]

The prevention, preparedness, and response plan must include measures to eliminate or reduce the potential consequences of an unauthorized release. These measures must include the use of safer design and maintenance. Safer design and maintenance includes (1) reducing vulnerability through the use of inherently safer technology; (2) reducing vulnerability through the use of secondary containment, and control or mitigation equipment; (3) reducing vulnerability by implementing security measures; and (4) reducing the potential consequences of any release through the use of buffer zones between the chemical source and surrounding communities. Inherently safer technologies use raw materials and processes that reduce the possibility of releases without using secondary containment and reduce the threat to public health of releases.[35]

The DHS Secretary shall, to the maximum extent permitted by the interest of national security, provide owners and operators with threat information for use in conducting assessments and preparing plans.

Not later than five years after the promulgation of the regulations for high priority categories and vulnerability and hazard assessment and prevention, preparedness, and response plans, the EPA administrator, in consultation with the DHS, shall review the regulations and revise them as needed. Additionally, the EPA may at any time designate additional substances of concern.[36]

Not later than one year after the EPA promulgates the regulations for vulnerability and hazard assessments and prevention, preparedness, and response plans, owners and operators of high priority category chemical sources shall certify to the EPA that they have conducted assessments and shall submit copies of the assessments to the agency. Not later than 18 months after promulgation of the regulations, owners and operators shall certify that they have completed prevention, preparedness, and response plans and submit copies of the plan to the EPA. Not later than five years after the initial submission and not less than every three years thereafter, owners and operators, in coordination with local law enforcement and first responders, must review the adequacy of their assessments and plans, certify that the review has been completed, and submit any changes to the EPA.[37]

5.3   Protection of Information

S. 157 protects against the disclosure of vulnerability and hazard assessments and prevention, preparedness, and response plans that could serve as a "how to" guide to attacking a chemical source. With the exception of certifications, all information provided to the EPA and all information derived from that information is exempt from disclosure under the Freedom of Information Act. As soon as practicable, but not later than one year after enactment, the EPA Administrator, in consultation with the DHS Secretary, must develop protocols to protect against the unauthorized disclosure of sensitive information submitted by owners and operators of chemical sources.

The protocols shall ensure that (1) copies of assessments and plans are maintained in a secure location, (2) only designated individuals have access to assessments and plans, and (3) no copies or information contained in or derived from assessments and plans shall be available to any person other than those designated by the EPA Administrator. However, the designated individuals may discuss the contents of assessments and plans with state and local officials.[38]

5.4   Recordkeeping and Entry

Owners and operators of chemical sources are required to maintain current copies of vulnerability and hazard assessments and prevention, preparedness, and response plans. The EPA Administrator shall have the right of entry to any chemical source or any premises where records of assessments and plans are maintained and may access and copy those records and other information necessary to enforce the Act or regulations under the provisions of S. 157.[39]

5.5   Enforcement and Penalties

The EPA Administrator, in consultation with the DHS Secretary, must review the vulnerability and hazard assessments and the prevention, preparedness, and response plan submitted by a chemical source to determine compliance with the Act. The EPA must review all of the assessments and plans submitted by all high priority chemical sources within three years of submittal and must establish a schedule for that review, taking into consideration the same factors in section 4(a)(2) considered when establishing the high priority categories of chemical sources.[40]

If the EPA determines that a chemical source is in compliance with the Act, the Administrator will issue a written certification. The Administrator's certification shall include a checklist confirming that the source considered use of each of the four elements of safer design and maintenance: (1) inherently safer technology, (2) secondary containment, (3) security measures, and (4) buffer zones.[41]

S. 157 authorizes the EPA to certify compliance based upon assessments and plans prepared before the promulgation of implementing regulations under S. 157. Assessments and plans submitted before the notice of proposed rulemaking requiring their submission shall be reviewed by the Administrator, in consultation with the DHS Secretary. Prior to promulgation of the final regulations, the EPA must determine whether the early submittals meet the assessment, planning, and consultation requirements of section 4(a)(3). If the EPA, in consultation with the DHS, determines that the early submitted assessments and plans meet the requirements of section 4(a)(3), then the Administrator shall certify compliance. The owners and operators of the chemical source will not be required to revise any assessment or plan for their initial certification.[42]

Upon review, the EPA may also find that assessments or plans (1) do not comply with regulations, (2) do not address existing threats, or (3) are not sufficiently implemented. The Administrator must notify the chemical source of its determination. The EPA, in coordination with the DHS and the Chemical Safety and Hazard Investigation Board, shall provide advice and technical assistance to address the deficiencies in the assessments and plans.[43]

If, after 30 days, the chemical source has not brought the assessments and plans into compliance, then the Administrator may issue a compliance order. The order may issue only after notice and opportunity for a hearing.[44] A compliance order also may issue if a chemical source has not complied with an entry or information request.

S. 157 also includes provisions to abate threats of terrorist attacks that are beyond the scope of any approved vulnerability assessments or prevention, preparedness, and response plans. The DHS Secretary shall notify the chemical source of these threats. If the chemical source does not take appropriate action to respond to the threat, the Secretary shall notify the EPA Administrator and the Attorney General. The Administrator or the Attorney General may obtain the necessary relief to abate the threat in United States District Court.[45]

An owner or operator of a chemical source that violates a compliance order may be subject to a civil penalty of not more than $25,000 for each day in which such violation occurs. Knowing violations of compliance orders are subject to criminal penalties. For a first violation, the owner or operator is subject to a fine of not less than $2,500 or more than $25,000 per day of violation, imprisoned for less than one year, or both. Subsequent violations are punishable by up to $50,000 per day of violation, imprisonment up to two years, or both.

The EPA Administrator may issue administrative penalty orders assessing fines up to $125,000. The Administrator must issue a notice of the proposed order and provide the opportunity for a hearing. The owner or operator must request a hearing not later than 30 days after receipt of the notice.

6.0 Key Differences Between S. 994 (Inhofe) and S. 157 (Corzine)

S. 994 and S. 157 differ in a number of significant respects. As a jurisdictional matter, S. 994 delegates authority for regulating chemical security to the DHS, while S. 157 grants this primary authority to the EPA. S. 157 does expressly provide that EPA shall consult with the DHS on most critical issues, as well as state and local authorities and the Chemical Safety and Hazard Investigation Board. S. 994 allows the DHS to request technical and analytical support from other federal agencies; however, it expressly prohibits "field work" by other agencies.[46]

The two bills also set forth somewhat different methodologies for identifying what chemical sources will be subject to vulnerability assessment and security planning requirements. Under S. 994, the DHS Secretary must develop a list of chemical sources from those Clean Air Act stationary sources that were required to file risk management plans with the EPA. The Secretary must consider certain factors, including the likelihood of a terrorist attack, nature and quantity of substances of concern on site, potential for harm, cost, and technical feasibility.

S. 157 would regulate so-called "high priority categories" of chemical sources by evaluating the combination of sources and substances of concern. The bill requires the EPA to consider the severity of harm, proximity to population centers, and threshold quantities of substances of concern when designating high priority categories. Chemical sources are defined more broadly as any stationary source, not merely those that had to submit risk management plans. The bill also defines substances of concern as those substances listed under the Clean Air Act accidental release program.

Senator Inhofe's bill would require owners or operators of listed chemical sources to conduct vulnerability assessments and prepare site security plans. Senator Corzine's proposal, on the other hand, would require owners and operators of high priority category chemical sources to conduct vulnerability assessments and hazard assessments and to prepare prevention, preparedness, and response plans. The requirements are similar because S. 994 vulnerability assessments must also identify the hazards that might result from a terrorist release. Moreover, the site security plans must include plans and procedures that would be implemented in case of a terrorist release. Prevention, preparedness, and response plans under S. 157, however, would require chemical sources to consider using safer design and maintenance, which includes the use of inherently safer technologies, secondary containment, security measures, and buffer zones.

Both bills would allow chemical sources to use assessments and plans prepared prior to enactment to satisfy the requirements of the proposed legislation. S. 994 allows the DHS Secretary to recognize existing chemical security protocols, such as those adopted by a number of industry associations. Any assessment or plan meeting an endorsed protocol satisfies the requirement of the bill for assessments and plans. Because S. 994 provides for endorsement of existing chemical security protocols, categories or groups of chemical sources could be "grandfathered." For example, if the Secretary were to endorse the American Chemistry Council's Responsible Care® Security Code of Management Practices, then all chemical sources that have implemented that code would have satisfied the S. 157 requirement for vulnerability assessments and site security plans.

Unlike S. 994, Senator Corzine's bill provides for case-by-case approval of vulnerability assessments; hazard assessments; and prevention, preparedness, and response plans. Under this early compliance provision, chemical sources would have to submit their assessments and plans for EPA review and approval. There is no provision for recognition of industry standards or protocols.

Perhaps the most significant difference between the bills concerns the requirements for submission of assessments and plans. S. 157 requires that owners and operators of high priority category chemical sources submit copies of vulnerability assessments; hazard assessments; and prevention, preparedness, and response plans to the EPA for review. The EPA would issue either a written certification approving the assessments and plans or a notice of non-compliance. However, S. 994 only requires submittal of vulnerability assessments and site security plans if requested by the DHS Secretary. Owners or operators would be required to submit routinely only certifications that assessments were conducted and plans prepared.

Another major difference between S. 994 and S. 157 is found in the penalty provisions. S. 994 does not include any criminal penalties for owners or operators of listed chemical sources that fail to comply with the requirements of the bill. However, owners or operators are subject to administrative penalties up to $250,000 and civil penalties of not more than $50,000 for each day of violation.

Senator Corzine's bill does include criminal penalties for owners and operators who knowingly violate compliance orders. First violations could result in fines up to $25,000 for each day of violation, imprisonment for up to one year, or both. The maximum fine and term of imprisonment are doubled for any subsequent violation.

7.0   Status and Outlook at Press Time

At press time, neither S. 994 nor S. 157 had seen Committee action. Given the Republican control of the Senate (albeit by a slim margin), the House of Representatives, and the White House, the chances of enactment of Senator Corzine's proposal are slim. Efforts to attach the earlier version of this legislation (S. 1602) to the Department of Homeland Security authorizing vehicle in the 107th Congress were defeated, as were more recent efforts to attach it to the wartime supplemental appropriations bill in April 2003.

Although, S. 994 has a greater chance of success, environmental groups have met it with vigorous opposition, while industry continues to evaluate it. Significant questions remain and will persist even if a comprehensive legislative proposal is adopted, including questions about jurisdictional issues, how vulnerability measures will be reflected in insurance rates, whether safeguards to protect sensitive information are adequate, and liability concerns with respect to what is "reasonable" post-9/11. In addition, expect to see continued attention from the DHS, EPA, and state and local governments using existing authorities on "critical infrastructure," which includes chemical plants.

Endnotes:

[1] 40 CFR § 68.220.

[2] 29 CFR § 1910.119. This regulation was promulgated pursuant to § 304 of the Clean Air Act Amendments of 1990, which is now codified at 29 U.S.C. § 655; however, it is enforceable under OSHA.

[3] See 40 CFR §§ 262.34, 264.14, 265.14, 265.31, and 265.51.

[4] The term ''stationary source'' means any buildings, structures, equipment, installations or substance emitting stationary activities (i) which belong to the same industrial group, (ii) which are located on one or more contiguous properties, (iii) which are under the control of the same person (or persons under common control), and (iv) from which an accidental release may occur. 42 U.S.C. §7412(r)(2).

[5] 42 U.S.C. § 7412(r)(7)(B)(ii).

[6] Section 4(a) requires owners to conduct vulnerability assessments and prepare site security plans.

[7] 42 U.S.C. § 7412(a).

[8] 42 U.S.C. § 7412(r)

[9] Section 2 of the Homeland Security Act of 2002; 6 U.S.C. § 101.

[10] The term "release" means any spilling, leaking, pumping, pouring, emitting, emptying, discharging, injecting, escaping, leaching, dumping, or disposing into the environment (including the abandonment or discarding of barrels, containers, and other closed receptacles containing any hazardous substance or pollutant or contaminant), but excludes (A) any release which results in exposure to persons solely within a workplace, with respect to a claim which such persons may assert against the employer of such persons; (B) emissions from the engine exhaust of a motor vehicle, rolling stock, aircraft, vessel, or pipeline pumping station engine; (C) release of source, byproduct, or special nuclear material from a nuclear incident, as those terms are defined in the Atomic Energy Act of 1954 (42 U.S.C. 2011 et seq.), if such release is subject to requirements with respect to financial protection established by the Nuclear Regulatory Commission under section 170 of such Act (42 U.S.C. 2210), or, for the purposes of section 9604 of this title or any other response action, any release of source byproduct, or special nuclear material from any processing site designated under section 7912(a)(1) or 7942(a) of this title; and (D) the normal application of fertilizer. Section 101 of the Comprehensive Environmental Response, Compensation, and Liability Act of 1980, 42 U.S.C. § 9601.

[11] The term "environment" means (A) the navigable waters, the waters of the contiguous zone, and the ocean waters of which the natural resources are under the exclusive management authority of the United States under the Magnuson-Stevens Fishery Conservation and Management Act (16 U.S.C. 1801 et seq.); and (B) any other surface water, ground water, drinking water supply, land surface or subsurface strata, or ambient air within the United States or under the jurisdiction of the United States. Section 101 of the Comprehensive Environmental Response, Compensation, and Liability Act of 1980, 42 U.S.C. § 9601.

[12] S. 994 Section 4(a)(1).

[13] S. 994 Section 4(a)(3).

[14] S. 994 Section 4(a)(4).

[15] S. 994 Section 4(e).

[16] S. 994 Section 4(c)(1).

[17] S. 994 Section 4(c)(2).

[18] Including vulnerability assessments and site security plans prepared before, on, or after the enactment date of the Act.

[19] S. 994 Section 4(d).

[20] S. 994 Section 4(g).

[21] S. 994 Section 4(b).

[22] S. 994 Section 4(h).

[23] S. 994 Section 4(i)(1) and (2).

[24] S. 994 Section 4(i)(3).

[25] S. 994 Section 7.

[26] S. 994 Section 5(a), (b), and (c).

[27] S. 994Section 7(d).

[28] S. 994 Section 8(a).

[29] S. 994 Section 8(b).

[30] 42 U.S.C. § 7412(r)(2).

[31] S. 157 Section 4(a)(1) and (2).

[32] S. 157 Section 4(a)(3)(A).

[33] This includes firefighters.

[34] The term "employee" means (A) a duly recognized collective bargaining representative at a chemical source, or (B) in the absence of such a representative, other appropriate personnel.

[35] S. 157 Section 4(a)(3)(B).

[36] S. 157 Section 4(a)(4) and (5).

[37] S. 157 Section 4(b).

[38] S. 157 Section 4(b)(4).

[39] S. 157 Section 6.

[40] S. 157 Section 5(a)(2)(D).

[41] S. 157 Section 5(a)(2)(A) and (B).

[42] S. 157 Section 5(a)(2)(C).

[43] S. 157 Section 5(b).

[44] S. 157 Section 5(c).

[45] S. 157 Section 5(d).

[46] S. 994 Section 6.

Chapter 6

Terrorism Risk Insurance

Powell Goldstein Frazer & Murphy LLP
Stacey Kalberman

1.0   Purpose of the Act

The Terrorism Risk Insurance Act of 2002, or TRIA,[1] was signed into law on November 26, 2002, by President Bush and became effective on that date. The Act resulted from concerns in the marketplace regarding the unavailability of commercial property and casualty insurance for terrorism risk and the danger this posed to financial stability in the economy.

The Act, which is a combination of public and private insurer compensation for insured losses, is limited to three years, terminating on December 31, 2005. It is anticipated by Congress that the insurance industry will have stabilized and recovered from its losses of September 11th by the end of this period and will be capable of providing fully funded private products at that time.

The most significant piece of the Act for U.S. companies and interests was the initial nullification of all terrorism insurance exclusions in commercial property and casualty policies as of the enactment date. The Act created immediate terrorism coverage for commercial property and casualty policyholders for a 90-day period during which insurers had to send notice to their policyholders of the premium for terrorist coverage. Although this period has expired, insurers are still responsible for offering terrorism coverage on each quote of a new commercial property and casualty policy.

The insurance program mandated by the Act is to be administered by the Treasury Department who also has the authority to issue regulations and procedures regarding the program.[2]

2.0 Components of the TRIA Insurance Program

The Act requires all insurers, as defined by the Act, to offer coverage for certified acts of terrorism to any policyholder purchasing commercial property and casualty insurance. The reach of the Act is very broad so that most commercial interests have the opportunity to purchase terrorism insurance if they wish. The following is an explanation of the components of the Act.

2.1 What is an Act of Terrorism Under the Act—Section 102(1)

The actual coverage offered under the Act is limited in scope as it only applies to acts of terrorism which are certified by the Secretary of the Treasury in concurrence with the Secretary of State and the Attorney General.[3] Although it is necessary for a terrorist act to be certified in order to be eligible for coverage under the Program, once an act is certified by the Treasury Secretary such certification is final and an insurer may not deny coverage under the Program.[4]

The following components must be present for an act to be certified as a terrorist act.[5] The act must

(i) Be violent
(ii) Be dangerous to human life, property, or infrastructure
(iii) Result in damage within the United States or outside the United States, in the case of an air carrier or vessel or the premises of a United States mission
(iv) Have been committed by an individual or individuals acting on behalf of any foreign interest, as part of an effort to coerce the civilian population of the United States, or to influence the policy or affect the conduct of the United States Government by coercion

Because the terrorist acts must be committed by an individual or individuals acting on behalf of a foreign person or foreign interest, domestic acts of terrorism, such as the Oklahoma City bombing, will not be provided coverage under the Act. Unless the insurer provides such coverage in addition to that mandated by the Act, most companies will not have insurance for such events.[6]

The United States is defined in the Act as including the states of the United States, territorial sea of the United States, and the continental shelf. Terrorist acts occurring outside the United States may only be certified if on an U.S. air carrier or vessel.[7]

In the final rules released by the Treasury Department on July 7, 2003, the Treasury determined "air carrier" to have the same definition as that found in 49 U.S.C. 40102, which is a United States citizen (individual, partnership, or corporation) that provides foreign or interstate air transportation. A United States flag vessel is one that is based principally in the United States, pays U.S. income tax, and complies with U.S. regulations regarding insurance. Losses due to a certified terrorism act on an air carrier or flag vessel occurring outside the United States are covered regardless of where they occur. However, insured losses does not include those incurred by third parties unless such losses are a result of the terrorist act taking place within the United States.

Additional limitations on the certification of a terrorist act by the Secretary include acts committed in the course of war as declared by Congress (except this limitation does not apply with respect to claims for workers' compensation) and an act which results in property and casualty losses that total less than five million dollars.[8] Again, unless the insurer provides separate coverage for losses which occur in the course of war or for losses which total in the aggregate less than five million dollars in damages, they will not be provided coverage under the Program.[9]

Section 102(1)(C) makes any certification of an act of terrorism by the Treasury Secretary final and not subject to judicial review. This section also makes any determination by the Secretary not to certify an act of terrorism a final determination. In either case, there is no recourse either by an insurer or policyholder as to whether an act of terrorism under the Program will be covered. The Treasury Secretary has the final word.

2.2   What is Commercial Property and Casualty

The Act defines property and casualty insurance as all commercial lines of property and casualty including excess insurance, workers' compensation insurance, and surety insurance.[10] The Act specifically excludes the following lines from coverage under the Program:

(i)   Federal crop insurance issued or reinsured under the Federal Crop Insurance Act, or any other type of crop or livestock insurance that is privately issued or reinsured (including crop insurance reported under either Line 2.1, Allied Lines, or Line 2.2, Multiple Peril (Crop) of the NAIC's Exhibit of Premiums and Losses

(ii)   Private mortgage insurance or title insurance

(iii) Financial guaranty insurance issued by monoline financial guaranty insurance corporations

(iv) Medical malpractice insurance

(v)   Health or life, including group life insurance

(vi) Flood insurance provided under the National Flood Insurance Act of 1968 or earthquake insurance reported under Line 12 of the NAIC's Exhibit of Premiums and Losses

(vii) Reinsurance

The Act does not cover personal lines of insurance. In its Final Rule issued on July 7, 2003, Treasury defined personal insurance as "coverage primarily designed to cover personal, family, or household purposes." In contrast, the final rule defines commercial property and casualty insurance as "commercial lines of property and casualty insurance, including excess insurance, workers' compensation insurance, and surety insurance" and means commercial lines within only the following lines of insurance from the NAIC's Exhibit of Premiums and Losses (commonly known as Statutory Page 14).[11]

Personal insurance policies which include both commercial and personal coverages are considered to be primarily personal policies if the commercial coverage comprises less than 25 percent of the total premium of the policy. If the policy is primarily personal, it will not be covered under the Act.

If a policy containing both personal and commercial covers is not primarily personal or contains more than 25 percent of commercial coverages, it will be considered to be commercial. The insurer will then need to allocate the portion of risk between commercial and personal coverages in order to determine what portion of the policy falls within the Program.

2.3   Who Is an Insurer

The Act requires the coverage to be offered by all insurers. The definition of insurer under the Act is very broad which ensures that the majority of policyholders with commercial risks have the ability to purchase coverage from their carrier.[12]

The term insurer under Section 102(6) of the Act includes all entities that are

(i)   Licensed and admitted to engage in the business of providing primary or excess insurance in any state[13]

(ii) Eligible surplus lines insurers (listed on the Quarterly Listing of Alien Insurers of the NAIC)

(iii) Approved by a federal agency for sales of maritime, energy or aviation[14]

(iv) State residual market insurance entity or state workers' compensation fund[15]

(v)   Captive insurers and other self-insurance arrangements[16]

The Act additionally requires that the entities listed above must receive direct earned premium for a commercial property and casualty policy in order to qualify as an insurer under the Program.[17] For instance, if a captive insurer does not receive direct earned premium and only receives reinsurance premium, it will not be an insurer for purposes of the Program.

Additionally, all requirements of the Act apply to non-U.S. insurers if they meet the definition of insurer under the Act but only with respect to premiums and losses as defined by the Act. The Act also gives the Treasury Secretary broad discretion to prescribe other criteria for determining which entities qualify as an insurer.[18]

2.4　Limits of Liability

The Act requires all insurers to offer coverage for terrorist acts on the same terms as losses arising from other events under its policy. Coverage offered for terrorist acts must, therefore, be granted using the same limits of liability and subject to the same conditions and exclusions as other losses or claims under the policy.[19]

2.5　Coverage Periods

Insurers must offer terrorism coverage on any new business or renewals for Program Year 1 (January 1, 2003, through December 31, 2003) and Program Year 2 (January 1, 2004, through December 31, 2004). The Secretary must decide by September 1, 2004, whether the Program will be extended into Program Year 3 (January 1, 2005, through December 31, 2005). The Act requires the Secretary to make this determination for extension of the Program into Year 3 in consultation with the NAIC,[20] representatives of the insurance industry, and representatives of policyholders. The determination is to be based on an assessment of the success of the Program as well as the capacity of the insurance industry to make terrorism coverage widely available and affordable.

3.0　Payment of Terrorism Losses

3.1　Insurer and Federal Government Payments for Loss

After the Secretary has certified an act as terrorism, the insurer and the Federal government will partition the losses pursuant to the Act. The scheme for sharing the losses includes insurer deductibles and co-payments as well as an insurance marketplace recoupment. The remainder of the losses up to a $100,000,000,000 aggregate are paid by the federal government.

3.2　Insurer Deductibles

The Act requires insurers to pay a percentage of their direct earned premium[21] as a deductible prior to receiving federal payment for losses under the Program. The insurer deductible increases with each subsequent year of the Program. Insurers are also responsible for a ten percent co-payment of all losses.

In Program Year One, the insurer is responsible for paying seven percent of its direct earned premiums as deductible. In Program Year 2, the deductible increases to ten percent and if the Program is extended by the Secretary into Program Year 3, the deductible rises to 15 percent. The federal government is then responsible for payment of 90 percent of the terrorism losses above the insurer deductible. The insurer retains responsibility as a co-payment for the remaining ten percent of losses.

3.3   Calculation of Insurer Deductible

In calculating an insurer's deductible, the Treasury will count direct earned premium of the insurer and any of its affiliates collectively as one insurer. A parent company and all affiliates that meet the requirements of an insurer under the Act will be treated as a consolidated entity for purposes of calculating the direct earned premium.[22] If an affiliate or a parent fails to meet one of the tests of an insurer under the Act, that affiliate or parent will not be included in the Program. For instance, if a parent company does not collect direct earned premium but is rather a holding company for its affiliate insurers, the parent does not qualify as an insurer under the Act

An affiliate is defined under Section 102(2) of the Act and in CFR 50.5(c)(1) as "an entity that controls, is controlled by or is under common control with the insurer."[23] An insurer is considered to be under control of another insurer if[24] (i) it controls or has power to vote 25 percent or more of any class of voting securities of the other insurer; (ii) it controls in any manner the election of a majority of the directors and trustees of the other entity; or (iii) the Secretary determines, after notice and opportunity for hearing, that the insurer directly or indirectly exercises a controlling influence over the management or policies of the other insurer, even if there is no control as defined in paragraph 50.5 (c)(2)(i) or (c)(2)(ii).

In order to clarify what constitutes a controlling influence under the (c)(2)(iii), the Treasury will apply the following presumptions that are rebuttable:[25]

(i)   If an insurer controls another insurer under any State law, and at least one of the factors listed in paragraph (c)(4)(iv) of this section applies, there is a rebuttable presumption that the insurer that has control under State law exercises a controlling influence over the management or policies of the other insurer for the purposes of paragraph (c)(2)(iii) of this section.

(ii)   If an insurer provides 25 percent or more of another insurer's captial (in the case of a stock insurer), policyholder surplus (in the case of a mutual insurer), or corporate capital (in the case of other entities that qualify as insurers), and at least one of the factors listed in paragraph (c)(4)(iv) of this section applies, there is a rebuttable presumption that the insurer providing such capital, policyholder surplus, or corporate capital exercises a controlling influence over the management or policies of the receiving insurer for purposes of paragraph (c)(2)(iii) of this section.

(iii) If an insurer, at any time during a Program Year, supplies 25 percent or more of the underwriting capacity for that year to an insurer that is a syndicate consisting of a group including incorporated and individual unincorporated underwriters, and at least one of the factors in paragraph (c)(4)(iv) of this section applies, there is a rebuttable presumption that the insurer exercises a controlling influence over the syndicate for the purposes of paragraph (c)(2)(iii) of this section.

(iv) If paragraphs (c)(4)(i) through (c)(4)(iii) of this section are not applicable, but two or more of the following factors apply to an insurer, with respect to another insurer, there is a rebuttable presumption that the insurer exercises a controlling influence over the management or policies of the other insurer for the purposes of paragraph (c)(2)(iii) of this section:

(A) The insurer is one of the two largest shareholders of any class of voting stock;

(B) The insurer holds more than 35 percent of the combined debt securities and equity of the other insurer;

(C) The insurer is party to an agreement pursuant to which the insurer possesses a material economic stake in the other insurer resulting from a profit-sharing arrangement, use of common names, facilities or personnel, or the provision of essential services to the other insurer;

(D) The insurer is party to an agreement that enables the insurer to influence a material aspect of the management or policies of the other insurer;

(E) The insurer would have the ability, other than through the holding of revocable proxies, to direct the votes of more than 25 percent of the other insurer's voting stock in the future upon the occurrence of an event;

(F) The insurer has the power to direct the disposition of more than 25 percent of a class of voting stock of the other insurer in a manner other than a widely dispersed or public offering;

(G) The insurer and/or the insurer's representative or nominee constitute more than one member of the other insurer's board of directors; or

(H) The insurer or its nominee or an officer of the insurer serves as the chairman of the board, chairman of the executive committee, chief executive officer, chief operating officer, chief financial officer or in any position with similar policymaking authority in the other insurer.

If an insurer wishes to rebut a presumption made under Section (c)(3) above, the insurer may request a hearing in which the insurer will be given an opportunity to refute the presumption of control. The Treasury will accept written submissions of evidence and, in its discretion, may hear oral presentations.[26]

3.4   Exclusion of Personal Insurance from the Insurer Deductible Calculation

Because coverage for personal insurance (coverage primarily designed to cover personal, family, or household risk exposures)[27] is excluded from the Program, any direct earned premium based on personal insurance should not included in the calculation of direct earned premium even if such premium is reported on Statutory Page 14. The Rule further states that exclusion of personal property and casualty premium applies even if the personal coverage contains an "incidental" amount of commercial coverage. Incidental is defined by the Rule as commercial coverage that comprises less than 25 percent of the total direct earned premium for the entire coverage. Personal property and casualty insurance coverage that includes "incidental" coverage for commercial purposes is primarily personal coverage, and therefore premiums are excluded from the calculation of direct earned premium.[28]

Where a property and casualty policy contains both commercial and personal exposures and the commercial exposures are not incidental to the coverage, insurers may allocate the premiums in accordance with the proportion of risk between commercial and personal components in calculating direct earned premium.[29]

3.5   Federal Government Payments

The federal share of compensation for insured losses under the Program is 90 percent of the losses of an insurer which exceed the insurer's deductible.[30] There is an aggregate limitation on all insured losses of $100,000,000,000, which applies to each Program Year. If losses from a terrorism event(s) exceed $100,000,000,000, neither the insurer nor the Treasury is liable for payment of these losses. However, should aggregate losses in any one Program Year exceed $100,000,000,000, the Secretary must notify the Congress of the estimated amount of loss and Congress has discretion to determine the source of any payment for the excess losses.[31]

3.6   Insurance Marketplace Aggregate Retention or Recoupment

Commercial Property and Casualty companies collectively will be responsible for recouping federal government terrorism losses within an "insurance marketplace aggregate retention." The amount of the insurance marketplace retention varies from 10 billion to 15 billion over the course of the Act.[32] The retention will be collected through a "terrorism loss risk-spreading premium" surcharge on all commercial property and casualty policies.

The Act requires the Secretary to recoup the difference between the insurance marketplace retention and the aggregate amount of losses paid by insurers under the insurer deductibles or losses that are not otherwise compensated by the Federal government's share.[33] If losses exceed the insurance marketplace retention, the Secretary is not required to recoup federal losses under the Program, however, the Secretary has discretion to do so under specified circumstances. If losses exceed the insurance marketplace retention, the Secretary has discretion to institute the terrorism premium surcharge based on the following economic factors:[34]

(i)   The ultimate cost to taxpayers of no additional recoupment
(ii) The economic conditions in the commercial marketplace, including the capitalization, profitability, and investment returns of the insurance industry and the current cycle of the insurance markets
(iii) The affordability of commercial insurance for small and medium sized business
(iv) Such other factors as the Secretary considers appropriate

3.7   Policy Surcharge for Terrorism Loss Risk-Spreading Premiums

The terrorism loss risk spreading premium surcharge is collected from policyholders by the insurer and remitted to the Treasury. The Secretary sets the amount of premium surcharge which must be based on a percentage of premium collected on the policy. While the size of the surcharge will be based on the amount of federal funds which are required to be recouped, the Act caps the surcharge at three percent of premium in any one policy year.

The premium surcharge is placed on those commercial and property casualty policies commencing in the year the Secretary institutes the premium surcharge.[35] The Act also gives the Secretary the authority to adjust the premium surcharge on a daily monthly or quarterly basis as appropriate in order to equally apply the surcharge to policies not based on a calendar year.[36] Although the Act is not clear on this point and regulations have yet to address it, the language of this section suggests that the Secretary may impose the surcharge on policies with commencement dates prior to the institution of the surcharge if the Secretary applies the surcharge on a pro rata basis such as monthly or quarterly.

The Act also grants the Secretary the authority to take into account regional differences as well as differences in lines of insurance when setting the amount of premium surcharge. The Secretary may make individual adjustments to the percentage of premium charged where factors such as the following warrant an adjustment:[37]

(i) The economic impact on commercial centers of urban areas, including the effect on commercial rents and commercial insurance premiums, particularly rents and premiums charged to small businesses, and the availability of lease space and commercial insurance with urban areas

(ii) The risk factors related to rural areas and smaller commercial centers, including the potential exposure to loss and the likely magnitude of such loss, as well as any resulting cross subsidization that might result

(iii) The various exposures to terrorist risk for different lines of insurance

3.8   Reinsurance

Insurers are permitted to purchase reinsurance to cover either the insurers individual deductible portion or any insured losses retained by the insurer. The purchase of reinsurance by an insurer shall not affect its calculation of deductibles or retentions under the Act.

4.0   Notification of Policyholders

As a condition to receiving federal payment for losses under the Program, the insurer must provide clear and conspicuous disclosure to the policyholder of the premium charged for terrorism coverage as well as the federal share of compensation for losses under the Program.[38] The notification must be made to the policyholder at the time of offer purchase or renewal of the policy and applies to all policies whether new or a renewal of an existing policy.[39]

The interim guidance issued by the Treasury on January 22, 2003, states that the insurer is deemed to be in compliance with the disclosure requirements if the insurer

(i) Makes the required disclosure to the policyholder or applicant no later than at the time the insurer first formally offers to provide insurance coverage or renew a policy for a current policyholder

(ii) Makes a clear and conspicuous reference back to that disclosure as well as the final terms of terrorism insurance coverage at the time the transaction is completed

(iii) Provides the disclosure as a separate line item
   (a) on the declarations page of the policy
   (b) elsewhere within the policy
   (c) in any rider or endorsement that is made a part of the policy

Treasury comments that the disclosures can be communicated by use of channels, methods, and forms of communication normally used to communicate similar policyholder information. Although it is not the only method of complying with the disclosure requirements of Section 103(b)(2), the above guidance is provided as a safe harbor method of issuing disclosure to policyholders. Treasury will be issuing future regulations with regards to insurer certification of compliance with the required disclosures to the policyholder.

5.0   Federal Cause of Action

TRIA creates an exclusive federal cause of action for any property damages, personal injury, or death arising out of or resulting from an act of terrorism. All state causes of action are preempted and the federal action will be the exclusive remedy for damages resulting from a terrorist act.[40] Punitive damages, if awarded, will not be considered insured losses and will not be covered under the Program.

The only exception to the federal action is in the instance where a determination has been made in a federal action that an organization, government, or person knowingly participated in, conspired to commit, aided or abetted, or committed any act of terrorism. Where such a finding has been made in a federal action, the Act will not limit the liability of such a government, person, or organization against whom such finding was made.[41]

Endnotes:

[1] Public Law 107-297, 116 Stat. 2322.

[2] The Treasury Department issued a final rule (31 CFR Part 50) on July 7, 2003. Citations in this chapter to any interim rules are current but were unchanged by the final rule.

[3] Section 102 (1)(A).

[4] Section 102 (1)(C).

[5] Section 102 (1)(A).

[6] Several insurers offer stand-alone terrorism policies which cover acts of domestic terrorism. Depending on the nature of the risk, a policyholder may purchase the standalone policy in conjunction with or separately from coverage under the TRIA program.

[7] Section 102 (15).

[8] In its Final Rule, Treasury commented that "in the aggregate" means losses suffered by all policyholders and not losses suffered by only one policyholder.

[9] Section 102 (1)(B).

[10] Section 102 (12)

[11] The following are the lines to be included from Statutory Page 14 of the NAIC Annual Statement: Line 1–Fire; Line 2.1–Allied Lines; Lines 3–Farmowners Multiple Peril; Line 5.1–Commercial Multiple Peril (non-liability portion); Line 5.2–Commercial Multiple Peril (liability portion); Line 8–Ocean Marine; Line 9–Inland Marine; Line 16–Workers' Compensation; Line 17–Other Liability; Line 18–Products Liability; Line 19.3–Commercial Auto No-Fault (personal injury protection); Line 19.4–Other Commercial Auto Liability; Line 21.2–Commercial Auto Physical Damage; Line 22–Aircraft (all perils); Line 24–Surety; Line 26–Burglary and Theft; and Line 27–Boiler and Machinery.

[12] Section 102 (6).

[13] In its final rule, Treasury clarified its definition of admitted insurer to include the following: "...State licensed captive insurance companies, State licensed or admitted risk retention groups, and State licensed or admitted farm and county mutuals, and, if a joint underwriting association, pooling arrangement, or other similar entity, then the entity must

    1. Have gone through a process of being licensed or admitted to engage in the business of providing primary or excess insurance that is administered by the State's insurance regulator, which process generally applies to insurance companies or is similar in scope and content to the process applicable to insurance companies;

    2. Be generally subject to State insurance regulation, including financial reporting requirements, applicable to insurance companies within the State; and

    3. Be managed independently from other insurers participating in the program."

[14] In its Interim Final Rule, Treasury states that only insurers which have received Federal Agency approval to sell insurance in connection with maritime, energy, or aviation activity and do not otherwise fall under categories 102(6)(i) and (ii) are eligible to participate in the Program. Other federally approved insurers which do not sell insurance related to maritime, energy, or aviation are not covered by the Program. Treasury specifically lists the following federal programs and statutes as federally approved insurers included in the Program:

- Approval of Underwriters for Marine Hull Insurance (maritime Administration, U.S. Department of Transportation)
- Aircraft Accident Liability Insurance (U.S. Department of Transportation)
- Oil Spill Financial Responsibility for Offshore Facilities (Minerals Management Service, U.S. Department of the Interior)
- Oil Spill Financial Responsibility for Vessels (United States Coast Guard, U.S. Department of Transportation)
- Longshoremen's and Harbor Workers' Compensation Act (Employment Standards Administration, U.S. Department of Labor)
- Price Anderson Act (Nuclear Regulatory Commission, U.S. Department of Energy)

[15] In its interim guidance published on December 18, 2002, Treasury listed the state residual insurance market and workers compensation funds that it considered to qualify as insurers under the Program. The list was developed in conjunction with the NAIC.

[16] In its final rule, Treasury states that so long as a captive or self-insured arrangement received direct earned premium and was licensed or admitted with a State, it would be considered to be an insurer under section 102(6). If a captive is not State licensed or admitted, then it is not in the Program unlless brought in under Section 103(f), which gives discretionary authority to the Secretary to add to the Program other classes or types of cative insurers.

[17] Section 102 (6)(B).

[18] Section 102 (6)(C).

[19] Section 103 (c)(1)(B).

[20] Section 103 (c)(2); The NAIC is the National Association of Insurance Commissioners which acts as a joint governing body for the various State Insurance Departments.

[21] In its initial interim guidance issued on December 3, 2002, Treasury clarified its definition of direct earned premium as, "the direct premium earned as reported to the NAIC in the Annual Statement in column 2 of the Exhibit of Premiums and Losses (Statutory Page 14).

[22] Section 102 (6)(A), (B) and (C).

[23] Section 102 (2).

[24] Section 102 (3).

[25] 31 CFR 50.5 (c)(4).

[26] 31 CFR 50.5 (c)(5).

[27] 31 CFR 50.5 (d)(ii).

[28] 31 CFR 50.5 (d)(iii).

[29] 31 CFR 50.5 (d)(iv).

[30] Section 103 (e)(1)(A).

[31] Section 103 (e)(2).

[32] Section 103 (e)(6) The insurance marketplace retention is as follows: 10 billion in Program Year 1, 12.5 billion in Program Year 2, and 15 billion in Program Year 3.

[33] Section 103 (e)(7).

[34] Section 103 (e)(7)(D).

[35] Section 103 (e)(8)(A).

[36] Section 103 (e)(8)(E).

[37] Section 103 (e)(8)(D).

[38] Section 103 (b)(2).

[39] Section 103 (b)(2)(c).

[40] Section 107 (a).

[41] Section 107 (a)(b).

Chapter 7

Public Health and Bioterrorism

Powell Goldstein Frazer & Murphy LLP
Larry Gage

1.0 Introduction[1]

The law of homeland security is one of the nation's newest bodies of law, perhaps one of the most rapidly formed in history. Yet in public health, as in most other areas, it rests on a broad foundation of federal, state, and local laws, regulations, and programs that pre-exist this new statutory framework.

The federal role in health care generally is a broad one. Over 80 million individuals receive insurance coverage through Medicare and the federal/state Medicaid program. The National Institutes of Health (NIH) provides both resources and leadership in the advancement of medical research. Other federal agencies fund a nationwide network of primary care centers or conduct research in a range of other areas, from alcoholism, drug abuse, and mental health to environmental and occupational health. Much of this federal role in the nation's health system, however, relates only tangentially to what we think of traditionally as "public health."

Like other essential "frontline" aspects of homeland security, such as police and fire protection, public health in America is traditionally the province of state and local governments. While the federal government has historically conducted or regulated certain public health activities with national implications, its role in many of the traditional areas of public health has been primarily that of a funding source for state and local activities.

Perhaps the single most important federal agency in public health is the Federal Centers for Disease Control and Prevention (CDC). The CDC is an essential cross-cutting public health resource for both national and world health. The CDC is responsible for some of the most important public health breakthroughs in history, including the eradication of smallpox, the control of many other diseases, and the early detection and diagnosis of new diseases and micro-biological agents. The long experience of CDC in identifying and responding to outbreaks of new or exotic germs and organisms provides a reassuring basis for building a new system of heightened responsiveness to the potential use by terrorists of chemical or biological agents as weapons of mass destruction.

Other federal departments and agencies also play a role related to the public health needs of homeland security. The Food and Drug Administration (FDA) is responsible for the regulation of the safety of drugs and pharmaceuticals, including many food additives. The Department of Agriculture (USDA) monitors and regulates the quality and safety of our food supply, the Environmental Protection Administration (EPA) concerns itself with our air, water and other vital aspects of the environment, and the Occupational Safety and Health Administration (OSHA) is responsible for promoting workplace safety programs and standards.

Each of the bodies of law surrounding the activities and programs of these agencies provides an important foundation for considering new statutes governing the public health aspects of homeland security.

1.1   Evolution and Current State of America's Public Health Infrastructure

It is important to understand how the new mandates and directives of homeland security will relate to America's state and local public health infrastructure. The evolutionary story of public health in America, as in many parts of the developed world, has until recently been a positive one. Perhaps a century ago, several important factors combined to change the nature of public health in our nation. In 1900, the three leading causes of death in America were pneumonia, tuberculosis, and diarrhea/enteritis, and the crude death rate for infectious diseases was 800 per 100,000 population per year. By 1980, that rate had shrunk to less than 40, due to a combination of factors that included improved sanitation, safer drinking water, vaccines, and antibiotics. The leading causes of death had shifted to heart disease, cancer, stroke, chronic lung disease, injury, etc. Among infectious diseases, only two—pneumonia and influenza (taken together) and HIV—were among the top ten causes of death in 1997 in America.

The most recent trends, however, have not been quite so positive. In fact, the death rate from infectious diseases has actually been increasing slowly, but steadily, since 1980 in the United States. Moreover, there have been other indicia of deterioration (such as persistently high infant mortality and substantial differences in morbidity and mortality among certain minority populations). At the same time, the U.S. and the world have seen the emergence in recent decades of potent new diseases and microbiological organisms to challenge our public health infrastructure. HIV and AIDS have been the most highly publicized of these challenges, representing a public health crisis of major proportions for America and many parts of the world. Our public health infrastructure has also been seriously tested in recent years by the emergence of multi-drug resistant viruses and microbiological organisms, and of other new and previously unknown diseases like West Nile Virus or the alarming new form of pneumonia being called SARS (Severe Acute Respiratory Syndrome).

As a result, many observers believe that our present public health infrastructure is in many respects underfunded, understaffed, and underequipped to meet both current public health needs and the heightened needs of homeland security.[2] All of the key areas of public health important to homeland security—surveillance, detection, prevention, response, and treatment—have suffered from the need to stretch scarce resources to cover ever-increasing threats in recent years.

At the same time, it is important to bear in mind that the health-related aspects of homeland security are typically far more broad than the services and personnel usually identified as "public health." The emergency personnel, physicians, hospitals, and other institutional caregivers who are first responders are also under pressure from other quarters. They are contending with Medicare and Medicaid reimbursement cuts, critical staff shortages, increased exposure to malpractice liability, rising uncompensated costs due to increased numbers of uninsured, and increased competition from providers who do not share the public health "safety net" role.

1.2   Threat of Biological and Chemical Terrorism: The Need for Heightened Public Health Readiness

Our awareness of new threats of human-induced chemical or biological terrorism has been elevated for years, well before the tragic events of 2001. Many signs had already begun to point to heightened threat of the introduction (or reintroduction) by human agents of deadly chemicals or little seen diseases into the American environment. Such attacks even found their way into popular culture in the 1990s, in the form of novels like Richard Preston's "The Cobra Event" and Tom Clancy's "Executive Orders" as well as in numerous movies and television plot lines.[3]

While intentional acts of chemical and biological terrorism have been rare in America, they have occurred. A religious sect in Oregon intentionally introduced salmonella into a restaurant salad bar in 1984, for example, and *Yersinia pestis* was sent through the mail to victims in Ohio in 1995. While there have been more hoaxes than actual events in recent years (including anthrax hoaxes in Los Angeles and Washington D.C. and ricin toxin hoaxes in Arkansas and

Minnesota), the prospect of biological or chemical terrorism was taken very seriously even before September 11, 2001. This concern was reinforced by occasional deadly attacks overseas—most notably the 1994 use of sarin gas in the Tokyo subway, which killed eight people and sickened over 4,000 others and the reported use of chemical agents to suppress uprisings in Iraq following the 1991 Gulf war.

In 2000, the first major citywide response exercise, known as "Top Officials 2000" (or TOPOFF), was held in Denver, Colorado. While that exercise (which simulated the release of *Yersinia pestis*, the bacteria that causes plague) was largely considered successful, it did raise a number of questions and concerns about public health readiness. Of particular concern was the ability to gain sufficiently rapid access to usable drugs and supplies from the federal stockpile and the inability of some of the key players to communicate effectively with one another. Similar issues arose in the "Dark Winter" exercise, which simulated a smallpox outbreak in Oklahoma City. The issue of effective communication also arose in New York City during and immediately after the events of September 11, 2001. (Another TOPOFF II exercise was held in Chicago in May 2003)[4]

In some respects, America's public health infrastructure is historically more capable of responding to chemical attacks and to those that result in traumatic injuries than to biological attacks. In part, this is because most state and local public or environmental health departments already have well-established hazardous material (HAZMAT) plans and protocols, and injury-inducing accidents involving toxic chemicals are not nearly as rare as intentional terrorist attacks. The nation's public health care infrastructure is also better equipped to respond to mass disasters, such as earthquakes, hurricanes, industrial accidents, and plane and train accidents, than to biological attacks. There are lessons to be learned from these experiences.

For example, in the early morning hours of June 9, 2001, tropical storm Allison dumped between 12 and 15 inches of rain on Houston in a nine-hour period, overwhelming drainage systems and flooding large swaths of the city. The Texas Medical Center was at the epicenter of devastation, incurring 40 percent of the $5 billion in damages attributed to Allison. Fortunately, the core of the public health infrastructure in the district—the Harris County Hospital District's Ben Taub Hospital—was relatively unscathed. Within hours, Ben Taub simultaneously accepted 50 intensive care patients and became the city's only Level I trauma center when neighbor Memorial Hermann Hospital had to shut down due to flooding. Public health officials believe that because 100 percent of those patients were critically ill, it was the equivalent of treating 500 patients during a mass casualty incident.

Officials identified several opportunities to improve response to future disasters. Chief among them was better coordination with other hospitals and the city's emergency response system. After the Allison experience, Texas Medical Center hospitals individually established incident command centers and collectively began holding emergency preparedness meetings, meetings that had not occurred previously. Since Allison, the Hospital District also has put in place a more rigorous hazard vulnerability analysis and developed emergency response performance measures. Procedures to facilitate a return to normal operations were developed, and the hospital's medical staff has been included more comprehensively in emergency preparedness.

Bioterrorism is thus the area that presents the greatest potential obstacles to full preparedness. In part, this is because with bioterrorism, the list of potential agents is long and harrowing. It includes, in addition to anthrax, such terrifying scourges as smallpox, botulism, cholera, glanders, plague (bubonic and pneumonic), Q-fever, and tularemia, among others. Some scientists estimate that 50 or more potential diseases could be used by terrorists, including many that have never been seen by most physicians practicing today. For example, the last case of recorded human-to-human transmission of bubonic plague occurred in 1934. The last recorded case of smallpox in the world was in Somalia in 1977. The World Health Assembly certified that the world was free of smallpox in 1980. Yet, as we all know, official reservoirs remained in the United States and Russia, and unofficial strains are now feared to be in the hands of several rogue states or terrorist organizations. Both the CDC and a number of major American teaching hospitals have established protocols for hospital response, ranging from tools for disease surveillance and initial diagnosis of a range of biological and chemical agents to detailed patient placement and transport precautions; guidelines for disinfection and sterilization of equipment and environment; and even discharge management and post-mortem care. Many helpful procedures, protocols, and benchmarks for hospitals and public health departments can be found on the CDC website.[5] These include protocols for responding to chemical attacks and incidents involving traumatic injury, as well as for biological attacks.

In addition, many state and local organizations have played a leadership role in developing protocols for swift and effective response to chemical and biological public health emergencies. For example, the University of North Carolina has developed a comprehensive "bioterrorist agents" diagnosis and treatment chart for distribution to appropriate hospital personnel. It includes concise information about symptoms, diagnosis, transmission, and treatment options for anthrax, botulism, pneumonic plague, and smallpox and can be obtained from the North Carolina Statewide Program for Infection Control and Epidemiology.

1.3 What Are the Key Public Health Elements of Homeland Security?

In order to fully understand the implications of the new federal laws described below, it may be helpful to identify the principal elements (and key players) of public health that are most directly related to homeland security. According to the CDC, there are five primary priorities for public health preparedness:

- Emergency preparedness and response
- Enhanced surveillance and epidemiology
- Enhanced laboratory capacity for rapid diagnosis
- Enhanced information technology to promote rapid and effective collaboration
- Strategically located stockpiles of necessary drugs and other pharmaceuticals to ensure ready availability in the event of a crisis

Those priorities must be addressed through a plan that involves all of the key first responders to any crisis, including primary care personnel, hospital emergency room staff, EMS personnel, public health professionals, laboratories, and law enforcement officers.

The CDC places its highest premium on having a plan in place that incorporates and addresses each of these elements and players, and much of the federal support and new statutory provisions governing public health and homeland security are aimed at strengthening each of them. The CDC web site lists resources for assistance in developing bioterrorism response plans, available at <www.bt.cdc.gov>.

The CDC has codified and refined its planning criteria into a series of what it calls "critical benchmarks for bioterrorism preparedness planning." Those benchmarks can be summarized as follows:

- Designate a Senior Public Health Official within the state health department to serve as Executive Director of the state bioterrorism Preparedness and Response Program and a Coordinator for hospital preparedness planning.
- Establish an advisory committee to include representatives from (included but not limited to):
  - State and local health departments and government
  - Emergency Management Agencies
  - Emergency Medical Services
  - Office of Rural Health
  - Police, fire department, emergency rescue workers, and occupational health workers

- Other health care providers, including university, academic medical, and public health
- Community health centers
- Red Cross and other voluntary organizations
- The hospital community (to include Veterans Affairs and military hospitals)

- Prepare a timeline for the development of a state-wide plan for preparedness and response for a bioterrorist event, infectious disease outbreak, or other public health emergency.
- Prepare a time for the development of regional plans for bio-preparedness and response for a bioterrorist event, infectious disease outbreak, or other public health emergency.
- Prepare a time line for assessment of emergency preparedness and response capabilities related to bioterrorism, other outbreaks of infectious disease, and other public health emergencies with a view to facilitating planning and setting implementation priorities.
- Establish a hospital bio-preparedness planning committee, (affiliated with the state-wide bioterrorism advisory committee) whose composition includes representation from (but not limited to):
  - Emergency Medical Services
  - Emergency Management Agencies
  - Office of Rural Health
  - State hospital associations
  - Veterans Affairs and military hospitals
  - Primary care associations

- Develop a timeline for implementation of regional hospital plans that would accommodate in at least 500 patients in an emergency.
- Assess statutes, regulations, and ordinances within the state that provide for credentialing, licensure, and delegation of authority for executing emergency public health measures.
- Develop a plan and identify personnel to be trained to receive and distribute critical stockpile items and manage a mass distribution of vaccine and/or antibiotics on a 24 hours a day, seven days a week basis.
- Develop a plan to receive and evaluate urgent disease reports from all parts of the jurisdiction on a 24 hour a day, seven days a week basis.
- Assess epidemiologic capacity with provision for at least one epidemiologist for each Metropolitan Statistical Area with a population greater than 500,000.

- Develop a plan to improve working relations and communications between Level A laboratories (clinical) and Level B/C laboratories, (Laboratory Response Network laboratories) as well as other public health officials.
- Develop a plan that ensures that 90 percent of the population is covered by the CDCs Health Alert Network.
- Develop a plan for communications systems that provides for a 24/7 flow of critical health information between hospital emergency departments, state and local health officials, and law enforcement.
- Develop a plan to enhance risk communication and information dissemination to educate the public regarding exposure risks and effective public response.
- Assess training needs with special emphasis on emergency department personnel, infectious disease specialists, public health staff, and other health care providers.[6]

1.4   Cost

While the key elements of homeland security are by now fairly clear, the ability of state and local public health departments, hospitals, and other first responders to develop and implement such plans depends in large part on the availability of additional resources. Many observers believe that federal resources allocated to date are inadequate to meet all of the needs of the public health infrastructure, at least without crowding out other essential public health activities.[7]

For chemical and biological terrorism, a combination of improved community-wide surveillance, increased availability of vaccines, stockpiled medicines and antibiotics, physicians trained to recognize symptoms early, and increased attention to general readiness (such as the availability of isolation facilities) are all part of the solution. Nevertheless, these steps are not free, and the cost of effective responsiveness is a major concern.

For example, the American Hospital Association initially estimated it would cost upwards of $27 billion just to adequately prepare U.S. hospitals to respond to an attack. The AHA later scaled back its estimate to $11.3 billion. This translates to $3 million for each metropolitan area hospital and $1.4 million for each rural hospital (based on estimates of 1,000 casualties per hospital in an urban area and 200 per hospital in rural areas). Funds are said to be needed by hospitals for

- Improved disease surveillance
- Maintenance of a 24-hour pharmaceutical stockpile
- Decontamination facilities
- Personal protective equipment for staff (including self-contained breathing apparatus and chemical-resistant suits for 50 staff members)

As described in Section 3.0 below, fiscal year 2002 appropriations for the public health aspects of homeland security totaled only $2.9 billion, with just $135 million of that allocated to hospitals.[8] Even those funds were delayed, at least in part, in their allocation. Much of the progress that has been made to date by state and local public health systems has been funded primarily from other sources. As further discussed below, additional funds for public health preparedness were included in the omnibus fiscal year 2003 spending bill passed by the Congress in January of 2003. Many state and local public health officials, confronting severe deficits due to the weak national economy, hope that those funds will be allocated more swiftly and effectively now that a new federal apparatus is in place.

2.0 Public Health Security and Bioterrorism Preparedness and Response Act of 2002 (PL 107-188)

2.1 Introduction

The Public Health Security and Bioterrorism Preparedness and Response Act was one of the first major laws enacted by the Congress following the events of September 11, 2001. While the passage of this legislation was motivated in part by lessons learned in the aftermath of those attacks, the subsequent anthrax crisis was perhaps an even greater motivation for a Congress that was itself being directly attacked.[9]

The 2001 U.S. anthrax attack uncovered some serious flaws in the nation's public health preparedness. We learned several things from that outbreak—not all of them encouraging. For one thing, much of the response-planning prior to that attack had centered around a model of mass infection of a population, with many casualties in a concentrated area. This model was based primarily on the accidental release of anthrax from a bioweapon factory in Sverdlosk, Russia, in 1979. In that case, just two grams of weapon-grade spores were carried downwind, resulting in 94 cases of inhalation anthrax and 66 deaths.

The actual threat in America materialized much more stealthily and (while infecting fewer individuals) was spread across a far broader geographic area. Upwards of a dozen different hospitals in six states and the District of Columbia were asked to diagnose anthrax in just one or a small number of individuals, in some cases with no advance warning as to the nature of the patient's illness. While much attention was paid to potentially infected U.S. Senators and Senate staff, for example, the deadly exposure of postal workers was not immediately anticipated. Perhaps understandably under the circumstances, some public health systems and hospitals responded more effectively than others did.

Of equal concern is the fact that hospitals across the country were also required to cope with instances of often hysterical patients presenting with symptoms similar to those described in the media as anthrax-related. Hospitals and laboratories were also confronted with the need to analyze many suspicious substances, presented by the concerned public as well as by local law enforcement officials.

One sorely underestimated aspect of bioterrorism response planning was the need for extensive collaboration. In a January 6, 2002 analysis of lessons learned from the U.S. anthrax attack, the New York Times quoted CDC spokesperson (now Director) Dr. Julie Gerberding: "In retrospect, we were certainly not prepared for layers and levels of collaboration" among a vast array of governmental agencies and professional organizations "that would be required to be efficient and successful" in the anthrax outbreak. [10]

The Times further reported that this lack of coordination also extended to hospitals and healthcare providers, pointing out that the New York City Health Department "had prepared itself for" an outbreak of "inhalation anthrax in recent years, building liaisons between hospitals and specialists in infectious disease, pulmonary disease, and emergency room care. But health officials overlooked dermatologists and surgeons who treated the first anthrax cases—the skin form."

Based on these concerns and other issues that had been previously identified in disaster planning events such as TOPOFF 1 (discussed above), Congress passed a sweeping new law whose stated purpose was "to improve the ability of the United States to prevent, prepare for, and respond to bioterrorism and other public health emergencies." The remainder of this part will provide a section-by-section summary of the new law.

2.2 National Preparedness for Bioterrorism and Other Public Health Emergencies

Subtitle A of Title I of the new law (National Preparedness and Response Planning, Coordinating, and Reporting) amends the Public Health Service Act to add a new Title XXVIII: National Preparedness for Bioterrorism and Other Public Health Emergencies.

Title XXVIII directs the Secretary of Health and Human Services to further develop and implement a coordinated strategy for carrying out health-related activities to prepare for and respond effectively to bioterrorism and other public health emergencies. Acknowledging the need to build on current core federal public health capabilities, the new law directs the Secretary to prepare a plan to coordinate federal activities with activities of the states, including local governments. [11]

The new law requires the provision of effective assistance to state and local governments in the event of bioterrorism or other public health emergency. It also seeks to ensure that state and local governments have the appropriate capacity to detect and respond effectively to such emergencies, including capacities for

- Effective public health surveillance and reporting mechanisms at the State and local levels
- Appropriate laboratory readiness
- Properly trained and equipped emergency response, public health, and medical personnel
- Health and safety protection of workers responding to such an emergency
- Coordination of health services (including mental health services) during and after such emergencies
- Participation in communications networks that can effectively disseminate relevant information in a timely and secure manner to appropriate public and private entities and to the public

The law specifically requires the Secretary to

- Develop and maintain medical countermeasures (such as drugs, vaccines and other biological products, medical devices, and other supplies) against biological agents and toxins that may be involved in such emergencies
- Ensure coordination and minimize duplication of federal, state, and local planning, preparedness, and response activities, including during the investigation of a suspicious disease outbreak or other potential public health emergency
- Enhance the readiness of hospitals and other health care facilities to respond effectively to such emergencies

Section 102 of the new law establishes in the Department of Health and Human Services an Assistant Secretary for Public Health Emergency Preparedness to coordinate efforts on behalf of the Secretary and provides for the operation of a National Disaster Medical System. This new system is a coordinated effort to provide health and health-related social services, and other appropriate auxiliary services, to respond to the needs of victims of a public health emergency. It also seeks to ensure that there is a federal presence at locations that the Secretary has determined to be at risk of a public health emergency.

Section 103 revises provisions of the Public Health Service Act which provide for revitalizing the Centers for Disease Control and Prevention to authorize the Director of the Centers to design, construct, and equip new facilities, or renovate existing facilities, to enable CDC to better combat threats to public health. Such facilities include laboratories, laboratory support buildings, scientific communication facilities, trans-shipment complexes, secured and isolated parking structures, office buildings, and other facilities and infrastructure.

This section of the new law also directs the Secretary to provide for the establishment of an integrated system or systems of public health alert communications and surveillance networks between and among federal, state, and local public health officials; public and private health-related laboratories, hospitals and other health care facilities; and any other entities determined appropriate by the Secretary.

Section 103 also authorizes appropriations to carry out its various purposes, including appropriations to CDC and funds to be specifically earmarked for state and local services (including public health departments, laboratories, hospitals, etc).

Section 104 provides for advisory committees that will issue expert recommendations to assist working groups in carrying out their respective responsibilities under provisions providing for the following:

- A joint interdepartmental working group on preparedness and readiness for the medical and public health effects of a bioterrorist attack on the civilian population
- A joint interdepartmental working group to address the public health and medical consequences of a bioterrorist attack on the civilian population

This section requires the establishment of the National Advisory Committee on Children and Terrorism, and its termination (one year after enactment of this Act), following the submission of its recommendations. It also requires the establishment of the Emergency Public Information and Communications Advisory Committee, and its termination (one year after enactment of this Act), following the submission of its recommendations.

This section also directs the Secretary to develop a strategy for effectively communicating information regarding bioterrorism and other public health emergencies, and to develop means by which to communicate such information. This section recommends that Congress establish an official federal Internet site on bioterrorism.

Section 105 directs the Secretary to

- Develop materials for teaching the elements of a core curriculum for the recognition and identification of potential bioweapons and other agents that may create a public health emergency, and for the care of victims of such emergencies
- Develop a core curriculum and materials for community-wide planning by state and local governments, hospitals and other healthcare facilities, emer-

gency response units, and appropriate public and private sector entities to respond to a bioterrorist attack or other public health emergency

- Develop materials for proficiency testing of laboratory and other public health personnel for the recognition and identification of potential bioweapons and other agents that may create a public health emergency
- Provide for dissemination and instruction of the materials, which may include telemedicine, long-distance learning, or other such means

Section 106 authorizes grants and cooperative agreements for the purpose of loans and other cost-sharing forms of assistance for the education and training of individuals in any health profession for which there is a shortage, and for which the Secretary determines is necessary to prepare for or respond effectively to bioterrorism and other public health emergencies. This section authorizes appropriations.

Section 107 requires the establishment of an advance registration system of health professions volunteers who would verify credentials during public health emergencies. This section authorizes appropriations.

Section 108 directs the Secretary, in coordination with the Secretary of Agriculture, the Attorney General, the Director of Central Intelligence, the Secretary of Defense, the Secretary of Energy, the Administrator of the Environmental Protection Agency, the Director of the Federal Emergency Management Agency, the Secretary of Labor, the Secretary of Veterans Affairs, and with other federal officials as appropriate, to establish a working group on prevention, preparedness, and response to bioterrorism and other public health emergencies.

Section 109 revises provisions concerning combating antimicrobial resistance and authorizes appropriations for such provisions.

Section 110 permits the provision of supplies and services, rather than award funds, to grant recipients, upon the recipient's request.[12]

2.3 Strategic National Stockpile; Development of Priority Countermeasures

Subtitle B of Title I directs the Secretary of Health and Human Services, in coordination with the Secretary of Veterans Affairs, to maintain a stockpile of drugs, vaccines and other biological products, medical devices, and other supplies that would provide emergency health security in the event of a bioterrorist attack or other public health emergency. In carrying out this duty, the Secretary must ensure that a sufficient amount of vaccine against smallpox is available to meet the health security needs of the United States. The law authorizes appropriations for this function. (See description in Part 3 below.)

Section 122 directs the Secretary of Health and Human Services to designate a "priority countermeasure" as a fast-track product, in accordance with the Federal Food, Drug, and Cosmetic Act (FDCA).

Section 123 requires the FDA to issue a final rule within 90 days allowing reliance on animal trials for priority countermeasures for public health emergencies.

Section 124 directs the Secretary, in consultation with the Attorney General and the Secretary of Defense, to provide security to persons or facilities that conduct the development, production, distribution, or storage of priority countermeasures.

Section 125 requires the Secretary to give priority to accelerated countermeasure research and development.

Section 126 directs the Secretary to promptly establish a program to periodically evaluate new and emerging technologies that would improve or enhance the ability of public health or safety officials ability to conduct public health surveillance activities relating to a bioterrorist attack or other public health emergency.

Section 127 directs the president to

- Make available to state and local governments, through the national stockpile, potassium iodide tablets for stockpiling and for distribution to public facilities in quantities that would adequately protect the population within 20 miles of a nuclear power plant
- Request the National Academy of Sciences conduct a study to determine the most effective and safe way to distribute and administer potassium iodide tablets on a mass scale

2.4 Improving State, Local, and Hospital Preparedness for Response to Bioterrorism and Other Public Health Emergencies

Subtitle C of Title I of the new law directs the Secretary to enhance the security of the United States with respect to bioterrorism and other public health emergencies. It authorizes appropriations for this purpose and directs the Secretary to make awards of grants or cooperative agreements to eligible entities for the purpose of

- Developing coordinated state and community-wide plans for responding to bioterrorism and other public health emergencies
- Addressing deficiencies in public health needs

- Purchasing or upgrading equipment supplies, pharmaceuticals, or other priority countermeasures to enhance preparedness for and response to bioterrorism or other public health emergencies
- Conducting exercises to test the capability and timeliness of public health emergency response activities
- Developing and implementing the trauma care and burn center care components of the state plans for the provision of emergency medical services
- Improving training or workforce development to enhance public health laboratories
- Training public healthcare personnel
- Developing, enhancing, coordinating, or improving systems by which disease detection and information about biological attacks and other public health emergencies can be rapidly communicated
- Enhancing communication to the public regarding bioterrorism and other public health emergencies, including through the use of 2-1-1 call centers
- Addressing the health security needs of children and other vulnerable populations with respect to bioterrorism and other public health emergencies
- Providing training and developing methods to enhance the safety of workers and workplaces in the event of bioterrorism
- Preparing and planning for contamination prevention efforts related to public health
- Preparing a plan for triage and transport management in the event of bioterrorism or other public health emergencies
- Enhancing the training of health care professionals to recognize and treat the mental health consequences of bioterrorism or other public health emergencies
- Enhancing healthcare professional training to include instruction concerning appropriate health care for large numbers of individuals exposed to a bioweapon
- Enhancing training and planning to protect the health and safety of personnel involved in responding to a biological attack
- Improving surveillance, detection, and response activities to prepare for emergency response activities including biological threats or attacks
- Developing, enhancing, and coordinating or improving the ability of existing telemedicine programs to provide healthcare information and advice as part of the emergency public health response to bioterrorism or other public health emergencies.

This section also directs the Secretary to make awards of grants or cooperative agreements to eligible entities that will enable them to improve community and hospital preparedness for bioterrorism and other public health emergencies. The section authorizes appropriations for the purposes outlined above.[13]

2.5   Emergency Authorities; Additional Provisions

Subtitles D and E of the new law provides extensions for certain reporting deadlines during a public health emergency, amends the Robert T. Stafford Disaster Relief and Emergency Assistance Act to require providing information to the public in a coordinated manner, and enacts certain additional provisions.

Section 142 expands the authority of the Secretary, in consultation with the Surgeon General and under certain conditions, to specify communicable diseases that are subject to individual detention orders.

Sec. 143 amends title XI of the Social Security Act to add provisions with the purpose of ensuring that in any emergency area during an emergency period

- Sufficient healthcare items and services are available to meet the needs of individuals in such area enrolled in the Medicare, Medicaid, and the State Children's Health Insurance Program (SCHIP)
- Healthcare providers furnishing such items and services in good faith, but that are unable to comply with one or more specified requirements, may be reimbursed for such items and services and exempted from sanctions for such noncompliance, absent any determination of fraud or abuse

Section 144 sets forth provisions for determining the expiration of public health emergencies.

Section 152 directs the Secretary of Energy and the Administrator of the National Nuclear Security Administration to expand, enhance, and intensify research relevant to the rapid detection and identification of pathogens likely to be used in a bioterrorism attack. This section authorizes appropriations and applies to other agents that may cause a public health emergency.

Section 153 directs the Secretary, acting through the Director of the National Institute of Occupational Safety and Health, to enhance and expand research on the health and safety of workers at risk for bioterrorist threats or attacks in the workplace.

Section 154 directs the Secretary of Veterans Affairs to take appropriate actions to enhance the readiness of Department of Veterans Affairs medical centers to protect the patients and staff from chemical or biological attack, or otherwise to respond to such an attack. This section authorizes appropriations.

Section 155 reauthorizes a grant program, through 2006, that develops projects focusing on the behavioral and biological aspects of psychological trauma response. The program also develops research that will help treat psychiatric disorders of children and youth resulting from witnessing or experiencing a traumatic event.

Section 156 expresses the sense of Congress regarding the many excellent university-based programs already functioning and developing important biodefense products and solutions throughout the United States.

Section 157 requires a General Accounting Office (GAO) report to Congress on Federal bioterrorism-related activities; coordination activities; and state, local, and private sector activities.

Section 158 amends the Public Health Service Act public health emergency provisions to authorize awards for expenses in addition to authorizing grants.

Section 159 directs the Secretary, with respect to the Community Access to Emergency Defibrillation Act of 2002, to award grants to states, political subdivisions of states, Indian tribes, and tribal organizations, to develop and implement public access defibrillation programs. This section authorizes appropriations.

2.6 Enhancing Controls on Dangerous Biological Agents and Toxins

Title II of the new law amends the Public Health Service Act to provide for enhanced control of certain biological agents and toxins. In particular, Subtitle A of Title II directs the Secretary to

- Establish and maintain (and review at least biennially) a list of each biological agent and each toxin that has the potential to pose a severe threat to public health and safety.
- Provide for regulation of transfers of listed agents and toxins.
- Provide for the establishment and enforcement of standards and procedures governing the possession and use of listed agents and toxins.
- Require registration with the Secretary of the possession, use, and transfer of listed agents and toxins.
- Provide appropriate safeguard and security requirements for persons possessing, using, or transferring a listed agent or toxin commensurate with the risk such agent or toxin poses to public health and safety. It authorizes the Secretary to inspect persons subject to the above requirements to ensure their compliance with such regulations (including the risk of use in domestic or international terrorism).

The new law authorizes exemptions for clinical or diagnostic laboratories and other persons who possess, use, or transfer listed agents or toxins that are contained in specimens presented for diagnosis, verification, or proficiency testing, provided that

- Identification of such agents or toxins is reported to the Secretary, and when required under federal, state, or local law, to other appropriate authorities
- That such agents or toxins are transferred or destroyed in a manner set forth by the Secretary by regulation

The new law authorizes exemptions for products that are, bear, or contain listed agents or toxins and are cleared, approved, licensed, or registered under specific regulations. The Secretary may determine that applying additional regulation to a specific product is necessary to protect public health and safety. The law authorizes exemptions for an investigational product that is, bears, or contains a listed agent or toxin when such product is being used in an investigation authorized under any federal act. The Secretary may establish that it is not necessary to apply additional regulation to such a product to protect public health and safety. The new law also authorizes exemptions, as specified, for public health and agricultural emergencies. It authorizes appropriations and sets forth

- Rules governing disclosure of information
- Penalties for violators
- Reporting requirements

Section 202 requires all persons (unless exempt) in possession of biological agents or toxins listed under the Public Health Service Act to notify the Secretary of Health and Human Services of such possession.[14]

2.7 Public Health Responsibilities of the Department of Agriculture

Subtitle B of Title II provides specific public health activities to programs under the control of the Department of Agriculture. Characterized as the Agricultural Bioterrorism Protection Act of 2002, this subtitle directs the Secretary of Agriculture to establish and maintain a list of each biological agent and toxin that the Secretary determines has the potential to pose a severe threat to animal or plant health, or to animal or plant products. It authorizes appropriations for its provisions and sets forth criteria for list inclusion and review, and for the regulation of

- Transfers of listed agents and toxins
- Possession and use of listed agents and toxins
- Registration, identification, and maintenance of a database of listed toxins
- Security and safeguard of persons possessing, using, or transferring a listed agent

This subtitle further requires that information regarding the identification of certain registered persons be submitted to the Attorney General and requires the Attorney General to promptly determine if any of the persons are within any specified criminal, immigration, national security, or other categories. It sets forth procedures concerning

- The process regarding persons seeking to register
- Administrative review

This subtitle requires prompt notification of the Secretary and appropriate federal, state, and local law enforcement agencies of the theft or loss of listed agents and toxins. It sets forth exemptions concerning clinical and diagnostic laboratories, products, investigational use, agricultural emergencies, and public health emergencies. It also sets forth

- Rules governing disclosure of information
- Penalties for violators
- Reporting requirements

2.8   Miscellaneous Provisions of Title II

Subtitle C of Title II ("Interagency Coordination Regarding Overlap Agents and Toxins") directs the Secretary of Agriculture and the Secretary of Health and Human Services to coordinate activities regarding overlap agents and toxins.

Subtitle D of title II ("Criminal Penalties Regarding Certain Biological Agents and Toxins") amends federal criminal code provisions concerning the possession of listed biological agents and toxins to provide that whoever

- Transfers a select agent to a person who the transferor knows or has reasonable cause to believe is not registered as required shall be fined, or imprisoned for not more than five years, or both
- Knowingly possesses a biological agent or toxin where such agent or toxin is a select agent for which such person has not obtained a required registration shall be fined, or imprisoned for not more than five years, or both.[15]

2.9   Protecting Safety and Security of Food and Drug Supply Subtitle

Title III of the 2001 statute addresses the safety and security of the nation's food and drug supplies. Subtitle A of this title ("Protection of Food Supply") directs the President's Council on Food Safety (as established by Executive Order), in consultation with the Secretary of Transportation, the Secretary of the Treasury, other relevant federal agencies, the food industry, consumer and producer groups, scientific organizations, and the states, to develop a crisis communications and education strategy with respect to bioterrorist threats to the food supply.

Section 302 of the new law amends the Federal Food Drug and Cosmetic Act [21 U.S.C. 300] to direct the Secretary of Health and Human Services to

- Give high priority to increasing the number of inspections under this section for the purpose of enabling the Secretary to inspect food offered for import at ports of entry into the United States, with the greatest priority given to inspections to detect the intentional food adulteration
- Give high priority to making necessary improvements to the information management systems of the FDA that contain information related to foods imported or offered for import into the United States for purposes of improving the ability of the Secretary to allocate resources, detect the intentional adulteration of food, and facilitate the importation of food that is in compliance with this Act
- Improve linkages with other regulatory agencies of the federal government that share responsibility for food safety, and shall, with respect to such safety, improve linkages with the states and Indian tribes
- Provide for research on the development of tests and sampling methodologies whose purpose is to test food in order to rapidly detect the adulteration of the food

The new law sets forth reporting requirements and authorizes appropriations.

Section 303 of the new law permits an officer or qualified employee of the FDA to order the temporary detention (in a secured facility) of any article of food that is found during an inspection, examination, or investigation if the officer or qualified employee has credible evidence or information indicating that such article presents a threat of serious adverse health consequences or death to humans or animals, but only if the Secretary or an official designated by the Secretary approves the order. This section also sets forth procedures for the appeal of such orders.

Section 304 provides for the debarment of importers for repeated or serious food import violations.

Section 305 directs the Secretary, by regulation, to require that any facility (domestic and foreign) engaged in manufacturing, processing, packing, or holding food for consumption in the United States be registered with the Secretary.

Section 306 authorizes the Secretary, if the Secretary has a reasonable belief that an article of food is adulterated and presents a threat of serious adverse health consequences or death to humans or animals, to have access to and copy all records relating to such article that are necessary to determine whether the food is adulterated and presents a threat of serious adverse health consequences or death to humans or animals.

Section 307 requires food importers to give the Secretary specified prior notice (including specified information about the source of the food) of the importation of any food for the purpose of enabling the food to be inspected.

Section 308 permits the Secretary to require the owner or consignee of food refused admission into the United States, but not ordered destroyed, to affix to the container of the food a label that clearly and conspicuously bears the statement: UNITED STATES: REFUSED ENTRY.

Section 309 prohibits an importer from port shopping with respect to food that has previously been denied entry.

Section 310 requires the Secretary, if the Secretary has credible evidence or information indicating that a shipment of imported food presents a threat of serious adverse health consequences or death to humans or animals, to provide notice regarding such threat to the appropriate states.

Section 311 authorizes the Secretary to make grants to states, territories, and Indian tribes that undertake specified examinations, inspections, and investigations, and related activities.

Section 312 authorizes grants to states and Indian tribes to expand participation in networks to enhance federal, state, and local food safety efforts, including meeting the costs of establishing and maintaining the food safety surveillance, technical, and laboratory capacity needed for such participation. This section authorizes appropriations.

Section 313 directs the Secretary, through the Commissioner of Food and Drugs and the Director of the Centers for Disease Control and Prevention, and the Secretary of Agriculture to coordinate the surveillance of zoonotic diseases.

Section 314 authorizes the Secretary to commission officers and qualified employees of other federal departments or federal agencies, pursuant to a memorandum of understanding between the Secretary and the head of the Department or agency of such other Federal employees, to conduct examinations and inspections for the Secretary under the FDCA.

Subtitle B of Title III amends the FDCA to mandate annual registration, through electronic means, of foreign manufacturers (as well as the importers) engaged in the import of drug and device products into United States.

Section 322 mandates a chain of possession identification (manufacturer, processor, packer, distributor, and other possessors) for those firms that seek to import components of drugs, devices, food additives, color additives, or dietary supplements for further processing and export. This section requires certificates of analysis for components containing any chemical substance or biological substance intended for export.

Subtitle C of Title III of the new law ("General Provisions Relating to Upgrade of Agricultural Security ") authorizes the Secretary of Agriculture to utilize existing authorities to give high priority to enhancing and expanding the capacity of the Animal and Plant Health Inspection Service in order to conduct specified inspection activities. It authorizes automated recordkeeping for the Service as well as appropriations.

Section 332 authorizes the Secretary to utilize existing authorities to give high priority to enhancing and expanding the capacity of the Food Safety Inspection Service to conduct food safety inspection activities, and authorizes appropriations.

Section 333 authorizes appropriations for the purpose of enabling the Agricultural Research Service to conduct building upgrades to modernize specified existing facilities.

Section 334 authorizes grants to colleges and universities with programs in food and agricultural sciences to review security standards and practices at their facilities in order to protect against bioterrorist attacks. This section authorizes appropriations.

Section 335 authorizes the Secretary to utilize existing research authorities and research programs to protect the food supply of the United States by conducting and supporting research specified bioterrorism agricultural research and development activities. This section authorizes appropriations.

Section 336 revises federal criminal code provisions concerning animal enterprise terrorism penalties.[16]

2.10   Drinking Water Security and Safety

Title IV of the 2001 statute amends the Safe Drinking Water Act to require each community water system serving a population of greater than 3,300 persons to

- Conduct an assessment of the vulnerability of its system to a terrorist attack or other intentional acts intended to substantially disrupt the ability of the system to provide a safe and reliable supply of drinking water
- Certify that the system has conducted and submitted a written copy of the assessment
- Prepare or revise, where necessary, an emergency response plan that incorporates the results of the vulnerability assessments

This title provides for guidance and support, and authorizes appropriations.

Section 401 requires a review of current and future methods to prevent, detect, and respond to the intentional introduction of chemical, biological, or radiological contaminants into community water systems and source water for community water systems, as specified. This section requires a review of methods and means by which terrorists or other individuals or groups could disrupt the supply of safe drinking water or take other action against water collection, pretreatment, treatment, storage, and distribution facilities which could render such water significantly less safe for human consumption, as specified.

Section 403 increases penalties under the Safe Drinking Water Act for tampering with drinking water systems and authorizes appropriations.[17]

2.11   Additional Unrelated Provisions

Title V enacts several additional provisions unrelated to the primary purpose of the new law.

Subtitle A of Title V is characterized as the Prescription Drug User Fee Amendments of 2002. It amends the FDCA to revise provisions concerning definitions and the authority to assess and use drug fees. It also provides for appropriations.

Section 505 provides for public accountability with respect to goals for the review process concerning human drug applications.

Section 506 revises provisions concerning reports of post-marketing studies.

Section 507 sets forth an effective date, savings, and sunset clauses for the amendments adopted by Subtitle A.

Subtitle B of title V enacts certain funding provisions regarding the FDA. This subtitle provides for reserves, from amounts appropriated to the FDA, in amounts specified for the Office of Drug Safety.

Section 522 authorizes appropriations for the Division of Drug Marketing, Advertising, and Communications.

Section 523 authorizes appropriations for the Office of Generic Drugs.

Subtitle C of Title V directs the Federal Communications Commission to take certain actions intended to promote the orderly transition to digital television and to promote the equitable allocation and use of digital channels by television broadcast permittees and licensees.

Section 532 of Title V enacts certain provisions related to Medicare, and in particular provides for specified delays in the lock-in procedures for

Medicare+Choice plans; the deadline for Medicare+Choice plans to submit information on Medicare benefits, premiums, cost sharing, supplemental benefits, and actuarial values of such coverage; and the annual election period for Medicare enrollees to select a Medicare+Choice plan.[18]

3.0 Public Health Provisions of The Homeland Security Act of 2002 (PL 107-296)

While many of the public health elements of homeland security were addressed in the 2002 law described in the previous part, the Homeland Security Act of 2002 (HSA) included several additional public health provisions. Moreover, while the major DHHS agencies responsible for public health preparedness (CDC, FDA, etc.) remained with that department, the HSA did transfer certain responsibilities from DHHS to the new Department of Homeland Security.

Section 302 of the law identifies agencies and functions relevant to chemical, biological, radiological, and nuclear countermeasures that are to be transferred to the Department of Homeland Security. This transfer includes the select agent registration enforcement programs and activities of the Department of Health and Human Services.

Section 303 of the law requires the Secretary of Homeland Security to carry out civilian human health-related biological, biomedical, and infectious disease defense research and development responsibilities, through agreements with the Department of Health and Human Services, unless the president otherwise directs, and gives the Secretary specific transfer authority to fund such agreements. In carrying out these responsibilities, however, the Secretary retains full authority to establish the research and development program. The section also provides the Secretary with specific authority to fund other research and development projects that the Secretary elects to carry out through the Department of Health and Human Services or other federal agencies.

Section 502 of the law identifies agencies and functions relevant to emergency preparedness and response that are to be transferred to the Department of Homeland Security. The section identifies these offices within the Department of Health and Human Services: the Office of the Assistant Secretary for Public Health Emergency Preparedness (including the Office of Emergency Preparedness, the National Disaster Medical System, and the Metropolitan Medical Response System) and the Strategic National Stockpile of the Department of Health and Human Services.

Section 505 of the law requires the Secretary of Homeland Security to carry out the following responsibilities through agreements with the Department of

Health and Human Services, unless the president otherwise directs, and gives the Secretary specific transfer authority to fund such agreements: (1) all biological, chemical, radiological, and nuclear preparedness-related construction, renovation, and enhancement of security for research and development or other facilities owned or occupied by that Department; and (2) all public health-related activities being carried out by that department on the effective date of the bill (other than activities under functions transferred by the bill to the Department of Homeland Security) to assist state and local government personnel, agencies, or authorities, non-federal public and private healthcare facilities and providers, and public and non-profit health and educational facilities, to plan, prepare for, prevent, identify, and respond to biological, chemical, radiological, and nuclear events and public health emergencies. The Secretary retains full authority to establish the preparedness and response program when carrying out these duties.

Section 905 of the law amends certain provisions of the Public Health Security and Bioterrorism Preparedness and Response Act of 2002 (Pub. L. No. 107-188) by replacing references to the Department and Secretary of Health and Human Services with references to the Department and Secretary of Homeland Security.

Section 906 of the law amends certain provisions of the Public Health Service Act and Public Health Security and Bioterrorism Preparedness and Response Act of 2002, by replacing references to the Department and Secretary of Health and Human Services with references to the Department and Secretary of Homeland Security. [19]

4.0 Appropriations for the Public Health Aspects of Homeland Security

4.1 FY 2003 Appropriations

The fiscal 2003 omnibus appropriations bill, which President Bush signed into law as P.L. 108-7 on February 20, 2003, includes $3.5 billion in homeland security funds for first responders. The law authorizes homeland security funding for 22 agencies and divisions that are now a part of the Department of Homeland Security. Congressional appropriators provided the National Institutes of Health with $27.17 billion and the CDC with $4.3 billion for fiscal year 2003. The law omitted controversial language from the Homeland Security Act (PL 107-296) that would have protected pharmaceutical companies from lawsuits related to a mercury-based vaccine preservative that is the subject of contentious debate.[20]

Appropriations for first responders included funding for various campuses to establish first responder training programs. One such program is a center established by George Washington University and run in cooperation with George Mason University and Shenandoah University. This particular center researches best practices related to terrorism response.[21]

HHS on March 20, 2003, announced the availability of $1.4 billion to states for funding bioterrorism and public health preparedness. This amount includes $498 million specifically for hospital preparedness. Federal funding allocations to states is now, as it was for fiscal year 2002, contingent upon HHS approval of state plans. One exception to this requirement is funding immediately available to support implementation of the administration's smallpox vaccination program as well as activities already approved for fiscal year 2002.[22] Concerning the distribution process, states have reported difficulty in drawing down federal funds from fiscal year 2002 appropriations while HHS officials maintain that states have neglected to collect millions of dollars in available funds by failing to submit funding plans. Local governments, in the meantime, report having to shift valuable resources away from planned projects to boost counterterrorism programs.[23]

4.2   FY 2002 Appropriations

President Bush on January 10, 2002, signed supplemental appropriations legislation providing $2.9 billion for HHS for bioterrorism preparedness funding. As the lead federal agency in bioterrorism threat preparation, HHS plans to work closely with states, local governments, and the private sector to expand the public health infrastructure and research into potential bioterror diseases. With these supplemental appropriations, HHS Secretary Tommy Thompson announced on January 25, 2002, an initial installment of more than $200 million in funding for state and local resources. HHS in fiscal year 2002 focused its appropriations on

- Fortifying the federal/state/local public health network ($940 million)
- Helping hospitals prepare to cope with bioterror incidents ($135 million)
- Support for community emergency preparedness [OEP] ($51 million)
- Expanding the National Pharmaceutical Stockpile ($645 million)
- Purchasing new smallpox vaccine ($512 million)
- NIH-supported research ($248 million)
- FDA food safety and drug/vaccine preparedness ($145 million)
- Enhanced CDC capacity, especially lab capacity ($116 million)[24]

HHS on January 25, 2002, also announced more than $200 million in funding for the first installment of $1 billion designated for rebuilding state and local public health infrastructures. This funding was specifically focused on the Metropolitan Medical Response System (MMRS), the Lab Network, Hospital Planning, the Health Alert Network, and the National Emergency Stockpile.[25]

MMRS funding would add 25 new cities to those that have already received funding in past years and will mean that 80 percent of the U.S. population will be covered by an MMRS plan. This funding will be used to expand the MMRS lab network and to enhance lab capabilities. Funds targeting hospital planning would be used by states to create regional hospital plans to respond in the event of a bioterror attack. Funds also targeted the Health Alert Network (HAN), which is a developing communications network used by the CDC to communicate with state and local health departments regarding possible disease outbreaks or to provide warning if a disease outbreak is known to exist somewhere in the country. Another funding target was the National Emergency Stockpile. Funds in the $2.9 billion supplemental bill increased the number of available Push Packages that contain medical supplies that would be needed in a disaster including a bioterror attack.

On January 31, 2002, HHS Secretary Tommy G. Thompson sent letters to governors detailing how much of $1.1 billion in funding, from the $2.9 billion announced on January 10, 2002, each state would receive to help them strengthen public health emergency response capacity. The funds were designed to support developing comprehensive bioterrorism preparedness plans; upgrading infectious disease surveillance and investigation; enhancing the readiness of hospital systems to deal with large numbers of casualties; expanding public health laboratory and communications capacities; and improving connectivity between hospitals, and city, local and state health departments to enhance disease reporting.

Funding for states and communities was divided into three parts. The first part was provided by the Centers for Disease Control and Prevention (CDC) and targeted supporting bioterrorism, infectious diseases, and public health emergency preparedness activities statewide. Each state's allocation consisted of an initial $5 million award, supplemented by an amount based on its population. HRSA distributed the second portion of the funds, to be used by states to create regional hospital plans to respond in the event of a bioterrorism attack. The third portion of the funds was to be awarded by the HHS Office of Emergency Preparedness for the support of the Metropolitan Medical Response System (MMRS). The MMRS funding will adds 25 new cities to those that have already received funds in past years. This funding establishes that 80 percent of the U.S. population will be covered by an MMRS plan. MMRS contracts are intended to improve local jurisdictions' ability to respond to the possible release of a chemical or biological disease agent, but it also serves to improve local response to any event involving mass casualties. [26]

States have authorization to immediately begin spending up to 20 percent of their allotments. Release of the remaining 80 percent of the $1.1 billion is contingent on submission of a state budget plan that HHS reviews and approves. HHS must complete its review of each plan within 30 days of receipt. Each statewide plan must outline how it would respond to a bioterrorism event and other outbreaks of infectious disease, and also how it plans to other strengthen essential public health capacities. Finally, a state's governor must endorse the statewide plan.

A state must designate a Coordinator for hospital preparedness planning and a Senior Public Health Official within its primary health department to serve as Executive Director of the State Bioterrorism Preparedness and Response Program. A state must also establish an advisory committee to include representatives from (included but not limited to)

- State and local health departments and government
- Emergency Management Agencies
- Emergency Medical Services
- Office of Rural Health
- Police, fire department, and emergency rescue workers and occupational health workers
- Other healthcare providers, including university, academic medical, and public health
- Community health centers
- Red Cross and other voluntary organizations
- The hospital community (to include Veterans Affairs and military hospitals)[27]

A state must submit timelines for various aspects of its preparedness plan, addressing statewide and regional plans, along with other implementation priorities. A state must establish a hospital bio-preparedness planning committee, (affiliated with the state-wide bioterrorism advisory committee) whose composition includes representation from emergency medical services, emergency management agencies, an Office of Rural Health, state hospital associations, Veterans Affairs and military hospitals, and primary care associations. A state must assess statutes, regulations, and ordinances that provide for credentialing, licensure, and delegation of authority for executing emergency public health activities. It must develop a plan and identify personnel to be trained to receive and distribute critical stockpile items and manage a mass distribution of vaccine and/or antibiotics on a 24 hours a day, seven days a week basis. It must also develop a plan to receive and evaluate urgent disease reports from all parts of the jurisdiction on a 24 hours a day, seven days a week basis. A state must develop a plan to improve working relationships and communication between Level A (clinical) laboratories and Level B/C laboratories, (i.e., Laboratory Response Network laboratories) as well as with other public health officials. [28]

The CDC proposal for public health preparedness asked states to designate a senior public health official to head a state bioterrorism program, establish a bioterrorism advisory committee, prepare timelines for state and regional incidence response plans, and create plans to improve communications among health and law enforcement officials. The HRSA awards were designed to target hospital preparedness, including designating a hospital bioterrorism preparedness coordinator and planning committee to work with state health departments, and creating a preparedness plan for handling epidemics.[29]

HHS on June 6, 2002, announced its approval of 24 state and two city bioterrorism preparedness plans, thereby releasing 80 percent of their share of nearly $1.1 billion in bioterrorism grants. Twenty-four states and one city received only a portion of their designated funding, pending full approval of their preparedness plans.[30]

California received the largest grant ($56.6 million) under the HHS funding plan. Los Angeles received $13.6 million, with another $9 million pending CDC's approval of California's state plan. Florida's bioterrorism funding award of $32.5 million was among the larger awards, and Florida will likely gain additional HRSA funding, pending state plan approval. Funding for the states is generally proportional to population size, with rural states receiving lowest grant awards.

President Bush on June 12, 2002, signed into law bioterrorism bill H.R. 3448, a bill to improve prevention, preparation for, and response to bioterrorism and other public health emergencies. The law authorized $1.6 billion in fiscal year 2002 grants for states and local governments to dedicate to hospital and clinic preparedness activities, including the training of healthcare professionals. Of this amount, Congressional conferees earmarked $1.1 million for state and local governments, including $520 million for hospital preparedness. As noted above, states must submit applications, essentially bioterrorism response plans, meeting HHS criteria to qualify for the funding. The legislation authorizes $1.15 billion for the HHS National Pharmaceutical Stockpile, including $509 million for building up a stockpile of smallpox vaccines. The CDC was designated to receive $300 million for fiscal years 2002 and 2003, to upgrade its facilities. Additional allocations include $133 million for the Department of Veterans Affairs to secure its medical and research facilities, for training, and for establishing a system for tracking pharmaceuticals.[31]

President Bush signed homeland security fiscal year 2002 supplemental spending legislation (H.R. 4775; Public Law 107-206) on August 2, 2002. The new law emerged following negotiations over how to limit spending to $28.8 billion, in accordance with instructions to Congress from President Bush to limit discretionary spending to that amount. Congressional conferees agreed on a measure that was $100 million above the president's target and passed it, appropriating $14.5 billion for national defense and the war on terrorism, with $387 million for bioterrorism response. The bioterrorism response funding was for strengthening toxicology and infectious disease laboratory capacity.[32]

Fiscal year 2002 bioterrorism funding can be summarized as follows:

Congress provided a total of $5.138 billion for bioterrorism response, including $1.408 billion through the regular fiscal year appropriations process and an additional $3.730 billion in the fiscal year spending supplemental. The supplemental funding includes $2.5 million for HHS to support a number of activities, including

- $865 million for upgrading state and local health capacity
- $135 million for grants to hospitals to increase capacity
- $100 million for upgrading capacity at CDC
- $85 million to NIAID for bioterrorism-related research
- $70 million for NIAID to construct a biosafety laboratory and related infrastructure costs
- $71 million for improving lab security at the NIH and CDC
- $593 for the National Pharmaceutical Stockpile
- $512 million for the smallpox vaccine
- $10 million for the Substance Abuse and Mental Health Services Administration
- $55.8 million to the Office of the Secretary for coordination of the Department's activities concerning preparedness and response[33]

5.0   National Pharmaceutical Stockpile and Project BioShield

5.1   Overview

A release of selected biological or chemical agents targeting the U.S. civilian population will require rapid access to large quantities of pharmaceuticals and medical supplies. Such quantities may not be readily available without maintenance of a stockpile. As part of the Department of Health and Human Services

1999 Bioterrorism Preparedness and Response Program, CDC led an effort working with governmental and non-governmental partners to upgrade the nations' public health capacity to respond to biological and chemical terrorism and establish a Bioterrorism Preparedness and Response Program. This initiative must ensure that capacity development at federal, state, and local levels. The National Pharmaceutical Stockpile Program (NPSP) is one response component of CDC's larger Bioterrorism Preparedness and Response Initiative.[34]

The goal of the CDC NPSP is to ensure the availability of pharmaceuticals, antibiotics, and chemical interventions as well as medical, surgical and patient support supplies, and equipment for prompt delivery to the site of a disaster, including a possible biological or chemical terrorist attack. The NPSP has resources to supplement the initial response to an incident of biological or chemical terrorism, from local and state emergency, medical, and public healthcare personnel. NPSP would provide critical drugs and medical material that would otherwise be unavailable to local communities.

The CDC coordinates with national security agencies to obtain updates and analyses of threat agents and to ensure that the NPSP reflects current needs. The CDC convenes expert panels to prioritize biological agents such as smallpox, anthrax, pneumonic plague, tularemia, botulinum toxin, and viral hemorrhagic fevers. Anthrax, plague, and tularemia can be effectively treated with antibiotics that are immediately available; therefore, these products are a purchasing priority for the NPSP formulary. The NPSP maintains a cache of vaccine available to address smallpox threats. The NPSP includes medical equipment that would be essential for treatment, including airway supplies, bandages and dressings, and other emergency medications. These particular items are ones that local clinicians may find in short supply in the event of a terrorism incident. A CDC team of five or six technical advisors will also deploy at the same time as the first shipment. Known as a Technical Advisory Response Unit (TARU), this team is comprised of pharmacists, emergency responders, and logistics experts who will advise local authorities on receiving, distributing, dispensing, replenishing, and recovering NPS material.[35]

5.2 Components of the National Pharmaceutical Stockpile

The NPSP has two basic components. The first consists of eight 12-hour Push Packages for immediate response that are fully stocked, positioned in environmentally controlled and secured warehouses, and ready for immediate deployment to reach any affected area within 12 hours of a federal decision to release the assets. A 12-hour Push Package is a preassembled set of supplies, pharmaceuticals, and medical equipment ready for quick delivery. Each package contains 50 tons of material intended to address a mass casualty incident. The packages would permit emergency medical staff to treat a variety of different agents, since the actual threat may not be identified at the time of the stockpile deployment.

The second component is comprised of Vendor Managed Inventory (VMI) material. Distribution of VMI packages would begin if an incident requires a larger or mulit-phased response and would arrive to their intended destination within 24 to 36 hours. The VMI packages contain pharmaceuticals and supplies in quantities estimated to effective address a suspected or confirmed agent or combination of agents.

These packages are stored in strategic locations around the United States to ensure rapid delivery anywhere in the country. Following a decision to deploy, the NPS will typically arrive by air or ground in two phases. The first phase shipment is the 12-hour Push Package, and the second phase is the VMI packages.

The NPS Program was tested in response to the tragic events of September 11th when New York State and local officials requested large quantities of medical material and logistical assistance. The CDC has since determined that all facets of the New York operation performed as intended, with the support of local and state public health and emergency response officials. The NPS Program also assisted states and cities with pharmaceutical and logistical support to areas affected by the anthrax attacks in October and November 2001.

To receive NPS assets, an affected state can directly request the deployment of the NPS from the Director of CDC. Once requested, the Director of CDC has the authority, in consultation with the Surgeon General, and the Secretary of Health and Human Services, to order the deployment of the NPS.

5.3   Training and Education

CDC is charged with leading a nationwide preparedness training and education program for state and local healthcare providers, first responders, and governments (to include Federal officials, Governors' offices, state and local health departments, and emergency management agencies). This training alerts state and local emergency response officials to the important issues they must plan for in order to receive, secure, and distribute NPS assets.

5.4   Project Bioshield

President Bush announced Project BioShield during his 2003 State of the Union address. The goal of Project BioShield is to ensure that resources are available to pay for effective drugs and vaccines to protect against attack by biological and chemical weapons or other dangerous pathogens. The legislation that would implement the president's proposal is called the Biodefense Improvement and Treatment for America Act. The measure would would ensure that the availability of "next-generation" medical countermeasures. Project BioShield would allow the government to buy improved vaccines or drugs for smallpox, anthrax, and botulinum toxin. The cost of the project is estimated to be $6 billion over ten years. Funds would be available through the project to purchase countermeasures to protect against other dangerous pathogens, such as Ebola and plague, as soon as scientists verify the safety and effectiveness of these products. The project would strengthen development capabilities at the National Institutes of Health by speeding research and development on medical countermeasures, based on emerging scientific discoveries. It would direct the Food and Drug Administration to make promising treatments quickly available in emergency situations.[36] The Senate's Health, Education, Labor, and Pensions Committee (HELP) on March 19, 2003, approved S 15, the Project BioShield legislation. The measure was reported to the Senate on March 25, 2003.[37]

6.0   Lessons of SARS: The Dilemmas of Privacy, Isolation, and Quarantine

The recent outbreak of Severe Acute Respiratory Syndrome (SARS), caused by a virulent and previously unknown virus, provides many lessons for public health authorities preparing for bioterrorism. Indeed, the manner in which SARS has been spread beyond China's Guangdong Province, where the virus is thought to have made its first leap into humans, is virtually identical to one method terrorists might use to intentionally release a biological weapon. Infecting one individual (or a small group) with a little known but highly infectious biological agent, then sending such individuals out to infect whole populations, is certainly one method of attack for which we must be prepared. This process of infection is precisely what happened with SARS, in places as diverse as Vietnam, Singapore, Hong Kong, and Toronto.

This experience points to areas where the legal system and not just the public health infrastructure may require further attention. By the time SARS was identified as a new and potentially deadly disease, broad exposure had already occurred, particularly in public areas, such as airplanes and hotels, and among healthcare workers caring for the early cases. In the process of continuing to learn about SARS and the behavior of the virus that causes it, public health officials have learned the importance of early communication about the disease, early identification of its symptoms, rapid and effective isolation of infected patients, and quarantine of healthy individuals who might have been exposed to the virus. At the same time, we have also learned that the legal framework in each of these areas, at least in the United States, may not be adequate to implement the required protections.

One area where there is a potential clash between legal constraints and the need for rapid response is in the area of the privacy and confidentiality of patient records and information. Privacy and confidentiality is now regulated by the Health Insurance Portability And Accountability Act Of 1996 (P.L. 104-191). Yet, the interaction between HIPAA requirements and the need to move quickly to respond to an act of bioterror or other public health emergency remains ambiguous.[38]

On the one hand, HIPAA's rules governing the privacy[39] and security[40] of confidential patient information provide strong protections for patients. Additionally, they establish relatively narrow parameters for compliance by doctors, hospitals, and entities covered by the new law (known as "covered entities"). The law does permit covered entities to release a patient's "protected health information" (PHI) under certain circumstances, which includes a "public health emergency." Even in such an emergency, there would remain limits on the release of PHI sufficient to contribute to the already substantial concern (and confusion among many covered entities over complying with the new law).

At the same time, there is concern (especially among civil libertarians) that the public health emergency "loophole" may itself be overly broad. This could afford public health officials too much discretion in determining that an emergency exists and overly broad powers in demanding the release of PHI or fashioning an appropriate response. Further clarification of these concerns and ambiguities is clearly warranted.[41]

Once the existence of a highly infectious biological agent in a population of people is confirmed, it is also clear from the SARS experience that rapid reaction must include both isolation of the sick and quarantine of the healthy. It is best, of course, if such steps can be implemented rapidly on a voluntary basis. This appears to have been the case thus far with SARS in the United States, and it is credited with minimizing its spread (and the risk), at least as of this writing. Of course, luck also plays a role in minimizing the impact of a new or alien disease, but while the voluntary response to date by both providers and the public has been encouraging, some observers are nevertheless concerned that we may not be able to rely only on luck and voluntarism in every case. As a number of commentators have recently noted, U.S. laws governing isolation and quarantine are often archaic or ambiguous, and thus potentially ineffective in a major emergency.

There have been sporadic attempts to impose isolation and quarantine requirements on various segments of the population since the early history of the United States. The CDC website provides an excellent history of the federal laws of isolation and quarantine. Even before 1776, protecting citizens from exposure to imported diseases was considered a local matter, to be addressed by the colonies. Yellow fever epidemics of the mid-nineteenth century resulted in the passage of federal quarantine legislation by Congress in 1878. This legislation affirmed states' rights but also served to increase federal involvement in quarantine activities. In 1892, cholera outbreaks necessitated a reinterpretation of the law to provide the federal government with authority to impose quarantine requirements. Congress in 1893 further clarified the federal role in quarantine activities, establishing additional federal oversight of local quarantine stations, and by 1921 federal jurisdiction over quarantine was complete.[42]

The codification of the Public Health Service Act in 1944 established quarantine authority for the federal government to prevent the introduction, transmission, and spread of communicable diseases from foreign countries into the United States. Quarantine, originally part of the Treasury Department, was, by 1967, transferred to the National Communicable Disease Center, now known as the Centers for Disease Control and Prevention. Quarantine by this time had developed into a large organization with 55 quarantine stations located at every port, international airport, and major border crossing. The CDC reduced the size of the quarantine program during the 1970s and altered its focus from one of routine inspection to program management and problem intervention. The Division of Global Migration and Quarantine currently has authority to detain, medically examine, or conditionally release individuals suspected of carrying a communicable disease. The list of quarantinable diseases, contained in an Executive Order of the President, includes cholera, diphtheria, infectious tuberculosis, plague, smallpox, yellow fever, and viral hemorrhagic fevers, such as Marburg, Ebola and Congo-Crimean.[43]

Federal laws and regulations governing quarantine powers can be found in the United States Code at 42 U.S.C. §264, and the Code of Federal Regulations at 42 C.F.R. §71. While state and local health departments constitute a primary source of cooperation for quarantine activities, CDC responsibilities include but are not limited to

- Monitoring the quality of medical examinations and documentation of aliens abroad and in the United States
- Notifying state and local health departments of the arrival of refugees in their jurisdiction
- Overseeing the screening of arriving international travelers for symptoms of illness that could be of public health significance
- Providing travelers with essential health information through publications, automated fax, and the Internet
- Undertaking special projects in response to immigration emergencies and/or threats posed by emerging infections

- Collecting and disseminate worldwide health data
- Ensuring timely distribution of investigational drugs and immunobiologics to patients in order to minimize morbidity and mortality
- Performing inspections of maritime vessels and cargos for infectious disease threats[44]

The CDC has Quarantine Stations in the international airports in New York, Chicago, Miami, Atlanta, Los Angeles, San Francisco, Seattle, and Honolulu. Each station has responsibility for all ports, seaports, and international airports in an assigned region. Public Health Advisors stationed in various countries oversee medical screening of immigrants and refugees and monitor individuals for illness and imported items for other public health significance.[45]

To a certain extent, this entire regulatory and bureaucratic framework is inadequate to thwart both intentional acts of bioterrorism and inadvertent introduction of new or mutant diseases. For one thing, it was developed to respond to threats with largely known parameters—immigrants arriving on our shores, often en masse, from parts of the world where known diseases posed known risks. The SARS experience to date clearly shows that a small number of individuals travelling on international flights can spread disease today in a matter of hours to the far corners of the earth. Even as public health officials began to know what to look for, the disease's pre-symptom gestation period, and the fact that some of its symptoms mirror that of influenza or the common cold make effective reaction a challenge. The danger of over-reaction in some cases, and under-reaction in others, is very real. Add to this mix an intent to deceive which would be part of a bioterror attack and which would effectively thwart all but the most knowledgeable and observant "first responders," it is clear that our federal system and the laws and regulations that underpin it are simply inadequate.

7.0   Model State Emergency Health Powers Act

Quarantine laws at the state level are also often inadequate, a problem that the authors of the Model State Emergency Health Powers Act (MSEHPA) sought to address. Twenty-two states have passed all or part of the MSEHPA, thereby expanding state authority in the event of an emergency.[46]

7.1   Overview

The Model State Emergency Health Powers Act is a guide for states to establish a legislative framework for responding rapidly to public health emergencies. The basic premise of the Act is that each state is responsible for safeguarding the public health and security of its citizens. It specifies the powers and duties of states to compile data and to ascertain and meet threats to the public health and sets limits to prevent unlawful discrimination and other civil rights violations. The Centers for Disease Control and Prevention in 2001 funded the Center for Law and the Public's Health at Georgetown and Johns Hopkins Universities to develop a Model State Emergency Health Powers Act. The current draft provides an outline of the issues state policymakers must consider as they assess the adequacy of their existing emergency powers statutes. Such consideration includes recognizing measures to detect and track potential and existing public health emergencies, provisions to define and declare a public health emergency, powers to control property and persons during a state of emergency, requirements related to public communication, and provisions to mandate planning for an emergency.

Critics of the draft model law maintain that government is already empowered with the authority to deal with crisis situations and that this statutory language is unnecessary. Others critics have identified gaps in the model language relating to the regulation of healthcare financing (for example, the power of insurers to exclude from coverage treatments related to public health emergencies). Civil rights advocates have voiced concern that the model statute places excessive emphasis on public health powers at the expense of individual civil liberties.

Supporters insist that the new era of heightened security requires change, or at least substantive debate, about public health powers and authorities and that this model statute provides a framework for discussing important, if controversial, issues.

The issues addressed by the model law include defining who can declare a public health emergency and the circumstances under which this action can be taken, the extent of government power to detain individuals and seize property, and the balance of decision-making authority between governors and state legislatures.

Thirty-six state legislatures and the District of Columbia have introduced the model law, in whole or part, through bills or resolutions. Twenty states (Arizona, Delaware, Florida, Georgia, Hawaii, Maine, Maryland, Minnesota, Mississippi, New Hampshire, New Mexico, North Carolina, Oklahoma, South Carolina, South Dakota, Tennessee, Utah, Vermont, Virginia, Wisconsin) and the District of Columbia have passed bills or resolutions that include provisions from, or that are closely related to, the model law. In 2002, 29 state legislatures indicated that public health preparedness would be a priority during their legislative session.[47]

The model law authorizes the Governor to appoint a Public Health Emergency Planning Commission. In the event of a public health emergency, it would authorize the Governor to inform the state's public, activate state and local disaster response, use stockpiled resources, suspend regulations that hinder necessary action, and mobilize organized militia.

7.2   Key Provisions of MSEHPA

The model law would authorize the Public Health Authority (the state's primary public health agency) to transfer management of healthcare institutions, seize facilities, compel services, and control disposal of corpses and infectious waste. The Public Health Authority would be authorized to evacuate and/or control facilities, roads, and public areas; ration/control distribution of healthcare supplies, food, fuel, clothing, firearms, etc. for emergency response; compel people to submit to medical examination, isolation, quarantine, vaccination, and treatment; collect specimens and test people or animals; and follow chain-of-custody procedures. It also establishes specific reporting requirements.

The model law further authorizes the Public Health Authority to

- Identify and investigate any health condition that poses substantial risk of a significant number of fatalities or disabilities and ensure they are subject to proper control.
- Interview people thought to have been exposed to relevant health conditions so that it can ensure positive identification.
- Seize any facility or material when a danger to public health is suspected. The PSA shall enforce any order the PHA gives to carry out these powers, and it also shall report any threatening conditions, clusters, or suspicious events.

The model law provides for isolating or quarantining and states that anyone isolated or quarantined may petition the state court for release or remedy according to procedures specified. State agencies and officials acting under this Act are not liable for those actions except in cases of gross negligence or willful misconduct. The liability of private parties acting under state direction pursuant to a state of public health emergency under this Act is also limited. If property is commandeered or otherwise used in coping with a declared state of public health emergency, compensation is calculated according to the procedures for eminent domain.

8.0   Smallpox Vaccination Efforts

8.1   Overview

One of the most controversial anti-terrorism actions taken by the Bush administration thus far is its smallpox immunization plan. Announced in December 2002, the plan involves the mandatory immunization of 500,000 military personnel and the voluntary vaccination of as many as 10.5 million medical workers and emergency responders, using live vaccinia of the kind that had last been used over 30 years ago, prior to the eradication of smallpox in the United States and globally. The first phase of voluntary immunizations was launched in January 2003 under an ambitious timetable to vaccinate 500,000 hospital and public health workers by March 1, 2003. Actual participation in the initiative, however, failed to meet administration expectations. As of April 25, 2003, only 34,531 individuals had received the vaccination under the program.[48]

Hospitals, public health departments and individual healthcare providers have expressed a variety of concerns about implementing the program. There are numerous clinical issues behind these concerns. They include the risk and severity of vaccinia side effects and the risk of newly immunized workers spreading smallpox to co-workers, family members, and immuno-compromised patients. It is also generally acknowledged that smallpox is one of a relatively large number of potential agents that might be used as a biological weapon and is likely more difficult to use than many others.

As a result, many hospitals and public health departments have elected not to immunize workers until there is a smallpox outbreak, until the pathogen is found outside of laboratories in the United States and Russia where it is known to be stored, or until the federal government articulates a more specific threat of smallpox being used as a bioterrorism weapon.

At the same time, in part due to the possibility that an actual smallpox case could present and be contagious before the patient developed the tell-tale scabs associated with the disease, other hospitals and health departments have volunteered to move ahead with the vaccination program. Such providers have implemented several mechanisms to reduce the clinical risk associated with the vaccine, including only vaccinating employees who have already been immunized— usually as children, before the United States stopped requiring smallpox immunizations in 1972. Furthermore, any employee living with individuals at high-risk for complications from vaccinia can be barred or discouraged from participating in the program. Certain categories of employees were also excluded, including those who routinely work with vulnerable patients and those not likely to be on the front lines of any smallpox outbreak. Doctors and nurses in the neonatal intensive care unit could also be exempt from participation

Most hospitals and health departments require staff who volunteer to be immunized to also complete extensive informed consent documents issued by the CDC. Precautions can also be taken once a volunteer receives the vaccine, such as requiring that they wear long sleeves and dressings covering the inoculation site during the three-week period when the newly immunized are potentially infectious.

8.2 Liability Issues

For as long as there have been mass immunization initiatives in America, there has been a legal debate over issues related to liability and legal responsibility. As long ago as 1905, the U.S. Supreme Court ruled that the greater benefits to society permitted states to enact laws requiring individuals to be punished if they refused to be vaccinated against smallpox.[49] In the early 1970s, fear over a new and potentially deadly influenza virus known as swine flu prompted an unprecedented initiative to vaccinate tens of millions of Americans. In order to induce manufacturers to produce the needed vaccine quickly, the Congress passed a law partially relieving them of liability and instead providing federal compensation for patients who might be injured by the swine flu vaccine.[50] Indeed, while the swine flu itself never materialized as a major health threat, a number of individuals were injured by the vaccine itself and in some cases received substantial compensation.

The Homeland Security Act of 2002 sought to address the issue of liability and immunity in Section 304. However, as summarized in the Smallpox Injury and Law Guide of the Smallpox Vaccine Injury Law Project, the protections afforded by those provisions were considered unacceptably ambiguous and inadequate by much of the provider community.[51] These concerns have been heightened by reports of possibly deadly (and previously unknown) risks for individuals with a history of cardiac problems.

Because liability and risk management concerns have thus continued to be impediments for many hospitals and health departments, Congress proposed, debated, and negotiated various compensation packages, including the administration's compensation proposal. Ultimately they agreed on the Smallpox Emergency Personnel Protection Act of 2003 (H.R. 1770) and President Bush signed it into law on April 30, 2003 (PL No. 108-20). Under the law, individuals who become permanently disabled from the vaccine may qualify for up to $50,000 per year in lost wages, with no cap on the amount compensation over a lifetime. The law provides that individuals who receive the vaccine and become partially disabled may also qualify for up to $50,000 per year in lost wages, although with a lifetime cap of $262,100. A spouse of an individual who receives the vaccine and dies as a result may qualify for $262,100. If there are dependent children, the surviving spouse may receive a $262,100 lump sum, or $50,000 per year until the youngest child reaches age 18. The law authorizes a person who is dissatisfied with the compensation to file suit under the Federal Tort Claims Act.[52]

9.0   Joint Commission

The Joint Commission on Accreditation of Healthcare Organizations (JCAHO), is a voluntary accrediting body that has also developed guidelines to enhance community mobilization to develop emergency response capabilities for terrorist attacks.[53] In a March 2003 report, JCAHO identifies barriers to optimal public health emergency response capabilities. The accrediting organization notes that severe staffing shortages currently facing many hospitals could further reduce the capacity of these facilities to deliver emergency care. The report cites increasing liability insurance premiums for physicians that are limiting the availability of critical specialists in certain jurisdictions as a problem. Other possible barriers include current state budget shortfalls that are resulting in cuts to the Medicaid rolls, Medicare cuts in hospital reimbursement, and increasing numbers of uninsured. JCAHO highlights a need for a "surge capacity"—the ability to care for perhaps hundreds to thousands more patients at a given time—but notes that many hospitals are already operating at full capacity. The federal government's plan enlisted state governments to allocate federal funds to their hospitals beginning in 2001. In many states, however, the money has not yet reached hospitals and some local public health agencies. Hospitals and their communities are working understand how to begin preparing for a public health emergency.

JCAHO highlights a need for templates or scalable models of community-wide preparedness to guide planning before an emergency and actions taken during and after an emergency. Given the urgency for community-based emergency preparedness and the barriers to achieving this goal across the country, JCAHO convened a Public Policy Roundtable to discuss emergency preparedness issues and propose steps medical facilities and local communities can take to prepare for a terrorist attack or other emergencies. The discussants determined that community participation is essential for local response preparation; coordinators should focus on aspects of the preparedness system that will preserve the ability of community health care resources to care for patients, protect staff, and serve the public; and coordinators must establish accountability, oversight, leadership, and sustainment of community preparedness systems.

The JACHO guidelines are as follows:

I.   Enlist the Community in Preparing the Local Response

- Initiate and facilitate the development of community-based emergency preparedness programs across the country.
- Constitute community organizations that comprise all of the key participants—as appropriate to the community—to develop the community-wide emergency preparedness program.
- Encourage the transition of community health care resources from an organization-focused approach to emergency preparedness to one that encompasses the community.
- Provide the community organization with necessary funding and other resources and hold it accountable for overseeing the planning, assessment, and maintenance of the preparedness program.
- Encourage the pursuit of substantive collaborative activities that will also serve to bridge the gap between the medical care and public health systems.
- Develop and distribute emergency planning and preparedness templates for potential adaptation by various types of communities.

II.   Focus on the Key Aspects of the Preparedness System That Will Preserve the Ability of Community Healthcare Resources to Care for Patients, Protect Staff, and Serve the Public

- Prospectively define point-in-time and longitudinal surge capacity at the community level.
- Establish mutual aid agreements among community hospitals and other healthcare organizations.
- Ensure a 48 to 72 hour stand-alone capability through the appropriate stockpiling of necessary medications and supplies.
- Fund and facilitate the creation of a credentialing database to support a national emergency volunteer system for healthcare professionals.
- Make direct caregivers the highest priority for training and for receipt of protective equipment, vaccinations, prophylactic antibiotics, chemical antidotes, and other protective measures.
- Support the provision of decontamination capabilities in each hospital.
- Maintain the ability to provide routine care.
- Make provision for the graceful degradation of care.

- Provide for waiver of regulatory requirements under conditions of extreme emergency.
- Adopt incident management approaches that provide for simultaneous management involvement by multiple authorities and fluidity of authority.
- Make provisions for accommodating and managing the substantial acute mental health needs of the community.
- Directly address the fear created by terrorist acts through targeted education, application of risk reduction strategies, and the teaching of coping skills.
- Provide public education about emergency preparedness.
- Actively engage the public in emergency preparedness planning.
- Anticipate the information needs of the community.
- Create redundant, interoperable communications capabilities.
- Develop a centralized community-wide patient locator system.
- Engage the mass media in the emergency preparedness planning process.
- Regularly test, at least yearly, community emergency preparedness plans through reality-based drills.
- Ensure the inclusion of all community emergency preparedness program participants in the plan tests.

III. Establish Accountability, Oversight, Leadership, and Sustainment of Community Preparedness Systems

- Develop and implement objective evaluation methods for assessing the substance and effectiveness of local emergency preparedness plans.
- Provide funding at the local level for emergency preparedness planning.
- Explore alternative options for providing sustained funding for hospital emergency preparedness activities.
- Initiate and fund public-private sector partnerships that are charged to conduct research on and develop relevant, scalable templates for emergency preparedness plans that will meet local community needs.
- Disseminate information about existing best practices and lessons learned respecting existing emergency preparedness initiatives.
- Clarify the applications of EMTALA, HIPAA, EPA, and other regulatory requirements in emergency situations.
- Coordinate domestic and international emergency preparedness efforts.

Endnotes:

1   The author is indebted to Laura Ogelman for her assistance in researching and writing this chapter and to David Inoue for his research assistance.

2   Garrett, Laurie. 2000. Betrayal of Trust: The Collapse of Global Public Health (Hyperion).

3   Annas, George J. "Bioterrorism, Public Health, and Civil Liberties." *NEJM*, 346: 17. 1337–1342. 25 April 2002.

4   Clarke, David. "Amid Terror Attack Warnings, Hospitals Say They Are Ready." *CQ Homeland Security—Local Response.* 13 March 2003.

5   U.S. Centers for Disease Control and Prevention, available at http://www.cdc.gov.

6   U.S. Department of Health and Human Services. "17 Critical Benchmarks for Bioterrorism Preparedness Planning." 6 June 2002.

7   Kady, Martin II. "Underfunded First Responders Put Conservatives in a Bind." *Congressional Quarterly Weekly—Homeland Security.* 29 March 2003. 760.

8   U.S. Department of Health and Human Services. "Bioterror Funding Provides Blueprint to Build a Strong New Public Health Infrastructure." HHS Press Office. 25 January 2002.

9   Congressional Research Service. CRS Report for Congress. "Public Health Security and Bioterrorism Preparedness and Response Act (P.L. 107-188): Provisions and Changes to Preexisting Law." Penny Hill Press. 21 August 2002.

10 Altman, Lawrence K., and Gina Kolata, "A Nation Challenged: Anthrax; Anthrax Missteps Offer Guide to Fight Next Bioterror Battle." *The New York Times.* 6 January 2002. A1.

11 Library of Congress. Thomas, H.R. 3448 Bill Summary and Status for the 107th Congress, Congressional Research Service summary. Available at http://thomas.loc.gov.

12 *Ibid.*

13 *Ibid.*

14 *Ibid.*

15 *Ibid.*

16 *Ibid.*

17 *Ibid.*

18 *Ibid.*

19 The White House. Analysis for the Homeland Security Act of 2002, available at http://www.whitehouse.gov/deptofhomeland/analysis/hsl-bill-analysis.pdf.

20 Kady, Martin II. "Funding Homeland Security." *CQ Weekly Publications.* 15 February 2003.

21 Clark, David. "University Medical Schools Join Homeland Security Funding Bonanza." *CQ Homeland Security—Local Response.* 7 March 2003.

22 U.S. Department of Health and Human Services. "HHS Announces Bioterrorism Aid for States, Including Special Opportunity for Advance Funding." HHS Press Office. 20 March 2003.

23 Logan, Christopher. "Local Governments Say (Again) They Need $9 Billion More for Homeland Security." *CQ Homeland Security—Local Response.* 26 March 2003.

24 U.S. Department of Health and Human Services. "Bioterror Funding Provides Blueprint to Build a Strong New Public Health Infrastructure. HHS Press Release." 25 January 2002.

25 *Ibid.*

[26] U.S. Department of Health and Human Services. "Federal Funds for Public Health Infrastructure Begins to Flow to States." HHS Press Release. 25 January 2002.

[27] U.S. Department of Health and Human Services. "HHS announces $1.1 billion in Funding to States for Bioterrorism Preparedness." HHS Press Release. 31 January 2002.

[28] U.S. Department of Health and Human Services. "17 Critical Benchmarks for Bioterrorism Preparedness Planning." *Public Health Preparedness, CDC.* 6 June 2002.

[29] U.S. Health Resources and Services Administration. Jane Ball, RN, DrPH, and Evelyn Boekler, RN, HRSA Bioterrorism Hospital Preparedness Program, Cooperative Agreement CFDA 93.003.

[30] U.S. Department of Health and Human Services. "Bioterrorism Preparedness Grants." HHS Press Office, 6 June 2002; U.S. Department of Health and Human Services. "HHS Approves State Bioterrorism Plans So Building Can Begin: States, Cities to Receive Additional Funds for Strengthening Public Health Systems." HHS Press Release, 6 June 2002.

[31] *CQ Homeland Security.* CQ Homeland Security Bill Watch, HR 3448.

[32] *CQ Homeland Security.* CQ Homeland Security Bill Watch, HR 4775.

[33] American Association of Medical Colleges, Government Affairs and Advocacy. "Bioterrorism Preparedness, FY 2002 Funding." Available at http://www.aamc.org.

[34] Centers for Disease Control and Prevention National Pharmaceutical Stockpile Information, available at http://www.bt.cdc.gov/stockpile/.

[35] *Ibid.*

[36] The White House. "President Details Project BioShield." Office of the Press Secretary. 3 February 2003.

[37] *Ibid.*

[38] Bruce, Julie. 2003. "Bioterrorism Meets Privacy: An Analysis of the Model State Emergency Health Powers Act and the HIPAA Privacy Rule." *Ann. Health L.* 12:75.

[39] 45 CFR Parts 160 and 164, 67 Federal Register 157 (14 August 2002).

[40] 45 CFR Part 162, 68 Federal Register 34 (20 February 2003).

[41] Annas, April 2002.

[42] The Centers for Disease Control and Prevention. "Division of Global Migration and Quarantine: History of Migration." 25 March 2003. Available at http://www.cdc.gov/ncidod/dq/history.htm.

[43] *Ibid.*

[44] *Ibid.*

[45] The Centers for Disease Control and Prevention. "Division of Global Migration and Quarantine." 13 June 2001. Available at http://www.cdc.gov/ncidod/dq/mission.htm.

[46] Chase, Marilyn. "With Few Cases in U.S., Patients Accept Isolation and Quarantine." *The Wall Street Journal.* 30 April 2003.

[47] The Center for Law and the Public's Health at Georgetown and Johns Hopkins Universities. "Model Public Health Laws." Available at http://www.publichealthlaw.net/Resources/Modellaws.htm.

[48] The Centers for Disease Control and Prevention, Office of Communication, Media Relations, Smallpox Vaccination Program Status by State, April 25, 2003.

[49] *Jacobson v. Commonwealth of Massachusetts*, 197 U.S. 11 (1905).

[50] National Swine Flu Immunization Program of 1976 (Swine Flu Act), originally codified as 42 USC § 247b(j)-(l) (1976).

[51] Richards, Edward P., and Rathbun, Katharine C. "Smallpox Vaccine Injury and Law Guide, Smallpox Vaccine Injury Law Project." Louisiana State University School of Law (26 March 2003).

[52] The White House, Statement by the Press Secretary. 30 April 2003; The Kaiser Network. *Administration News: Federal Officials Partly Responsible for Problems With Smallpox Vaccination Program, GAO Study Says.* 30 April 2003; The Kaiser Network, *Administration News: Bush Signs Smallpox Vaccine Compensation Fund Into Law.* 1 May 2003.

[53] Joint Commission on Accreditation of Healthcare Organizations. "Health Care at the Crossroads: Strategies for Creating and Sustaining Community-wide Emergency Preparedness Systems." March 2003.

Chapter 8

Immigration and Border Security

Powell Goldstein Frazer & Murphy LLP
Rebecca L. Sigmund

1.0 Overview of Recent Acts Impacting Immigration

September 11, 2001, marked the starting point for far-reaching legal changes in the immigration laws. In record time, Congress passed and President George W. Bush signed into law the USA PATRIOT Act,[1] the most expansive antiterrorism measure in history. The Act, among other things, gives law enforcement agencies broad new powers to conduct searches, employ electronic surveillance, and detail suspected terrorists. The climate of war has added to this focus on heightened security, which has led to substantial changes in our immigration processes and significant security measures.

Legislative initiatives continued to stem from Presidential Directives and new regulations that placed aliens seeking entry into the United States under even more scrutiny. Beginning with the Executive Order establishing a White House Office of Homeland Security,[2] President Bush then created, by Presidential Directive, a Foreign Terrorists Tracking Task Force, mandated to coordinate efforts to deny entry into the United States aliens associated with, suspected of being engaged in, or supporting terrorist activities. This Task Force was further mandated to locate, detain, prosecute, or deport any such alien already in the United States. Lastly, it was charged with a thorough review of the student visa policies.[3] Additional Directives were issued (and regulations promulgated) that subjected certain men from certain countries suspected of harboring terrorists to "voluntary" interviews and required men seeking entry from those countries to undergo extensive background checks.[4] Another Directive implemented a new entry-exit system that imposed expanded registration and fingerprint requirements on certain nonimmigrants deem to be a national security risk, which was later expanded by regulation to include additional countries.[5]

The Enhanced Border Security and Visa Entry Reform Act (Border Security Act)[6] followed the enactment of the USA PATRIOT Act and continued many of the themes reflected in the PATRIOT Act and the related Presidential Directives and Executive Orders. Specifically, the Border Security Act provides for greater information sharing between government agencies and an interoperable electronic immigration data system; the implementation of entry-exit and foreign student tracking systems; and limitations and enhanced security measures on visa issuance to applicants from countries designated as state sponsors of terrorism. Further, embassies and consulates were required to establish "terrorist lookout committees" to identify potential terrorists within the country of operation.

Shortly thereafter, Congress enacted the Homeland Security Act of 2002, which marked the first government reorganization of its magnitude since the Truman era.[7] Of major significance is the abolishment of the Immigration and Naturalization Service and a total reorganization and restructuring of our immigration function. The Act essentially separates the enforcement function and the service function of our country's current immigration system. All Acts prior to the Homeland Security Act refer to the Immigration and Naturalization Service as a whole. Regulations implementing these laws will now need to designate the specific immigration agency responsible for certain actions as mandated.

2.0   USA PATRIOT Act

President Bush, on October 26, 2001, signed into law the USA PATRIOT Act, a bill that never made its way through the standard committee process. The Senate Bill, once introduced, went straight to the Senate floor.[8] Two versions of the Bill that passed the Senate and the House were never sent to a conference committee for further consideration and a resolution of the conflicting provisions. Rather, differences between the two bills were worked out informally among the House and Senate leadership.[9] This law set the tone for subsequent homeland security laws enacted, and served as an outline for a more enhanced and defined law created by the Border Security Act.

Titles IV and VI of the USA PATRIOT Act comprise the law's immigration provisions. Certain key provisions discussed below are unique to the PATRIOT Act. Generally, these provisions expand the definition of terrorism, create new grounds of inadmissibility for aliens with terrorist ties, authorize the detention of aliens reasonably believed to be connected to terrorism or otherwise posing a national security threat, and expand the authority of enforcement agencies. Title VI also created saving provisions to preserve the immigration benefits of those non-citizen victims of the attacks of September 11th and their families.

Other provisions of the PATRIOT Act (that subsequently have been enhanced by the Border Security Act and thus are discussed under Section 3) impose stricter controls on countries participating in the Visa Waiver Program,[10] require interagency information sharing, and call for a quick implementation of the entry-exit and foreign student tracking systems required by the Illegal Immigration Reform and Immigrant Responsibility Act of 1996 (IIRIRA).[11]

2.1   New Grounds of Inadmissibility

The PATRIOT Act expands the definition of "terrorist" and adds new grounds of inadmissibility to the Immigration and Nationality Act (INA) Section 212(a)(3)(B). Individuals who are deemed "terrorist" and are now inadmissible include representatives of foreign terrorist organizations or of certain groups that publicly endorse terrorism (as designated by the Department of State under INA Section 219); a member of a political, social, or other similar group who has publicly endorsed acts of terrorist activities; a person who has used his position of prominence within a country to endorse terrorist activity or persuade such support; and any spouse or child of a person deemed inadmissible for terrorist activities if the activity occurred within the last five years.[12] The law provides exceptions to the inadmissibility of a spouse or child first, in the case that a consular officer believes that the individual has renounced the activity, or second, in the case that the spouse or child did not know or could not reasonably have known of the activity taking place.

Further added to the grounds of inadmissibility is the act of having any association with terrorist organization. The new INA section 212(a)(3)(F) provides that persons deemed to have been associated with a terrorist organization and engaged solely or incidentally in activities that could endanger the welfare and safety of the United States will be inadmissible. These grounds include persons who have contributed funds or material support to, or solicited funds for, or membership in, an organization that has been designated as a terrorist organization. Further, by contributing to, or soliciting in or for any nondesignated terrorist organization, a person will be found inadmissible or deportable unless the alien can "demonstrate that he did not know and should not reasonably have known, that the act would further the organization's terrorist activity."[13] For purposes of this Act, the Palestine Liberation Organization is considered to be engaged in terrorist activities as defined.[14]

2.2   Foreign Terrorist Organizations

The Department of State has redesignated 39 organizations as "foreign terrorist organizations" based on its authority under INA Section 219.[15] The Department of State is allowed to designate an organization if the group is a foreign organization, engages in terrorist activity as defined in INA Section 212(a)(3)(B), and threatens the security of U.S. nationals or the national security of the United States.[16] The Department of State must notify Congress of the intent to designate a particular organization as terrorist and must publish the designation in the *Federal Register*. Further, a recent court decision in the U.S. Court of Appeals for the D.C. Circuit ruled that the Secretary of State must give notice to the "foreign terrorist organization" that such a designation is impending and that the organization must be granted an opportunity to present evidence.[17]

The designation of an organization as a terrorist organization lasts for two years, at which time the Department of State may redesignate it for another two years. Congress may block or revoke a redesignation at any time. U.S. citizens may not support designated terrorist organizations, and U.S. financial institutions are required to freeze their assets.[18] The AEDPA already prohibits assistance or funding to designated organizations and requires U.S. financial institutions to block funds that belong to these organizations.[19]

2.3　Certification and Detention of Potential Terrorists

The PATRIOT Act provides for the "certification" by the Attorney General or the Deputy Attorney General of any person he reasonably believes to be a terrorist or a person who is engaged in any other activity that endangers the national security of the United States. This law goes further to require that such persons so certified be retained in custody, regardless of whether they are eligible for, or are granted, relief from removal for as long as the Attorney General continues to certify that there are reasonable grounds to believe that the person is involved in terrorist activity.[20] If the individual is finally determined not to be removable, he or she must be released. For those who are detained indefinitely, the Attorney General must review the detention every six months, and at that time, if the person cannot be removed to another country in the "reasonably foreseeable future," continued detention is permissible upon a showing that his or her release would jeopardize the national security of the United States or the safety of any individual or community.[21]

This provision of the USA PATRIOT Act opened the door for the detention of those individuals who met a certain profile, and who the government suspected would have knowledge of the terrorist acts of September 11th. It was reported that up to 5,000 males between the ages of 16 and 33 and from Middle Eastern countries were detained during the few months following the enactment of the USA PATRIOT Act. The law authorized enforcement agencies to detain these individuals indefinitely or until there was no criminal or immigration charges against them. Although there is a provision in Section 412 of the USA PATRIOT Act that permits a detention of only seven days for determination of immigration or criminal charges against an individual, the government often used the broader "national security" provisions to mandate the ongoing detention of certain persons.

2.4 Preserving Benefits to Noncitizen Victims of September 11th Attacks

The attacks of September 11th included victims from 40 countries. The destruction in New York City also indirectly impacted many immigration filings in the northeast. Congress recognized the need to preserve certain benefits for noncitizen victims of the attacks as well as their families. The USA PATRIOT Act created a special immigrant status to any person whose family or employment-based immigrant petition, fiancé visa, or application for labor certification was revoked or terminated (or otherwise rendered null) due to the death, disability, or loss of employment (due to the physical damage or destruction of the business) of the petitioner, applicant, or beneficiary as a direct result of the terrorist attacks on September 11th. The relief was also available to the spouses and children who were either accompanying the principal applicant or who were following to join the applicant up to two years later (September 11, 2003). The grandparents of any child whose parents died in the attacks would also qualify for this status if the parents were U.S. citizens or legal permanent residents.[22] In determining eligibility for an immigrant visa, the public charge grounds of inadmissibility were not applied to these special immigrants.[23]

3.0 Border Security Act Expands and Enhances PATRIOT Act

The primary theme in immigration since 2001 has been the initiation of changes to improve immigration processes and procedures with a focus on national security. The Border Security Act sets forth these objectives with a mandate for action. Specifically, this Act doubles or triples the funding and appropriations set forth in the PATRIOT Act and shortens, in many cases, the time frame for taking certain actions also provided by the PATRIOT Act.

3.1 Interagency Information Sharing

The PATRIOT Act and the Border Security Act attempt to resolve the problems associated with the lack of communication between and among federal law enforcement agencies and the federal intelligence community as well as within the various agencies. The PATRIOT Act expanded the scope of information sharing in an effort to address terrorism concerns. Section 203 of the PATRIOT Act amended Rule 6(c) of the Federal Rules of Criminal Procedure and various provisions of the criminal code to allow for the sharing of grand jury and electronic, wire, and oral interception information related to foreign intelligence or counterintelligence with a range of federal law enforcement and other officials, including immigration officials, in order to assist those officers in the performance of their duties.[24] Further, the PATRIOT Act amended the National Security Act of 1947 to require federal law enforcement agencies to expeditiously disclose to the Director of the Central Intelligence Agency foreign intelligence acquired in the course of a criminal investigation.[25]

Attorney General John Ashcroft released three memoranda on September 23, 2002, that set forth new guidelines for the sharing of information. The memorandum setting forth guidelines for the implementation of Section 203 of the PATRIOT Act mandates that all grand jury or electronic, wire, or oral interception information which identifies a "United States person" as defined by federal law must be labeled to indicate that it contains such identifying information prior to disclosure. Such information must be marked if it identifies any U.S. person, even if that person is not the target or subject of the investigation or surveillance, but the U.S. person must be identified by name, nickname, or alias. The memorandum goes further to define a non-U.S. person as an individual known or believed to be outside the United States or identified as an alien who has not been admitted for lawful permanent residence.[26]

More specific to immigration, Title II of the Border Security Act requires that law enforcement and intelligence agencies make a concerted effort to share information relevant to the admissibility and deportability of aliens with the immigration agencies and the Department of State pending the development of a comprehensive datashare system. The lack of coordination and access to such information has been recognized as a critical problem and was first addressed in the USA PATRIOT Act, which required that the system be in place within two years.[27] The Border Security Act advances this time period to 15 months, after which the President must certify a technology standard (biometric identifier) for use in identifying aliens seeking admission into the United States and changes from 18 months to one year, the period after which the president must first report to Congress on the progress.[28]

Other communication problems exist not only among various enforcement agencies but also within agencies. To resolve some of these problems, Section 202 of the Border Security Act calls for the immigration agencies to integrate all of its data systems into one system as part of an interoperable interagency system called the CHIMERA system.[29] To identify aliens, it must be available to consular officers and other officers responsible for determining admissibility, investigating, or identifying aliens.[30] The interoperable electronic data system must include sophisticated, linguistically sensitive name-matching algorithms that could account for transliterations of the same name.[31] The new algorithms are required for at least four languages as deemed high priority by the Secretary of State.[32] CHIMERA represents the future of lookout systems as it combines a "lookout" component, using algorithms for distinguishing names, as well as a "name check or security advisory opinion" component, which screens individuals who are not yet on the list.[33]

Once a visa is issued to an applicant, the Department of State is to provide Immigration with an electronic version of the visa file of that alien to ensure that the data is available to Immigration inspectors before the arrival of the alien at the Port of Entry. (The Department of State has been able to provide 100 percent of visa data to Immigration since December 1, 2001; however, Immigration's capabilities currently limit the transfer of the data.)[34]

3.2   Visa Issuance, Inspection, and Admission

The Border Security Act requires the Department of State to implement enhanced security measures for the review of visa applications.[35] In following this mandate, the Department of State began requiring interviews for all visa applicants over the age of 16 who are from one of the countries that have been deemed to sponsor international terrorism.[36] Additionally, these applicants must complete an additional Form DS-157[37] and are subject to a Visas Condor clearance prior to the issuance of a visa. (Visas Condor is an in-depth security check instituted in January 2002 by which the names of visa applicants are sent for analysis by appropriate U.S. government agencies.)[38]

The Border Security Act goes further to require the implementation of an integrated entry and exit database containing arrival and departure information from machine-readable visas, passports, and other travel and entry documents possessed by travelers.[39] The systems for the databases as well as the machine-readable visas and passports were to be implemented pursuant to the USA PATRIOT Act for the purpose of visa integrity and security.[40] For the technology to fully meet the objectives of this law, entry and exit documents must be machine readable, tamper resistant, and otherwise contain biometric identifiers. The ports of entry will utilize equipment and software to allow biometric comparison and authentication of travel documents as mandated by the PATRIOT Act.[41]

Certain benefits to travelers will be unavailable if the passports are not machine-readable. By October 26, 2004, countries currently eligible for participation in the Visa Waiver Program must have its government certify that it has a program to issue to its citizens machine-readable passports that are tamper-resistant and which incorporate biometric and authentication identifiers that satisfy the standards of the International Civil Aviation Organization.[42] After

October 26, 2004, an alien seeking admission under the Visa Waiver Program must present such a passport, unless the alien's passport was issued prior to that date.[43] The Border Security Act also shortens from five years (called for by the PATRIOT Act) to two years the period of time between the required periodic reviews of a program country's compliance with the requirements for continued participation in the Visa Waiver Program.[44] Subsequent to this Act, Argentina and Uruguay were removed from the program. Further, the Department of State is authorized to increase fees for those applicants without machine-readable passports.[45]

3.3　Terrorist Lookout Lists and Committees

The Secretary of State, under Section 304 of the Border Security Act, must establish a terrorist lookout committee to identify known and potential terrorists and to develop information on those individuals utilizing cooperative resources of all elements available.[46] The committee is charged with bringing this information to the attention of consular officers and ensuring that names are entered into the appropriate lookout databases.[47] Currently, the Department of State has a terrorist reporting program called the Visas Viper Program that will be expanded to implement this provision.[48] There is also a Consular Lookout and Support System (CLASS) that contains information on members and supporters of foreign terrorist organizations, NARCO-traffickers, and international criminals. In addition to these systems, the Department of State's Bureau of Intelligence and Research maintains a database known as TIPOFF. The information is classified and includes persons who may be considered terrorists.[49] While these systems are modified to properly implement the committee's ultimate databases, modifications to the training of consular officers regarding improved terrorist identification will also occur as mandated by the Border Security Act.[50]

3.4　Restriction on Issuance of Visas to Nonimmigrants from Countries Deemed State Sponsors of Terrorism

The Border Security Act has placed restriction on the issuance of nonimmigrant visas to citizens from countries that have been designated as state-sponsors of terrorism.[51] The term "state sponsor of terrorism" has been defined in Section 306 as "any country the government of which has been determined by the Secretary of State under any of the laws specified in paragraph (2) to have repeatedly provided support for acts of international terrorism."[52] This broad definition will bring in the Export Administration Act of 1979, the Arms Export Control Act, and the Foreign Assistance Act of 1961.[53] An exception to this restriction will be based on a determination by the Secretary of State that the applicant in question does not pose a safety or national security threat to the United States.[54] As indicated above, the Department of State initially determined that Cuba, Iran, Iraq, Lybia, North Korea, Sudan, and Syria comprised the countries that sponsored international terrorism.[55] This list has been expanded to include a total of 25 countries that have been designated as state sponsors of international terrorism.

3.5   NSEERS

The National Security Entry-Exit Registration System (NSEERS) was originally proposed to be a lookout system or a name check/security system. Instead, it is both a "special registration" and a tracking device for gathering entry and exit data, monitoring people in the United States, and otherwise keeping tabs on nationals of the designated state sponsors of terrorism as well as other nationals of certain other countries determined to require monitoring.[56] An inspector at the port of entry has the authority to require any person that they deem requires "monitoring" while they are visiting the United States to register. The Attorney General has determined certain pre-existing criteria that can be considered by Inspectors including unexplained travel to certain troublesome countries, overstays, identification by intelligence agencies as needing "monitoring," and demeanor or behavior raising suspicion.[57]

The first phase of the NSEERS program commenced on September 11, 2002, at selected ports of entry. By October 1, 2002, the program expanded to all ports of entry, including land, air, and sea. The NSEERS program by November 2002 consisted of several components that apply to certain nationals of the Department of Justice's list of suspect countries.[58] The main components include registration upon entry into the United States, which consists of being fingerprinted, photographed, and interviewed; compliance interviews between 30 and 40 days after entry; re-registration each year; and registration upon departure at specific points of departure listed in the NSEERS packet provided to the individuals.

NSEERS was expanded to include certain foreign nationals in the United States in some longer-term nonimmigrant status who had not traveled recently and, therefore, were not registered at the ports of entry. For this special registration, all males between 16 and 45 years of age who had been in the United States prior to September 30, 2002, and who are citizens or nationals of the designated countries requiring registration were required to report to Immigration for a "call-in" interview. This internal special registration required compliance of the various nationals affected in a three-phase process. Citizens and nationals of Iran, Iraq, Libya, Sudan, and Syria must have complied with the special registration requirements by December 16, 2002. Nationals of Afghanistan, Algeria, Bahrain, Eritrea, Lebanon, Morocco, Amman, Qatar, Somalia, Tunisia, United Arab Emirates, and Yemen must have complied by January 10, 2003. Saudis and Pakistanis had until February 21, 2003, to comply. Considering the difficulties of publicizing and administering this special registration, these deadlines were extended. Also, the government was not finished adding other countries (and still is not finished). The NSEERS program was expanded in January 2003 to include Bangladesh, Egypt, Indonesia, Jordan, and Kuwait. The registration for these countries was set to expire March 28, 2003, but was also extended.[59]

3.6   Passenger Manifests

The Border Security Act amends the passenger manifest provisions in Section 231 of the Immigration and Nationality Act by expanding the information to be provided to Immigration officers regarding passengers.[60] Specifically, commercial flights and vessels coming to the United States from any place outside the country must provide manifest information about each passenger, crew member, and other occupant prior to the arrival in the United States.[61] Also, every vessel or aircraft departing the United States for any destination outside the United States must provide manifest information before departure.[62] The information that must be provided for each individual includes name, date of birth, citizenship, sex, passport number and country of issuance, country of residence, U.S. Visa number, date, place of issuance, and, when applicable, the alien registration number and U.S. address while in the United States.[63] Beginning, January 1, 2003, the manifest is to be transmitted electronically to the port of entry. Section 402 also calls for a feasibility study of extending these manifest requirements to land carriers transporting persons to the United States and raises existing penalties against noncomplying carriers from $300 to $1,000. These provisions are expected to be difficult for carriers to fulfill as they conflict with the privacy laws in other countries.

3.7   Foreign Students and Exchange Visitors

As background, Section 641 of the Illegal Immigration Reform and Immigrant Responsibility Act (IIRIRA) established the implementation of a foreign student visa monitoring program.[64] To fully implement and expand the program, Section 416 of the USA PATRIOT Act required that this program include all approved educational institutions, even flight schools, language training schools, and vocational schools.[65] Section 501 of the Border Security Act heightens and strengthens the "monitoring" aspect of the student information collection requirements set forth in Section 641 of IIRIRA and also mandates the collection of additional data.[66] Specifically, Section 501 requires the establishment of an electronic means to monitor and verify various steps involved in the admittance to the United States of foreign students, including the issuance of documentation of acceptance of a foreign student by an educational institution or exchange visitor program; the transmission of such documentation to the Department of State's Bureau of Consular Affairs; the visa issuance and the student's admission to the United States; the registration and enrollment of the student in his or her institutional program; and any other relevant acts such as changing schools or terminating studies for program participation.[67] The reporting requirements also include notifying Immigration if a student does not report to school more than 30 days after the deadline for registering for classes.[68] Additional data that must be collected under the Act includes the student's date of entry, port of entry, date of school enrollment, date the student leaves school (e.g., graduates, quits), and the degree program or field of study.[69] Student visa applicants must also provide additional information to the Consular officer including their address, names and addresses of relatives, and names of contacts in the country of residence who can verify information about the student visa applicant and previous work history, if any, including the name and addresses of employers.[70] There have been concerns by schools regarding the ability and feasibility of disseminating this information due to privacy issues and technology.

3.7.1 Overview of the Student and Exchange Visitor Information System (SEVIS)

The INS published a final rule in the *Federal Register* on December 11, 2002, to amend and enhance the regulations governing the retention and reporting of information regarding students and exchange visitors. This rule implements the Student and Exchange Visitor Information System (SEVIS), and establishes a process for electronic reporting by designated school officials of information required by the Border Security Act. Once this system is fully operational, Immigration expects to track nearly 1 million nonimmigrant foreign students and exchange visitors during their stay in the United States with the assistance of the attending schools.[71] In addition, Immigration will review and allow schools to enroll in SEVIS under a two-tier process allowing schools to gain access to SEVIS. The first tier is a preliminary enrollment period for certain schools that meet the basic criteria, and the second tier is a full certification review for schools either that were ineligible for the preliminary enrollment or that did not apply during the preliminary enrollment period.[72]

As of January 30, 2003, all schools must now utilize SEVIS in order to issue a certificate of eligibility for non-immigrant students (using the new form I-20). Generally, re-certification encompassing an on-site visit is required prior to May 14, 2004.[73] Preliminary enrollment is not available to flight schools, even if they had been accredited by an agency recognized by the Department of Education and had been participating as a Service-Approved school for the past three years, which is required by other schools for preliminary enrollment.[74]

SEVIS and the rules implementing the program do not change the existing regulations governing the student and exchange visitor programs.[75] The process and program is for the purpose of information gathering and tracking of the visitors during their stay. Further, it does not take the place of reporting requirements under other programs or regulations. For example, SEVIS requires the timely reporting and updating of a change in actual and current U.S. address of an exchange visitor. However, this does not satisfy the address reporting requirements imposed by the National Security Entry-Exit Registration System (NSEERS).[76]

3.7.2 The Interim Student and Exchange Authentication System (ISEAS)

On September 11, 2002, the Department of State introduced the Interim Student and Exchange Authentication System (ISEAS), which is a web-based design that allows consular officers to verify the acceptance of foreign students and exchange visitors who apply to enter the United States as a student or exchange visitor. This system was created pursuant to Section 501 of the Border Security Act. Specifically, Section 501 provides that a visa may not be issued to a student or exchange visitor unless the Department of State has received from the approved school or program electronic evidence of their acceptance to the school.[77] Without this system, consular officers would be unable to issue visas to foreign students and exchange visitors until the SEVIS program was fully implemented.

ISEAS is the means by which INS-approved educational institutions and department-designated exchange programs can meet the legislative requirements of the Border Security Act. This is only an interim system and is therefore limited in capacity.[78] As a backup, the Department of State permits schools to e-mail status verifications directly to the consular posts.[79]

The Department of State is currently responsible for the J-1 exchange visitor program; therefore, the SEVIS implementation for J-1 participants is currently the responsibility of the Bureau of Educational and Cultural Affairs (ECA) of the State Department. Responsibilities include regulatory writing, developing the SEVIS-ready form, and serving as liaison with exchange program sponsors.

4.0   Homeland Security Act of 2002

The Homeland Security Act of 2002 completely reorganized and merged 22 federal agencies with 170,000 employees under the umbrella of the new Department of Homeland Security. This marks the first government reorganization of its magnitude since the Truman era. Of major significance is the abolishment of the Immigration and Naturalization Service and a total restructuring of our immigration function, which became effective March 1, 2003. The Act essentially separates the enforcement function and the service function of our current immigration system, creating the Bureau of Citizenship and Immigration Services (BCIS) to handle services, and the Bureau of Immigration and Customs Enforcement (BICE) to handle enforcement. A third agency, the Bureau of Customs and Border Protection (BCBP), enforces immigration and customs law at and between the 307 ports of entry into the United States. As a result of the reorganization of the former INS under the Homeland Security Department, the BICE and the BCBP are both under the Directorate of Border and Transportation Security while the BCIS was created separately and reports to the Deputy Secretary of Homeland Security.

The BCIS's exclusive focus is administering immigration benefits and services. These services include family-sponsored and employment-based petitions, naturalization applications, asylum and refugee cases, and special registration.[80] The BCIS will conduct operations within the same physical infrastructure used by the former INS, namely, four service centers, three regional offices, and 33 district offices located at the same locations as the corresponding INS buildings.

The BICE's (internally referred to as ICE) focus is enforcement of both the immigration laws and customs laws as well as protecting over 8,000 federally owned and leased buildings within the United States and its territories. The BICE is composed of former customs service and INS special agents, INS detention and deportation officers, INS's immigration litigation section, federal protective service employees, and part of the former INS customs and FFPS intelligence sections.[81]

Immigration enforcement by the BICE will include immigration investigations, detention, removal, and intelligence. The BICE's immigration enforcement strategy is a "comprehensive interior enforcement strategy to systematically combat illegal immigration inside the United States by attacking its causes, not merely its symptoms."[82] The BICE is also responsible for maintaining the student and exchange visitor monitoring program and special registration databases.[83]

BCBP enforces immigration and customs laws at the borders. Employees include former inspectors from the customs service, the INS and the agricultural quarantine inspection program, and 10,000 former border patrol agents.[84]

With this lack of direct coordination of the agencies, a centralized source will need to be responsible to coordinate the interagency systems and related technology. In order to provide some congruency between the three immigration-related bureaus, the Homeland Security Act established a Director of Shared Services. The Director of Shared Services will report directly to the Deputy Secretary of the Department of Homeland Security and is mandated to coordinate and manage resources used by all three bureaus. Because of the separation of the enforcement agencies and the service agency, this director of shared services will play a vital role in coordinating a consistent immigration policy for the entire system.[85]

Endnotes:

[1] Uniting and Strengthening America by Providing Appropriate Tools Required to Intercept and Obstruct Terrorism (USA PATRIOT) Act, Pub. L. No. 107-56, 115 Stat. 272. (2001).

[2] Exec. Order No. 13, 228, 66 Fed. Reg. 51812-17 (10 October 2001).

[3] *See* 78 Interpreter Releases 1703, 1707 (Nov. 5, 2001) and Stichter, "Homeland Security Meets Immigration: A Review of Recent Government Activity and Pending Legislation," 2-10 Immigration Briefings (October 2002).

[4] *See* 78 Interpreter Releases 1816 (3 December 2001) and 79 Interpreter Release 138 (28 January 2002).

[5] Fed. Reg. 52584-92 (12 August 2002), discussed and reproduced in 79 Interpreter Releases 1230 (19 August 2002). *See also* 79 Interpreter Releases 899 (10 June 2002).

[6] Enhanced Border Security and Visa Entry Reform Act, Pub. L. No. 107-173, 116 Stat. 543. (2002).

[7] Homeland Security Act, Pub. L. No. 107-296, 116 Stat. 2135, signed into law on 25 November 2002.

[8] *See* 78 Interpreter Releases 1609, 1610 (15 October 2001).

[9] *See* 78 Interpreter Releases 1673 (October 2001).

[10] The Visa Waiver Program (VWP) waives the visa requirements for citizens of certain countries entering the United States for business or tourism for specified periods of time. For a discussion of the VWP, see Vazquez-Azpiri, "The Visa Waiver Pilot Program: A Guide to the Benefits and Risks," 96-8 Immigration Briefings (August 1996).

[11] Illegal Immigration Reform and Immigrant Responsibility Act of 1996. Pub. L. No. 104-208, 110 Stat. 3009.

[12] USA PATRIOT Act, *supra* note 1, Section 411.

[13] *Ibid.*

[14] *See* 78 Interpreter Releases 1871 (December 2001), which provides the text of a State Department cable (No. 2001-State-190946) of November 2, 2001.

[15] Al-Ittihad al Islami (AIAI), Al-Wafa al-Igatha al-Islamia, Asbat al-Ansar, Darkazanli Company, Salafist Group for Call and Combat (GSPC), Islamic Army of Aden, Libyan Islamic Fighting Group, Makhtab al-Khidmat, Al-Hamati Sweets Bakeries, Al-Nur Honey Center, Al-Rashid Trust, Al-Shifa Honey Press for Industry and Commerce, Jaysh-e-Mohammed, Jamiat al-Ta'awun al-Islamiyya, Alex Boncayao Brigade (ABB), Army for the Liberation of Rwanda (ALIR)—aka, Interahamwe, Former Armed Forces (EX-FAR), First of October Antifascist Resistance Group (GRAPO)—aka, Grupo de Resistencia Anti-Fascista Premero De Octubre, Lashkar-e Tayyiba (LT)—aka, Army of the Righteous, Continuity Irish Republican Army (CIRA)—aka, Continuity Army Council, Orange Volunteers (OV), Red Hand Defenders (RHD), New People's Army (NPA), People Against Gangsterism and Drugs (PAGAD), Revolutionary United Front (RUF), Al-Ma'unah, Jayshullah, Black Star, Anarchist Faction for Overthrow, Red Brigades-Combatant Communist Party (BR-PCC), Revolutionary Proletarian Nucleus, Turkish Hizballah, Jerusalem Warriors, Islamic Renewal and Reform Organization, The Pentagon Gang, Japanese Red Army (JRA), Jamiat ul-Mujahideen (JUM), Harakat ul Jihad I Islami (HUJI), The Allied Democratic Forces (ADF), and The Lord's Resistance Army (LRA).

[16] Immigration and Nationality Act, Section 219, subparagraphs (D) and (E) added by Section 356 of IIRIRA, Pub. L. 104-208, 110 Stat. 3009, effective as if included in the enactment of Title IV, Subtitle A, of the Antiterrorism and Effective Death Penalty Act of 1996 (AEDPA), Pub. L. 104-132, 110 Stat. 1214.

[17] *National Council of Resistance of Iran v. Department of State*, 25 F.3d 192 (DC Cir. 2001).

[18] *See* 78 Interpreter Releases 1603 (November 2001) citing CNN television broadcast, 5 October 2001.

[19] *See supra* note 16. Also *see* 73 Interpreter Releases 521 (22 April 1996) cited in 78 Interpreter Releases 1603 (November 2001).

[20] USA PATRIOT Act, *supra* note 1, Section 412.

[21] *Id.*

[22] USA PATRIOT Act, *supra* note 1, Section 412.

[23] *Id.* INA Section 212 (a)(4); 8 U.S.C. 1182 (a)(4).

[24] 79 Interpreter Releases 1504. 7 April 2002.

[25] *Id.*

[26] *See* 79 Interpreter Releases 1504 discussing and reproducing the Ashcroft memoranda of September 23, 2002 at Appendix IV.

[27] *See* USA PATRIOT Act, *supra* at note 1.

[28] Border Security Act, *supra* note 6, Section 201.

[29] Statement of Michael Cronin, Assistant Commissioner for Inspections, before the Committee of the Judiciary, 9 October 2002. Posted on AILA Infonet at Doc. No. 02101043 (10 October 2002).

[30] *Id.*

[31] *Supra* note 29.

[32] Border Security Act, *supra* note 6, Section 101.

[33] Sindelar, Richard. "CHIMERA, NSEERS, Lookout and Security Checks: The New Age." *Bender's Immigration Bulletin* 8: 2. (15 January 2003).

[34] "DOS Cable Summarizes New Border Security Law" posted on AILA Infonet at Doc. No. 02052045 (20 May 2002).

[35] Border Security Act, *supra* note 6, Section 101.

[36] The Department of State initially listed as state sponsors of international terrorism Cuba, Iran, Iraq, Libya, North Korea, Sudan, and Syria. *See* "Patterns of Global Terrorism" (May 2002). Available at http://www.state.gov/s/ct/rls/pgtrpt/2001/

[37] The Supplemental Nonimmigrant Visa application DS-157 requests information that will lead to a security advisory opinion, in some cases. It is generally required of male nonimmigrant applicants between the ages of 16 and 45 but required of every applicant coming from one of the terrorist sponsoring states. *See* "Visa Policy Telegram P 110032Z, a New Form—DS-157, Supplemental Nonimmigrant Visa Application." 11 January 2002, available at http://travel.state.gov/state006020.html

[38] *See* "The Consul and the Visas Condor" posted on AILA InfoNet at Doc. No. 03012240 (22 January 2003).

[39] Border Security Act, *supra* note 6, Section 302.

[40] USA PATRIOT Act, *supra* note 1, Section 44.

[41] *Id.*

[42] "DOS Cable Summarizes New Border Security Law" posted on AILA Infonet at Doc. No. 02052045 (20 May 2002).

[43] *Id.*

[44] Border Security Act, *supra* note 6, Section 307.

[45] Border Security Act, *supra* note 6, Section 103.

[46] Border Security Act, *supra* note 6, Section 304.

[47] "DOS Cable Summarizes New Border Security Law" posted at AILA Infonet at Doc. No. 02052045 (20 May 2002).

[48] *Id.* The Visas Viper Program originated in 1993 after the World Trade Center bombing to correct deficiencies in the systems in place with DOS and INS at the time. *See* Foreign Affairs Manual § 40.32, Note N11.

[49] Scofield, Eileen, et al. "Privacy versus Security on the 'Visa Lookout' List." *Immigration and Nationality Law Handbook*, 2002-03, Vol. I. p. 271.

[50] *Id.*

[51] *See supra* at note 37.

[52] Border Security Act, *supra* note 6, Section 306.

[53] AILA summary of the Enhanced Border Security and Visa Entry Reform Act of 2002, posted on AILA InfoNet at Doc. No. 02052445 (4 May 2002).

[54] Border Security Act, *supra* note 6, Section 306.

[55] DOS Cable, *supra* note 42.

[56] Availabe on AILA InfoNet at Doc. No. 02121333 (13 December 2002). *See also, supra* note 33, p. 110.

[57] *Id.*

[58] Those nationals subjected to NSEERS include nationals from state sponsors of terrorism—Iran, Iraq, Syria, Libya, Sudan and North Korea. This list was expanded by the Department of Justice to include Afghanistan, Algeria, Bahrain, Eritrea, Lebanon, Morocco, Amman,

Qatar, Somalia, Tunisia, United Arab Emirates, and Yemen. In December 2002, further added were Armenia, Saudi Arabia, and Pakistan and specifically applied to males, ages 16 to 33, admitted into the United States prior to September 30, 2002, and remaining in the United States after February 21, 2003.

[59] "NSEERS Program Expanded Again." *Bender's Immigration Bulletin* 8: 183. (1 February 2003). *See also*, "NSEERS Program Registration Deadlines," *Bender's Immigration Bulletin.* 8: 47. (1 January 2003).

[60] 68 Fed. Reg. 2 (3 January 2003). *See also* Section 231 of the Immigration and Nationality Act. Pub. L. No. 82-414, 66 Stat. 163, 8 U.S.C. 1221.

[61] Border Security Act, *supra* note 6, Section 402.

[62] *Id.*

[63] Border Security Act, *supra* note 6, Section 402.

[64] IIRIRA, *supra* note 3, Section 641.

[65] USA PATRIOT Act, *supra* note 1, Section 416; IIRIRA, *supra* note 3, Section 641.

[66] Border Security Act, *supra* note 6, Section 501. *See also supra* note 53.

[67] Border Security Act, *supra* note 6, Section 501.

[68] *Id.*

[69] *Supra* note 68.

[70] *Supra* note 68.

[71] Office of Public Affairs, Immigration and Naturalization Service. "Preliminary Enrollment in the Student and Exchange Visitor Information System." Available at www immigration.gov (2 July 2002).

[72] *Id.*

[73] 67 Fed. Reg. 76308 (11 December 2002).

[74] *Supra* note 72.

[75] *Supra* note 74.

[76] *Id.* at 76309. *See also* www.immigration.gov for a discussion on NSEERS.

[77] Border Security Act, *supra* note 6, Section 501.

[78] "DOS answers to AILA questions" posted on AILA InfoNet at Doc. No. 02100340 (3 October 2002)

[79] *Id.*

[80] *See* "Transition Questions from Bureau of Citizenship and Immigration Services Field Offices." (13 March 2003). Available at www.aila.org/infonet (Document No. 03032031).

[81] *See* www.bice.immigration.gov.

[82] INS, *Backgrounder* at www.immigration.gov\graphics\shared\lawensor\interiorens \strategy.htm.

[83] *See supra*, note 82.

[84] *See* DHS, "Welcome to the Bureau of Customs and Border Protection." Available at cbp.customs.gov.

[85] Homeland Security Act, supra note 1, Section 475.

Chapter 9

Cybersecurity

Kelley Drye & Warren LLP
Glenn B. Manishin

1.0   Overview

The security of electronic networks and information (*i.e.,* of what has become
known as cyberspace—hence, the common term "cybersecurity") is an increasingly important issue affecting American government and businesses nationwide. Nonetheless, the scope of private-sector obligations regarding
cybersecurity—and the legal risks faced by individual businesses and industry
segments—is highly unclear and rapidly changing. Despite a focus on
cybersecurity by the White House and the recent establishment of the new
federal Department of Homeland Security, virtually all federal and state industry-specific regulators have yet to establish any rules protecting electronic networks and the information they store or transmit, let alone specifically addressing
vulnerability assessment, risk analysis, security and reporting requirements, and
the like.

Limited segments of some markets and certain critical infrastructure industries have become subject to express security regulations. These include the
financial and health transactions covered by congressional mandates and the
Federal Energy Regulatory Commission's rules on electricity transmission
cybersecurity. For the most part, however, the government has yet to mandate
substantial new security obligations. That has prompted one leading state, California, to enact its own consumer-oriented cybersecurity statute. Nevertheless,
overall corporate legal exposure to security risks, both for physical assets and
cybersecurity, clearly exists as matter of public company financial reporting,
tort law, and products liability law, regardless of whether the federal or state
governments enact legislation defining affirmative corporate obligations to protect electronic information.

This chapter outlines in broad terms the current legal framework governing
cybersecurity obligations and risks for private industry. By necessity it raises
issues more than it provides clear or settled answers. As a result, and especially

in an era when so much public attention is focused on matters of homeland security, corporate counsel and executives are well advised to acknowledge the fluid nature of corporate law by proactive management. Although the scope of legal risks remains largely undefined, the first step in managing homeland security legal exposure is rigorously assessing the existence, likelihood, and consequences of security vulnerabilities.[1] Only then can any corporate officer be in a position to take responsible positions on the evolving law of cybersecurity.

1.1   Definition of Cybersecurity

There are a number of different elements encompassed within the concept of cybersecurity. A common misunderstanding, however, is that cybersecurity involves the relationship between government and private parties with respect to access to the latter's electronic networks. For instance, the USA PATRIOT Act of 2001 defines the rights of governments to access ISP networks and to obtain customer records in the absence of a subpoena.[2] Yet these and similar provisions are not properly considered "cybersecurity" statutes because they do not relate to the *security* of those networks. Security by definition involves excluding unauthorized access to a company's physical facilities, information technology (IT) networks, or electronic information; since these type of laws govern *authorized* access, particularly by the government, they are not appropriately classified as part of a company's cybersecurity obligations.[3]

Cybersecurity is the protection of electronic networks (and the information they store or transmit) from the threat of intentional access or misappropriation by unauthorized third-parties for malicious purposes.[4] The Homeland Security Act of 2002 includes several references to cybersecurity, as discussed below, but does not expressly define the term.[5] H.R. 4246, the Cybersecurity Information Act, would define cybersecurity as

> The vulnerability of any computing system, software program, or critical infrastructure to, or their ability to resist, intentional interference, compromise, or incapacitation through the misuse of, or by unauthorized means of, the Internet, public or private telecommunications systems, or other similar conduct that violates federal, state, or international law, that harms interstate commerce of the United States, or that threatens public health or safety.

Cybersecurity involves phenomena as diverse as distributed denial of service attacks on Internet Web sites, "hacking" of computer systems, unauthorized release of internal corporate information stored electronically, cyber terrorism, and compromised integrity of electronic data storage, among others. Cybersecurity has existed as long as IT systems have been around, although the form and scope of security threats and vulnerabilities has changed—indeed, it has expanded exponentially—with the advent of near-ubiquitous Internet connectivity and broadband communications.

1.2   National Policy on Cybersecurity

In February 2003, the Executive Branch released a document tilted "The National Strategy to Secure Cyberspace," part of the Bush Administration's response to the September 11 attacks and a companion to its "National Strategy for the Physical Protection of Critical Infrastructures and Key Assets." Described as a "call for national awareness and action by individuals and institutions throughout the United States, to increase the level of cybersecurity nationwide and to implement continuous processes for identifying and remedying cyber vulnerabilities,"[6] the National Strategy includes a simple yet elegant declaration by President Bush:

> The policy of the United States is to protect against the debilitating disruption of the operation of information systems for critical infrastructures and, thereby, help to protect the people, economy, and national security of the United States.[7]

The National Strategy includes a high-level evaluation of the risks faced by critical infrastructures and IT systems, presents recommendations for the development of "best practices" by private sector industries, and calls for a public-private partnership in increasing America's cybersecurity preparedness. It does not, however, include proposals for any mandatory regulations affecting cybersecurity, and it stresses that the vast majority of critical infrastructures in the United States are privately owned. Thus, the National Strategy explains that "the private sector is best equipped and structured to respond to an evolving cyber threat" and that there are only a few "specific instances...where federal government response is most appropriate and justified." The National Strategy limits government's role in cybersecurity (in addition to "ensuring the safety of its own cyber infrastructure") to situations "where high transaction costs or legal barriers lead to significant coordination problems; cases in which governments operate in the absence of private sector forces; resolution of incentive problems that lead to under provisioning of critical shared resources; and raising awareness."[8]

Despite the National Strategy, political controversy developed in early 2003 over the Administration's elimination of the president's Critical Infrastructure Protection Board and the resignation of White House cybersecurity "czar" (Special Advisor to the President for Cyberspace Security) Richard Clarke.[9] In April 2003 congressional testimony, Clarke later complained that the federal government has failed to "recruit a cadre of nationally recognized cybersecurity experts," leaving federal agencies and the private sector more vulnerable to malicious electronic intrusions.[10]

Little legislation affecting cybersecurity has been introduced or is under consideration at the federal level. The National Cyber Security Leadership Act of 2003, introduced by Sen. Edwards (D-S.C.), would require the appointment of a CIO for each federal agency and empower the National Institute on Standard and Technology (NIST) to create technology standards for the protection of federal IT systems. The bill finds that

> [f]ederal agencies must take significant steps to better protect themselves against cyber attacks, including:
>
> (a) identifying significant vulnerabilities in their computer networks and the tools needed to detect such vulnerabilities;
> (b) monitoring for new vulnerabilities in their computer networks;
> (c) assessing risks of cyber attacks;
> (d) testing computers against identified vulnerabilities; and
> (e) ensuring that computers and networks are adequately protected against such vulnerabilities[11]

The bill would mandate the use of these NIST-developed technology standards by federal agencies and require every agency to report on its progress in implementing cybersecurity measures annually to the Office of Management and Budget (OMB) under 44 U.S.C. 3545(e). Earlier bills from the 107th Congress, such as a 2002 measure that would have established a nonprofit, nongovernmental consortium of academic and private sector experts to promulgate "best practices" for private sector cybersecurity, have not been re-introduced.[12]

1.2.1 DHS Private Sector Office

Contemporaneous with its release of the "National Strategy to Secure Cyberspace," the Bush Administration (in a politically controversial move) eliminated the President's Critical Infrastructure Protection Board, the body which had overseen development of the National Strategy and implementation of information security sharing plans by many industry segments.[13] As a partial substitute, Section 102(f) of the Homeland Security Act establishes the position of Special Assistant to the Secretary for the Private Sector[14] for which Alfonso Martinez-Fonts, formerly Chairman of JP Morgan Chase Bank in El Paso, Texas, has been confirmed.

The Special Assistant, as the position's title indicates, serves as the key interface between the Department and the private sector and has been placed in charge of the Department's Private Sector Office. The Special Assistant and his relatively small authorized staff (31 in total) serve as the focal point for input on the impact of Department policies and regulations on the private sector, and they advise the Secretary on private sector projects, partnerships, and practices to address homeland security issues. It is expected that the Private Sector Office will be the principal vehicle for coordination of the public-private partnership on cybersecurity proposed in the National Strategy.

1.3   Prosecution of Cyber Crimes

Despite its prominent role under the Homeland Security Act of 2002, the Department of Homeland Security (DHS) is not responsible for investigating or prosecuting crimes involving cybersecurity. Indeed, combating any form of terrorism, as either a law enforcement or military matter, is *not* within the scope of the Department's responsibilities. The Act specifies clearly that primary responsibility for investigating and prosecuting acts of terrorism remains with federal, state, and local law enforcement agencies, except for specific enforcement responsibilities held by agencies transferred to the Department.[15]

The Act does modify the federal penalties associated with criminal computer trespass and cyber attacks. The Cybersecurity Enhancement Act of 2002 (CSEA), enacted as Section 225 of the Homeland Security Act,[16] directs the United States Sentencing Commission to review its sentencing guidelines and policies applicable to certain computer crimes and submit a report to Congress of actions taken. Specifically, the CSEA requires that the Commission review the sentencing guidelines and policy statements applicable to persons convicted of an offense under 18 U.S.C. 1030[17] to ensure that the sentencing guidelines and policy statements reflect the serious nature of such offenses, the "growing incidence" of such offenses, and the need for "an effective deterrent and appropriate punishment" to prevent these types of crimes.[18]

1.4   Criminal Procedure and Investigations

Section 225 of the Homeland Security Act allows Internet service providers (ISPs) to voluntarily provide government agents with access to the contents of customer communications without consent based on a "good faith" belief that an emergency justifies the release. This is intended to ease fear of lawsuits on the part of ISPs due to information sharing with law enforcement. The Act also specifies that an existing ban on the "advertisement" of any device that is used primarily for surreptitious electronic surveillance applies to online ads. It introduces fines and 20-year prison terms for offenders who "knowingly" or "recklessly" cause or attempt to cause serious bodily injury and provides up to a life sentence for computer intrusions that "knowingly" or "recklessly" put others' lives at risk. It permits limited surveillance without a court order, including the installation of pen register and trap and trace devices, when there is an "ongoing attack" on a "protected computer"[19] or "an immediate threat to a national security interest." Surveillance is limited to obtaining a suspect's telephone number, Internet address, or e-mail header information—not the contents of online communications or telephone calls.

2.0 Regulation of Private Sector Cybersecurity Obligations

Consistent with the "National Strategy to Secure Cyberspace," current federal law does not impose any mandatory requirement on private sector entities—with only a few scattered exceptions in the health, financial services, and electric utility industries—for the development or implementation of cybersecurity measures. That is unlikely to change even with the creation of the Department of Homeland Security.

In general, the Secretary of DHS assumes the rulemaking power "as exists on the date of enactment" held by agencies and offices transferred to the Department,[20] but is not otherwise granted the power to promulgate substantive regulations imposing security-related obligations on industries already regulated by existing administrative agencies not transferred to DHS, such as the Federal Communications Commission, the Federal Energy Regulatory Commission, etc. Indeed, the Act states expressly that with only a few specified exceptions, "this Act vests no new regulatory authority in the Secretary or any other Federal official."[21]

One major exception to this limited regulatory authority is the power of DHS to define the procedures for sharing of cybersecurity information between private industry and the federal government. The Act requires that the Secretary establish "uniform procedures" within 90 days for the "receipt, care, and storage" by federal agencies of certain cybersecurity information voluntarily submitted to the government[22] as part of its role in protecting critical infrastructure information under Section 133 of the Act (the "Critical Infrastructure Protection Act of 2002").

Few federal agencies have promulgated rules expressly mandating cybersecurity obligations for regulated entities except as specifically required by Congress for the healthcare (*see* Section 2.4) and financial services (*see* Section 2.5) industries. One principal exception is the Federal Energy Regulatory Commission, also discussed below (*see* Section 2.3). Far more common is the approach of the Federal Communications Commission, which formed a "Homeland Security Policy Council in November 2001 to assist the Commission in achieving several very general objectives:

- Evaluating and strengthening measures for protecting U.S. tele-communications, broadcast, and other communications infrastructure and facilities from further terrorist attacks
- Ensuring rapid restoration of U.S. telecommunications, broadcast, and other communications infrastructure and facilities after disruption by a terrorist threat or attack
- Ensuring that public safety, public health, and other emergency and defense personnel have effective communications services available to them in the immediate aftermath of any terrorist attack within the United States

The FCC's Homeland Security Policy Council is comprised of senior staff from each of the Commission's Bureaus and is directed by the Chief of Staff for the Commission.[23] It has yet to take reported action or make express recommendations to the FCC to date.

On the other hand, Congress has been active in a variety of technology areas over the past decade, and may be persuaded to move more rapidly to a legislative solution than the Executive Branch would prefer. Indeed, in July 2003, the Chairman of the House Government Reform Subcommittee on Technology announced that he plans to introduce legislation to mandate computer security standards for the private sector. Rep. Adam Putnam (R.-Fla.) also publicly said that neither the government nor private enterprise has done a good job in securing the nation's electronic infrastructure and that there was a lack of "attention and understanding" as to the nature of the cybersecurity threat.[24]

2.1 Cybersecurity Preparedness

The Department of Homeland Security will play a principal role in encouraging the private sector to identify and secure vulnerabilities in critical infrastructures and electronic networks. In fact, DHS succeeds to the functions of a number of federal agencies involved in academic and scientific research, or engineering coordination, in connection with information security issues. These include the following:

- The Critical Infrastructure Assurance Office (CIAO) of the Department of Commerce[25]
- The National Infrastructure Simulation and Analysis Center of the Department of Energy
- The Federal Computer Incident Response Center (FedCIRC) of the General Services Administration[26]

Pursuant to Section 223 of the Act, DHS's Under Secretary for Emergency Preparedness is expected to coordinate with the Under Secretary for Information Analysis and Infrastructure Protection to provide analysis, warnings, crisis management support, and technical assistance to state and local entities, and to the private sector upon request, to assist in response to threats or attacks on "critical information systems."[27] Under Section 201 the Under Secretary for Information Analysis and Infrastructure is charged directly with developing a national plan for securing telecommunications systems that constitute critical infrastructure.[28]

In June 2003, DHS announced that it had formed within the Information Analysis & Infrastructure Directorate a 60-person National Cyber Security Division (NCSD), charged with addressing potential security breaches to private sector and government computer systems.[29] The NCSD builds upon the existing capabilities transferred to DHS from the former Critical Infrastructure Assurance Office, the National Infrastructure Protection Center, the Federal Computer Incident Response Center, and the National Communications System. The creation of the NCSD both strengthens government-wide processes for response and also improves protection of critical cyber assets through maximizing and leveraging the resources of these previously separate offices. Robert Liscouski, the Assistant Secretary of Homeland Security for Infrastructure Protection, will oversee NCSD.[30]

The new Division is organized into three sections, each of which has a specific mission:

- Identify risks and reduce the vulnerabilities to government's cyber assets; coordinate with the private sector to identify and help protect America's critical cyber assets
- Oversee a consolidated Cyber Security Tracking, Analysis, & Response Center (CSTARC), which will detect and respond to Internet events; track potential threats and vulnerabilities to cyberspace; and coordinate cyber security and incident response with federal, state, local, private sector and international partners
- Create, in coordination with other appropriate agencies, cyber security awareness and education programs and partnerships with consumers, businesses, governments, academia, and international communities

NCSD is expected to coordinate with the Office of Management and Budget and the National Institute of Standards and Technology regarding the security of federal systems and "best practices" for private sector cybersecurity technologies and processes.

In addition, Section 223 of the Homeland Security Act requires that the Secretary provide to state and local governments, and upon request to private sector entities that own or operate critical information systems, analysis and warnings related to threats and vulnerabilities of critical information systems.[31] To protect against cyber attacks, Section 224 of the Act permits the Under Secretary to create a national corps of volunteers with expertise in science and technology (to be known as "NET Guard") to "assist local communities to respond and recover from attacks on information systems and communication networks."[32]

2.2   Critical Infrastructure Information

Critical infrastructure protection has been a governmental priority at the federal level since at least 1998, when President Clinton issued Presidential Decision Directive/NSC-63 (PDD 63). PDD 63 found that "because our economy is increasingly reliant upon interdependent and cyber-supported infrastructures, non-traditional attacks on our infrastructure and information systems may be capable of significantly harming both our military power and our economy."[33] On October 16, 2001, President Bush issued Executive Order 13231, which continued many PDD 63 activities by focusing on cyberthreats to "critical infrastructure in the information age." The order also created the President's Critical Infrastructure Protection Board to coordinate federal cybersecurity efforts.

As set forth more recently in President Bush's February 2003 "National Strategy for the Physical Protection of Critical Infrastructures and Key Assets" (the "CIP Strategy"), the objective of critical infrastructure protection is "to identify and assure the protection of those assets, systems, and functions that we deem most 'critical' in terms of national-level public health and safety, governance, economic and national security, and public confidence." The CIP Strategy advocates a dual policy of ensuring protection of infrastructure and assets that "face a specific, immediate threat" and, over the longer-term as risk and criticality vary, "pursue collaborative measures and initiatives to ensure the protection of other potential targets that may become attractive over time."[34]

To partially address these concerns, Section 214 of the Homeland Security Act—known as the Critical Infrastructure Information Act of 2002—provides that information voluntarily provided by non-federal parties to DHS which relates to the security of critical infrastructure or protected systems shall be exempt from disclosure under Section 552 of the Freedom of Information Act (FOIA) when accompanied by an express statement specified in the Act.[35] Such information should not lose its protected character if forwarded by DHS to other federal agencies. Moreover, information voluntarily provided is not subject to rules concerning *ex parte* communications and may not be used in any civil action if such information has been submitted in good faith. The provisions of this section preempt state law to ensure that the information is not disclosed by state openness laws. The Act provides for punishment, including fines and imprisonment for up to one year, of any DHS employee for disclosing any voluntarily submitted critical infrastructure information that is not customarily in the public domain.

The extent of the protection actually accorded by this provision is as yet uncertain.[36] The Homeland Security Act does not expressly amend FOIA, and application of the statutory definition of "voluntary" may be subject to interpretation. Procedures for the receipt and storage of critical infrastructure information are to be established by DHS within 90 days of the enactment of the Act.[37] However, there is no deadline for the establishment by the president of the new procedures required under Section 892 for sharing of homeland security information with "appropriate state and local personnel," although a progress report must be submitted to Congress within one year.

2.3 Federal Energy Regulatory Commission

The Federal Energy Regulatory Commission (FERC) has recently finalized regulations, initially proposed in an NOPR in September 2002, setting new criteria for protection by the agency (including removal from public access) of Critical Energy Infrastructure Information (CEII).[38] In addition, the FERC-led process of defining a "Standard Market Design"—a new approach to competition in bulk power transmission—includes cybersecurity standards developed by the North American Electric Reliability Council (NERC).[39]

These FERC rules, scheduled to become effective in January 2004, are designed "to reduce risks to the reliability of bulk electricity systems from any compromise of critical cyber assets." They are the first-ever substantive cybersecurity regulations applicable to the private sector promulgated by a federal agency. The content of the FERC rules, although far from specific (consisting mainly of requirements that utilities assess cyber vulnerabilities and prepare a plan for security and response to attacks), represents an effort to encourage more long-range cybersecurity planning in the private sector. They require the identification of cyber assets and the development of a written cybersecurity policy by any entity performing transmission, generation, interchange, balancing, or load-serving functions. The proposed standards define critical cyber assets to include IT systems (computers, software, and communications networks) that "support, operate, or otherwise interact with the bulk electric system operations."

2.4 Security of Medical Records and Patient Information

The Health Insurance Portability and Accountability Act of 1996 (HIPAA)[40] requires the promulgation of regulatory standards for the privacy and security of healthcare information. The substantive security requirement is established by Section 1173(d)(2), which requires every healthcare provider and healthcare "clearinghouse" to "ensure the integrity and confidentiality" of health information and "to protect against reasonably anticipated...unauthorized uses of disclosures of [health] information."[41] The implementing security and privacy rules, promulgated by the Department of Health and Human Services (DHHS) as Section 164 of Title 45 of the Code of Federal Regulations and effective as of April 14, 2003,[42] require that every "covered entity" follow standards for use and disclosure of health information. The security standards have been described as "less a series of checklists and more a description of principles for each covered entity to evaluate and apply, based on the entity's specific situation."[43] Although the regulations plainly have a substantial impact on cybersecurity in the healthcare system because they prohibit unauthorized use and disclosure of protected information by any means, the DHHS standards do not establish any special rules applicable to health care IT systems or electronic databases or require any specific cybersecurity planning.

2.5 Security of Financial Information

The Gramm-Leach-Bliley Act (the Financial Modernization Act of 1999)[44] requires financial institutions to implement a "comprehensive information security program" to (a) ensure the security and confidentiality of customer information, (b) protect against any anticipated threats or hazards to the security or integrity of such information, and (c) protect against unauthorized access or use.[45] The statute gives authority to eight different federal agencies and the states to administer and enforce financial privacy rules and security safeguards. The most significant of these is the right of notice and opt-out from use of a customer's personal or financial information by a financial institution.

In addition, pursuant to Gramm-Leach-Bliley the Federal Trade Commission (FTC) has promulgated standards, known as the "safeguards rule," for ensuring the "security, confidentiality, integrity, and protection" of financial customer records and information. The FTC's safeguards rule provides that a financial institution must have a security plan that encompasses certain general elements, but the rule does not require specific technology measures or performance criteria nor is reporting of security lapses or intrusions mandated.[46] Instead, the safeguards rule requires each affected entity to conduct a risk assessment and then develop, implement, and revise a security plan appropriate to its business and the vulnerabilities it faces.

3.0   State Regulation of Cyber Security

In landmark legislation (Senate Bill 1386) that took effect on July 1, 2003, California became the first state in the nation to require disclosure by private companies of intrusions into their IT networks and electronic databases.[47] Under the new state statute, companies must warn California customers of security holes in their corporate computer networks and must disclose unauthorized intrusions or release of personal information to third-parties.

The legislation applies to any company that stores data electronically and does business in California. It specifies that a company "shall disclose any breach of the security of the system following discovery or notification of the breach in the security of the data to any resident of California whose unencrypted personal information was, or is reasonably believed to have been, acquired by an unauthorized person."[48] The Act defines "personal information" as an individual's first name or initial and last name, with one of the following: social security number, driver's license number, state identification number, or credit or debit card account number and security code. Except when disclosure would impede a criminal investigation, companies must notify consumers "in the most expedient time possible," with an e-mail or letter. If a hacker gains access to data for 500,000 or more customers, the company might have to notify people through e-mail, a "conspicuous" posting on a web site, and disclosure to a major media outlet.

Politicians call the statute the first of its kind in the United States, and it could become the model for a nationwide law. Senator Dianne Feinstein (D-Cal.) reportedly plans to introduce similar legislation at the federal level. "Corporate and government databases are increasingly becoming targets of identity thieves seeking Social Security numbers and other sensitive personal data," Feinstein has said. "Under current law, all too often people are unaware that an identity thief has gained this information and may be using it to run up credit card bills or use it to manufacture a new identity."[49]

California's new statute contrasts with the Bush Administration's relatively hands-off treatment of the technology industry, particularly when it comes to controversial e-commerce issues such as privacy and fraud. Although the FBI and the Federal Trade Commission have investigated web site operators involved in fraudulent sales and auctions, proponents of the laissez-faire approach worry that regulations would hamper innovation in a fledgling industry. "You cannot legislate good behavior," said eBay chief security officer Howard Schmidt, who resigned along with Richard Clarke in 2003 as a cybersecurity adviser to

President Bush. "The Administration's policy was not to look to legislation or regulation to improve security, but to look to market forces to drive it."[50]

No provisions similar to the California legislation currently apply at the federal level. However, a bill introduced in 2003, the Consumer Identity and Information Security Act (H.R. 2617), would make it unlawful to display social security numbers on the Internet or to require disclosure of social security numbers in an e-commerce transaction, unless the web site uses a secure connection or encryption and otherwise fashions protections for personal identity information.

4.0 Corporate Liability for Cybersecurity Breaches and Losses

FERC's proposed cybersecurity standards (*see* Section 2.3) include a risk and security governance component and focus on accountability in senior management. They also establish financial incentives for private sector compliance by requiring self-certification as a condition of receiving transmission services for interstate power distribution. These measures obviously impose some legal constraint on the ability of electric utilities to ignore responsibility for protection of critical infrastructures.

More generally, however, little attention has been paid to date to the application of traditional sources of corporate liability to the security arena. Nonetheless, that does not mean that companies can afford to ignore either physical or cybersecurity without consequences. An analogy to the Y2K issue is appropriate in this regard. When the so-called "millennium bug" was first discussed in the early 1990s, few companies took it seriously, and almost none undertook any study of necessary changes to their IT systems. After the Security and Exchange Commission defined risk disclosures to include Y2K assessments and "readiness statements"—and subsequent legislation provided limited liability for companies making Y2K disclosures—the rate of Y2K risk disclosures and preventative actions skyrocketed.

This suggests, quite clearly, that standard corporate exposure to traditional forms of shareholder and governmental legal accountability may and likely will be applied in the event of security losses in a variety of industries, well beyond the specific areas of healthcare, financial services, and electricity transmission governed by current regulations. In the absence of an SEC safe harbor, the failure of companies to disclose (at least in general terms) their security risks and preventative steps may be the basis for asserting Securities Act liability for withholding information on "material risk" affecting stock prices. Likewise, traditional tort and consumer protection causes of action provide ample flexibility to impose liability on companies that fail to take reasonable security precautions in the event of a cybersecurity breach that damages third-parties or the company itself.[51] Although this is a highly unsettled and embryonic area, developments to date suggest that the law seems to be recognizing what security consultants have been saying for some time: security is a process, not a product. Consequently, legal compliance with a security obligation involves a process applied to each case in order to achieve the objective of appropriate security measures, rather than hard and fast rules dictating the implementation of standard security measures in all cases.

On the other hand, many corporate CEOs and CIOs, especially in today's distressed market environment, hesitate to allocate substantial funds to enhancing either physical or cybersecurity in the absence of an identifiable, near-term threat. However shortsighted, this reluctance is driven by the hard economic reality that the expense of ensuring complete protection is infinite and that the costs of self-insuring against a security incident appear relatively modest in relation to the perceived level of risk.[52] That may or may not be a correct assessment. As a business matter, the only way to assess the scope and extent of an entity's legal exposure to claims arising from security matters is first to evaluate the existence and size of potential vulnerabilities and the operational and financial consequences to the organization of a security breach. By conducting such an empirical analysis, moreover, CEOs and CIOs would be well-positioned not only to make the security investment decisions they have largely deferred to date but also to legitimately argue that liability should not be imposed, even in the event of a massive security event, because the company has taken reasonable precautions to identify and prevent cybersecurity breaches.

Endnotes:

[1] *See generally* "Cybersecurity Today and Tomorrow: Pay Now or Pay Later," Computer Science and Telecommunications Board, National Research Council (2002). Available at http://csrc.nist.gov/publications/reports/ CSTBNRC-report.pdf.

[2] Pub. L. 107-56, codified at 18 U.S.C. 2703(2), 2510. The USA PATRIOT Act, among other things, (a) increases search warrant availability for e-mail and voicemail access and provides for subpoena access to ISP personal information (billing, etc.) and for government monitoring, ISP immunity for disclosures if harm imminent, and ISP rights to allow government monitoring; (b) expands the scope of trap and trace orders and pen registers; (c) overrides the Cable Communications Act immunity for electronic communications carried by cable companies; (d) provides lower threshold standards for and allows for multi-device search warrants for foreign intelligence gathering; (e) provides immunity to communication service providers in exchange for cooperation with government investigative requests; (f) promotes data sharing among agencies (foreign intelligence and domestic); (g) increases funding for

DOJ, INS border agents, and the Customs Service; and (h) increases monitoring requirements of aliens and visa holders (especially foreign students).

3 Another example is the Digital Millennium Copyright Act of 1998 (DMCA), which includes "anti-circumvention" provisions that allow copyright holders in certain circumstances to obtain, without a warrant, the identities of ISP customers who allegedly engage in the unauthorized distribution of copyrighted materials, such as software and songs. 17 U.S.C. 512, 1201. In 2003, Verizon was successfully sued under the DMCA by the Recording Industry Association of America and required to reveal the names of customers who allegedly had participated in "file sharing" of MP3 files via peer-to-peer software. *See, e.g., In re Verizon Internet Services Inc.,* 258 F. Supp.2d 24 (D.D.C. 2003). Although the DMCA and *Verizon* are about access to electronic networks without the affirmative permission of the network's owner or user, they relate to *legally authorized* access and do not involve cybersecurity.

4 The American National Standards Institute and the Alliance for Telecommunications Industry Solutions define cybersecurity as "the protection of [electronic] information against unauthorized disclosure, transfer, modification, or destruction, whether accidental or intentional." *Telecom Glossary 2000.* 28 February 2001. Available at http://www. atis.org/tg2k/. CRN, the Comprehensive Risk Analysis and Management Network project of the Swiss Federal Technical Institute at Zurich, defines cybersecurity more narrowly as "threats of electronic, radio-frequency, or computer-based attacks on the information or communication components that control critical infrastructures." Available at http://www.isn.ethz.ch/crn/issueareas/index.cfm?service=cybersecurity&menu=1. Of course, one need not "penetrate" an IT system to do major damage. This was demonstrated by the distributed denial-of-service attacks on Yahoo and others in 2000 and 2001, which showed that the Internet and other electronic networks can be disrupted or prevented without any form of penetration. *See, e.g., Cyber Security: Beyond The Maginot Line,* Statement of Wm. A. Wulf, Ph.D., President, National Academy of Engineering and AT&T Professor of Engineering and Applied Science, University of Virginia, before the House Science Committee, U.S. House of Representatives. (10 October 2001). Available at http://www.house.gov/science/full/oct10/wulf.htm.

5 Section 1001 of the Homeland Security Act, known as the "Federal Information Security Management Act of 2002," defines "information security" as, *inter alia,* "protecting information and information systems from unauthorized access, use, disclosure, disruption, modification or destruction." 44 U.S.C. 3532(b)(1). Subtitle B of Title II of the Act, known as the "Critical Infrastructure Information Act of 2002," defines "critical infrastructure information" (CII) and establishes confidentiality protections for voluntarily shared CII. 6 U.S.C. 131(3), 133.

6 "National Strategy" at 2.

7 *Id.* at iv.

8 "National Strategy" at ix.

9 *See* "Homeland Cybersecurity Efforts Doubted." *Security Focus.* 11 March 2003. Available at http://www.securityfocus.com/news/3043.

10 "Former Bush Official Blasts Government Cybersecurity." *InfoWorld.* 8 April 2003. Available at http://www.infoworld.com/article/03/04/08/HNcyberbush_1html. "Who is the highest level official in the Department of Homeland Security whose full-time job is cybersecurity?" Clarke reportedly asked. "What office in the Department of Homeland Security does nothing but cybersecurity? How many people in OMB have that full-time responsibility? The answers to those questions are pretty frightening." *Id.* Clarke repeated these criticisms in July 2003.

See "Clarke: U.S. Cybersecurity Efforts Lacking." *CRN.* 15 July 2003. Available at http://www.crn.com/ sections/BreakingNews/dailyarchives.asp?ArticleID=43267.

[11] S.187, 108th Cong., 1st Sess. (2003).

[12] *See* Cyberterrorism Preparedness Act of 2002, S.1900, 107th Cong., 2nd Sess. (2003); Cong. Rec. S176-83 (28 January 2002).

[13] *See* Section 1.2.

[14] 6 U.S.C. 102(f).

[15] 6 U.S.C. 111(b)(2).

[16] 6 U.S.C. 145.

[17] This statute criminalizes a variety of conduct relating to the misuse of computers, including obtaining and communicating restricted information (18 U.S.C. 1030(a)(1)), the unauthorized accessing of information from financial institutions, the United States government, and "protected computers" (18 U.S.C. 1030(a)(2)), the unauthorized accessing of a government computer (18 U.S.C. 1030(a)(3)), fraud (18 U.S.C. 1030(a)(4)), the damaging of a protected computer resulting in certain types of specified harms (18 U.S.C. 1030(a)(5)), trafficking in passwords (18 U.S.C. 1030(a)(6)), and extortionate threats to cause damage to a "protected computer" (18 U.S.C. 1030(a)(7)). The statutory maximums for violations of Section 1030 range from one year to life, depending upon the subsection violated and, in certain cases, whether certain aggravating factors are present. CSEA also increased the statutory maximum term of imprisonment for convictions under 18 U.S.C. 1030(a)(5)(A)(i) when aggravating conduct is present. The statute now provides a maximum term of imprisonment of 20 years' imprisonment if the offender knowingly or recklessly caused or attempted to cause serious bodily injury and provides a statutory maximum of life imprisonment if the offender knowingly or recklessly caused or attempted to cause death.

[18] The Commission explained in its December 2002 Notice of Amendments that its revised guidelines for computer crime sentencing should consider, among other factors, "the potential and actual loss resulting from the offense, the level of sophistication and planning involved in the offense, whether the offense was committed for purposes of commercial advantage or private financial benefit," and "whether the violation was intended to, or had the effect of, significantly interfering with or disrupting critical infrastructure." 67 Fed. Reg. 77532 (18 December 2002). Available at http://www.ussc.gov/FEDREG/fedr1202.htm.

[19] As defined, any computer involved in interstate commerce or communications qualifies as a "protected computer."

[20] 6 U.S.C. 877(a).

[21] *Id.*

[22] 6 U.S.C. 133(e)(1). The Department's Notice of Proposed Rulemaking on this subject was released for public comment on April 15, 2003. *See* 68 Fed. Reg. 18524, to be codified at 6 C.F.R. 29.1 *et seq.*

[23] *See* Press Release, "FCC Announces Creation of Homeland Security Policy Council." 14 November 2001. Available at http://hraunfoss.fcc.gov/edocs_public/ attachmatch/DOC-217676A1.pdf.

[24] "Lawmaker Promises Cybersecurity Laws." *InternetNews.com,* 11 July 2003. Available at http://dc.internet.com/news/article.php/2234091. Rep. Pete Sessions (R.-Tex.), vice chairman of the Homeland Security Subcommittee on Cybersecurity, reportedly said that the federal government has been "asleep at the wheel" when it came to cybersecurity matters. *Id.*

[25] The Planning and Partnerships Office (PPO) within the DHS Directorate of Information Analysis and Infrastructure Protection assumed many of the responsibilities previously held by CIAO. The office's primary focus is to raise issues that cut across industry sectors and ensure a cohesive approach to achieving continuity in delivering critical infrastructure services.

[26] FedCIRC is the federal civilian government's trusted focal point for computer security incident reporting, providing assistance with incident prevention and response.

[27] 6 U.S.C. 143(1)(B).

[28] 6 U.S.C. 121(d)(5).

[29] "Ridge Creates New Division to Combat Cyber Threats." DHS Press Release. 6 June 2003. Available at http://www.dhs.gov/dhspublic/ display?content=916.

[30] The Bush Administration is seeking modest funding for these and other private sector cybersecurity initiatives. President Bush signed the Cyber Security Research and Development Act, which authorized $880 million over five years for new cybersecurity research centers and grants, in November 2002, although the funds have yet to be appropriated by Congress. *See* "ITAA Calls for Cybersecurity Czar." *InternetNews.com.* 22 April 2003. Available at http://dc.internet.com/ news/article.php/2194871. Overall, however, DHS's $37.7 billion budget earmarks only $3 billion for cybersecurity. "Homeland Cybersecurity Efforts Doubted." *Security Focus.* 11 March 2003. Available at http://www.securityfocus. com/ news/3043.

[31] 6 U.S.C. 143.

[32] 6 U.S.C. 144.

[33] A February 2003 study on critical infrastructure protection conducted by the General Accounting Office for the House Committee on Energy and Commerce found that more than four years after the issuance of PDD 63, some federal agencies have still not completed "the fundamental step of identifying their critical infrastructure assets and the operational dependencies of these vital assets on other public and private assets." In the study, the GAO looked at four agencies—Health and Human Services, Energy, Commerce, and the Environmental Protection Agency—to gauge their compliance with PDD 63. The study also looked at five private-sector Information Sharing and Analysis Centers (ISACs) that exist in critical infrastructure areas (information technology, water, energy, telecommunications, and electricity) to gather, analyze, and share information with members, other sectors, and the federal government. *Critical Infrastructure Protection: Challenges for Selected Agencies and Industry Sectors,* GAO-03-233 (2003).

[34] The Department of Energy in September 2002 issued a set of "21 Steps" for improving the cybersecurity of supervisory control and data acquisition (SCADA) networks, recommendations timed to coincide with the White House's release of the "CIP Strategy" and its companion "National Strategy to Secure Cyberspace."

[35] 6 U.S.C. 133.

[36] The General Accounting Office has concluded that "it is too early to tell whether such restrictions will improve information sharing, and whether additional actions may be needed, such as the use of public policy tools, to encourage increased private-sector CIP efforts and information sharing with the federal government." *Critical Infrastructure Protection: Challenges for Selected Agencies and Industry Sectors,* GAO-03-233, at 6 (2003).

[37] *See* Section 2.0, n22 above.

[38] *Critical Energy Infrastructure Information, Final Rule,* Order No. 630, Docket Nos. RM02-4-000-000, PL02-1-000-000 (issued 21 February 2003).

[39] NERC also operates the electricity sector's Information Sharing and Analysis Center (ES-ISAC), serves as the electricity sector coordinator for CIP under PDD-63, and has begun to develop reliability standards for bulk electric systems under the auspices of the private-sector American National Standards Institute.

[40] Pub. L. 104-191, 42 U.S.C. 1301 *et seq.*

[41] 42 U.S.C. 1173(d)(2).

[42] 45 CFR § 164.534.

[43] Marks, R., and P. Smith, "Analysis and Comments on HHS's Just-Released HIPAA Security Rules." *Bulletin of Law/Science and Technology, ABA Section of Science and Technology.* April 2003. 124: 2.

[44] Pub. L. 106-102, 15 USC 6801-09

[45] 15 U.S.C. 6801(b)(1-(3); *see* 12 CFR Part 30, App. B.

[46] 16 CFR Part 314; *see* 67 Fed. Reg. 36484 (23 May 2002).

[47] Cal. Civil Code 1798.29 (2002). Section 1798.84(a) provides a private right of action for damages for individuals injured by violation of Section 1798.29. *See* "Computer Break-Ins: Your Right to Know." *BusinessWeek Online.* 11 November 2002. Available at http://www.businessweek. com/technology/content/nov2002/tc20021111_2402.htm.

[48] Cal. Civil Code 1798.29(a).

[49] "California Law Tells Firms To Warn Customers If Web Sites Are Breached." Associated Press. 13 July 2003. Available at http://www.kansascity.com/mld/kansascity/business/6259091.htm.

[50] *Id.*

[51] Just as a company can be held liable in tort for failure to take reasonable care in product design, there is no legal impediment to state law tort liability for failure to take reasonable care in the protection of IT networks and electronic databases, at least if the vulnerabilities and risks are foreseeable and actual harm to plaintiffs is caused by intrusions or unauthorized disclosures. Moreover, voluntary commitments a company makes to provide privacy or security are enforceable by the Federal Trade Commission, which has taken the position (crystallized in two well-publicized cases) that departures from a voluntarily adopted web privacy policy constitute a misleading trade practice that violates the Federal Trade Commission Act. *See In re Eli Lilly & Co.,* Decision and Order (FTC, 8 May 2002); *Federal Trade Commission v. Microsoft Corp.,* Consent Decree (FTC, 7 August 2002). Indeed, the FTC recently settled with Guess Inc., based on allegations that the company's privacy policy misrepresented the security of personal information stored on its network, in a 20-year consent decree requiring Guess to implement and maintain a comprehensive information security program. *See* "Guess Settles With FTC Over Cybersecurity Snafu." *SecurityFocus News.* 19 June 2003. Available at http://www.securityfocus.com/news/5968.

[52] That economic balance may well understate the risks of liability and the scope of potential monetary exposure. For instance, in January 2003 a government contractor was sued in a class action by 562,000 retired military personal whose personal information was allegedly stolen from computer hard disk drives improperly disposed of by the contractor. *Stollenwork v. TriWest Health Care Alliance Corp.* No. 2:03cv0015 (D. Ariz. filed 28 January 2003).

Chapter 10

Procurements, Grants, and Appropriations

Bracewell & Patterson LLP
Anthony H. Anikeeff and Albert. B. Krachman

1.0   Introduction and Overview

The events of September 11, 2001, have had a profound effect upon the nation. They caused many people to lose the sense of security grounded in the belief that the United States was to some degree isolated from the destructive forces of terrorism that much of the rest of the world has grappled with for years. They have instilled in many the fear of an unknown assailant whose targets and methods of attack are also unknown. And, they have engendered a desire to achieve some level of security and assurances of safety. It is to a large degree federal, state, and local government officials who are charged with establishing a system that accomplishes this difficult task.

The response to September 11th has resulted in substantial changes in the laws by which we are governed and in the institutions though which we govern ourselves. Governments at the federal, state, and local levels have undergone realignments to address their obligations with respect to the undefined boundaries that comprise homeland security. Governments also have realigned programmatic and budgetary priorities to meet emerging needs. At the Federal level, the signal event has been the creation of the massive Department of Homeland Security (DHS), into which 22 agencies have been merged.

Among the many changes that have occurred are potentially significant changes to the manner in which the federal government and others will procure products and services. More than ever before, the public sector will be looking to the skill, talent, and innovation of the private sector to develop homeland security solutions. As a result, significant portions of homeland security budgets will find their way to businesses, universities, non-profits, and other entities through contracts, grants, and other vehicles.

Navigating the evolving field of homeland security procurement has and will continue to require even long-time government contractors to reevaluate and retool their methodology to compete effectively in the new environment. The effort will be substantially greater for the many new entrants that aspire to enter this apparently lucrative market. At the Federal level, much of the homeland security procurement effort will be conducted through or in conjunction with the DHS. And, it is through that agency that much, if not all, of the homeland security budget will flow.

In this chapter, we provide an initial roadmap for those desiring to develop a strategy to tackle this market. Concentrating on the DHS, we examine (1) the structure, procurement drivers, and emerging procurement process; (2) the grants structure and process, which, increasingly, should be another target of an entity's marketing efforts; (3) the DHS's budget and appropriations process; and (4) third-party liability protection. An important caveat to our review is that the DHS is still in the nascent stage of its development, with positions unfilled, many regulations to be promulgated, and many polices and guidance as yet to be developed. Additionally, there is pending and likely future legislation that will adjust various aspects of the DHS and its operations. Thus, the DHS is an ongoing work in process and subject to any number of significant changes as its maturation continues.

2.0 Procurements—Selling to the Department of Homeland Security

2.1 DHS Creation and Overview

The Homeland Security Act of 2002 (HSA) created the Department of Homeland Security as a new executive Department of the United States in what may be the signal action by the federal government in response to the events of September 11th.[1] The Department centralizes much of federal effort to address the broad range of challenges encompassed by homeland security. To accomplish this, the DHS has absorbed 22 agencies and will employ an estimated 170,000 persons around the world. It will be the third largest agency of the federal government behind the Department of Defense and Department of Veterans Affairs. The DHS will be supported by a massive budget, amounting to $33.7 billion for fiscal year 2003 and a projected $36.2 billion for fiscal year 2004. These budgets will be compounded by those portions of other agencies' budgets, such as those of the Departments of Defense, Energy, Health and Human Services, and Justice that are devoted to the homeland security effort.

There is no doubt that the DHS presents an alluring target for experienced and new entrants to the federal market. Understanding what motivates the DHS's components and personnel to acquire goods and services is essential if one is going to be successful. This requires an assessment of numerous factors, including the DHS's mission, structure, needs, budget, and procurement process.

2.2 DHS Mission

The DHS has been tasked with an extremely broad mission, which encompasses (1) preventing terrorist attacks; (2) reducing the Nation's vulnerability to terrorism; (3) minimizing the damage from terrorist attacks; (4) assisting in the recovery from terrorist attacks that do occur; and (5) monitoring connections between terrorism and illegal drug trafficking, coordinating efforts to sever such ties, and contributing to drug interdiction efforts. In addition, the DHS is expected to continue with the many tasks previously carried out by the agencies absorbed into the DHS, including serving as the focal point for addressing natural and man made crises and emergency planning.[2]

The tasks assigned to the DHS are enormously broad and challenging. Continuing to build upon the already substantial procurements of the agencies under its aegis, the DHS eventually will generate a substantial and varied procurement demand, from the mundane of computer terminals and paper clips, to the facilities to house the DHS's personnel and operations, to information systems, border security devices, and disaster recovery aids, to advancing the boundaries of science and technology. Organizationally, the DHS has subdivided and assigned aspects of its mission to several directorates and independent organizations that will become the agency's programmatic customers. Knowing the responsibilities assigned to these elements of the DHS will be a first step in identifying appropriate targets for one's products and services.

2.3 DHS Structure and Responsibilities

The DHS will accomplish its mission primarily through four substantive directorates, each of which being headed by an Under Secretary. Management functions within the DHS are concentrated under a Directorate of Management that is also headed by an Under Secretary. In addition, the Coast Guard, Secret Service, and aspects of the Bureau of Citizenship and Immigration Service will maintain separate identities within the DHS and will report directly to the Office of the Secretary.

The four substantive directorates include the following: (1) Directorate for Information Analysis and Infrastructure Protection, (2) Directorate of Science and Technology, (3) Directorate of Border and Transportation Security, and (4) Directorate of Emergency Preparedness and Response. Each has distinct responsibilities that effectuate the DHS's overall mission.

The Directorate of Information Analysis and Infrastructure Protection is charged primarily with (1) gathering, analyzing, and integrating information generated by other public and private entities; (2) identifying, assessing, and detecting terrorist threats in terms of potential vulnerabilities; (3) carrying out a comprehensive assessment of vulnerabilities with respect to, and developing plans for, securing key resources and critical infrastructure; (4) identify priorities for protective and support measures; and (5) disseminating information as necessary to assist in achieving the agency's mission. This Directorate also will administer the Homeland Security Advisory System.[3]

The Directorate of Science and Technology is charged primarily with coordinating and prioritizing the Nation's civilian research and development efforts in order to identify and develop countermeasures to various chemical, biological, radiological, nuclear, and other emerging terrorist threats, through a variety of government and private sector programs. In doing so, the Directorate is to coordinate with and rely upon other agencies in areas for which they have specialized expertise or facilities.[4] In addition, the Directorate will house the Homeland Security Advanced Research Projects Agency (HSARPA), modeled on a similar agency within the Department of Defense, which will administer a fund to support basic and applied research to accelerate the development, testing, evaluation, and deployment of technologies that further DHS's mission[5]. The HSA also directs the Secretary to establish a Homeland Security Institute to test the vulnerabilities of the nation's infrastructure and the effectiveness of the defensive systems to protect those systems.[6]

The Directorate of Border and Transportation Security is by far the largest of the directorates. It is charged with (1) protecting the Nation's borders, waterways, airways, ports, terminals, and transportation systems from terrorism; (2) establishing policies for and administering the immigration and visa systems; (3) administering the Customs laws of the United States; and (4) conducting various agricultural inspections.[7] The largest element of this directorate is the Transportation Security Agency (TSA), which was transferred from the Department of Transportation. By statute, the TSA will retain its independent status and functions to provide for aviation and airport security, which may well include its unique procurement and dispute resolution procedures, for at least a two-year period.[8]

The Directorate of Emergency Preparedness and Response is charged with providing the federal government's response, and ensuring the effectiveness of the response of others, to terrorist attacks, major disasters, and other emergencies. The Directorate also is to develop a national incident management system and a comprehensive program for developing interoperative communications technologies that are to be made available to emergency response providers.[9]

Within these broad parameters, the tasks will be further divided among the 22 agencies that have been incorporated into the overarching directorates. As currently conceived, the DHS will provide centralized leadership from headquarters. However, at the execution level, much of the activity of the DHS will be decentralized and carried out through a regional office structure throughout the country. It is at that level that the DHS is likely to have greatest contact with state and local officials in executing the DHS's programs and in generating many of the DHS's requirements.

The Directorate of Management will be responsible for administering the management and support functions for the DHS, including (1) procurements, (2) grants and other assistance programs, (3) budget and appropriations, (4) human resources, (5) the DHS's information and communications systems, and (6) operations and administration.[10] From a procurement perspective, one unique aspect of the DHS is its collocating management of procurements and grants within the same management structure. To a greater extent than may be the practice in other agencies, this structure should facilitate the DHS's ability to use grants and procurements strategically to accomplish the agency's mission. Considering the substantial grants already and likely to be issued, those considering the homeland security market may well benefit from monitoring DHS grant opportunities in addition to traditional procurement opportunities.

2.4   DHS Requirements

As noted elsewhere throughout this book and chapter, the mission assigned to the DHS is extraordinarily broad. Moreover, the responsibilities assigned to the directorates also are broad. In assessing what the DHS will procure to meet those needs, one of the key drivers is that underlying all of DHS's responsibilities, and those of the individuals who work for and with the DHS, is the fact that they are confronting an unknown assailant. In carrying out the DHS's mission, the agency's personnel must address, among other things, the timing of a potential attack; the method of attack in terms of weapons, delivery, and personnel; and the target of any such attack. Added to the mix is the imbalance between the anonymity of success and the potentially catastrophic consequences of a failure. In response, as might be expected, the DHS is looking for solutions that will increase the likelihood that it can prevent, or minimize the consequences of, future attacks.

The requirements of each directorate and independent office within the DHS will vary according to its respective areas of responsibility. However, on a broader level, the needs of DHS might be categorized into the areas of technical solutions, integration of various solutions, and day-to-day operations support.

Because the DHS is delving into threat areas not previously addressed in a systematic manner, the DHS necessarily will be seeking novel technical solutions to address a host of discrete areas. In broad brush, these needs will focus upon the detection, identification, and prevention of future events, the protection of various assets, and the response to any events that do occur. The DHS also will require, at a higher level, the capability to integrate various technical solutions into existing and future systems. In addition, like any other entity, the DHS will require operational and administrative support for its many employees and systems. Moreover, despite the nature of its mission, the DHS will be required to evaluate along with other federal agencies which of its functions might appropriately be considered for outsourcing as not being inherently governmental. Considering how the products and services of one's own entity can best contribute to the DHS's missions and efforts and where the capabilities of one's own entity fit on the DHS's scale of needs should afford further insight into where best to target one's efforts.

2.5   DHS Budget and Appropriations

2.5.1   DHS Budget

The massive DHS budget has made the DHS an alluring marketing target for many, amounting to $33.7 billion for FY 2003 and $36.2 billion for FY 2004. A recent analysis of the FY 2003 and FY 2004 budgets reveals that approximately $6.13 billion and $7.21 billion, respectively, of the DHS budget for those years will be available for procurement.[11] Closer analysis of the details of the budget will afford strong indicators as to where funding will be available for new procurements and grants.[12]

The task of assessing priorities within the DHS budget and the larger homeland security arena should be facilitated, commencing with the FY 2005 budget, when the president will be required to include with the proposed budget a report to Congress that analyzes the gross and net appropriations or obligations authority that contribute to homeland security, by budget function, agency, and by initiative for the prior, current, pending, and future fiscal years.[13]

2.5.2   DHS Appropriations Process

Annually, Congress considers appropriations measures that provide funding for federal government activities. The power to appropriate funds is an exclusively legislative power. The Executive branch may spend only the amount appropriated by Congress and may only use funds for purposes articulated by Congress. Of course, the president has the power to veto or approve the measures. And, the president can influence spending through the annual budget proposal. After the president submits the proposed budget, the House and Senate Appropriations Committees hold subcommittee hearings on the portions of the budget over which they exercise jurisdiction. The House and Senate Appropriations Committees each have 13 subcommittees.

As Congress responds to the increased need and demand for homeland security legislation, the temptation to authorize expansive and expensive new programs increases. Legislators have also worked to authorize new grant programs to meet state and local needs in the war on terrorism. While federal legislation authorizes spending, the legislation does not appropriate the funds. Only the Congressional appropriations process does that. Given the realities of massive demand, reduced revenue, and risk of increasing deficits, the Appropriations Committee is the critical venue for allocation of funds to the authorized programs.

After September 11th, the House of Representatives and the Senate established homeland security appropriations subcommittees, which is a rare event. Rather than establish a new, fourteenth subcommittee, Congress merged the former Subcommittee on Transportation with the Subcommittee on Treasury, Postal Service, and General Government to form the Subcommittee on Transportation, Treasury, and General Government. Thus, there remain 13 appropriations subcommittees, notwithstanding the addition of the Subcommittee on Homeland Security.

The new homeland security appropriations subcommittees were established in February of 2003. They consolidate many pieces of homeland security formerly dispersed among the other appropriations subcommittees. At the time of writing, the full committees were determining the jurisdiction of the new subcommittees. Members of the House Subcommittee on Appropriations include nine Republicans and six Democrats: Harold Rogers (R-Ky.) chair; C.W. Bill Young (R-Fla.), vice chair; Frank R. Wolf (R-Va.); Zach Wamp (R-Tenn.); Tom Latham (R-Iowa); Jo Ann Emerson (R Mo.); Kay Granger (R-Tex.); John E. Sweeney (R-N.Y.); Don Sherwood (R-Pa.); Martin Olav Sabo (D-Minn.), ranking member; David E. Price (D-N.C.); Jose E. Serrano (D-N.Y.); Lucille Roybal-Allard (D-Cal.); Marion Berry (D-Ark.); Alan B. Mollohan (D-W.Va.).

Members of the Senate Subcommittee on Appropriations include nine Republicans and eight Democrats: Thad Cochran (R-Miss.) chair; Ted Stevens (R-Alaska); Arlen Specter (R-Pa.); Pete V. Domenici (R-N.Mex,); Mitch McConnell (R-Ky.); Richard C. Shelby (R-Ala.); Judd Gregg (R-N.H.); Ben Nighthorse Campbell (R-Colo.); Larry E. Craig (R-Idaho); Robert C. Byrd (D-W.Va.) ranking member; Daniel K. Inouye (D-Hawaii); Ernest F. Hollings (D-S.C.); Patrick J. Leahy (D-Vt.); Tom Harkin (D-Iowa); Barbara A. Mikulski (D-Md.); Herb Kohl (D-Wisc.); and Patty Murray (D-Wash.).

The demands made upon the homeland security appropriations subcommittees likely will be immense. Not only must they confront the demands at the federal level, but private and public entities, and state and local bodies also will be seeking funding to strengthen their unique homeland security efforts.

2.6   DHS Private Sector Policy

The HSA establishes as DHS policy an unusually strong commitment to encourage and invite the best and brightest of the Nation to participate with the DHS in finding solutions to the challenges of homeland security. For example, the HSA prescribes that there be a Special Assistant to the Secretary of DHS charged with creating and fostering strategic communications with the private sector, advising with respect to the impact of DHS activities on the private sector, and engaging in other efforts to promote interaction between the public and private sectors.[14] In that regard, the DHS has established an Office of Private Sector Liaison that is to serve as a single point of contact for business and other non-governmental entities.

The HSA further prescribes that the DHS use "commercial-off-the-shelf technology" to address agency needs,[15] and encourages the use of commercially available information technology solutions.[16] The HSA directs the HSARPA to conduct technology conferences to improve contact between technology developers, vendors, and acquisition personnel.[17] The HSA also directs the DHS to establish a program to encourage technological innovation in facilitating the mission of the DHS through creation of a technology clearinghouse, issuing announcements seeking unique and innovative technologies, and providing assistance to those seeking advice on how to develop or deploy new technologies.[18] It also instructs all agencies to conduct market research to identify the capabilities of new entrants and small businesses that are available to meet the DHS's needs.[19] And, lastly, as discussed below, the enhanced procurement options authorized by the HSA afford the DHS a variety of options to entice new entrants into the market.

2.7   DHS Procurement Process

Those selling to the DHS are likely to encounter an amalgam of familiar and novel organizations and principles with which they will need to grapple. If there is an overriding procurement principle in the HSA, however, it is the apparent effort to make the procurement process as attractive as possible to do business with the DHS.

2.7.1   Procurement Management

The Secretary of the DHS is vested with overall procurement authority to make contracts, grants, and cooperative agreements and to enter into agreements with other federal agencies.[20] This Secretary will manage the procurement process through the Under Secretary for Management,[21] who, in turn, will oversee the Office of the Chief Procurement Officer (CPO). The Office of the CPO will be comprised of five offices: (1) Competitive Sourcing, (2) Small and Disadvantaged Business Affairs (OSDBU), (3) Grants, (4) Acquisition Policy and Oversight, and (5) Acquisition Systems and Strategic Sourcing. The Office of Competitive Sourcing will be responsible for implementing government requirements for outsourcing and privatization. The OSDBU will be responsible for developing and implementing policy and procedures relative to small and disadvantaged business development. The Office of Grants will manage and coordinate the grants efforts within the DHS. The Office of Acquisition Policy and Oversight will be responsible for developing agency procurement polices. The Office of Acquisition Systems and Strategic Sourcing will manage the integration and coordination of the DHS's many elements and acquisition partners.

It is envisioned that the DHS CPO will provide a level of centralized policy direction for procurements by the DHS. Implementation, however, will likely occur on a more decentralized level that has yet to emerge. As of July 2003, the Office of CPO is still in the organizational stages such that significant changes could occur. The Office of Acquisition Policy, however, is currently developing procurement guidance that will become the Homeland Security Supplemental Acquisition Regulations (HSAR) and the Homeland Security Acquisition Manual (HSAM). Following the model of the Federal Aviation Administration, the HSAR is expected to address matters that have a substantive impact on vendors. The HSAM will address "back room" management issues that should not substantively affect vendors.

2.7.2   DHS Procurement Authorities

The DHS is afforded a variety of procurement vehicles with which to procure that which it needs as well as to attract vendors who may have previously declined to participate in the government market. They include (1) all of the traditional procurement methods; (2) new government-wide procedures made available for procurements related to the defense against or recovery from terrorism or nuclear, biological, chemical, or radiological attack;[22] (3) streamlined procurement authority for mission-critical DHS procurements;[23] and (4) particularly flexible procurement methods for research and development (R&D) and prototype projects.[24] What is unclear at this early stage of the DHS's evolution is whether and, also, how the DHS will utilize these various authorities.

2.7.2.1   Traditional Procurement Authorities

The DHS is a civilian Executive Department of the United States Government.[25] As such, it is subject to and may utilize all of the procurement-related statutes and regulations that apply to the other civilian agencies. They include (1) the Federal Property and Administrative Services Act of 1949, which establishes the general procurement requirements applicable to federal civilian agencies;[26] (2) the Competition in Contracting Act of 1984 (CICA), which establishes the principle of "fair and open competition" in government procurements;[27] (3) the Contract Disputes Act (CDA), which establishes the procedure for resolving disputes between the government and contractors;[28] and the Truth in Negotiations Act.[29] The DHS and those doing business with the DHS also will be required to observe the various procurement integrity and false claims statutes and regulations that apply to federal procurements.[30]

The DHS also is subject to the regulatory requirements set forth in the Federal Acquisition Regulation (FAR). The FAR is applicable to most federal agencies,[31] and establishes uniform rules regarding all phases of the procurement process from acquisition planning;[32] to contracting methods and types;[33] to the use and effect of various socioeconomic programs;[34] to general contracting requirements such as those governing intellectual property rights, cost accounting standards and cost principles, protests, and dispute resolution;[35] to contract management principles.[36] The DHS, like other federal agencies, is authorized to promulgate a supplement to the FAR to address the particular needs and requirements of the DHS.[37] As noted above, the CPO's office of Acquisition Policy & Oversight is currently in the process of developing the HSAR and companion HSAM.

In conducting procurements, the DHS is obliged, in the same manner as other agencies, to conduct solicitations in a manner to encourage "full and open competition," unless an exception authorizes otherwise.[38] "Full and open competition" is defined to mean that all responsible sources are permitted to submit sealed bids or competitive proposals on the procurement.[39]

The federal government traditionally conducts procurements through one of two methods: (1) sealed bidding pursuant to FAR part 14 or (2) negotiated procurements pursuant to FAR Part 15. Over the course of the last decade, however, Congress has effected changes intended to streamline the procurement process for commercial items and services and make it operate more like the commercial market. These changes were enacted through the Federal Acquisition and Streamlining Act of 1994,[40] extended through the Clinger-Cohen Act of 1996,[41] and implemented primarily through FAR Part 12.

Numerous benefits flow to those whose products or services qualify as a "commercial item."[42] The government is expected to rely more upon a contractor's published materials regarding proposed goods and services in lieu of requiring detailed technical proposals.[43] The government is also expected to rely upon a contractor's quality assurance system rather than its own inspection system, with any government inspection to be consistent with commercial practice.[44] The government, generally, is not to acquire data rights greater than those customarily provided to the public and is to presume that the data were developed at private expense.[45] The government, generally, is also not to acquire rights to commercial computer software or to related documentation under licensing other than to the extent provided to the public and shall not acquire technical information that is not customarily provided to the public or obtain downstream rights except as mutually agreed.[46] Subject to existing laws and customary practices, the parties may negotiate and tailor a number of the contract clauses to conform to market conditions of a particular purchase, as well as to incorporate commercial practices appropriate to the industry.[47] The government may use various forms of commercial financing procedures.[48] A number of the traditional contract clauses are modified or simplified and contractors are required to comply with only a limited number of the statutes, regulations, and other provisions that usually apply to government contracts.[49] In this regard, commercial items sales are exempted from both the requirements of the Truth in Negotiations Act[50] and also the Cost Accounting Standards.[51]

As a practical matter, the procurement procedures for a commercial item acquisition are generally simplified and more expedited than for other acquisitions. These procedures can be even more streamlined for the acquisition of commercial items under contracts that are less than $5million.[52] In addition, those who provide commercial itmes as a subcontractor to a federal contractor benefit from there being only a minimal impact upon their customary practices.[53]

In addition to these procurement options, the DHS also will be able utilize and procure items and services through any number of Multiple Award Schedule contracts, indefinite quantity contracts, Federal Supply Schedule Contracts, and Government Wide Acquisition Contracts. Entities desiring to sell through these vehicles may need either to secure the award of such a contract vehicle, if possible, or team with an entity that already holds such a contract vehicle.

At the other end of the scale, in appropriate circumstances, the DHS may enter into contracts following procedures that reflect "other than full and open competition."[54] Such procedures are authorized in circumstances where, for example, there is but one responsible source, or there are unusual and compelling circumstances, or revealing the agency's needs would compromise national security, or the agency head determines that public interest so dictates.[55]

The DHS is authorized to receive unsolicited proposals, by which an entity can propose what it perceives to be a unique product or solution to an agency. In some circumstances, this can lead to the award of a contract without providing for full and open competition.[56]

The DHS also is authorized by CICA to issue Broad Agency Announcements (BAA) to obtain proposals for basic and applied research or that part of a development effort not related to the development of a specific system or hardware procurement. In the months following September 11th, the Defense Department used the BAA process to solicit innovative proposals to combat terrorism and received some 12,000 proposals. The DHS is expected to make similar use of the BAA authority. Contracts awarded under these general solicitations meet the "full and open" competition requirements of CICA.[57]

2.7.2.2 Defense Production Act

The DHS also has available to it the authority established by the Defense Production Act (DPA).[58] The DPA authorizes the government, in times of national emergency, to compel private sector companies to provide needed goods and services that are essential to the national defense. Companies are required to accept and satisfy such orders on a priority basis even though it disrupts the company's own schedule. In return, they are afforded protection against liability related to the disruption of their other commitments.

2.7.2.3 Special Procurement Authorities

The HSA establishes several new streamlined procurement authorities that are available to the DHS, either exclusively or as an Executive Agency. They include (1) Federal Emergency Procurement Flexibility for the Defense Against or Recovery from Terrorism or Nuclear, Biological, Chemical, or Radiological Attack;[59] (2) Streamlined Acquisition Authority for DHS mission-critical procurements;[60] and (3) "Other Transactions" Authority for DHS R&D and prototype projects.[61] As with other aspects of the DHS, these provisions reflect another means to facilitate procurements by the DHS and potentially attract new entrants into the market.

2.7.2.3.1 Federal Emergency Procurement Flexibility

The HSA authorizes all executive agencies, for a one-year period following enactment of the HSA, through November 25, 2003, to utilize several streamlined procurement authorities if the agency head determines that the procurement is for the defense against or recovery from terrorism or nuclear, biological, chemical, or radiological attack.[62] The authority encompasses a very broad range of potential procurements and covers acquisitions to support both prospective actions as well as recovery actions. The DHS, as an executive department, is entitled to use this authority in addition to its own similar streamlined authority discussed below. Considering its short prescribed lifespan, the government promptly issued implementing regulations.[63]

The HSA establishes the following for eligible procurements:

(1) Increases the simplified acquisition threshold for procurements in "support of a humanitarian or peacekeeping operation or contingency operation," to $200,000 for contracts to be performed or purchases to be made in the United States and to $300,000 for contracts to be performed or purchases to be made outside the United States[64]

(2) Increases the threshold to make purchases without competitive quotations under the micro-purchase authority to $7,500[65]

(3) Authorizes agencies to utilize four enumerated statutes applicable to commercial items, without limitation as to the amount, in acquiring covered goods and services[66]

(4) Directs agency heads to utilize streamlined procurement authorities, including those that provide for other than full and open competition, where appropriate[67]

(5) Waives certain small business limitations when using streamlined acquisition authorities and procedures[68]

(6) Increases the small business set aside reserve requirements to the same limits as the increased simplified acquisition thresholds[69]

It remains to be determined how broad a scope of activities will be eligible for simplified acquisition procedures under the provisions for "humanitarian or peacekeeping operation or contingency operation."[70] Practical experience also will likely reveal what ramifications, if any, arise from Congress having specified that the commercial item authority be limited to the application of four statutes. Initial review suggests, however, that the cited statutes cover most, if not all, aspects of commercial item procurements. In the meantime, there are numerous benefits to be had for contractors if the government exercises its commercial item procurement authority. As discussed above, such procurements should be much less burdensome on contractors and the government alike. Significant issues, however, may arise if the government endeavors to utilize the commercial item authority to procure items or services that otherwise would not qualify for commercial item status. Because such items and services may lack the market exposure and price history attendant to traditional commercial item sales, they may not fit well into the model that has been created for such procurements. Disputes may arise with respect to the government's desire for more assurance about product capabilities or the price reasonableness of a product that has not been tested in the marketplace. Contractors may find the use of fixed-price contracts awkward for some types of service contracts. There also may be a need to address in greater depth various intellectual property rights associated with patent and data rights.[71]

2.7.2.3.2   Streamlined DHS Mission Critical Procurements

The HSA authorizes the Secretary of Homeland Security, for the period through September 30, 2007, to utilize three streamlined acquisition authorities in circumstances where the Secretary determines in writing that the mission of the Department "would be seriously impaired without the exercise of such authorities."[72] The Secretary is required to report the exercise of this authority to Congress within seven days of his determination and may only delegate his authority to a presidential appointee who has undergone Senate confirmation.[73]

The HSA authorizes the following for covered procurements:

(1) Increased threshold to make purchases without competitive quotations under the micro-purchase authority to $7,500 for a limited number of designated employees[74]

(2) Increased simplified acquisition threshold for procurements to $200,000 for contracts to be performed or purchases to be made in the United States, and to $300,000 for contracts to be performed or purchases to be made outside the United States[75]

(3) The DHS Secretary may "deem any item of service to be a commercial item for purposes of Federal procurement laws" up to a value of $7.5 million[76]

As a preliminary matter, the high-level approval required combined with the need to promptly report and justify the action to Congress raises some question about how often the DHS will be inclined to exercise the authority. In this regard, there also is an issue as to whether the Secretary could make a blanket designation to cover all DHS purchases for a specified period of time or would be required to make separate decisions and reports for each covered acquisition.

The primary benefit of this provision is the authority for the DHS to "deem" any item or service as a commercial item, thereby entitling the contractor to all of the attendant benefits that flow from such designation, as discussed above. Although this authority is more straightforward than that under the federal emergency authority, contractors may face many of the same types of issues discussed above, if the DHS uses the authority to procure items and services that are not inherently commercial.

2.7.2.3.3   Other Transactions

The HSA authorizes a five-year pilot project, through November of 2007, for the DHS to enter into "other transactions" (OT) for certain research and development (R&D) and prototype projects related to homeland security. The DHS program is modeled after and largely mimics the OT program at the Department of Defense.[77] In essence, the HSA extends the authority of the Defense Department to the DHS, under the authority of the Secretary, to carry "basic and advanced research and development projects" in the same manner as the Defense Department does through its Secretary. It is likely that this vehicle will be used by the HSARPA.

OTs refer to transactions other than contracts, grants, and cooperative agreements and are used when those vehicles are considered to be inappropriate or infeasible such that there is a need to utilize innovative business arrangements. They have proven attractive to technology and research companies that might otherwise have balked at doing business with the government because they are exempt from most statutes and regulations that govern government procurement. As a result, they afford the government and prospective contractors considerable flexibility in structuring their relationship.

Different criteria establish when the DHS may enter into OTs for R&D and prototype contracts. There are three conditions regarding the DHS's authority to enter into OTs for R&D projects. R&D OTs are authorized where the Secretary determines that (1) use of a contract, grant, or cooperative agreement for such a project is not feasible or appropriate,[78] and (2) the transaction does not duplicate research being conducted under a existing programs being carried out by the DHS.[79] In addition, where the Secretary determines that it is practicable, the program participants are to cover at least one-half of the costs of the project.[80] Considering the Secretary's authority under the HSA to delegate his functions, and in light of the practice at the Defense Department, one could expect that these determinations will be delegated down to lower level officials.[81]

Similar criteria govern the use of OTs for prototype OTs, although they generally do not all require secretarial determinations: (1) DHS must determine that use of a contract, grant, or cooperative agreement for such project is not feasible or appropriate;[82] (2) to the maximum extent practicable, the transaction is not to duplicate another DHS project; (3) to maximum extent practicable, DHS must award OTs based upon competitive procedures; (4) participants entering into OTs that exceed $5million generally must allow the General Accounting Office at least limited access to their books if they have held a government contract in the prior year that subjected them to government audit; and (5) DHS is to require the program participants to pay at least one-third of the costs, unless at least one nontraditional contractor participates significantly in the program or a senior procurement official waives the cost sharing requirement based upon exceptional circumstances.[83] Although the Defense Department's OT program restricts prototype OTs to projects directly relevant to "weapons or weapon systems proposed to be acquired by the Department of Defense,"[84] the DHS likely will not be held to this limitation but may restrict its OT program in some other like manner.

It is unclear at this stage whether and, if so, when the DHS will promulgate regulations or issue guidance regarding its OT programs. If it does do so, it will be able to draw upon the Defense Department model and considerable guidance as a base from which to work.

2.7.3   Coast Guard Procurement Authority

As noted above, the Coast Guard transitioned into the DHS as a distinct entity, whose Commandant will report directly to the Secretary of DHS.[85] In that regard, the Coast Guard will retain its structure, authorities, capabilities, and functions, which presumably includes its authority to contract. From a procurement perspective, the Coast Guard likely will remain at least somewhat distinct from the rest of the DHS in that it is subject to the Armed Services Procurement Act, rather than the Federal Property and Administrative Services Act that covers the otherwise civilian DHS.[86] It will, however, be entitled to make use of the streamlined procurement authority otherwise available to the DHS.

2.7.4   Transportation Security Administration Procurement Authority

The HSA transfers the Transportation Security Administration (TSA) from the Department of Transportation into the DHS as a distinct entity under the aegis of the Directorate of Border and Transportation Security, including the functions of the Secretary of Transportation and of the Under Secretary of Transportation for Security relating thereto.[87] The DHS is required to maintain the TSA's separate existence for two years.[88]

From a procurement perspective, it is unclear whether the TSA is to follow the general federal procurement system and rules that apply to the DHS or to continue to utilize the far more relaxed procurement system it was authorized to develop while within the Transportation Department, whereby it operated under its own Acquisition Management System that was exempt from most procurement laws and regulations. At least one commentator suggests that the TSA may and perhaps must continue to use the TSA's preexisting AMS.[89]

2.7.5   Bid Protests and Contract Dispute Resolution

DHS is generally subject to the procurement statutes and regulations. Accordingly, it likely will implement and otherwise be subject to a bid protest and dispute resolution system similar to other federal agencies. The TSA, however, may at least temporarily be the most significant exception.

2.7.5.1 Bid Protests

The FAR authorizes interested parties to submit agency level protests to challenge the solicitations or awards made by an executive agency such as the DHS. Such agency protests are relatively expeditious and informal proceedings that are useful to challenge readily apparent errors.[90] In addition, the General Accounting Office and the United States Court of Federal Claims possess protest jurisdiction over contract actions by the DHS.[91] One may appeal the decision of the Court of Federal Claims for to the United States Court of Appeals for the Federal Circuit[92] and from there seek further review before the United States Supreme Court.[93]

The TSA utilized an alternative protest system while at the Transportation Department.[94] It is unclear at this stage the extent to which it will be able to continue to utilize its preexisting system or will be required to adopt the more conventional system used by other agencies.

2.7.5.2 Contract Disputes

The DHS generally is subject to the Contract Disputes Act (CDA), which establishes a government-wide system for the resolution of contract disputes.[95] Under the CDA and the FAR disputes clause, a contractor first must present its disputed contract claim to an agency contracting officer.[96] The contacting officer may negotiate a mutually satisfactory resolution of the matter or issue a "final" decision denying the claim entirely or in part. If the contracting officer fails to issue a decision on the claim it is deemed to be denied.[97] Upon receipt of an adverse final decision, or based upon a deemed denial, a contractor may challenge the decision before the United States Court of Federal Claims or before the appropriate agency board of contract appeals.[98] At present, the DHS has neither established its own board of contract appeals nor designated another existing board to serve in that capacity, which it is authorized to do.[99] Contractors may appeal adverse decisions of the Court of Federal Claims and the boards of contract appeals to the United States Court of Appeals for the Federal Circuit,[100] and from there seek further review before the United States Supreme Court.[101]

2.7.6 Third-Party Liability

2.7.6.1 SAFETY Act

Potential third-party liability is likely to be a substantial concern of any entity considering sales either to the DHS or sales to others in the homeland security arena. With the potential for catastrophic losses and the likelihood of ensuing products liability lawsuits, companies are reasonably wary about putting their products on the front lines.

The HSA, through the incorporated "Support Anti-Terrorism by Fostering Effective Technologies Act of 2002 (SAFETY Act),[102] makes a substantial effort to protect contractors in these circumstances. Those entities whose "anti-terrorism technology" secures approval from the Secretary of Homeland Security and is deployed enjoy significantly limited tort liability from those who are injured by terrorist attacks. In July 2003, the DHS has issued proposed regulations that implement and interpret the requirements and benefits of the SAFETY Act.[103]

The SAEFTY Act limits a seller's liability to the amount of liability insurance coverage that the Act requires the seller to maintain, for all claims arising out of or relating to or resulting from an act of terrorism, where the seller's "qualified anti-terrorism technologies" have been deployed in defense against or response or recovery from such terrorist act.[104] Sellers, regardless of whether they intend to sell to the DHS or to some third party, may submit their technology to the Secretary for approval. In assessing whether to qualify the technology for protection, the Secretary is required to evaluate the technology according to the following criteria:

(1) Prior United States Government use or demonstrated substantial utility and effectiveness
(2) Availability of the technology for immediate deployment in public and private settings
(3) Existence of extraordinarily large or extraordinarily unquantifiable potential third party liability risk exposure to the seller or other provider of such anti-terrorism technology
(4) Substantial likelihood that such anti-terrorism technology will not be deployed unless protections under the system of risk management provided under this subtitle are extended
(5) Magnitude of risk exposure to the public if such anti-terrorism technology is not deployed
(6) Evaluation of all scientific studies that can be feasibly conducted in order to assess the capability of the technology to substantially reduce risks of harm
(7) Anti-terrorism technology that would be effective in facilitating the defense against acts of terrorism, including technologies that prevent, defeat or respond to such acts[105]

If approved by the Secretary, the Secretary will issue a certificate of conformance to the seller and place the anti-terrorism technology on an Approved Product List for Homeland Security. This, in turn, results in three benefits.

First, there is exclusive federal court jurisdiction over lawsuits against the seller of qualified antiterrorism technology for injuries that are proximately caused by the seller's products used in conjunction with the defense against or response to or recovery from a terrorist act. This means that such a lawsuit cannot be brought against the seller in state courts. The federal court is to apply the substantive law of the state where the terrorist act occurred, unless the federal law preempts the state law.[106] Here, the provisions of the SAFETY Act should preempt state law.

Second, the Act bars the award of punitive damages. It also limits recovery of non-economic damages (*e.g.,* for pain, suffering, inconvenience, impairment, and other non-pecuniary damages) to an amount directly proportional to the percentage of responsibility of the seller for the harm to that plaintiff. Further, non-economic damages may not be awarded unless the plaintiff suffered physical harm.[107]

Third, the Act establishes a cap on the seller's potential total liability in the amount of the liability insurance coverage that the Act requires the seller to obtain.[108] In that regard, the Act requires, as a condition of approval, that a seller obtain liability insurance in an amount "no greater than the maximum amount of liability insurance reasonably available from private sources on the world market at prices and terms that will not unreasonably distort the sales price of Seller's anti-terrorism technologies." The insurance must be of such a nature as to protect, in addition to the seller, contractors, subcontractors, suppliers, vendors, and customers of the seller as well as those same classes of entities vis-à-vis the customer, to the extent of their potential liability for involvement in the manufacture, qualification, sale, use, or operation of the qualified anti-terrorism technologies that are deployed in defense against or response or recovery from a terrorist act.[109] The seller must present evidence of its insurance to the Secretary. In addition, the seller and all other parties must agree to assume responsibility for their own losses for business interruptions or to their employees or property.[110]

The HSA also authorizes a seller to seek separate Secretarial approval that would entitle the seller to assert the "government contractor defense" in any covered action brought against it.[111] This separate approval process, which can be run simultaneously or separately from the "qualification" process, involves a heightened standard of review. The Secretary is required to conduct a "comprehensive review of the design of such technology and determine whether it will perform as intended, conforms to the seller's specifications, and is safe for use as intended."[112] Notably, the DHS expects that certain sellers will be able to obtain the protections that come with designation as a qualified anti-terrorism technology even if they have not satisfied the requirements for the government contractor defense.[113]

The benefits of qualifying for the government contractor defense are considerable. The HSA establishes a rebuttable presumption that the government contractor defense applies to covered lawsuits as a shield for the seller. In essence, this defense protects government contractors from liability to third parties under state law.[114] The SAFETY Act now extends that protection to approved sellers for sales to those outside the federal government. A party can overcome the presumption only through evidence demonstrating that the seller acted fraudulently or willfully in submitting information to the DHS as part of the Secretary's consideration of the seller's technology.[115]

2.7.6.2 Public Law 85-804

Public Law 85-804 provides for various forms of extraordinary contractual relief, including contractual indemnification.[116] As such, it serves as a congressionally approved exception to the prohibition on government indemnity of private contractors for situations involving unusually dangerous risks.[117]

The president has authorized many federal agencies to provide indemnification under Public Law 85-804 and recently extended such authority to the DHS. In doing so, however, the president imposed severe restrictions on all agencies regarding its use, apparently with the intention to force reliance upon the SAFETY Act where it might be applicable.[118] The president barred, subject to two limited exceptions, the use of Public Law 85-804 "with respect to any matter that has been, or could be, designated by the Secretary of Homeland Security as a qualified anti-terrorism technology [under the SAFETY Act]."[119]

The two exceptions are narrow. First, in the case of the Department of Defense, the Secretary of Defense must determine that the exercise of authority is necessary for the timely and effective conduct of United States military or intelligence activities. Second, in the case of any other executive department or agency, the Secretary of Homeland Security must advise whether the use of the SAFETY Act authority would be appropriate, and the Director of the Office and Management and Budget has approved the exercise of authority.

Given the limitations imposed by the president regarding Public Law 85-804, it is unlikely that the DHS will be able to make significant use of that provision in lieu of the SAFETY Act.

2.7.6.3 Targeted Protection

In addition to the general protection provisions, the HSA also affords two targeted forms of liability protection to the manufacturers of smallpox vaccines and aviation screening companies. The Secretary is authorized to activate the smallpox protection by declaring that an actual or potential bioterrorist incident or other actual or public health emergency makes it advisable to administer a smallpox vaccine. In effect, absent breach of contract or gross misconduct, the HSA bars a person injured by a vaccine from suing the manufacturer and transfers liability to the government. [120]

The HSA also limits the liability of most aviation screening companies for third party claims arising from the terrorist attacks on September 11, 2001.[121]

2.7.7 Prohibition on DHS Contracts with "Corporate Expatriates"

In response to concern about United States companies moving offshore to avoid taxes, the HSA bars the DHS from contacting with certain formerly United States companies that are acquired by a foreign entity, where the aggregate entity does not have substantial business in the foreign country where it is created or organized as compared with its total business activities.[122] The Secretary is authorized to waive this requirement in the interest of homeland security, to prevent loss of jobs in the United States, or to prevent the Government from incurring additional costs that otherwise would not occur.[123]

2.7.8 Transition Issues

The creation of the DHS involves a massive integration effort of a host of diverse agencies and offices, many of which have longstanding cultures and procedures that have withstood multiple reorganizations and changes in leadership. Those endeavoring to enter into the DHS market will need to remain sensitive to these cultures and the relationships that may have developed over the years. As a practical matter, it is likely that these entities will continue to operate somewhat independently for some time to come, as well as continuing their procurement traditions. In this regard, however, contractors should ensure that contracting officers with whom they do business possess the necessary contracting authority from the DHS. The adverse consequences of doing business with a government official who lacks the authority to bind the government can be substantial.

At a more formal level, the HSA makes a provision to ensure the continuity of operations during the transition process. The HSA specifies that upon transfer of an agency to the DHS, "the personnel, assets [which include contracts], and the obligations of the transferred agency shall be transferred to the Secretary," for appropriate allocation within the DHS. [124] The HSA savings provisions provide that completed administrative actions, including contracts and grants, shall not be affected by the transfer.[125] Similar continuity is provided for pending proceedings and civil actions.[126]

3.0   DHS Grants

3.1   Introduction and Overview

Like homeland security contracting, today's universe of homeland security grants is a patchwork of different programs administered by different agencies. Like contracting, there is also strong momentum to centralize, simplify, and streamline the homeland security grant process. Simplification is clearly needed. A month rarely passes without the announcement of some proposal to reform the fragmented federal grant application and award process. Despite the post-September 11th promises, until 2003, relatively little homeland security grant money found its way to state and local first responders, firemen, and other front line recipients. Congress and the Executive Departments have heard the message and are taking action on a number of fronts.

This subchapter will define a homeland security grant, contrast homeland security grants with procurement contracts, and will outline the statutory and regulatory framework for homeland security grants. The subchapter will also identify major grant sources, various categories of grants, and will describe the basic procedures to pursue and administer a homeland security grant. Finally, this subchapter will also address proposed legislation which is likely to significantly affect homeland security grant procedures.

3.2   Defining a Homeland Security Grant

Generally, a homeland security grant is a form of federal financial assistance intended to support or stimulate homeland security activity. [127] The parties to the grant are the federal agency and the award recipient. A homeland security grant differs from a homeland security contract in many ways, ranging from the intended purpose of the vehicles to closeout procedures. First, a grant vehicle is to be used when the principal purpose of the relationship is to transfer value to the recipient to carry out a public purpose.[128] In contrast, a contract vehicle should be used when the principal purpose of the relationship is to acquire services or supplies for the Federal Government's use.[129] Grants are governed by regulations and statutes applicable to financial assistance, while contracts are governed by the FAR and other contracting laws.[130]

Grants are generally awarded to specifically defined classes of eligible recipients, and the use of funds is carefully prescribed. Eligible recipients for homeland security grants will generally be defined on a case-by-case basis in the grant solicitation or announcement. States, counties, municipalities, educational institutions, and non-profit organizations receive the bulk of federal grant awards. Eligibility criteria for federal contracts are found in the form of responsibility criteria[131] and required contractor qualifications. The procedures to obtain homeland security grants from selected agencies are outlined below.

3.3   Statutory Framework for Homeland Security Grants

Before September 11, 2001, federal agencies awarded and administered what are now known as homeland security grants in a fragmented, duplicative, and non-coordinated fashion. The Departments of Justice, Health and Human Services, and Transportation, the Federal Emergency Management Agency, and others utilized their statutory authorities to administer scores of overlapping grant programs.[132] September 11, 2001, exposed the criticality of state and local response systems and the serious inadequacies in coordinated funding of state and local capability to respond to large-scale terrorist incidents. It also revealed the absence of a coherent federal grants program directed toward homeland security.

The USA PATRIOT Act[133] was the first comprehensive legislation to include a coherent homeland security focus on grants. The USA PATRIOT Act provides the statutory blueprint for many of the grant programs now administered by the DHS and focuses attention on the grant instrument as an important policy tool to promote counter-terror and homeland defense activities.

The USA PATRIOT Act includes several types of grants. Among the most important are the first responder assistance grants.[134] These grants, available to states and units of local governments, are designed to improve the ability of state and local law enforcement, fire departments, and other first responders to respond to and prevent acts of terrorism. These grants cover equipment, training, and technical assistance. Other general categories of grants provided by the USA Patriot Act include terror prevention[135] and antiterrorism training.[136]

The HSA built on the USA PATRIOT Act's emphasis on grant awards to effect homeland security activity at state and local levels. Broadly, the HSA charged the DHS with the responsibility to coordinate and issue federal grants to aid states, communities, and first responders in homeland protection.[137] Despite the broad charge, the HSA did not include the specifics on interagency coordination, state security plans, or timetables to expedite awards. These issues have been addressed more recently in proposed legislation, discussed below.

The DHS has made grant funding available for an increasing number of security-related activities. The grant awards have included funding for the following services and supplies:

- Equipment
- Training

- Planning and Exercises
- Information Sharing
- Radiological and Biological Defense Systems
- Vulnerability Self-Assessments
- Critical Infrastructure
- Emergency Management
- Law Enforcement Overtime Costs
- Port and Transit Security

In fiscal year 2003, the DHS Office for Domestic Preparedness made nearly $4 billion available to state and local governments to support first responders and to offset overtime costs.

3.4   Representative Grant Programs

The evolving nature of homeland security-related grant programs presents great challenges in any attempt to inventory them. Between the Office of Domestic Preparedness and the Federal Emergency Management Agency, 12 separate homeland security grant programs in those offices alone became consolidated within DHS. The diversity stimulated the government itself to mandate in proposed legislation a requirement to inventory all the grant programs.[138] There are, however, several representative programs which are likely to remain in their current structure for the near term and which merit attention.

3.5   Office for Domestic Preparedness Equipment Grants

The DHS Office for Domestic Preparedness (ODP) issues formula grants for equipment, training, and situational exercises to state and local first responders and direct grants to cities and counties.[139]

ODP's Equipment Grant Program provides funds to all 50 states, the District of Columbia, the Commonwealth of Puerto Rico, American Samoa, the Commonwealth of Northern Mariana Islands (CNMI), Guam, and the U.S. Virgin Islands. The authorized equipment falls into four categories: 1) personal protective equipment (PPE); 2) chemical, biological, or radiological detection equipment; 3) decontamination equipment; and 4) communications equipment.

3.6   Fiscal Year (FY) 2003 State Homeland Security Grant Program

Following the U.S. action in Iraq, the ODP provided additional financial assistance directly to states and territories under the Fiscal Year (FY) 2003 State Homeland Security Grant Program—Part II (SHSGP II).[140] This covers responder preparedness and mitigates the costs of enhanced security at critical infrastructure facilities. Funding was authorized for the procurement of specialized emergency response and terrorism incident prevention equipment.

Each state has established a state administrative agency (SAA), to apply for and administer the grant funds under this program. The State may elect to subgrant FY 2003 funding directly to cities or counties within the State or to retain the funds for use at the State level, provided that the State has complied with any pass through requirements that apply.

3.7   Directorate of Emergency Preparedness and Response

The Directorate of Emergency Preparedness and Response, formerly known as the Federal Emergency Management Agency, has also been a major source of grant funding. The Directorate has made funding available for state and local fire fighting, emergency planning, citizen and community preparedness, and operations centers.

The Directorate also awards Emergency Management Performance Grants (EMPG's). These grants provide states the flexibility to allocate funds according to risk vulnerability and to address the most urgent state and local needs in disaster mitigation preparedness and response recovery.

3.8   Transportation Security Grants

In the past, the Department of Transportation awarded transportation security grants through the Transportation Security Administration (TSA). That activity likely will shift to the DHS, with the transfer of the TSA to that agency.[141] Among the many TSA priority initiatives are port security grants. TSA's port security grants program covers port security assessment, strategies, and vulnerability identification.

With respect to domestic surface transportation, the Department of Homeland Security has identified the highest risk transit systems and has established grant programs for upgraded security. Among the Transit Security improvements to be funded by grants are physical barriers, area monitoring systems, integrated communications system, and prevention planning, training, and exercises

3.10   Obtaining a Homeland Security Grant

Obtaining a homeland security grant is a multi-step process that commences by identifying grant opportunities for which the applicant is eligible. The grant program website will typically identify eligibility requirements, and some sites require a pre-registration to determine eligibility and gain access to the application forms. The applicant must also obtain not only the relevant application forms but also any applicable financial assistance regulations or Office of Management and Budget Circulars.[142] With increasing frequency, the application forms can be completed and submitted electronically.

As of June 2003, there is no unified, one-stop source similar to the "FedBizOpps" portal for government contracts solicitation, through which one can search all federal grant opportunities. As a result, identifying grant opportunities and obtaining grant applications remains an agency-specific undertaking. Although DHS has consolidated its overall grants award and administration function within the DHS Directorate of Management, it remains necessary in 2003 to search the independent agencies and departments for grant opportunities.[143] This is, however, changing. Web sites at <www.grants.gov> and <www.fedgrants.gov> are beginning to assemble comprehensive links to grant opportunities government wide. Also, in June 2003, the Office of Management and Budget issued a final policy directive requiring agencies to adopt a uniform government-wide format for announcement of funding opportunities for discretionary grants and cooperative agreements.[144] The Senate Committee on Governmental Affairs is also considering a bill, S. 1245, called the Homeland Security Grant Enhancement Act of 2003. If enacted, this will also mandate better access to comprehensive grant information.

Until the DHS Grants office implements homeland security specific guidelines on writing grant proposals, writing a homeland security grant proposal will follow the pre-existing practice as dictated by the soliciting agency or department. Volumes have been written on writing successful grant proposals, and a well-established cottage industry of hired grant writers is available to advise on the grant proposals. Like any grant application, responsiveness to the solicitation requirements and close adherence to the evaluation criteria are essential. Two useful sites on grant writing applicable to homeland security grants can be found at <http://www.cfda.gov/public/cat-writing.htm> and <http://www.npguides.org/guide/index.html.> As the DHS Grants office matures, there is certain to be more and better information on writing homeland security specific grant proposals.

Once the closing date for receipt of grant proposals has passed, the government will begin evaluation and review of the proposals leading toward award decisions. The scope of the evaluation will vary widely depending on the subject matter of the award. Larger scale grant proposals, such as those involving port security, will receive multi-level review by field offices, regional state authorities, and then federal review. The evaluation process will often involve a pre-screen phase to first eliminate ineligible applications or incomplete proposals. The field of eligible recipients will then be narrowed according to the quality of the grant proposal.

An award recipient will need to ensure that it has systems in place to track grant reporting requirements and compliance with applicable OMB Circulars and other agency regulations. The grant application should describe each of the regulatory requirements, and applicants should not wait until receiving notice of award to first review them.

3.11 Major Legislative Proposals Affecting Homeland Security Grants

The grant process itself, and many of the regulatory requirements associated with grant awards, have been the subject of sharp criticism. Applicants and potential applicants have complained of paperwork overload, delays, lack of resource materials, lack of agency contacts, duplication of forms, and other deficiencies. Many improvements to the grant process, both internal to the government, and external to the public are underway.

One important structural change under consideration is the consolidation of certain grant activities in ODP. The president's budget request for Fiscal Year 2004 proposes that all monies for both ODP and fire grant programs (now administered by FEMA's successor, the Office of Emergency Preparedness) be administered through the Office for Domestic Preparedness. This would move state and local governments toward the much-needed "one-stop shop" they have been seeking, consolidate related functions within the DHS, and improve coordination between the programs.

On June 12, 2003, Senator Collins introduced the Homeland Security Grant Enhancement Act of 2003.[145] The bill offers a number of critical improvements to the Homeland Security Grant process. The bill is intended to improve the funding flow to first responders, eliminate duplicate planning requirements, simplify the grant application process, and coordinate the many grant programs on the books today.

The key features of the proposed legislation include formation of an interagency committee to first inventory the varied homeland security grant programs.[146] The committee is then required to recommend actions to coordinate and streamline the various grant application requirements. The interagency committee will be comprised of members from the agencies responsible for most of the homeland security grants: DHS, HHS, DOT, DOJ, and EPA. The president may add others to the committee.[147]

The bill also proposes to establish a homeland security clearinghouse.[148] The clearinghouse will maintain a web site and a single publication identifying and describing all the homeland security grants programs compiled by the inventory. The clearinghouse will also provide state and local governments with technical assistance and a best practices guidance for homeland security plans and programs.[149]

The bill will also codify the purposes for which homeland security grants may and may not be awarded. Under the bill, homeland security grants "shall be used to address homeland security matters related to acts of terrorism or major disasters and related capacity building" but shall not be used "to supplant ongoing first responder expenses or general protective measures."[150] The bill authorizes grant funds to be utilized for states to prepare comprehensive state homeland security plans.[151] To be eligible for the grant funding, states must first prepare a plan and then submit an application for reimbursement. The state plan must cover communications, first responder training, emergency response plans, protective measures for critical infrastructure owned by private owners, and other elements.[152]

The bill will also require detailed reporting of progress[153] and will require adherence to national performance standards.[154] Finally, in response to a problem cited by state and local authorities, the bill will afford new flexibility in allowing states to reallocate grant funds that could not be spent on certain authorized activities.[155]

3.12   Conclusion—Grants

Overall, the homeland security grant program is a work in process. There are scores of grant programs which can be classified as related to homeland security, and the mission to consolidate and simplify them is daunting. In 2003, grant applicants should continue to approach ODP, FEMA, the Department of Justice, the Department of Transportation, and the Department of Health and Human Services for the large grant awards. Significant changes are on the horizon, all for the better in terms of simplification and streamlining the process.

Endnotes:

[1] Homeland Security Act of 2002, Pub. L. 107-296, § 101(a), 116 Stat. 296 (25 November 2002), 6 U.S.C. § 111(a) (hereafter cited as HSA).

[2] HSA § 101(b), 6 U.S.C. § 111(b). For example, the Coast Guard will continue to perform all of its non-homeland security functions such as ensuring the marine safety, search and rescue, aids to navigation, fishing, law enforcement, maritime environmental protection, and ice operations. HSA § 888, 6 U.S.C. § 468.

[3] HSA § 201, 6 U.S.C. § 121.

[4] HSA § 302, 6 U.S.C. § 182.

[5] HSA § 307, 6 U.S.C. § 187.

[6] HSA § 312, 6 U.S.C. § 192. On a related note, the HSA also directs formation within the Justice Department of an Office of Science and Technology to serve as a focal point for improving the safety and effectiveness of law enforcement technology and improve access to such technology by Federal, state, and local law enforcement authorities. HSA §§ 231 *et seq.*, 6 U.S.C. §§ 161 *et seq.*

[7] HSA § 402, 6 U.S.C. § 202.

[8] HSA § 424, 6 U.S.C. § 234.

[9] HSA § 502, 6 U.S.C. § 312.

[10] HSA § 701, 6 U.S.C. § 341.

[11] S. Gould and C. Beckner, *The Homeland Security Market*, at 11 (The O'Gara Co. May 2003) (hereafter referred to as *HS Market*).

[12] *See HS Market, supra,* at 12 (*HS Market* report also providing detailed projected budget breakdown for various directorates and sectors of the DHS). *See also, U.S. Department of Homeland Security, Budget in Brief, 2004* (February 2003).

[13] HSA § 889, 6 U.S.C. § 889, *codified at* 31 U.S.C. § 1105(a)(33)(a)(i).

[14] HSA § 102(f), 6 U.S.C. § 112(f).

[15] HSA § 509, 6 U.S.C. § 319.

[16] HSA § 1001(b), *amending* 44 U.S.C. § 3531.

[17] HSA § 307(b), 6 U.S.C. § 187(b).

[18] HSA § 313, 6 U.S.C. § 193.

[19] HSA § 858, 6 U.S.C. § 428.

[20] HSA § 102(b)(2), 6 U.S.C. § 112(b)(2).

[21] HSA § 701(a), 6 U.S.C. § 341(a).

[22] HSA §§ 852 *et seq.*, 6 U.S.C. § 422 *et seq.*

[23] HSA §§ 833 *et seq.*, 6 U.S.C. §§ 393 *et seq.*

[24] HSA § 831, 6 U.S.C. § 391.

[25] See HSA § 876, 6 U.S.C. § 456. (barring military activities).

[26] 41 U.S.C.§ 251 *et seq.*

[27] 41 U.S.C. § 253.

[28] 41 U.S.C. §§ 601-613.

[29] 41 U.S.C. § 254b; FAR Part 15.4.

[30] *See e.q.*, FAR Part 3 (Improper Business Practices and Conflicts of Interest); 31 U.S.C. §§ 3729-3733 (False Claims Act).

[31] 41 U.S.C. § 405(a) (mandating use of FAR by all federal agencies); 41 U.S.C. § 403(1)(A) (citing 5 U.S.C. § 101) (defining an executive department to be an executive agency).

[32] FAR Parts 1-12.

[33] FAR parts 13-18.

[34] FAR parts 19-26.

[35] FAR Parts 27-41.

[36] FAR parts 42-51.

[37] FAR Subpart 1.3.

[38] 41 U.S.C § 253.

[39] 41 U.S.C § 403(6); see *also id.,* § 403(7) (defining "responsible source").

[40] Pub. L. No. 103-355, 108 Stat. 3243 (Oct. 13, 1994).

[41] National Defense Authorization Act for Fiscal Year 1996, Pub. L. 104-106, Div. D, 110 Stat. 186, 642 (10 February 1996).

[42] 41 U.S.C. § 403 (12); FAR § 2.101. Commercial items include a broad range of potential products and services, including (A) items that have been sold or offered for sale in the commercial market place, items that reflect technology advances on commercial items, items that reflect modifications to such items, and combinations of the forgoing types of items; (B) services that are ancillary to the sale of commercial items or that have been commoditized; (C) combinations of the foregoing; (D) certain sales to government entities; and (E) qualifying intercompany transactions. *Id.*

[43] FAR § 12.205.

[44] FAR § 12.208.

[45] FAR § 12.211. Although the presumption is rebuttable, it affords the contractor considerable protection.

[46] FAR § 12.212.

[47] FAR § 12.302 (tailoring); FAR § 12.213 (other commercial practices).

[48] FAR § 12.210.

[49] FAR §§ 12.301; 52.212-1 (Instructions to offerors); 52.212-3 (Offeror Representations and Certifications); 52.212-4 (Contract Terms and Clauses); 52.212-5 (Contract Clauses Required to Implement Statutes or Executive Orders); 12.503 (laws inapplicable or partially inapplicable to commercial item contracts).

[50] 41 U.S.C. § 254b(b)(1)(b). See FAR § 15.403(b)(3) & (c)(3).

[51] FAR § 12.214.

[52] *See generally* FAR Subparts 12.6 and 13.5 (streamlined procedures for certain commercial item procurements).

[53] FAR Section 12.504 strictly limits the number of clauses that can be flowed down from a prime contractor to a subcontractor under a commercial item prime contract. Similarly, FAR Subpart 44.4 provides similar limitations to the number of clauses that can be flowed down to a commercial item subcontractor from a prime contact that is for other than commercial items.

[54] 41 U.S.C. § 253(b); FAR Subpart 6.3.

[55] 41 U.S.C. § 253(c).

[56] FAR Subpart 15.6. *See also* HSA § 834, 6 U.S.C. § 394 (mandating modifications to the FAR).

[57] See FAR § 6.102 (Use of Competitive Procedures); FAR § 35.016 (Broad Agency Announcements).

[58] 50 U.S.C. App § 2061 *et seq.*

[59] HSA §§ 851-856, 6 USC §§ 422-426.

[60] HSA §§ 833, 6 U.S.C. § 393.

[61] HSA § 831, 6 U.S.C. § 391.

[62] HSA § 852, 6 U.S.C § 422.

[63] 68 Fed. Reg. 4048 (27 January 2003) (codified in FAR Parts 2, 10, 12, 13, 19, and 25).

[64] HSA § 853, 6 U.S.C. § 853. *See also* FAR Part 13 (setting forth simplified acquisition procedures authorized n such circumstances).

[65] HSA § 854, 6 U.S.C. § 424.

[66] HSA 425, 6 U.S.C § 825.

[67] HSA 856(a), 6 U.S.C. § 856(b).

[68] HSA 856(b), 6 U.S.C. § 426(b).

[69] HSA § 853(c). 6 U.S.C.§ 423(c).

[70] Some guidance is found in the definitions for these terms included in the FAR. "Contingency operation" is defined to mean "a military operation that—(1) Is designated by the Secretary of Defense as an operation in which members of the armed forces are or may become involved in military actions, operations, or hostilities against an enemy of the United States or against an opposing military force; or (2) Results in the call or order to, or retention on, active duty of members of the uniformed services...during a war or during a national emergency declared by the President or Congress." 10 U.S.C. § 101(a)(13)); FAR § 2.101. "Humanitarian or peacekeeping operation" is defined to mean a military operation in support of the provision of humanitarian or foreign disaster assistance or in support of a peacekeeping operation under chapter VI or VII of the Charter of the United Nations. The term does not include routine training, force rotation, or stationing." 10 U.S.C. § 2302(8); 41 U.S.C § 259(d); FAR § 2.101.

[71] *See* Zenner, W., J. Handwerker, and J. Catoe, "Fundamentals of Contracting with the Department of Homeland Security, Briefing Papers," No. 03-4, at 12-14, 15-16 (West Group Mar. 2003) (hereafter "DHS Fundamentals").

[72] HSA § 833(a), 6 U.S.C § 393(a). *See also* HSA § 101, 6 U.S.C. 611 (DHS mission).

[73] *Id.*

[74] HSA§ 833(b), 6 U.S.C. § 833(b).

[75] HSA § 833(c), 6 U.S.C. § 393(c). *See also* FAR Part 13 (setting forth simplified acquisition procedures authorized in such circumstances).

[76] HSA § 833(d), 6 U.S.C. § 833(d).

[77] HSA § 831, 6 U.S.C. § 391. Indeed, the HSA sets forth the scope and authorities of the DHS OT program by reference to the statutory authority for the Defense Department OT program. *Id.*, (citing 10 U.S.C. § 2371 and Section 845 of the National Defense Authorization Act for Fiscal Year 1994, Pub. L. 103-160, 10 U.S.C. § 2371, note).

[78] HSA § 831(a)(1); *see also* 10 U.S.C § 2371(e)(2).

[79] *See* 10 U.S.C. § 2371(e)(1)(A), *as referenced by* HSA § 831(a)(1), 6 U.S.C. § 391(a)(1).

[80] *See* 10 U.S.C. § 2371(e)(1)(B), *as referenced by* HSA § 831(a)(1), 6 U.S.C. § 391(a)(1).

[81] HSA § 102(b)(1), 6 U.S.C. § 112(b)(1).

[82] Unlike the other criteria applicable to prototypes, this requirement is derived from the HSA itself. *See* HSA § 831(a)(2), 6 U.S.C. § 391(a)(2) (authorizing prototype contracts pursuant to section 831(a)(1), 6 U.S.C. § 391(a)(1), which requires this determination).

[83] 10 U.S.C. § 2371 note §§ 845(b)(d).

[84] 10 U.S.C. § 2371 note §§ 845(a).

[85] HSA § 888, 6 U.S.C§ 468.

[86] 10 U.S.C. § 2303(a)(5); 41 U.S.C § 252(a)(1).

[87] HSA §§ 403, 424(a); 6 U.S.C. §§ 203, 234(a).

[88] HSA § 424(b); 6U.S.C. § 234(b).

[89] *See* DHS Fundamentals, *supra* at 4-5.

[90] FAR § 33.103.(agency level protest procedures).

[91] 28 U.S.C. § 1491(b) (Court of Federal Claims); 31 U.S.C. § 3551 *et seq.* (GAO).

[92] 28 U.S.C. § 1295(a)(3).

[93] 28 U.S.C § 1254.

[94] *See* DHS Fundamentals, *supra* at 5-6.

[95] 41 U.S.C. §§ 601 *et seq.* The CDA has been implemented through FAR Subpart 33.2.

[96] 41 U.S.C. § 605; FAR §§ 33.206-33.207.

[97] 41 U.S.C. § 605; FAR § 33.211.

[98] 41 U.S.C. § 609 (Court of Federal Claims); 41 U.S.C. § § 606, 607 (board of contract appeals).

[99] 41 U.S.C. § 607.

[100] 41 U.S.C. § 607(g); 28 U.S.C. §§ 1295(a)(3) & (a)(10).

[101] 28 U.S.C § 1254.

[102] HSA §§ 861-865, 6 U.S.C. §§ 101 note, 441-443.

[103] 68 Fed. Reg. 41419 (11 July 2003).

[104] HSA § 863(d)(2), 6 U.S.C. § 442(d)(2).

[105] HSA § 862(b), 6 U.S.C. § 441(b).

[106] HSA § 863(a), 6 U.S.C. § 442(a).

[107] HSA § 863(d)(1), 6 U.S.C. § 442(d)(1).

[108] HSA § 864(c), 6 U.S.C. § 443(c).

[109] HSA § 864(a), 6 U.S.C. § 443(a).

[110] HSA § 864(b), 6 U.S.C. § 443(b).

[111] HSA § 863(d)(2), 6 U.S.C. § 442(d)(2); *see* 68 Fed. Reg. 41419, 41422.

[112] HSA § 863(d)(2), 6 U.S.C. § 442(d)(2); Fed. Reg. 41419, 41422.

[113] See 69 Fed. Reg. 41419, 41422.

[114] HSA § 863(d), 6 U.S.C. § 442(d).

[115] HAS § 863(d)(1), 6 U.S.C. § 442(d)(1); *see* 69 Fed. Reg. 41419, 41422.

[116] 50 U.S.C. §§ 1431-1435; Executive Order 10789, 23 Fed. Reg. 8897 (Nov. 14, 1958).

[117] *See* FAR §§ 50.403-1 (indemnification requests for unusually hazardous or nuclear risks).

[118] Executive Order 13286 § 73(b) (28 February 2003).

[119] *Id.*

[120] HSA § 304(c), 6 U.S.C. § 604(c).

[121] *See* HSA § 890.

[122] HSA §§ 835(a) & (b), 6 U.S.C. § 395(a) & (b).

[123] HSA § 835(d); 6 U.S.C. § 395(d.).

[124] HSA § 1511 (d), 6 U.S.C. § 551(d). Section 2(3) of the HSA defines "assets" to include "contracts." 6 U.S.C. § 101 (3).

[125] HSA § 1512 (a), 6 U.S.C. § 552(a).

[126] *Id.,* §§ 1512 (b) & (c), 6 U.S.C. § 552 (b) & (c).

[127] A grant is a legal instrument that transfers property, money, or services to the recipient where there is no substantial involvement between the federal agency and the recipient during performance. *See*, Federal Grant and Cooperative Agreement Act of 1977, 31 U.S.C. § 6304 (2000).

[128] *Id.*

[129] *Id.* §§ 6301-6308.

[130] 48 C.F.R. §§ 1.000-53.303 (2002).

[131] 48 C.F.R. § 9.104-1 (2002).

[132] For example, among others, the Department of Justice and the Office for Domestic Preparedness administer the State Homeland Security Grant Program, the Local Law Enforcement Block Grant, and the Byrne Memorial Formula Grant Program. The Federal Emergency Management Agency assistance programs include the Assistance to Firefighters Grant Program and Citizen Corps grants. The Department of Health and Human Services administers the Public Health Bioterrorism Preparedness Program and the Hospital Bioterrorism Program. The Department of Transportation administers the Hazardous Materials Emergency Preparedness Program. An EPA Homeland Security related grant program is the Water Security Assistance Program.

[133] The USA PATRIOT Act of 2001. Pub. L. No. 107-56.

[134] USA PATRIOT Act § 1005, 28 U.S.C. § 509 note.

[135] *Id.* § 1005(b), 28 U.S.C. § 509 note.

[136] *Id.* § 1005(c), 28 U.S.C. § 509 note.

[137] HSA § 238, 6 U.S.C. § 238.

[138] *See* S. 1245, The Homeland Security Grant Enhancement Act of 2003, discussed infra.

[139] ODP also administers the Nunn-Lugar-Domenici (NLD) Domestic Preparedness Program, which was formerly managed by the Department of Defense (DOD). NLD grants focus on equipment for training purposes.

[140] Funding for the FY 2003 SHSGP II is authorized by 1) the Wartime Supplemental Appropriations Act of 2003, Pub. L. No. 108-11, 117 Stat. 559; 2) the USA Patriot Act of 2001, Pub. L. No. 107-56, 115 Stat. 272; and 3) the Homeland Security Act of 2002, Pub. L. No. 107-296, 116 Stat. 296.

[141] HSA §§ 403, 424; 6 U.S.C. §§ 203, 234.

[142] *See* OMB Circular Nos.: A-21, (Principles for Determining Costs Applicable to Grants Contracts, and Other Agreements with Educational Institution); A-87, (Cost Principles for State, Local, and Indian Tribal Governments); A-102, (Grants and Cooperative Agreements with State and Local Governments); A-110, (Uniform Administrative Requirements for Grants and Agreements with Institution of Higher Education, Hospitals, and Other Non-Profit Organizations); A-122, (Cost Principles for Non-Profit Organizations); A-133, (Audits of States, Local Government, and Non-Profit Organizations); and Exec. Order No. 12,372, (Intergovernmental Review of Federal Programs), 3 C.F.R. 197 (1983), reprinted as amended in 31 U.S.C. § 6506 note (2000).

[143] Only the Emergencies and Disasters Directorate at DHS currently has a grants index on its website.

[144] This format implements the Federal Financial Assistance Management Improvement Act of 1999, Pub. L. No. 106-107, 113 Stat. 1486.

[145] Homeland Security Grant Enhancement Act of 2003, S.1245, 108th Congress.

[146] *Id.* § 2(a).

[147] *Id.*

[148] *Id.* § 3(d).

[149] *Id.*

[150] *Id.* § 4(c)(1).

[151] *Id.* § 4(c)(2).

[152] *Id.* § 4(c).

[153] *Id.* § 4(h)(1).

[154] *Id.* § 4(h)(2).

[155] *Id.* § 5.

Chapter 11

Employment and Worksite Issues[1]

Bracewell & Patterson LLP
Nancy Morrison O'Connor

1.0   Introduction

Most of the victims on September 11, 2001, were engaged in their job duties
when tragedy struck. They were at their desks, in conference rooms, or in airline seats on behalf of their employers. It was, for many, an employment-related
event. As such, many of the repercussions and responsibilities of homeland
security efforts are in the workplace.

Since September 11, 2001, employers have repeatedly re-examined their
workplaces in light of new issues, issues that were once unthinkable but have
now acquired not only reality but priority, even urgency. These issues include
securing the workplace against the threat of an attack or natural disaster, revising policies to fit the circumstances of a changed world, addressing the special
issues associated with hiring employees from other countries or transferring
employees across borders, and ensuring the security of the workplace while
respecting the privacy rights of employees. These are issues that require constant attention and adjustment because they are in flux as the delicate balance
between competing concerns tips in synch with the changing surrounding environment.

Employers continue to face the challenge of balancing workplace privacy
with workplace security. Recognizing that security and privacy are interdependent, employers often find conflicting obligations in the workplace context.

2.0   Addressing the Threat of an Attack or Disaster

The events of September 11th have underscored the vulnerability of the workplace to criminal/terrorist activities and natural disasters. As a result, one of the

biggest challenges to employers is to re-examine their approach to issues of safety and security.

2.1 Infrastructure Security

Infrastructure security is of particular concern where multiple tenants or multiple employers share an office building.

2.1.1 Securing Ventilation Systems from CBR Attacks

The Centers for Disease Control and Prevention (CDC) and the National Institute for Occupational Safety and Health (NIOSH) collaborated with the Office of Homeland Security and 30 other federal agencies, state and local organizations, and professional associations in producing its 40-page guide to immediate actions to protect occupants from airborne chemical, biological, or radiological (CBR) attacks by reducing both the likelihood and the impact of such attacks. The agencies' recommendations include adoption of security measures for air intake and exhaust systems, evaluation of filtration systems, restricted access to building operations systems, and restricted dissemination of building design information.[2]

2.1.2 Options for Increasing Security

In securing premises, employers and landlords are adopting many and varied measures to protect employees and tenants, including

- Installing concrete or metal posts around the building perimeter to avoid the use of vehicles as potential weapons
- Limiting access to the building to one or two points of entry
- Stationing a security guard at each point of entry
- Requiring identification and registration of guests
- Authorizing security personnel to search bags or other items of personal property
- Developing a policy/procedure for escorting visitors to work locations beyond the reception area
- Issuing key cards to restrict and monitor employee access
- Issuing employee/guest identification badges and requiring their display for entry
- Developing a policy/procedure for vendor review and premises access
- Developing Emergency Action/Evacuation Plans

Considerations for employers drafting and implementing such measures include

- The potential for claims of false imprisonment, invasion of privacy, and related claims
- The need to provide adequate training to security personnel regarding appropriate/inappropriate searches
- The need to perform adequate employment screening for security personnel

2.1.3 Providing for the Security of Information Systems

In order to maintain the security of information systems, employers must consider a combination of firewalls, virus software, encryption, system backups, security policies, and employee training.

On January 17, 2002, the FBI's National Infrastructure Protection Center (NIPC) issued an Internet Content Advisory, advising companies to consider unintended audiences when posting information on their websites.[3] The Advisory encourages internet content providers to review the data they make available online to determine whether

- The information has been cleared/authorized for public release
- The website provides details concerning enterprise safety and security
- The website provides personal information on employees (such as biographies, addresses, etc.)
- The information could be used to target a company's personnel or resources, especially if used in conjunction with other publicly available information

The American Management Association Spring 2002 survey revealed that 83 percent of almost 500 responding employers had adopted a crisis management plan for technology system failure or loss of data and that "cyber threats" are of at least moderate concern to 72 percent of employers.[4]

2.1.4 Emergency Action/Disaster-Preparedness Plans

There are several reasons why emergency action plans and disaster-preparedness plans are popular and appropriate.

Occupational Safety and Health Admninstration (OSHA) Considerations: All employers should adopt Emergency Action/Disaster-Preparedness Plans. Employers with ten (10) or more employees must have those plans in writing.[5] An employer can be found negligent in the management of its premises and working conditions if it does not have an emergency action plan or train employees regarding alarms, evacuation procedures, and related matters and have the appropriate security equipment, devices, policies, procedures, and employee training in place.

Centers for Disease Control and Prevention (CDC) Considerations: The CDC urges employers to develop emergency action plans that describe the appropriate action to be taken when there is a known or suspected exposure of employees to Bacillus Anthracis (Anthrax).[6] The CDC is preparing models and funding research for prevention and response to other potential bioterrorist threats, such as smallpox, radiation, and botulism.[7]

The Federal Emergency Management Agency (FEMA) website provides sample emergency plans.[8] Drafting considerations include

- The development of an evacuation plan
- The development of a chemical/biohazard exposure and treatment plan
- The development of a process for employee education, information, and training
- The development of a decision-making chain of command
- The development of an emergency contact list (including federal emergency-management agencies such as FEMA and CDC as well as sources for weather and disaster information)
- The development of safety protocols (including the purchase of safety equipment and devices, the installation of air filters and detection systems, the training of employees, etc.)

Americans with Disabilities Act (ADA) Considerations in Evacuation Plans. The ADA requires employers to provide reasonable accommodations to qualified individuals with disabilities. This obligation may extend to providing reasonable accommodation during emergency evacuations. This may include providing "evacuation chairs" or "areas of refuge/rescue assistance."

On October 31, 2001, the Equal Employment Opportunity Commission (EEOC) issued guidance on the ADA considerations involved in the development of Emergency Evacuation Plans.[9] These guidelines permit an employer to inquire whether employees will require assistance because of a disability in the event of an evacuation. Such inquiries, however, can only be made

- After a conditional offer of employment has been extended
- Through periodic surveys of employees that explain the purpose for requesting the information and advise employees that the disclosure of information is voluntary and/or
- By requesting such information from an employee with a known disability

Employers may ask for details regarding the assistance needed but cannot inquire about the underlying impairment. Employers may share the information provided with the appropriate first aid and safety personnel but no other individuals. Reasonable accommodation remains an issue for consideration.

The National Organization on Disability provides numerous resources that address the needs of individuals with disabilities in the context of evacuation plans and emergency preparedness.[10]

2.2 Anthrax and the Mail

The CDC issued guidelines to assist employers in developing comprehensive programs to reduce the potential for anthrax exposure at locations where mail is handled or processed. These guidelines include recommendations for engineering controls, administrative controls, housekeeping controls, and personal protective equipment.

- With regard to engineering controls, the CDC recommends both the use of industrial vacuum cleaners with high efficiency particulate air (HEPA) filters in areas where aerosolized particles may be generated and the use of HEPA-filtered exhaust hoods in areas where dust can be generated.
- With regard to administrative controls, the CDC recommends that employers limit the number of employees or visitors in work areas where aerosolized particles can be generated.
- With regard to housekeeping controls, the CDC suggests that employers avoid the dry sweeping or dusting of potential areas of contamination, substituting wet cleaning.
- With regard to personal protective equipment, the CDC recommends

  - That all employees who sort or handle mail be provided with protective impermeable gloves
  - That employees who work at or near areas where aerosolized particles can be generated be issued and fitted with NIOSH-approved respirators that are at least as protective as an N95 respirator
  - That employees who work at or near equipment where oil mist is generated be issued and fitted with respirators containing p-type filters

2.2.1   OSHA Considerations

OSHA's Standard for Personal Protective Equipment requires employers to assess the workplace to determine whether hazards are present which would require the use of personal protective equipment. If so, then the employer must purchase the appropriate equipment, train employees, and ensure that the equipment is properly used.

OSHA's Respiratory Protection Standard also requires employers to test fit and train employees on the proper use of respirators and ensure their proper use. Employees must obtain medical clearance before they may be permitted to wear such respirators. For example, on the advice of health officials at the CDC, the U.S. Postal Service initially purchased approximately 4.8 million respirators after the first anthrax exposure to protect its 700,000 employees against the possibility of inhaling anthrax spores. Employees, however, were not permitted to use the respirators until they were fitted and trained as required by OSHA.

OSHA has also developed an anthrax matrix detailing employer responsibilities according to varying degrees of potential exposure.

As a practical measure, employers should develop respiratory protection programs that comply with OSHA's requirements and reduce such policies or programs to writing.[11]

2.2.2 Employer Voluntary Response

Surveys indicate that at least 50 percent of employers have modified their mail-handling procedures as a result of the recent anthrax exposure incidents.

By way of contrast and context, according to a recent American Management Association Survey of 428 respondents, only 49 percent of the organizations had a general crisis management plan, 41 percent had a written plan, and only 38 percent had a contingency plan. While 54 percent responded that they have a crisis management team, 61 percent reported that they have never conducted a drill or simulation and 71 percent reported that key management across all lines of business had not been trained in crisis management to ensure intra-company support. It is not surprising, then, that 65 percent reported that they offer no employee security training, including training on their own security plans or procedures. [12]

A Word of Caution for Employers with Unions: Any change in the terms and conditions of employment, whether the implementation of a new or revised safety program or a new or revised requirement to use personal protective equipment, may trigger an employer's duty to bargain with the recognized labor organization prior to implementation.

2.2.3 Revised NIOSH Respirator Requirements

On December 28, 2001, NIOSH issued new requirements for self-contained breathing apparatus (SCBA) to be used by first responders in terrorist events involving possible chemical, biological, radiological, or nuclear agents. The prior certification program protected workers from traditional workplace hazards, where the exposures and levels were known. After January 22, 2002, however, NIOSH will accept applications for special approval labels identifying SCBA's that are appropriate for use against chemical, biological, radiological, and nuclear agents. The new certification program is voluntary.

3.0   Revisiting and Revising Employment Policies after September 11th

In light of September 11th, employers must take a hard look at their existing policies. Special issues that have arisen since September 11th may affect the following:

3.1   Solicitation/Distribution Policies

Employer solicitations for employee contributions to disaster relief funds may undermine the enforceability of employer no-solicitation rules.

Under Section 8(a)(1) of the National Labor Relations Act (NLRA),[13] an employer commits an unfair labor practice if it prohibits or restricts union solicitations while permitting other forms of non-union solicitation.

In an effort to address post-September 11th concerns, the General Counsel for the NLRB issued a Memorandum to all Regional Directors addressing the conflict between employer no-solicitation rules and recent employer efforts to solicit employee contributions for disaster relief funds.[14]

The General Counsel noted that, although employers may sponsor a small number of charitable efforts as exceptions to a no-solicitation rule without vitiating the rule, the NLRB has not yet determined the exact number of times an employer may engage in such activity (or for how long) before triggering a finding of unlawful discrimination. The Board declined to make any specific exception, or provide any specific guidelines, for funds or solicitations relating to September 11th or any other specific disaster or issue. There has been no update to this Memorandum.

3.2   Harassment and EEO Policies

In light of the events of September 11th, the EEOC has asked employers to be "particularly sensitive to potential discrimination or harassment against individuals who are—or are perceived to be—Muslim, Arab, Afghani, Middle Eastern, or South Asian (Pakistani, Indian, etc.)." In this regard, the EEOC has requested that employers reiterate policies against harassment based on religion, ethnicity, and national origin; communicate procedures for addressing workplace discrimination and harassment; urge employees to report any such improper conduct; and provide training and counseling, as appropriate.

Because employers can expect an increase in both discrimination/harassment claims and claims regarding religious accommodation, they should consider

- Revising existing discrimination/harassment policies to include factors other than sex
- Revising existing policies to allow for religious accommodation
- Communicating such policies to employees on a periodic basis
- Training supervisors to enforce such policies and investigate all claims
- Establishing an effective complaint procedure
- Encouraging employees to report claims

The U.S. Equal Employment Opportunity Commission has released two Fact Sheets on "backlash discrimination," addressed to employers and employees respectively.[15] The EEOC notes that charges of discrimination based on religion and/or national origin—"backlash discrimination"—most commonly addressing harassment and termination of employment, had more than doubled between September 11, 2001, and June 2002. Some of the actual allegations in these charges are included in the scenarios posed and answered in the Fact Sheets. Charges filed by Islamic employees have witnessed a 150 percent increase over last year.[16]

The EEOC has initiated and publicized recent litigation that has initiated specifically associated with alleged post-September 11th activities by employers. By July 2003, the EEOC had received more than 800 charges of backlash discrimination by individuals who are—or who are perceived to be—Muslim, Arabic, Middle Eastern, South Asian, or Sikh. The most common allegations are harassment and discharge. Nearly 100 Charging Parties have received over $1.5 million through the EEOC's enforcement, mediation, conciliation, and litigation efforts.[17]

The EEOC has publicized much of this litigation. Since shortly after September 11, 2002, its webpage has consistently and prominently carried coverage of charges and litigation. For example, on July 17, 2003, the EEOC filed its sixth backlash discrimination lawsuit. In this case,[18] the EEOC alleged that Trans States, a commuter airline, unlawfully discriminated against former First Officer Mohammed Hussein because of his Islamic religious beliefs and his Arabic appearance. Hussein, a Pacific Islander and native of Fiji, was fired September 18, 2001, i.e. one week after the September 11 terrorist attacks, despite an allegedly excellent prior work record. Hussein filed a charge of religious, racial, and national origin discrimination with the EEOC, alleging that Trans States refused to provide a reason or other justification for his discharge. The EEOC's Complaint alleges that, contrary to its established policy, Trans States relied on but did not investigate, or even identify the author of, an anonymous report that Hussein was in a "drinking establishment" while in uniform, refused to inform Hussein of the allegations against him, and denied him the opportunity to respond to accusation. Hussein began his employment at Trans State in February 2001.

Less than a week earlier, on July 11, 2003, the EEOC filed a case[19] against a Houston restaurant, alleging unlawful backlash discrimination in its firing of Karim El-Raheb, a general manager, because of his Egyptian ancestry. The suit alleges that, shortly after September 11, 2001, Pesce's co-owner began making repeated references in front of the restaurant staff and patrons that El-Raheb could "pass for Hispanic" and should change his name to "something Latin" and then fired El-Raheb in November 2001 after openly speculating that his Egyptian name and physical appearance were to blame for the restaurant's decline in earnings in the months following the terrorist attacks.

The EEOC recently announced a settlement in a case involving The Herrick Corporation[20] in which the Commission alleged that the company, a steel fabrication plant, denied equal employment opportunities to and subjected four Pakistani-American and Muslim employees to a hostile working environment in violation of Title VII based on their national origin (Pakistani) and religion (Islam). The employees, who were primarily machine operators, were hassled over an extended period of time during their daily Muslim prayer obligations, mocked because of their traditional dress, and repeatedly called "camel jockey" and "raghead." In the consent decree resolving the case, the company agreed to a total payment of $1.11 million to the four claimants and an agreement to avoid future employment discrimination at the facility on the basis of national origin or religion. The company also agreed to make policy changes to establish a more effective complaint and investigation procedure and to provide for supervisor accountability for national origin or religious harassment.

3.3   Workplace Aggression

According to the Spring 2002 American Management Association Survey of almost 500 employers, nearly three-quarters of responding employers have at least "moderate" concern for workplace violence.[21] However, most employers do not have a strong workplace aggression policy, and if they do, it is often not enforced.

The definition of "workplace aggression" has expanded. Workplace aggression is no longer limited to employee threats and physical altercations. It also includes documents or phone messages containing any form of threat (including the threat of anthrax or other diseases); hate mail, messages, and e-mail; the desecration of religious articles and symbols; the removal of safety guards on machinery and equipment; and the workplace spillage of chemicals and toxic substances.

In order to address concerns of workplace aggression, employers must review, revise, and republish policies and then enforce them. Employers must institute training regarding the nature and scope of workplace aggression, the fact that such aggression will not be tolerated, the manner of reporting threats or incidents of aggression, and mechanisms for mitigating threats.

3.4   Workplace Restraining Orders

In 2002, Tennessee, Colorado, and Indiana joined Arizona, Arkansas, California, Georgia, Nevada, and Rhode Island in providing employers the right to obtain restraining orders or injunctions against individuals who have threatened violence against their worksites. In most states, only individuals can secure this protection, which attaches only to the individual. These statutes protect the work location rather than individuals. As such, they do not protect employees outside the worksite or outside the scope of their job duties. The combination of remedies, however, protects both and significantly enhances the employer's ability to protect the worksite from known threats.

3.5   Concealed Weapons Policies

Employers should examine and republish concealed weapons policies in light of safety concerns and potential workplace aggression. These policies should include new definitions or descriptions of "weapons" and "workplace."

3.6   Workers' Compensation

Employers should bear in mind that workers' compensation benefits will more than likely be paid to workers injured in their place of employment as a result of workplace aggression or terrorist attacks. Workers' compensation benefits may also be available to employees who are emotionally injured as a result of workplace aggression.[22]

According to data from the Bureau of National Affairs, workers' compensation claims filed through December 2001 as a result of the events of September 11th, approximated $4 billion. Dramatic increases in the cost of premiums are expected, as are limitations upon terrorist-related claims.

3.7   Reasonable Accommodation

Employers should also note that employees who are physically or emotionally injured as a result of workplace aggression or terrorist attacks may be entitled to reasonable accommodation under the Americans with Disabilities Act (ADA)[23] and comparable state legislation. These employees' claims may be covered under Employee Assistance Plan benefits, health plan benefits, or workers' compensation benefits.

3.8　Special Issues Relating to Hospital Workplace Violence

According to data compiled by the U.S. Bureau of Labor Statistics, hospital workers experience workplace violence four times more often than the general working population. Unlike in other work sites, these attacks come most often from patients and authorized visitors rather than from co-workers or trespassers. HHS, through the CDC and NIOSH, has released *Violence: Occupational Hazards in Hospitals* (May 2002) to help hospital administrators and employees implement strategic preventive measures for increased employee safety and secure premises.[24]

3.9　Religious Accommodation

Courts have continued to respond to challenges to the requirements of employer accommodation of religion. Many of these challenges have been brought by the EEOC, which filed 16 religious accommodation lawsuits FY 2002.[25] These suits have covered discipline for Sabbath observance, restrictions on compliance with religious grooming or garb requirements, and prayer breaks. Some of the EEOC's positions on these subjects are included in its recent Fact Sheets described above. [26]

In *EEOC v. Chemisco*, a Missouri district court denied summary judgment to an employer relying on a collectively bargained no fault/no excuses attendance policy as a defense to claims of religious discrimination when the employer terminated an employee for absences and refusals to work overtime due to the employee's observance of a Saturday Sabbath and religious holidays. Although the court agreed that an employer is not required to violate the terms of a collective bargaining agreement to provide accommodation on the basis of religion, "the burden remains on the employer to make an effort to resolve the conflict before terminating the employee." The court also rejected the employer's challenge to the sincerity of the employee's purported religious beliefs based on her failure to belong to any organized religion since 1997; her working on several religious holidays; her inconsistent definition of her Sabbath hours; and her having had a child out of wedlock, an act prohibited by her religion. In preserving this question for the jury, the court noted: "No one advocates or challenges the proposition that adopting any particular religious belief is itself a guarantee that the adherent will never fall below the vows of the order."

3.9.1 Legislation Proposed to Increase Accommodation Obligation

The proposed Workplace Religious Freedom Act, sponsored by Sens. John Kerry (D-Mass.) and Rick Santorum (R-Pa.), would make it easier for employees to obtain workplace accommodations for their religious beliefs by expanding the Title VII definition of "undue hardship" and increasing the requirement for employers to provide reasonable accommodations to employees to be more in line with that under the Americans with Disabilities Act.

4.0 Other policies/procedures and issues

Other policies/procedures and issues that employers should re-examine or implement in light of recent events include the following:

- Consistent employment application and screening procedures
- Consistent procedures for reference checks (and their limitations)
- Consistent procedures for background checks, criminal record checks, and credit checks (including limitations imposed by the Fair Credit Reporting Act and other federal and state legislation)
- Complete, accurate, and consistent I-9 procedures
- Immigration limitations and recent legislation
- Workplace surveillance and search policies
- Workplace safety audits
- Employer policies on telecommuting
- Employer travel requirements and employee obligations
- Leave policies (including military leave) and medical benefits
- Employee Assistance Programs
- Layoffs and reductions in hours
- Hiring freezes, furloughs, and temporary office/plant closures
- Delays in the payment of wages
- Post-employment reference and reporting responsibilities and limitations, including responsibilities imposed by the Uniting and Strengthening America by Providing Tools to Intercept and Obstruct Terrorism (USA PATRIOT) Act
- General liability insurance coverage
- Director and officer liability coverage

5.0 Addressing Military Leaves of Absence and Veteran Reemployment Rights

The Uniformed Services Employment and Reemployment Rights Act (USERRA)[27] is the primary federal law that applies to employees in military service. It is enforced by the U.S. Department of Labor, which has posted a user-friendly summary and compliance guide.[28] The Act applies to all employers, regardless of size, and provides job and benefit protection rights for members of the uniformed services and covers all U.S. citizens and permanent resident aliens working in foreign countries for companies that are either organized or incorporated in the United States or controlled by an entity organized in the United States.

The purpose of the Act is to prohibit employers from discriminating or retaliating against members of the uniformed services. Employees are required to provide their employers with advance notice of the proposed leave, unless military necessity precludes such notice. Employers are not required to compensate employees for absences due to military leave. However, employers must comply with all other legal obligations, e.g., the Fair Labor Standards Act (FLSA), when addressing issues of temporary leave.

Employees on military leave are entitled to the same benefits as are provided to employees on other forms of leave. Employees also have the right to reinstatement upon completion of their period of service, provided they give their employer notice of their intent to return to work, as provided under the Act. The amount of time for providing such notice will vary, depending upon the length of the employee's service. The notice period may also be extended for up to two years if the employee is hospitalized or convalescing from a service-related injury or illness.

Employees who served fewer than 90 days must be reinstated to the same position they would have held had they remained continuously employed, provided they qualify for the position. The employer may not offer reinstatement to "other jobs" of like status. Employees who served more than 90 days may be reinstated either to the same position they would have held had they remained continuously employed, provided they qualify for the position, or to another position of equivalent status, seniority and pay. If they fail to qualify after training, however, then the employer may offer reinstatement to the position they held at the time they commenced their leave.

Upon their return to work, employees are entitled to seniority and benefits as if they had never been absent on leave. They are also entitled to accrue vacation upon their return at the same rate they would have attained had they remained continuously employed, and they are entitled to any non-seniority-based rights or benefits that were established by policy, practice, or agreement prior to the commencement of their leave or implemented during their absence.

Employers must also provide the option of health benefits during the employee's period of leave, similar to that provided under COBRA.

Upon reinstatement, there will be a period of time during which employees may only be discharged for cause (depending upon the length of military service).

Finally, it should be noted that USERRA supersedes individual employee agreements and Collective Bargaining Agreements if the rights provided by the statute exceed those of those agreements. Additional or greater rights and privileges, however, may be negotiated above any USERRA requirements.

6.0　Employee Privacy Versus Workplace Security

Few employment law issues have commanded as much attention in recent times as workplace privacy. Most employment decisions (including hiring, verification, surveillance, and technology decisions) raise employee privacy issues. These issues, however, promise to become even more prevalent as concerns regarding workplace security increase.

Sources of workplace privacy law include

- Federal Law
    - The U.S. Constitution
    - Federal Statutes and Regulations
    - The Americans with Disabilities Act of 1990
    - The Family and Medical Leave Act
    - Title VII of the Civil Rights Act of 1964
    - The Age Discrimination in Employment Act
    - The Employee Polygraph Protection Act of 1988
    - The Electronic Communications Privacy Act of 1986 and
    - The Fair Credit Reporting Act
- State law
- Common law

Invasion of privacy includes

- The unauthorized appropriation of a person's name or likeness
- The public disclosure of private facts
- Placing another person in a false light
- The unauthorized intrusion into a person's seclusion

6.1   Invasion of Privacy in Employment

In the employment context, invasion of privacy claims tend to arise when employees are subjected to searches or investigations, when personal information is sought, or when employees are required to undergo testing or other scrutiny.

6.2   Searches and Investigations

Workplace privacy concerns tend to arise when the employer searches items that belong to the employee, items under an employee's control, or the employee. Items "under an employee's control" may include desks, office furniture, computer equipment, telephones, voice mail, physical mail, electronic communications, and lockers. Related issues include:

- The extent to which an employee has an expectation of privacy
- The extent to which notice of and consent to the search have been provided
- The extent to which a search (particularly of the individual) is conducted in an appropriate/inappropriate manner

Additional issues include

Mail Appropriation. Federal law prohibits the interception of mail for purposes of obstructing or prying into its contents "before it has been delivered to the person to whom it has been directed."

Fingerprinting. At least one court has rejected the argument that fingerprinting, in the employment context, does not constitute an invasion of privacy. Further, certain states (including New York) prohibit employers from requiring applicants or employees to provide fingerprints as a condition of employment.

Wiretapping. Employer efforts to record employee conversations secretly may result in challenges under wiretapping statutes, both state and federal. At least one court has held that the "complete interception of personal [employee] phone calls...[can never] be protected behavior under the business-extension exemption."[29] Even the "fear of bomb threats" will not be considered a valid business reason for secretly recording employee telephone conversations.[30]

In a case of first impression in Maryland, the state's highest court found that the use of recording equipment to monitor employees who interact with customers by telephone is a violation of the Maryland Wiretap Act. In *Schmerling v. Injured Workers' Insurance Fund,*[31] the Maryland Court of Appeals ruled that the use of recording equipment, added years after the basic telephone system, did not "further the use of or functionally enhance the telecommunications system," and is not "telephone equipment.or a component thereof" within the meaning of the exemption to the Maryland Wiretap Act. Thus, the Court found immaterial the purported "valid business purpose" of recording incoming and outgoing calls to monitor calls for customer service quality in the ordinary course of business. The Court noted that, while the Maryland wiretap statute was modeled after Title III of the federal Omnibus Crime Control and Safe Streets Act, "our State Legislature unequivocally has demonstrated its intent to create an Act more protective of privacy interests than that which is promoted by Title III."

Similarly, in *Karch v. BayBank FSB, N.H.,*[32] the Supreme Court of New Hampshire refused to dismiss a bank employee's claims for invasion of privacy, wrongful discharge, intentional infliction of emotional distress, and violation of the state wiretap law when the bank constructively discharged her after learning of an intercepted telephone call in which she privately criticized the bank. The employee's Saturday night telephone conversation with a co-worker was intercepted by a couple with a radio scanner who reported the conversation to their friend, one of the bank's vice presidents. This bank officer promptly disciplined the employee and threatened to fire her. She failed to return from a medical leave, claiming the hostile environment at the bank prevented her continued employment. The Court noted that the employee may bring additional claims under the state workers' compensation statute.

6.3 No Reasonable Expectation of Privacy in Sexually Explicit E-Mails

A federal court in Massachusetts found in *Garrity v. John Hancock Mutual Life Ins. Co.*[33] that employees who send sexually explicit e-mails through their employers' e-mail system have no reasonable expectation of privacy, and that their employer's reading their e-mails after they are transmitted is not an "interception" within the meaning of the Massachusetts Wiretap Statute. When a co-worker complained of receipt of an offensive e-mail, the company initiated an investigation of employee e-mail folders. Upon finding the sexually explicit materials, the company terminated the originating employees for violation of the company's e-mail policy. The court relied on similar rulings by Pennsylvania and Texas courts.

6.4 False Imprisonment

False imprisonment claims may arise in the course of a workplace search or investigation if an employee is, or feels, confined to an area or denied permission to leave an area against his or her will.

6.5   Video Surveillance

While video surveillance of employees has become increasingly popular, it has also come under attack as an unnecessary form of invasion of privacy. Courts have generally upheld an employer's right to monitor employees if they are in plain view at work. However, courts have also increasingly limited an employer's right to monitor employees where they have a reasonable expectation of privacy (such as employee dressing areas and lounges), or where employees are on their "own time" (such as on break or eating lunch). Surveillance can also constitute unlawful harassment.

6.6   Electronic Monitoring

Electronic monitoring in the workplace (including telephone, computer, and e-mail monitoring) is still an evolving area of the law and also poses some risk.

In 1986, Congress amended the Omnibus Crime Control and Safe Streets Act of 1968[34] specifically to address e-mail communications and other forms of electronic communications. It is unclear to what extent Congress intended to protect the individual employee from privacy intrusions by the employer. However, the law does not apply to conduct authorized by the person or entity providing a wire or electronic communication service or by a user of that service, with respect to a communication by or for that user. The business-extension exception applies to employers who monitor communications that are made in the ordinary course of business. The prior-consent exception applies when the individuals subject to the interception grant their consent. Although there is disagreement among courts as to how narrowly this exception should be interpreted, some cases suggest courts will find implied consent where individuals were put on notice that their communications might be monitored.

7.0   Background Investigations and Personal Information

Where employers fail to undertake thorough background investigations or fail to act on the information contained therein and compliance with federal and state limitations imposed upon such investigations, concerns arise concerning liability for workplace violence, negligent hiring, and negligent retention claims.

The USA PATRIOT Act[35] requires persons seeking to transport hazardous materials to undergo a criminal background check.[36] On May 5, 2003, the Transportation Security Administration (TSA) and the U.S. Department of Transportation issued an interim final rule requiring background checks on commercial drivers who are certified to transport hazardous materials, including explosives.[37] Under this rule, approximately 3.5 million commercial drivers with hazardous material endorsements must undergo a routine background check that includes a review of criminal immigration and FBI records. Any driver who has been convicted or found not guilty by reason of insanity in the past seven years, who was released from prison in the past five years, who is wanted or under indictment for committing certain felonies, or who has been found mentally incompetent will not be permitted to obtain, retain, transfer, or renew the hazardous materials endorsement. The background checks are also implemented to verify that the driver is a U.S. citizen or a lawful permanent resident, as required by law.

The USA PATRIOT Act also prohibits states from issuing a commercial drivers license endorsement for transporting hazardous materials unless the Department of Transportation has first determined that the applicant does not pose a security risk.

Airport screeners will also have to pass pre-hire security clearance, a pre-appointment drug screening test, a pre-hire medical examination, and an aptitude test currently being developed. These requirements were announced by the U.S. Department of Transportation, Transportation Security Administration (TSA), on December 19, 2001.[38] By June 2003, the TSA had terminated the employment of some 1,300 screeners because of problems in the background checks and the securing and analysis of the background checks.[39]

Additionally, a Transportation Department task force has actively explored development of a national transportation-worker identity card. One type of the electronic card would have an encoded biometric description of the owner to ensure that the person using the card is in fact the person identified therein.

It is important for an employer to provide notification to employees regarding the restrictions it intends to place on their privacy rights. A written policy enumerating the employer's rights with regard to searches and investigations is advisable. Employers should also ensure that applicants/employees understand the employer's rights by signing an acknowledgment and/or consent form. Additionally, employers should ensure they comply with the notice requirements of the Fair Credit Reporting Act (FCRA) where background or other investigations are conducted by third parties.

8.0   Employee Identity and Authorization to Work in the United States, Social Security Concerns, and Assistance

8.1   Social Security Administration (SSA) Offers Assistance in Verification of SSNs

The Social Security Administration now offers employers complimentary assistance in verifying the accuracy of employee and applicant provided Social Security information for tax and INS work authorization (I-9) purposes. Details of these programs are available More information is available online at the EVS website <http://www.ssa.gov/employer/ssnv/htm> through the following link: Enumeration Verification Service (EVS).

8.2   IRS Announces Fines for Mismatched W-2 Data

The IRS announced May 15, 2002 that, beginning with forms filed for tax year 2002, it will assess penalties for employees' mismatched W-2 forms. Errors in names and social security numbers will result in employer fines up to $50 per incorrect form. Notices of the proposed penalties, however, will not be issued until June 2004. It is unclear whether false social security numbers provided to the employer will be subject to this penalty provision.

Social Security will send the 2003 letters only to employers with more than ten mismatches or for whom mismatched employees represented .5 percent of the W-2 forms the company filed. This will reduce the number of notices from the 900,000 sent in 2002 to an estimated 130,000 letters. SSA will now also send a no-match letter to each no-match employee several weeks before sending the no-match letter to the employer, unless it does not have a valid employee address.

In addition, the 2003 no-match letters have dropped the reference to possible IRS penalties which was contained in the 2002 letters.

9.0   Employment Issues in the International Arena

Whenever an employer conducts business in multiple jurisdictions, employment and security issues are bound to arise. Examples include the following:

9.1   Export Controls

Since the early 1990s, there has been a steady increase in the number of foreign nationals who are either employed in technical positions within the United States or employed by U.S. companies in technical positions abroad. This increase has led to the application of export licensing controls to employment situations that previously would *not* have been subject to licensing requirements.

In 1994, the U.S. Department of Commerce's Bureau of Export Administration (BXA) amended the Export Administration Regulations (EAR) to broaden the scope of items and information "deemed exports." Prior to 1994, technical data were only "deemed" exports if they were released, transported or shipped from the U.S. to a foreign country with the "knowledge or intent" to export. In 1994, the BXA amended the Export Administration Regulations to remove the "knowledge and intent" requirement. The result of this modification was to broaden the definition of an "export" to include the release of *any* technical data, know-how, or source codes (that were not specifically excluded from the regulations) to foreign nationals, under virtually any circumstance.

Under the revisions to the EAR, technology or software will be deemed "released"

- If a foreign national "visually inspects" U.S.-origin equipment or facilities
- If there is an oral exchange of information with foreign nationals in the U.S. or abroad
- If the technology is made available to foreign nationals by practice or application under the guidance of persons with knowledge of the technology
- If personal knowledge or technology experience acquired in the United States is applied abroad

The 1994 revisions, therefore, make it possible for U.S. companies to violate export controls simply by employing foreign nationals in positions with access to technology or software not excluded under the regulations.

The "deemed export" rule requires employers to seek export licenses prior to disclosing unpublished software or technology to foreign nationals employed in the U.S. or abroad. There is also a potential conflict between the export license requirements of the Department of Commerce and other U.S. legislation (including EEO legislation).

Legislation such as Title VII of the Civil Rights Act of 1964 ("Title VII") and the Immigration Reform and Control Act of 1986 prohibits employers from undertaking certain pre-employment inquiries or discriminating against employees who are foreign-looking or foreign-sounding. Export license regulations require expansive biographical information. In some situations, this conflict can be resolved by

- Obtaining the required biographical information from an applicant or employee's resume or curriculum vitae (after verification)
- Obtaining the required information through the visa process
- Obtaining the remaining information after a conditional offer of employment

Post-employment inquiries, however, may prove inefficient given the processing delays associated with obtaining export licenses and the need to have employees work with restricted technology upon arrival.

Problems may also arise from "deemed re-exports." The term "deemed re-export" is often used to indicate the transfer of a controlled U.S. technology to a foreign national of a third country overseas. For example: A U.S. exporter transfers its controlled proprietary technology to a firm in Country A. The firm in Country A, in turn, employs an individual from Country B, who is a permanent resident of neither Country A nor the United States and who will need the proprietary technology to perform his/her assigned duties. If the U.S. exporter intends to transfer the controlled technology to the Country B national (who is employed by the firm in Country A) the U.S. exporter will have to obtain a deemed export license, just as if the company were transferring the technology to Country B. If, however, the Country A firm is the entity that intends to transfer the technology to the employee from Country B, then the Country A firm will be responsible for obtaining the deemed re-export license from the Bureau.

9.2   Visa Restrictions and Immigration Issues

Although employers are still bringing foreign nationals into the United States on non-immigrant visas, they can expect more stringent visa requirements as a result of the September 11th terrorist attacks. Employees overstaying their visas or violating visa restrictions also face an increased likelihood of detection and detention.

9.3   Privacy Issues

In addition to complying with domestic legislation, U.S. companies operating abroad must consider the impact of European legislation and European Union (EU) Directives on workplace security.

For example, the EU Privacy Directive, which became effective on October 5, 1998, requires EU member states to enact comprehensive legislation within three years of passage that implement personal data policies. The Privacy Directive mandates that member states protect the "fundamental rights and freedoms of natural persons, and in particular their right to privacy with respect to the processing of personal data."

Under the terms of the Directive, all EU member states as well as any non-member state doing business in the EU are required to follow minimum standards for personal data safety. It also prohibits the transfer of personal information to countries outside the EU that do *not* ensure the "adequate" protection of personal data. If foreign companies do not comply, they may be denied access to the EU market or be subjected to penalties for failing to protect the privacy of EU citizens.

Additionally, in a precedent-setting case, France's highest court ruled last year that employers do not have the right to read their employees' electronic mail or personal computer files.[40] It is expected that the ruling will have a dramatic impact on other cases currently under review in both France and the European Union.

9.3.1 The Impact of EU Privacy Regulations on International Background Searches

From 1998 to 2001, companies specializing in background investigations have reported that between 12 percent and 30 percent of those applicants screened have failed to disclose some portion of prior criminal records. Since September 11th, requests for criminal background searches have increased, including requests for international background searches. With regard to the latter, however, most companies have found that the EU's privacy requirements make it difficult to acquire meaningful information on job applicants.

10.0 Developments under the National Labor Relations Act

10.1 Recent National Labor Relations Board Actions

10.1.1 D.C. Court of Appeals Upholds NLRB's Extension of "*Weingarten*" Rights to Non-Union Employees in *Epilepsy Foundation*, 331 N.L.R.B. 676 (2000).

On July 10, 2000, the NLRB ruled that federal labor law protections providing union-represented employees the right to have a representative present during a disciplinary interview should extend to employees in nonunion workplaces. Prior to this ruling, the NLRB had taken precisely the opposite position for 12 years, and nonunion employers were not required to provide employees with this prerogative. This ruling significantly affects the way all employers must now handle any conference with an employee where the employee believes the meeting might reasonably lead to any type of disciplinary action.

The right to representation at disciplinary meetings is commonly referred to as a *Weingarten* right (after the employer party in a 1975 Supreme Court decision).[41] The NLRB's opinion states that *Weingarten* rights "should be extended to employees in nonunionized workplaces, to afford them the right to have a co-worker present at an investigatory interview which the employee reasonably believes might result in disciplinary action." The Board reasoned that, because the *Weingarten* case was grounded in the section of the National Labor Relations Act allowing employees to engage in protected concerted activity (commonly referred to as "Section 7" rights), affording nonunion employees the right to a representative at disciplinary meetings "greatly enhances the employees' opportunities to act in concert to address their concern 'that the employer does not initiate or continue a practice of imposing punishment unjustly.'"

The Board's 3-2 ruling was sharply divided, with the minority voicing strong opposition to the ruling, citing practical concerns such as employers being unaware of the requirement and the likelihood that a nonunion employee would likely pick any coworker on the spur of the moment (as opposed to union employees, who customarily select a designated and experienced union steward), thereby decreasing the value of the representative's presence at the investigatory interview.

Although the Board's decision was reversed in part by the D.C. Circuit, the essential holding of the case remains good law.[42] The key portion of the Board's interpretation of the NLRA, i.e., that an employer's denial of any employee's request that a co-worker be present at an investigatory interview which the employee reasonably believes might result in disciplinary action constitutes an unfair labor practice, was upheld by the court. The Court held that the Board erred, however, in retroactively applying this interpretation. At the time of the employee's scheduled interview, it was well-settled law that employees in nonunion workplaces had no statutory right to have a coworker present, and the Epilepsy Foundation's decision to discharge him for refusing to meet alone with his supervisors was not unlawful under then-current Board interpretation of his Section 7 rights under the NLRA.

10.2 Section 7 Rights and Electronic Correspondence

The right to engage in concerted activity under Section 7 of the NLRA fundamentally encourages employees to communicate with one another. In an age in which computers, e-mail, and the Internet are commonplace in the workplace, employees can now exercise their Section 7 rights by means of these new technologies.

The most obvious thing that non-union employees can do under Section 7 is to complain to management about the terms and conditions of their employment. This protected right to express opinions takes on an added significance with advances in technology, which have simplified the dissemination of information. On the one hand, employees may liberally use the "cc:" button on their e-mail to rally support for collective action. Meanwhile, employers may use the technology to monitor employee communications.

A recent NLRB case,[43] illustrates these issues. On October 31, 2001, employee Jeborah Diebold sent an e-mail message to a number of her fellow employees in which she stated that anthrax had been found at the plant and that all employees were being tested. Diebold further stated in her e-mail that the facility was responsible for sending out bills and, as a result, another facility was being tested. In truth, the facility had received a letter purporting to contain anthrax. Subsequent testing, however, determined that the facility had not been contaminated. Moreover, the facility was not responsible for sending out bills and no other facilities were placed in danger. Citing a zero-tolerance policy for anthrax hoaxes, the company terminated Diebold on November 5th. Diebold filed an unfair labor practice charge with the Board complaining that her e-mail constituted protected concerted activity under Section 7 of the Act and that she was terminated for engaging in protected concerted activity in violation of Section 8(1) of the Act.

The Board held that e-mail communications regarding the health and safety of employees within a worksite constitutes protected concerted activity under the Act. However, the concerted activity loses its protected status when an employee disseminates information that she knows to be false. Diebold had reason to believe that anthrax had been located at the facility on October 31st and that Sprint was closing the facility in order to conduct further tests. The Board concluded, however, that she had no basis to believe that Sprint had confirmed the presence of anthrax at the facility or that other facilities may have been contaminated. Rather, the evidence suggests that Diebold purposely fabricated that portion of her e-mail. Because Diebold had no reasonable belief in the veracity of portions of her e-mail but instead sent it knowing of its falsity, the communication was not protected by Section 7. Accordingly, the Board held that Sprint did not commit an unfair labor practice when it terminated Diebold's employment.

Although the Board held Diebold's actions not to be protected because she knew her statements to be false, the case demonstrates the concerns employers should have about concerted activity in the technological workplace. Complaints about workplace conditions that are circulated via e-mail will be protected concerted activity. Accordingly, employers are prohibited from taking action against employees for circulating such e-mails.

10.3 Employer Concerns and Recommended Courses of Action

10.3.1 Extension of *Weingarten* Rights

Under the Board's recent *Epilepsy Foundation* decision, the employer is required to permit an employee to have a witness present during a meeting that the employee reasonably believes could lead to termination. This is the case even in workplaces that do not have a union. Failure to permit the employee to have a witness during such a meeting will constitute an unfair labor practice under the Act.

In light of this decision, employers may wish to amend their employee handbooks to inform employees of their right to have a witness present at all meetings that they believe could result in termination. At the outset of such a meeting, the management employee conducting the meeting should consider asking the employee if he wishes to have another employee sit in to act as a witness on his behalf. Although this offer is not technically required by the Board's decision, it may prevent an unfair labor practice charge in the future and will demonstrate good will towards the employee.

Employers should also inform their managers, supervisors, and human resources consultants that employees must be allowed to bring a witness to all disciplinary meetings that are of serious consequence. Procedures for handling requests to have a co-employee witness present at a disciplinary meeting should be codified and distributed by the human resources department.

10.3.2 Surveillance of Concerted Activity in the High Tech Workplace

E-mail and Internet access in the workplace permit employees to engage in protected concerted activity without ever leaving their desk. In general, employers are prohibited from conducting clandestine surveillance of employees who are participating in concerted activity. However, an employer may observe employee activity that takes place on or near company property so long as the observation is consistent with the protection of legitimate employer interests in good order and productivity.

In the high-tech workplace, this prohibited surveillance may include intercepting employee e-mails. As with ordinary photographing and surveillance, however, the employer may act to protect its legitimate business interests. In order to clarify its concerns with employee e-mail use, the employer should set forth a policy regarding use of company e-mail. The policy should state that e-mail is to be used for company business only and that the use of company e-mail for personal reasons is inappropriate and will not be tolerated. The policy should further clarify that the reason for this measure is to ensure continued employee productivity and good order in the workplace. By following such a policy, the employer reduces the risk that it will be charged with an unfair labor practice if it intercepts employee e-mail.

10.3.3 Terminating Employees for Internet Abuse

Company e-mail systems have become popular venues not only for exchanging business information but also for communicating complaints about the employer. When an employee forwards a complaint to other employees, it should be considered to be a protected concerted activity. The employer should not take action against the employee unless it can demonstrate that the employee knew her complaints were false at the time that she made them.

Endnotes:

[1] The author gratefully acknowledges the contribution of Victoria M. Garcia, Parnter, Bracewell & Patterson LLP, San Antonio, Texas.

[2] In *Guidance for Protecting Building Environments from Airborne Chemical, Biological or Radiological Attacks* (May 2002), these agencies identify available safety measures, with immediate implementation recommended a more comprehensive plan is developed and implemented. The document contains a list of website resources for building security and prevention of CBR terrorist attacks. (Available at: http://www.cdc.gov/niosh/hhs-ventrel.html) (Accessed 30 June 2003).

[3] *See* http://www.nipc.gov/warnings/advisories/2002/02-001.htm (Accessed 30 June 2002).

[4] *2002 AMA Survey: Crisis Management and Security Issues.*

[5] OSHA provides an analysis for determining whether a written plan is required. http://www.osha.gov/SLTC/etools/evacuation/do_i_need.html (Accessed 30 June 2003).

[6] http://www.bt.cdc.gov/. *See also* http://www.fema.gov/library/bizindex.shtm (Accessed 30 June 2003).

[7] *Id.*

[8] http://www.fema.gov/ (Accessed 30 June 2003).

[9] http://www.eeoc.gov/facts/evacuation.html. (Accessed 30 June 2003). This Guidance expands upon its earlier Enforcement Guidance (26 July 2000) addressing Disability-Related Inquiries and Medical Examinations of Employees Under the ADA.

[10] *See* http://www.nod.org/ (Accessed 30 June 2003). *The National Organization on Disability's Emergency Preparedness Initiative Guide on the Special Needs of People with Disabilities* is linked to the site at http://www.nod.org/content.cfm?id=1267 (Accessed 30 June 2003).

[11] http://www.osha.gov/bioterrorism/anthrax/matrix/index.html (Accessed 30 June 2003).

[12] *2002 AMA Survey: Crisis Management and Security Issues.*

[13] 29 U.S.C. §§ 151 *et seq.* (1994).

[14] http://www.nlrb.gov/gcmemo/gc01-06.html (Accessed 30 June 2003).

[15] *Questions and Answers About Employer Responsibilities Concerning the Employment of Muslims, Arabs, South Asians, and Sikhs* (May 2002) and *Questions and Answers About the Workplace Rights of Muslims, Arabs, South Asians, and Sikhs Under the Equal Employment Opportunity Laws* (May 2002). *See also* Note 14.

[16] The Fact Sheet for employers is available at http://www.eeoc.gov/facts/backlash-employer.html; the Fact Sheet for employees is available at http://www.eeoc.gov/facts/backlash-employee.html (Accessed 30 June 2003).

[17] *See* EEOC Press Releases, 17 July 2003, http://www.eeoc.gov/press/7-17-03a.html (Accessed 28 July 2003) and 11 July 2003, http://www.eeoc.gov/press/7-10-03.html (Accessed 28 July 2003).

[18] *EEOC v. Trans States Airlines, Inc.*, In the United States District Court for the Eastern District of Missouri, Case No. 4:03CV00964 TCM; *see* EEOC Press Release, 17 July 2003, http://www.eeoc.gov/press/7-17-03a.html (Accessed 28 July 2003). *EEOC v. Pesce, Ltd.*, In the United States District Court for the Southern District of Texas, Case No. _____ (11 July 2003); *see* EEOC Press Release, 11 July 2003, at http://www.eeoc.gov/press/7-10-03.html (Accessed 28 July 2003).

[19] *EEOC v. Pesce, Ltd.*, In the United States District Court for the Southern District of Texas, Case No. _____ (11 July 2003); *see* EEOC Press Release, 11 July 2003, at http://www.eeoc.gov/press/7-10-03.html (Accessed 28 July 2003).

[20] *EEOC v. The Herrick Corporation d/b/a Stockton Steel*, No.S-00-0102-MCE-DAD (E.D. Cal. 18 March 2003); *see also* http://www.eeoc.gov/litigation/settlements/settlement03-03.html (Accessed 30 June 2003).

[21] *2002 AMA Survey: Crisis Management and Security Issues.*

[22] The CDC and NIOSH have released *The Changing Organization of Work and the Safety and Health of Working People* (April 2002), which discusses safety and health issues related to the impact on employees of recent trends in corporate restructuring and downsizing, nontraditional employment practices, and more flexible and efficient production techniques. Copies of the document are available at http://www.cdc.gov/niosh/02-116pd.html (Accessed 30 June 2003).

[23] 42 U.S.C. § 12101 *et seq.* (1994).

[24] Copies of the document are available at http://www.cdc.gov/niosh/riskassault.html (Accessed 30 June 2003).

[25] U. S. Equal Opportunity Commission, Office of General Counsel, Annual Report, Fiscal Year 2002, "Issues Alleged," available at http://www.eeoc.gov/litigation/02annrpt.html#IIIBissuesalleged (Accessed 28 July 2003).

[26] *See* Section 3.2.

[27] 38 U.S.C. § 4301 *et seq.* (1994).

[28] http://www.dol.gov/vets/programs/fact/vet97-3.htm (Accessed 30 June 2003).

[29] *Smith v. Devers*, 2002 U.S. Dist. LEXIS 1125 (M.D. Ala. Jan. 17, 2002).

[30] *Sanders v. Robert Bosch Corp.*, 10 Indiv. Empl. Rts. Cas. (BNA) 1 (4th Cir. 1994).

[31] 795 A.2d 80 (Md. 2002).

[32] 794 A.2d 763 (N.H. 2002).

[33] 2002 U.S. Dist. LEXIS 8343 (D. Mass. 2002).

[34] 42 U.S.C. 33789d (1994)

[35] Uniting and Strengthening America by Providing Appropriate Tools Required to Intercept and Obstruct Terrorism Act of 2001 ("USA PATRIOT Act "), Pub. L. 107-56, 115 Stat. 272 (2001).

[36] Section 44936 of Title 49, U.S. Code, requires the Under Secretary of Transportation for Security to issue regulations requiring employment investigations, including a criminal history records check (CHRC), for screeners of the Transportation Security Administration (TSA), flight crew members, or individuals seeking unescorted access to Secure Identification Display Areas (SIDA) of an airport. On February 22, 2002, TSA issued regulations to implement this portion of the statute concerning individuals with unescorted access to secure areas of an airport, and screening personnel. See 49 C.F.R. §§ 1542.209, 1544.229 and 1544.230.

[37] 49 CFR §§ 1570-72 (May 5, 2003).

[38] Section 44936 of Title 49, U.S.C., requires the Under Secretary of Transportation for Security to issue regulations requiring employment investigations, including a criminal history records check (CHRC), for screeners of the Transportation Security Administration (TSA), flight crew members, or individuals seeking unescorted access to Secure Identification Display Areas (SIDA) of an airport. On February 22, 2002, TSA issued regulations to implement this portion of the statute concerning individuals with unescorted access to secure areas of an airport, and screening personnel. See 49 C.F.R. §§ 1542.209, 1544.229 and 1544.230.

[39] *Washington Post*, June 5, 2003, page A1.

[40] *Nikon France v. Frederic Onos*, Cour de Cassation, Chambre Sociale, Arret. No. 41-64. 2 October 2001.

[41] *NLRB v. J. Weingarten, Inc.*, 420 U.S. 251, 95 S.Ct. 959 (1975).

[42] *Epilepsy Found. v. N.L.R.B.*, 268 F.3d 1095 (D.C. Cir. 2001); *cert denied*, 122 S. Ct. 2356 (2002).

[43] *Sprint/United Mgmt. Co.*, 2002 NLRB LEXIS 485 (Sept. 30, 2002)

Part III

Organizational Structure of the Department of Homeland Security

Chapter 12

Management Structure and Leadership

Kelley Drye & Warren LLP
Glenn B. Manishin

1.0   Overview

The foremost objective of the Homeland Security Act of 2002 was to establish a new Cabinet-level agency designed to coordinate America's domestic war on terrorism, headed by a single Cabinet official whose primary mission is to protect the American homeland from terrorism. The Act is comprised principally of organizational mandates for transferring personnel, functions, and agencies from a wide spectrum of governmental entities into the new Department of Homeland Security (DHS). As a result, although DHS has some independent regulatory authority, its mission is largely to engage in planning, coordination of existing resources, and administration of a number of security-related governmental functions, such as borders, emergency response, and the like.

The new Department will also be taking a leading role in establishing the relationship of the federal government to private sector industries. And because as much as 85 percent of America's critical infrastructures are privately owned and operated, DHS is likely to have a pronounced effect, directly or indirectly, on how these industries—including telecommunications, energy, transportation, agriculture, and others—will be charged with protecting the security of the United States.

1.1   Effective Date and Transition Period

Effective January 24, 2003,[1] the Act required the Department of Homeland Security to be largely in place by March 1, 2003, and to be fully operational within a one-year "transition period."[2] Former Pennsylvania Governor Tom Ridge, who previously served as the Director of the White House Office of Homeland Security, has been appointed and confirmed as the first Secretary of

Homeland Security. Gordon England, formerly Secretary of the Navy, has been confirmed as the first Deputy Secretary of Homeland Security.

With more than 170,000 personnel and a budget for fiscal year 2003 of greater than $35 billion,[3] the Department will have a significant impact on virtually every industry in the United States. Secretary Ridge's first and perhaps principal objective, however, is to manage what has been described as the most massive reorganization of the federal government since World War II.[4] For companies desiring to do business with the Department and for those concerned with new security obligations DHS may impose under its rulemaking powers, the organizational structure of the Department is an important matter.

1.2   Mandate of the Department

The mandate of the new Department is extremely broad in scope and stated very generally in the Act. The actual limits and contours of the mandate necessarily will be refined through agency interpretation and action as well as through legal challenge. The Department's mission encompasses at least the following areas of responsibility:

- Collecting, analyzing, and maintaining databases of intelligence information on terrorist threats and perceived vulnerabilities of the country
- Establishing and coordinating responses to national emergencies, including but not limited to terrorist attacks
- Serving as a single federal focal point and resource for assistance to "first responders" and other state and local entities in combating terror and preparing responses to any future national emergencies
- Providing border, coastline, and transportation security and administering immigration laws
- Coordinating efforts to address challenges of nuclear, chemical, biological, and cyber terrorism, and encouraging academic and private sector research and development on new technologies
- Coordinating the use of private sector technologies, goods, and services in homeland security preparations

It is important to note that investigating and combating terrorism, as either a law enforcement or military matter, are *not* within the scope of the Department's responsibilities. The Act specifies clearly that primary responsibility for investigating and prosecuting acts of terrorism remain with federal, state, and local law enforcement agencies, except for specific enforcement responsibilities held by agencies transferred to the Department.[5]

1.3 Office of the Secretary and Directorates

Created through a massive reorganization of the federal government involving the transfer of offices and functions from more than 22 existing agencies, including over 100 separate organizations,[6] the Department is comprised principally of the Office of the Secretary and four Directorates. An Under Secretary for Management and an Inspector General assist in managing the Department under the direction of the Secretary.[7] There are, in addition, a number of specific agencies and bureaus, such as the Secret Service, that will continue to exist as separate organizational entities within DHS. The sheer size and complexity of the DHS reorganization indicates it is likely to require considerable time before the Department's organization is settled.[8]

The four Directorates, each organized with its own Under Secretary appointed by the president and operating pursuant to a separate title of the Act, are

- Title II   Directorate of Information Analysis
               and Infrastructure Protection
- Title III   Directorate of Science and Technology
- Title IV   Directorate of Border Transportation and
               Security
- Title V   Directorate of Emergency Preparedness

The Office of the Secretary includes many officers to be designated by presidential appointment. The president also will appoint other members of the management team. Certain distinct entities transferred to or created within the Department will report directly to the Secretary, including the Secret Service, the Coast Guard, the Office for State and Local Government Coordination, the Office for International Affairs, the Office for National Capital Region Coordination, the Homeland Security Institute, and the Nuclear Incident Response Team.

It is important to note that the Department's organizational structure is not fixed permanently by the Act's creation of four Directorates. To the contrary, Section 872 provides that with notice to Congress and subject to a few exceptions (for instance, the Secretary may not "abolish" any agency or function "established or required to be maintained" by the Act) the Secretary is empowered to "allocate or reallocate" functions among the offices of the Department and may "establish, consolidate, alter or discontinue" organizational units within DHS.[9] This administrative flexibility is paralleled in the Act's provisions on personnel, which provide the Secretary with the power, jointly with the Director of the Office of Personnel Management, to establish a new "human resources management system" that bypasses most provisions of the federal civil service rules.[10]

1.4   Powers, Practices, and Procedures

1.4.1   Powers and Responsibilities

In the service of its broad mandate, the Department has been given wide-ranging powers and responsibilities, some of which are unique to DHS among federal agencies. Many powers are transferred along with the Department's constituent agencies and offices, and disentangling the complexities of the rearrangement of powers among the numerous offices and agencies involved is likely to be a time-consuming challenge. Several powers and practices granted to the Secretary also are subject to checks and balances, particularly to ensure the protection of individual rights and liberties.

1.4.1.1   Regulations

The Secretary is granted limited new rulemaking powers under the Act. These include the authority to issue regulations concerning "research, development, demonstration, testing, and evaluation activities of the Department, including the conducting, funding, and reviewing of such activities"; regulations necessary to implement the Support Anti-Terrorism by Fostering Effective Technologies (SAFETY) Act of 2002;[11] regulations governing "uniform procedures" for "critical infrastructure information that is voluntarily submitted to the Government";[12] and regulations necessary for the protection and administration of federal property in connection with homeland security. In general, the Secretary assumes the rulemaking power "as exists on the date of enactment" held by agencies and offices transferred to the Department[13] but is not otherwise granted the power to promulgate substantive regulations imposing security-related obligations on industries already regulated by existing administrative agencies not transferred to DHS, such as the Federal Communications Commission, the Federal Energy Regulatory Commission, etc. Indeed, the Act states expressly that with only a few specified exceptions, "this Act vests no new regulatory authority in the Secretary or any other Federal official."[14]

1.4.1.2   Plans, Priorities and Policy-Making

Virtually every Directorate is responsible for the recommendation of national plans and policies to address homeland security issues in their areas of jurisdiction. The plans and policies to be developed include

- A "comprehensive national plan for securing key resources and critical infrastructure"[15]
- A "national policy and strategic plan for identifying priorities, goals, objec-

tives, and policies for.efforts to identify and develop counter measures to chemical, biological, radiological, nuclear, and other emerging terrorist threats,"[16] as well as priorities for directing, funding, and conducting national research

- "[S]trategic technology development plans" and "national immigration enforcement policies and priorities"[17]
- A "single coordinated national [emergency] response plan"[18]

The establishment and implementation of these plans, priorities, and policies will have a significant impact with respect to the responsibilities and obligations that may be imposed on the private sector in connection with homeland security. In many areas, the Secretary is responsible for coordinating among and consulting with a variety of federal and state agencies as well as private sector entities in the establishment and implementation of national plans and policies.

1.4.1.3   Administration and Program Implementation

A large portion of the Secretary's duties is focused on program implementation and administration. For example, program functions in the immigration and border control areas under Title IV, and terrorism preparedness and emergency response programs under Titles IV and V. The procedures and practices to be used in fulfilling administrative functions have yet to be determined.

1.4.1.4   Adjudication, Investigation and Enforcement

The Secretary has the power to adjudicate visa matters. Under the Act, the Secretary also is deemed to be a federal law enforcement, intelligence, protective, national defense, immigration, or national security official for the purpose of receiving information from law enforcement agencies. In certain arenas, however, the Secretary's enforcement powers are circumscribed. Notably, primary responsibility for investigating and prosecuting acts of terrorism remain with federal, state, and local law enforcement agencies, except for specific enforcement responsibilities held by agencies transferred to the Department.[19]

1.4.1.5   Information Gathering and Analysis

One of the primary functions of the Department, particularly in the area of critical infrastructure protection, is the gathering and analysis of information. Information gathered will inform a wide range of the Department's decisions, including the assessment of terrorist threats, steps required to protect critical infrastructure and other areas of vulnerability, and the identification of technologies and other products and services deserving of promotion, funding, and liability protection. The Act requires that the Secretary establish uniform procedures within 90 days of the enactment of the Act for the "receipt, care, and storage" by federal agencies of certain critical information to be protected from disclosure.[20]

1.4.1.6 Promoting Research and Technology Development

The Act includes several ways in which the Secretary is directed to promote research and development of homeland security technologies. These include standards-setting, conducting and promoting research, funding technology development, and providing anti-terrorism risk protection. However, Section 313(c)(1) of the Act caveats that this authority does not extend to "set[ting] standards for technology to be used by the Department, any other executive agency, any state or local government entity or any private sector entity."[21]

1.4.1.7 Streamlined Contracting for Commercial Goods and Services

The Act requires in several places that the Department promote the participation of the private sector in homeland security activities. In particular, the Secretary must rely to the "maximum extent practicable" on the use of private sector networks and infrastructure for emergency response.[22] The Act also includes several provisions that aim to facilitate and streamline the ability of private industry to contract with the Department for technologies, goods, and services.[23] Notably, Section 835 prohibits contracts with "corporate expatriates," which are companies or partnerships with substantial U.S. business or assets that are incorporated or organized abroad to avoid tax or other fiduciary duties in the United States.[24]

1.4.1.8 Reports to Congress

The Act requires that the Secretary and numerous other government officials report periodically to different Congressional committees on various activities, resource inventories, program implementation developments and status, compliance plans, public impact, and legislative requirements. Tracking of such reports will provide critical insight into the way the Department's policies, procedures, and practices are taking shape.

1.4.2 Presidential Directive Authority

In addition to the specific powers granted the Secretary of Homeland Security under the Act, on March 1, 2003, President Bush issued a Homeland Security Presidential Directive that provides the Secretary with the responsibility to manage major domestic incidents by establishing a single, comprehensive national incident management system. Components of the Directive include the following:

- The Secretary is responsible for coordinating federal operations to prevent, prepare for, respond to, and recover from all domestic incidents when any of the following conditions apply: (1) the initial lead federal department or agency has requested assistance; (2) the resources of state and local authorities are overwhelmed and assistance has been requested by the state and local authorities; (3) more than one federal agency has become substantially involved in responding to the incident; or (4) he has been directed to assume responsibility for the domestic incident by the president.
- All federal departments and agencies shall cooperate with the Secretary in the Secretary's domestic incident management role and shall participate in and use domestic incident reporting systems and protocols established by the Secretary.
- The Secretary will provide assistance to state and local governments to develop all-hazards plans and capabilities, including those of greatest importance to the security of the United States homeland, such as the prevention of terrorist attacks and preparedness for the potential use of weapons of mass destruction, and ensure that state, local, and federal plans are compatible.
- The Attorney General has the lead responsibility for criminal investigations and intelligence operations concerning terrorist attacks and shall also work to ensure that members of the law enforcement community will work with the Secretary as the official responsible for domestic incident management, to detect, prevent, preempt, and disrupt terrorist attacks against the United States.
- The Directive transfers the authority for developing, implementing, and managing the national Homeland Security Advisory System (color-coded advisory system), previously held by the Attorney General, to the Secretary.

1.5 Limitations on Private Rights of Action

Several provisions of the Act constrain private rights of action. Section 215 specifies that no private right of action is created by any provision of Title II Subtitle B (providing for the protection of the confidentiality of voluntarily provided critical infrastructure information) for enforcement of any provision of the Act.[25] Section 428(f) provides that there is no private right of action to challenge a decision of a consular officer or other U.S. official or employee to grant or deny a visa.[26] Subtitle G of Title VIII pertaining to the SAFETY Act limits actions for recovery for damages from sellers of protected anti-terrorism technologies.[27] In a politically divisive area, the Act also provides immunity from products liability and other civil actions for manufacturers of smallpox vaccines.[28]

1.6   Protection of Individual Rights and Liberties

The Act establishes several officers charged specifically with protecting individual rights and liberties. The Secretary is directed to appoint a Privacy Officer to ensure compliance of the Department with the Privacy Act and that the use of technologies by the Department does not erode privacy protections for personal information. A Citizenship and Immigration Services Ombudsman, reporting to the Deputy Secretary, will assist individuals in resolving any problems with, and recommending improvements in the responsiveness of, the Bureau of Citizenship and Immigration Services. The Secretary is also required to appoint an Officer for Civil Rights and Civil Liberties who is responsible for "reviewing and assessing information alleging abuses of civil rights, civil liberties, and racial and ethnic profiling by employees and officials of the Department."[29]

1.7   Directly Reporting Agencies

For several historically important security agencies, the Act transfers functions to DHS but does not abolish the agencies outright. Although this approach was not applied to the Immigration and Naturalization Service, which no longer exists, the Secret Service, the Coast Guard and the relatively new Transportation Security Administration all continue on as "distinct entit[ies] within the Department."[30] The Commandant of the Coast Guard and the Director of the Secret Service, who remain presidential appointees, are specifically called out (along with a CFO, CIO, and other internal DHS officials) as statutorily required officers of DHS.[31] The Customs Service now is part of the Directorate of Border and Transportation Security.[32]

In addition to these organizationally distinct agencies, several other relatively less formal organizations also report directly to the president, to the Secretary of Homeland Security, or to a Deputy or Under Secretary. These include

- The Bureau of Citizenship and Immigration Services, reporting directly to the Deputy Secretary, charged with adjudicating visa, immigration, and naturalization applications and providing related "consumer" immigration services formerly offered via the Immigration and Naturalization Service.[33]
- The National Homeland Security Council, established by Title IX of the Act,[34] comprised of the president, vice-president, Secretary of Homeland Security, Attorney General, and such others as the president may designate, which is charged with oversight of homeland security policies and making recommendations to the president.

- The Homeland Security Institute, a federally funded research and development center, authorized for three years only to conduct risk analysis, design metrics, and evaluate standards for homeland security technologies and policies.[35]
- The Office of International Affairs, headed by a Director appointed by the Secretary, charged with promoting "information and education exchange with nations friendly to the United States."[36]
- The Office of National Capital Region Coordination, headed by a Director appointed by the Secretary, charged with oversight and coordination of federal programs, and relations with state and local officials, in the Washington, D.C. metropolitan area.[37]
- The Office for State and Local Government Coordination, charged with oversight and coordination of the Department's programs for and relationships with state and local governments.[38]
- The Homeland Security Advanced Research Projects Agency, modeled on DARPA and reporting to the Under Secretary for Science and Technology, charged with administering a fund that awards competitive grants and contracts supporting basic and applied homeland security research.[39]
- The Office of Domestic Preparedness, headed by a presidentially appointed Director, charged with primary Executive Branch responsibility for coordinating federal preparedness for acts of terrorism.[40]
- The Homeland Security Science and Technology Advisory Committee, charged with recommending research areas of potential importance to homeland security, reporting to the Under Secretary for Science and Technology.[41]

The Secretary of Homeland Security is empowered to create and appoint the members of advisory committees, which are largely exempt from the public disclosure provisions of the Federal Advisory Committee Act (which requires, among other things, meetings open to public participation).[42] In addition, the Act creates a number of agencies not within the Department of Homeland Security, such as an Office of Science and Technology in the Justice Department.[43]

1.8 Private Sector Office

Section 102(f) of the Act establishes the position of Special Assistant to the Secretary for the Private Sector[44] for which Alfonso Martinez-Fonts, formerly Chairman of JP Morgan Chase Bank in El Paso, Texas, has been confirmed. The Special Assistant, as the position's title indicates, serves as the key interface between the Department and the private sector and has been placed in charge of the Department's Private Sector Office. The Special Assistant and his relatively small authorized staff (31 in total) serve as the focal point for input on the impact of Department policies and regulations on the private sector, and advise the Secretary on private sector projects, partnerships, and practices to address homeland security issues.

The Special Assistant enjoys broad discretion under the Act to create mechanisms for "strategic communications" between the Department and the private sector,[45] including the creation of private sector advisory councils to advise the Secretary on such issues as private sector products and technological solutions to homeland security challenges.[46] The Special Assistant also is charged with working with the private sector to develop technologies for homeland security missions, promoting public-private sector partnerships, and assisting in the development of private sector best practices to secure critical infrastructure.

The development and evolution of the role of the Special Assistant to the Secretary, as well as the establishment, function, and opportunities for participation in private sector advisory councils, will have a substantial effect on the nature and extent of impact the new Department has on the private sector as well as on new opportunities for businesses in the homeland security arena.

1.8.1   Private Sector Participation

DHS is specifically directed under the Act to use private sector networks and infrastructure, and purchase commercial off-the-shelf technology, to the maximum extent practicable.[47] This is just one example of how, in several respects, the Act creates opportunities for private sector entities to actively participate—and even to partner with—the new Department in activities addressing homeland security concerns. Such participation may take many different forms, and the nature and extent of such opportunities will require time to evolve as the Department becomes fully operational.

The statute expressly provides that, in addition to input that may be offered to the Special Assistant to the Secretary and the Private Sector Office, private sector companies and individuals can

- *Consult* with the Under Secretary for Information Analysis and Infrastructure Protection, and with the Homeland Security Institute.
- *Serve* as analysts of critical infrastructure information.
- *Request technical assistance* from the Department with respect to emergency recovery plans to respond to major failures of critical information systems.
- *Volunteer* to participate in the "NET Guard" to be established to provide scientific and technological expertise to assist local communities to respond to and recover from attacks on information systems and communication networks.[48]

- *Compete* for grants from the Acceleration Fund for Research and Development of Homeland Security Technologies ($500 million to be appropriated in 2003) to be administered by the Director of the HSARPA.[49] Other research and development grants also may be available through the Directorate of Science and Technology's "Extramural Programs."[50]
- *Enter into agreements* for cooperative research and development or licenses with a Department of Energy national laboratory utilized by the Secretary of Homeland Security.
- *Participate* in advisory committees to be established by the Secretary (*see generally* Section 871), such as the Technology Advisory Committee to assist in the development of an Internet-based system to permit individuals and employers to gain online access to information regarding the processing status of immigration-related applications.[51]
- *Provide* off-the-shelf commercially developed information technologies and other goods and services for use by the Department in the conduct of its business.
- *Benefit* from the use of streamlined procurement procedures for property or services.
- *Obtain* a Certificate of Conformance, as well as a listing on the Secretary's Approved Product List for Homeland Security, for the sale of certain qualified anti-terrorism technology.[52]

1.9   Transition

The Office of the Secretary was established as of January 24, 2003. Also as of that date, many of the offices were effective, including several within the Secretary's Office, the Bureau of Border Security, the Bureau of Citizenship and Immigration, and the Director of Shared Services, who is responsible for the coordination of information resources for the Bureau of Border Security and Bureau of Citizenship and Immigration Services.

Certain federal agencies were abolished as a result of the Act, with the functions, assets, and liabilities of such entities transferred to various entities within the Department and elsewhere (*e.g.,* the Immigration and Naturalization Service). In other instances, only certain portions or duties of the federal agency were transferred to the Department (*e.g.,* the Coast Guard), and in still other instances, an agency will continue to exist as a distinct entity within the Department (*e.g.,* the Secret Service.) The transfers are not supposed to affect the completed administrative actions or the pending proceedings of a transferred agency.

The Department's initial reorganization plan, prepared by the White House, was submitted to Congress on November 25, 2002, pursuant to Section 1502 of the Act.[53] All agency transfers were substantially complete by March 1, 2003, with the exception of the Plum Island Animal Disease Center of USDA, which will not be transferred until June 1, 2003.[54] Also as of June 1, 2003, the Homeland Security Science and Technology Advisory Committee was expected to be established. All incidental transfers of personnel, assets, and liabilities of various entities to be transferred to the Department are scheduled to be completed by September 1, 2003.

Regardless of the statutory transition deadlines, the Department faces a substantial practical and logistical challenge in centralizing administrative functions for such a large number of transferred agencies, eliminating duplication, and selecting physical locations. As of May 2003, the Department is planning to locate its permanent central headquarters in Washington, D.C., although that issue could become politically charged. In addition, the Act allows the Secretary to consolidate or eliminate branch and regional offices of any of the Department's constitute Directorates or agencies, which could also have a pronounced effect on the Department's offices and organizational structure.

Endnotes:

[1] 6 U.S.C. 101 note.

[2] 6 U.S.C. 544(d)(1), 541(2).

[3] The DHS budget for fiscal year (FY) 2004 proposed by President Bush includes a total of $36.2 billion, 7.4 percent more than the 2003 level and over 64 percent more than the FY 2002 level for these activities. Approximately half of the requested amount, $18.1 billion, is allocated to the Directorate for Border and Transportation. Next is the Directorate for Emergency Preparedness and Response, which is designated to receive $5.9 billion, an increase of 16 percent ($838 million) over FY 2003. The Directorate for Information Analysis and Infrastructure Protection is provided $829 million; the Directorate for Science and Technology is allocated $803 million. The FY 2004 request also includes $12.2 billion for non-homeland security functions, such as the Coast Guard's search and rescue activities and Secret Service protection of currency and financial integrity.

[4] The Department itself has described the reorganization as "the most significant transformation of the U.S. government since 1947, when Harry S. Truman merged the various branches of the U.S. Armed Forces into the Department of Defense to better coordinate the nation's defense against military threats." DHS Organization. Available at http://www.dhs.gov/dhspublic/themehome1.jsp. *See, e.g.,* "Homeland Security Will Drastically Reshape American Government." *Wall Street Journal*, 22 November 2001. A1.

[5] 6 USC 111(b)(2).

[6] The Department's Directorate of Information Analysis and Infrastructure Protection is authorized to enter into "personnel detailing" agreements with the State Department, CIA, FBI, NSA, the National Imagery and Mapping Agency, and the Defense Intelligence Agency on either a reimbursable or non-reimbursable basis, effectively expanding the already impressive human resource assets of the Department. 6 U.S.C. 201(f).

[7] 6 U.S.C. 113(a)(7), (b). The Under Secretary for Management is responsible for budget, appropriations, expenditure of funds, and accounting and finance; procurement; human resources and personnel; information technology systems; facilities, property, equipment, and other material resources; and identification and tracking of performance measurements relating to the responsibilities of the Department. 6 U.S.C. 341. The Under Secretary for Management Designate is Janet Hale. The Inspector General serves as an independent inspection, audit, and investigative body to promote effectiveness, efficiency, and economy in the Department's programs and operations, and to prevent and detect fraud, abuse, mismanagement, and waste in such programs and operations. 6 U.S.C. 371-72. Clark Kent Ervin has been Acting Inspector General since January 24, 2003, the first day of the Department.

[8] The Congressional Research Service has observed that new and reorganized agencies experienced substantial startup problems—delays in obtaining key officials prevented timely decisionmaking; delays in obtaining needed staff impeded first-year operations; insufficient funding necessitated additional budget requests; and inadequate office space contributed to inefficient handling of workload and morale problems. CRS. *Homeland Security: Department Organization and Management—Implementation Phase.* 5 March 2003. 3.

[9] 6 U.S.C. 452(a). The Act does require that this organizational power be exercised by the Secretary as part of the reorganization plan mandated by Section 1502 (6 U.S.C. 542), but that plan may be modified until the end of the one-year transition period established by the Act.

[10] 6 U.S.C. 411. *See* M. Daniels, "Homeland Security: Do It Right." *Washington Post*, 23 July 2002. A17. The Office of Personnel Management (OPM) has indicated that it intends to have the new personnel system of the Department of Homeland Security operational by June 1, 2003. Among other issues, OPM will be attempting to reconcile differences among 15 basic pay systems, 12 special pay systems, ten hiring methods, eight overtime pay rates, seven payroll and benefit systems, five locality pay systems, and 19 performance management systems coming to the department. The Bush Administration reportedly will be soliciting input from a variety of sources, including federal employees, union representatives, personnel experts, and government reform organizations. *See* "OPM Promises Homeland Security Personnel System by June." *Federal Times.* 2 December 2002. 1, 5; "OPM Begins Sorting Security Personnel." *Washington Post.* 9 December 2002. A21.

[11] 6 U.S.C. 441(c).

[12] 6 U.S.C. 133(e)(1). The Department's Notice of Proposed Rulemaking on this subject was released for public comment on April 15, 2003. *See* 68 Fed. Reg. 18524, *to be codified at* 6 C.F.R. 29.1 *et seq.*

[13] 6 U.S.C. 877(a).

[14] 6 U.S.C. 877(a).

[15] 6 U.S.C. 121(d)(5).

[16] 6 U.S.C. 182(2).

[17] 6 U.S.C. 402(5).

[18] 6 U.S.C. 312(6).

[19] 6 U.S.C. 111(b)(2).

[20] 6 U.S.C. 133(c)(1), *see* n12 *supra.*

[21] 6 U.S.C. 193(c)(1).

[22] 6 U.S.C. 318.

[23] 6 U.S.C. 853, 856, 858.

[24] 6 U.S.C. 395.

[25] 6 U.S.C. 134.

[26] 6 U.S.C. 236(f).

[27] 6 U.S.C. 421 *et seq.*

[28] 6 U.S.C. 184(c).

[29] 6 U.S.C. 345.

[30] 6 U.S.C. 381 (Secret Service), 468(b) (Coast Guard), 234(a)(TSA). The Transportation Security Administration's protected status as a distinct entity within DHS sunsets two years after enactment. 6 U.S.C. 234(b).

[31] 6 U.S.C. 103(c), (d)(1).

[32] 6 U.S.C. 211.

[33] 6 U.S.C. 271.

[34] 6 U.S.C. 491-96.

[35] 6 U.S.C. 192.

[36] 6 U.S.C. 459.

[37] 6 U.S.C. 462.

[38] 6 U.S.C. 261.

[39] 6 U.S.C. 187.

[40] 6 U.S.C. 238.

[41] 6 U.S.C. 191.

[42] 6 U.S.C. 451.

[43] 6 U.S.C. 161.

[44] 6 U.S.C. 102(f).

[45] 6 U.S.C. 102(f)(1).

[46] 6 U.S.C. 102(f)(4).

[47] 6 U.S.C. 318, 319.

[48] 6 U.S.C. 224.

[49] 6 U.S.C. 307.

[50] 6 U.S.C. 308.

[51] *E.g.,* 6 U.S.C. 451.

[52] 6 U.S.C. 863(d)(3).

[53] 6 U.S.C. 542. The reorganization plan is available at http://www.whitehouse.gov/news/releases/2002/11/reorganization_plan.pdf

[54] 6 U.S.C. 190.

Chapter 13

Organization and Functions of the DHS Directorates

Kelley Drye & Warren LLP
Glenn B. Manishin

1.0 Information Analysis and Infrastructure Protection Directorate (Title II)

1.1 Organization

The Directorate of Information Analysis and Infrastructure Protection (IAIP)[1] was created through the transfer on March 1, 2003, of five agencies into the Department:

- The National Communications System of the Department of Defense
- The National Infrastructure Protection Center of the FBI (other than the Computer Investigations and Operations Section)
- The Critical Infrastructure Assurance Office (CIAO) of the Department of Commerce[2]
- The National Infrastructure Simulation and Analysis Center of the Department of Energy
- The Federal Computer Incident Response Center (FedCIRC) of the General Services Administration[3]

Other personnel from the State Department, CIA, FBI, NSA, the National Imagery and Mapping Agency, and the Defense Intelligence Agency are to be detailed to the Department to assist with analytic and related functions.

The IAIP Directorate is divided into two operational units, each headed by an Assistant Secretary appointed by the president. The Assistant Secretary for

Information Analysis and the Assistant Secretary for Infrastructure Protection are specifically charged under the Act merely with "assit[ing] the Under Secretary ... in discharging the responsibilities" of Title II.[4] Nonetheless, it is apparent that the IAIP Directorate will organizationally be separated between information collection/analysis and infrastructure protection, with each Bureau or subunit responsible for substantially different areas of concern.

1.2   Critical Functions

The IAIP Directorate merges under one roof the capability to identify and assess current and future threats to the homeland, map those threats against known vulnerabilities, issue timely warnings, and take preventive and protective action. The critical functions of the Directorate are as follows:

- To designate critical infrastructure and develop a national plan to secure key resources and critical infrastructure
- To collect and receive certain intelligence and other information from all federal agencies for analysis in service of the Department's mandate to protect critical infrastructure
- To issue threat assessment and warnings
- To engage in information sharing, privacy protection and security assurance

1.2.1   Assurance of Cybersecurity

The Act places substantial emphasis on cybersecurity. Section 223 requires that the Secretary provide to state and local governments, and upon request to private sector entities that own or operate critical information systems, analysis and warnings related to threats and vulnerabilities of critical information systems.[5] To protect against cyber attacks, Section 224 of the Act permits the Under Secretary to create a national corps of volunteers with expertise in science and technology (to be known as "NET Guard") to "assist local communities to respond and recover from attacks on information systems and communication networks."[6]

Further, Section 225 of the Act incorporates the entire text of the Cyber Security Enhancement Act (CSEA), which was previously approved by the full House.[7] The CSEA directs the United States Sentencing Commission to review its guidelines applicable to certain computer crimes and submit a report to Congress, by May 1, 2003, of actions taken. The Act allows Internet service providers (ISPs) to voluntarily provide government agents with access to the contents of customer communications without consent based on a "good faith" belief that an emergency justifies the release. This is intended to ease fear of lawsuits on the part of ISPs due to information sharing with law enforcement.

The Act also specifies that an existing ban on the "advertisement" of any device that is used primarily for surreptitious electronic surveillance applies to online ads. It introduces fines and 20-year prison terms for offenders who "knowingly" or "recklessly" cause or attempt to cause serious bodily injury and provides up to life sentence for computer intrusions that "knowingly" or "recklessly" put others' lives at risk. It permits limited surveillance without a court order, including the installation of pen register and trap and trace devices, when there is an "ongoing attack" on a "protected computer"[8] or "an immediate threat to a national security interest." Surveillance is limited to obtaining a suspect's telephone number, Internet address, or email header information—not the contents of online communications or telephone calls.

1.3   Major Issues

1.3.1   Designation of Critical Infrastructure

It is unclear what facilities will actually be designated as critical infrastructure by the Secretary or the president. The Act references Section 1016 of the USA PATRIOT Act, which in turn defines "critical infrastructure" as "systems and assets, whether physical or virtual, so vital to the United States that the incapacity or destruction of such systems and assets would have a debilitating impact on security, national economic security, national public health or safety, or any combination of those matters."[9] The definition is certainly open to interpretation. The transfer of such offices as CIAO and the National Infrastructure Simulation and Analysis Center to the Department puts the interpretation of the USA PATRIOT Act provisions under the Secretary's jurisdiction. Thus, as a practical matter, the determination of what constitutes critical infrastructure will fall to the Secretary.

The consequences of a critical infrastructure designation, however, are more informational than substantive. As discussed in the next section, the Act provides for the protection of critical infrastructure information voluntarily shared with the federal government, but does not otherwise provide substantive regulations or standards for protection of such critical assets.

1.3.2   Protection of Confidential Information

The protection of information regarding critical infrastructure and vulnerabilities to terrorist attack is of paramount concern, particularly as the Act provides for the widespread dissemination of homeland security information among federal, state, and local authorities as well as the private sector.

To address these concerns, Section 214—known as the Critical Infrastructure Information Act of 2002—provides that information voluntarily provided by non-federal parties to the Department that relates to the security of critical infrastructure or protected systems shall be exempt from disclosure under Section 552 of the Freedom of Information Act (FOIA), when accompanied by an express statement specified in the Act.[10] Such information should not lose its protected character if forwarded by the Department to other federal agencies. Moreover, information voluntarily provided is not subject to rules concerning ex parte communications and may not be used in any civil action if such information has been submitted in good faith. The provisions of this section preempt state law to ensure that the information is not disclosed by state openness laws. The Act provides for punishment, including fines and imprisonment for up to one year, of any Department employee for disclosing any voluntarily submitted critical infrastructure information that is not customarily in the public domain.

The extent of the protection actually accorded by this provision is as yet uncertain. The Homeland Security Act does not expressly amend FOIA, and the application of the statutory definition of "voluntary" may be subject to interpretation. Procedures for the receipt and storage of critical infrastructure information are to be established within 90 days of the enactment of the Act. However, there is no deadline for the establishment by the president of the new procedures required under Section 892 for sharing of homeland security information with "appropriate state and local personnel," although a progress report must be submitted to Congress within one year.

1.3.3 Environmental Protection Issues

One of the critical areas that the new Homeland Security Department may seek to address through regulations are eco-security programs to protect against harm to people and/or the environment, for example, from the possible release of hazardous materials due to terrorist or other criminal attacks against nuclear and other electric power plants, petroleum and natural gas pipelines, chemical manufacturing and storage facilities, and other industrial facilities. Such protective programs are not expressly required under the Act, but the need for eco-security programs for critical infrastructure likely will be examined in the context of the Department's threat assessment analysis. Any regulatory proposals regarding eco-security for critical infrastructure would raise a number of serious questions, such as which facilities should be encouraged or required to implement these programs, whether security measures should be federally-mandated or only voluntarily implemented, and whether facility assessments and other business information relating to security evaluations would be legally protected from disclosure.

2.0 Science and Technology Directorate (Title III)

2.1 Organization

Under the direction of Under Secretary Dr. Charles McQueary, the Science and Technology (S&T) Directorate was created through the transfer of programs and activities from other agencies, including the Environmental Measurements Laboratory and the advanced scientific computing research program and activities at Lawrence Livermore National Laboratory. The Department of Defense National Bio-Weapons Defense Analysis Center, including related functions of the Secretary of Defense, are also scheduled to be transferred.

The Homeland Security Advanced Research Projects Agency reports to the Under Secretary for the S&T Directorate.[11] The Under Secretary is empowered by the Act to create one or more "federally funded research and development centers" to provide independent analysis of homeland security issues[12] and one or more "university-based centers for homeland security" to support extramural and intramural programs for homeland security.[13]

2.2 Critical Functions

The Directorate of Science and Technology generally is responsible for research and development efforts in support of homeland security, including

- Identifying and developing countermeasures to chemical, biological, radiological, nuclear, and other emerging terrorist threats
- Assessing and testing vulnerabilities and possible threats
- Establishing priorities for directing, funding, and conducting research and for developing, testing, evaluating, and procuring technology and systems to prevent the importation of chemical, biological, radiological, nuclear, and related weapons and material
- Detecting, preventing, protecting against, and responding to terrorist attacks

The Act establishes several principal areas of responsibility in support of the Department's science and technology agenda, discussed individually in the following sections.

2.2.1 Collaboration with Other Agencies

The Under Secretary is responsible for coordinating with other executive agencies in carrying out the Department's science and technology agenda. The Act specifies that the Department will collaborate with the Department of Agriculture, the Department of Health and Human Services, and the Department of Energy.

2.2.2   Research, Development, Testing, and Evaluation

The primary science and technology mission of the Act—research, development, demonstration, testing, and evaluation—will be carried out through a combination of "extramural" and "intramural" programs. Extramural programs, including university-based centers for homeland security and programs with the private sector, are to be established within one year of the date of enactment.[14] Criteria for selection will include (1) demonstrating expertise in relevant areas such as food safety; emergency medical services; chemical, biological, radiological, and nuclear countermeasures; port and waterway security; (2) having a nationally recognized program in information security; and (3) having strong affiliations with diagnostic laboratories, among other factors.

The Department will be allowed to draw on the expertise of any laboratory of the federal government, whether operated by a contractor or the government itself. A Department headquarters laboratory and additional laboratory units may be established at any laboratory or site. Furthermore, the Under Secretary may establish or contract with federally funded research and development centers to provide independent analysis of homeland security issues or to carry out other responsibilities under the Act.

2.2.3   Homeland Security Advanced Research Projects Agency

The Director of the Homeland Security Advanced Research Projects Agency (HSARPA), who will report to the Under Secretary, will administer the Acceleration Fund for Research and Development of Homeland Security Technologies; award competitive grants and contracts to public and private entities; and support accelerated research, testing, and deployment of critical homeland security technologies to promote homeland security and address vulnerabilities.[15] HSARPA also will coordinate with other research agencies, and possibly operate joint projects. For fiscal year 2003, $500 million has been authorized (but not yet appropriated) for the Fund.[16]

2.2.4   Homeland Security Science and Technology Advisory Committee

The Under Secretary will appoint 20 members to the Advisory Committee, which will make recommendations and identify research areas of potential importance to national security.[17]

2.2.5   Homeland Security Institute

The Institute is a federally funded research and development center, administered as a separate entity by the Secretary.[18] Its operations will be determined by the Secretary, and may include systems analysis, risk analysis, simulation and modeling to determine vulnerabilities, economic and policy analysis, design and support for conduct of homeland security-related exercises and simulations, and creation of strategic technology development plans to reduce vulnerabilities in the critical infrastructure. The Institute will consult widely with private and public entities.

2.2.6 Technology Clearinghouse

The Technology Clearinghouse is intended to encourage technological innovation in service of the mission of the Department,[19] and will include the following five components:

- A centralized federal clearinghouse relating to technologies that would further the mission of the Department
- Issuance of announcements seeking unique and innovative technologies
- Establishment of a technical assistance team to assess the merits of proposals
- Provision of guidance to other government agencies and private sector efforts to evaluate and implement the technologies
- Provision of information for persons seeking guidance on how to develop or deploy such technologies

However, the Clearinghouse will not set standards for technology to be used by the Department.[20]

2.3 Major Issues

2.3.1 New Regulations for Contractors

It would not be surprising to see a number of new rules and regulations resulting from the creation of the S&T Directorate. The Under Secretary will have the authority to issue new regulations with respect to research, development, demonstration, testing, and evaluation activities of the Department, including conducting, funding, and reviewing of such activities. In this respect, implementation of the Act should provide a number of contracting opportunities for private organizations. However, companies contracting with federal agencies pursuant to the Act also will face new regulations and compliance requirements.

2.3.2 Funding

Although Title III contemplates the funding of various "extramural programs" for research, development, demonstration, evaluation, and testing of homeland security technologies, including by private sector entities, the Act does not expressly authorize appropriations for such funding. Consequently the amount, nature, and terms and conditions of any such funding are unclear.

3.0   Border and Transportation Security Directorate (Title IV)

3.1   Organization

Led by Under Secretary Asa Hutchinson, the Directorate of Border and Transportation Security (BTS) has been created out of the functions transferred from a number of existing federal agencies and offices. Chief among these is the INS, which is abolished and largely replaced by the new BTS Directorate.[21] Other offices transferred to the BTS Directorate include the Customs Service of the Department of Treasury (except customs revenue functions, such as assessing and collecting customs duties, which will not transfer); the Transportation Security Administration (TSA) of the Department of Transportation; the Federal Law Enforcement Training Center (FLETC) of the Department of the Treasury; and the Office for Domestic Preparedness of the Office of Justice Programs. BTS also incorporates the Federal Protective Service (General Services Administration) to perform the additional function of protecting government buildings, a task closely related to the Department's infrastructure protection responsibilities. Certain agricultural inspection functions of the Secretary of Agriculture also will be transferred.

3.2   Critical Functions

The Secretary, acting through the Under Secretary for Border and Transportation Security, is responsible for preventing the entry of terrorists and instruments of terrorism into the United States; securing the borders and transportation systems; carrying out immigration enforcement functions; establishing and administering rules governing the granting of visas or other forms of permission for non-citizens to enter the United States; and establishing national immigration enforcement policies and priorities.

3.3   Directorate Organization

The BTS Directorate is organized into two separate bureaus, one governing border security and the other governing citizenship and immigration services. The Act creates the position of Director of Shared Services within the Office of Deputy Secretary,[22] responsible for the coordination of resources for the two bureaus, including information resources management, records and file management, and forms management. The former INS is similarly divided between separate enforcement and service bureaus designed to allow for more efficient processing of immigration petitions and applications.

3.3.1 Bureau of Customs and Border Protection (CBP)

The Bureau of Customs and Border Protection (referred to in the Act as the "Bureau of Border Security") is headed by an Assistant Secretary who reports directly to the Under Secretary for Border Security.[23] The Assistant Secretary (now known as the Commissioner of Customs and Border Security) controls and establishes policy for the Border Patrol program, as well as the detention and removal program, the intelligence program, the investigations program, and the inspections program. Among other things, the Assistant Secretary is charged with establishing policies and overseeing the administration of the immigration functions and administering the Student and Exchange Visitor Information System and other programs established to collect information relating to foreign students and other exchange program participants.

CBP is comprised of 35,000 federal employees, which includes 17,000 inspectors and canine enforcement officers from the APHIS-Agricultural Quarantine Inspection program, INS inspection services, and the Customs Service, and 10,000 Border Patrol Agents. Robert C. Bonner is Commissioner of the Bureau of Customs and Border Protection.

Unifying the border agencies—a good government reform advocated by many studies over the past 30 years—is designed to improve the way the U.S. government manages the border. The CBP Bureau is dedicated to combining skills and resources to make sure that border security in the future will be more effective and efficient than it was when border responsibilities were fragmented into four agencies, in three different departments of government. CBP's strategy to improve security and facilitate the flow of legitimate trade and travel includes

- Improving targeting systems and expanding advance information regarding people and goods arriving in the United States
- Pushing America's "zone of security outward" by partnering with other governments as well as with the private sector
- Deploying advanced inspection technology and equipment
- Increasing staffing for border security
- Working in concert with other agencies to coordinate activities with respect to trade fraud, intellectual property rights violations, controlled deliveries of illegal drugs, and money laundering

The Act creates two additional positions within the Bureau of Customs and Border Protection. A Chief of Policy and Strategy is responsible for consulting with personnel in local offices, researching policy issues, analyzing and making policy recommendations on immigration enforcement issues, and coordinating immigration policy. The Legal Advisor provides legal advice to the

Assistant Secretary for Border Security and will represent the Bureau in all exclusion, deportation, and removal proceedings before the Executive Office for Immigration Review (EOIR).[24]

3.3.2   Bureau of Immigration and Customs Enforcement

As part of its March 1, 2003, reorganization, the functions of several border and security agencies—including the Customs Service and the FPS—were transferred into the BST Directorate and reorganized into the Bureau of Immigration and Customs Enforcement (ICE).

The Bureau of Immigration and Customs Enforcement brings together approximately 14,000 Federal employees who focus on the enforcement of immigration and customs laws within the United States, the protection of specified federal buildings, and air and marine enforcement. By unifying previously fragmented investigative functions, it is hoped that the new Bureau will deliver effective and comprehensive enforcement. The Bureau is led by an Assistant Secretary who reports directly to the Undersecretary for Border and Transportation Security. Michael Garcia, former Acting INS Commissioner, has been nominated by President Bush to fill this role.

The Bureau of Immigration and Customs Enforcement is comprised of the following primary program areas:

- *Immigration Investigations*—Responsible for investigating violations of the criminal and administrative provisions of the Immigration and Nationality Act (INA) and other related provisions of the United States Code
- *Customs Investigations*—Responsible for investigating a range of issues including terrorist financing, export enforcement, money laundering, smuggling, fraud—including Intellectual Property Rights violations—and cyber crimes
- *Customs Air and Marine Interdiction*—Responsible for protecting the Nation's borders and the American people from the smuggling of narcotics, other contraband, and terrorist activity with an integrated and coordinated air and marine interdiction force
- *Federal Protective Service*—Responsible for providing a safe environment in which federal agencies can conduct their business by reducing threats posed against the over 8,800 General Services Administration (GSA)-controlled facilities nationwide
- *Detention and Removal*—Responsible for promoting the public safety and national security by ensuring the departure from the United States of all removable aliens through the fair enforcement of the nation's immigration laws.

- *Immigration Intelligence*—Responsible for the collection, analysis, and dissemination of intelligence to immigration staff at all levels to aid in making day-to-day, mid-term, and long-term operational decisions; acquiring and allocating resources; and determining policy
- *Customs Intelligence*—Responsible for the collection, analysis, and dissemination of strategic and tactical intelligence data for use by the operational elements of customs enforcement

In June 2003, the Department implemented a substantial reorganization of the Bureau of Immigration and Customs Enforcement.[25] The reorganization established five divisions at ICE headquarters in Washington: (1) investigations, (2) intelligence, (3) detention and removal, (4) air and marine interdiction, and (5) federal protective services. The new divisions integrate previously separate INS and Customs investigations and intelligence operations. The air and marine interdiction division comes from the Customs Service. The detention and removal division is composed of former INS staff, and the federal protective services division, which is charged with protecting federal buildings, was formerly part of the General Services Administration. The yet-to-be-named division heads will report to ICE Acting Assistant Secretary Michael Garcia.

3.3.3 Bureau of Citizenship and Immigration Services

The service and benefit functions of INS have been transferred into the Department as the Bureau of Citizenship and Immigration Services (BCIS).[26] BCIS is headed by a Director, who is charged with establishing national immigration services policies and priorities. BCIS is organizationally separate from the BTS Directorate and reports to the Deputy Secretary of DHS. The Bureau has authority for several functions previously administered by the Commissioner of the INS, all adjudications previously performed by the INS, including adjudications of immigrant visa petitions, naturalization petitions, asylum, and refugee applications, and adjudications performed at service centers.

Eduardo Aguirre, current Vice Chairman and Chief Operating Officer of the Export-Import Bank of the United States, was appointed by President Bush as Acting Director of the BCIS. The functions of BCIS include

- Adjudication of immigrant visa petitions
- Adjudication of naturalization petitions
- Adjudication of asylum and refugee applications
- Adjudications performed at the service centers
- All other adjudications performed by the INS

The immediate priorities of the new BCIS are to promote national security, continue to eliminate immigration adjudication backlogs, and implement solutions for improving immigration customer services.[27] Fifteen thousand (15,000) federal employees and contractors working in approximately 250 headquarters and field offices around the world comprise the BCIS.

A Citizenship and Immigration Services Ombudsman will serve to identify problem areas between individuals or employers and the Citizenship and Immigration Bureau, to assist with resolution of such problems, and to propose changes to mitigate future such problems.[28]

The Act vests in the Secretary of Homeland Security (acting through the Secretary of State) exclusive authority to administer and enforce all laws, and to issue regulations relating to the functions of consular officers in the granting or refusal of visas, including the authority to develop programs of homeland security training for consular officers.[29]

While granting authority over administration and enforcement of laws related to visa issuance, the Act does not give the Secretary of Homeland Security the authority to alter or reverse the decision of a consular officer to refuse a visa. The Act does, however, authorize the Secretary of State to direct a consular officer to refuse a visa to an alien if the Secretary of State deems such refusal necessary or advisable in the foreign policy or security interests of the United States. In addition, the Secretary of State continues to retain authority under certain areas of the Immigration and Nationality Act.

3.3.4 Office of Domestic Preparedness

The Directorate for Border and Transportation Security also contains the Office of Domestic Preparedness,[30] headed by a Director who reports directly to the Deputy Secretary of the Department. This Office bears the primary responsibility within the Executive Branch for preparing the United States for acts of terrorism and for coordinating preparedness efforts at all levels and in all matters pertaining to combating terrorism on behalf of the United States.

4.0 Emergency Preparedness and Response Directorate (Title V)

4.1 Organization

Headed by Under Secretary Mike Brown, the Directorate of Emergency Preparedness and Response (EP&R) was established by Section 501 of the Act.[31] Agencies and functions related to emergency preparedness transferred to the new Directorate include

- Federal Emergency Management Agency (FEMA)
- The Integrated Hazard Information System of the National Oceanic and Atmospheric Administration, which will be renamed "FIRESAT"
- The National Domestic Preparedness Office of the FBI, including related functions of the Attorney General
- The Domestic Emergency Support Teams of the Department of Justice, including the related functions of the Attorney General
- The Office of Emergency Preparedness
- The National Disaster Medical System
- The Metropolitan Medical Response System of the Department of Health and Human Services, including the related functions of the Secretary of Health and Human Services and the Assistant Secretary for Public Health Emergency Preparedness
- The Strategic National Stockpile of the Department of Health and Human Services, including the related functions of the Secretary of Health and Human Services

Functioning as separate and distinct entities assisting in emergency preparation and response, yet under the direct authority of the Secretary, are the Nuclear Incident Response Team,[32] which is activated in cases of actual or threatened terrorist attack; the United States Secret Service; and the Homeland Security Institute, a federally funded research and development center whose duties may include systems/risk analyses to determine vulnerabilities in the nation's critical infrastructures and assessment of alternative approaches to enhancing security.

4.2   Critical Functions

The EP&R Directorate is charged with aiding to ensure the effectiveness of emergency response providers to terrorist attacks, major disasters, and other emergencies. According to DHS, to fulfill its mission of preparing for natural disasters and man-made catastrophes, the EP&R Directorate will build upon the Federal Emergency Management Agency, which has a long and solid track record of aiding the nation's recovery from emergency situations. The EP&R Directorate will continue FEMA's efforts to reduce the loss of life and property and to protect our nation's institutions from all types of hazards through a comprehensive, risk-based emergency management program of preparedness, prevention, response, and recovery. It will also further the evolution of the emergency management culture from one that reacts to disasters to one that proactively helps communities and citizens avoid becoming victims. In addition, the Directorate will develop and manage a national training and evaluation system to design curriculums, set standards, evaluate, and reward performance in local, state, and federal training efforts.

4.2.1   Response Plans

The critical functions of the Directorate of Emergency Preparedness and Response include the establishment of a comprehensive national (federal, state, local) emergency response plan and management system including coordination with the Department of Health and Human Services, the Federal Emergency Management Agency, and the Nuclear Incident Response Team.

4.2.2   Emergency Response Supplies

The Act may potentially benefit the private sector and create a new market for existing technology. Specifically, it requires the Secretary, to the extent possible, to use off-the-shelf commercially developed technologies.[33] The Secretary must use such technology to ensure that the Department's information systems allow the Department to collect, manage, share, analyze, and disseminate information securely over multiple channels of communications. Furthermore, in order to avoid competition with the private sector, the Secretary should rely on commercial sources to supply the goods and services needed by the Department.[34] This is in line with existing federal policies to avoid commercial competition with the private sector.

4.3   Major Issues

4.3.1   Use of Private Sector Networks

Section 508 requires that the Secretary use national private sector networks and infrastructure, to the extent practicable, for emergency response to chemical, biological, radiological, nuclear, or explosive disasters and other major disasters.[35] This section does not define the phrase "national private sector networks and infrastructure" and sets no parameters for the prescribed use. The terms and conditions of the use of such networks are not addressed, and it is not clear whether the Act contemplates or permits the appropriation of private sector networks and infrastructure in the event of such emergencies. It is further unclear if the use may occur only in times of emergency and major disasters, *i.e.,* a temporary takeover of the infrastructure and networks, if the Department should use these private facilities in its everyday operations in preparation for response to such emergencies and disasters or if requirements and obligations may be imposed on private networks to ensure that they are serviceable to the Department in the event of an emergency. The extraordinary breadth and vagueness of this provision raises significant concerns and will require close monitoring of its implementation.

4.3.2　Impact on Communications Policy and Providers

Several provisions of the Act have potential significance for the establishment of communications policy and the operation of communications networks by public as well as private sector entities. Section 502(7) requires that the Under Secretary for Emergency Preparedness and Response develop "comprehensive programs for developing interoperative communications technology, and help[ ] to ensure that emergency response providers acquire such technology."[36] Pursuant to a related provision, Section 223, the Under Secretary for EP&R is expected to coordinate with the Under Secretary for IAIP to provide analysis, warnings, crisis management support, and technical assistance to state and local entities, as well as to private sector upon request, to assist in response to threats or attacks on "critical information systems."[37]

Under Section 201 the Under Secretary for Information Analysis and Infrastructure is charged directly with developing a national plan for securing telecommunications systems that constitute critical infrastructure.[38] Meanwhile, the Office of Science and Technology established in the Department of Justice is charged in Section 232(b)(7) with administering "a program of research, development, testing, and demonstration to improve the interoperability of voice and data public safety communications."[39] Finally, pursuant to Section 430, the Office of Domestic Preparedness in the BTS Directorate has primary responsibility within the executive branch for "coordinating or, as appropriate, consolidating communications and systems of communications relating to homeland security at all levels of government."[40]

These provisions raise a number of significant questions. As an initial matter, they are very broadly written and lack any definitions of the terms "communications technology," "communications systems," "critical information systems," and "interoperability." Conceivably the provisions apply to all manner of communications technologies and systems, regardless of the technology employed (*i.e.,* wireline or wireless) and without distinction between private commercial systems, private non-commercial systems (*e.g.,* utility), and public sector systems (*e.g.,* municipal or other government and public safety). The authority of various officials of the Department of Homeland Security and/or the Department of Justice to mandate technologies, standards, protocols, or procedures for response to threats or attacks, to achieve "interoperability," or to ensure availability for Department use in the event of an emergency is completely unclear.

The diffusion of responsibility for these issues promises to create confusion at best, and direct conflicts at worst, in the obligations, expectations, and standards imposed on communications systems by various homeland security officials. Significant conflict may also arise between the Department of Homeland

Security and other communications authorities, including the Federal Communications Commission and the Department of Commerce's National Telecommunications and Information Administration. This is particularly true with respect to spectrum allocation and utilization for critical infrastructure and public safety, but also with respect to network reliability and cybersecurity. The availability of spectrum, avoidance of interference, and standards for interoperable use for any and all communications systems that may need to be used in a national emergency will present a complex set of issues with many masters that will have to be carefully navigated over the coming months.

Endnotes:

[1] On March 20, 2003, the president announced his intention to nominate Frank Libutti, currently the New York City Police Department's Deputy Commissioner of Counter Terrorism, as Under Secretary for Information Analysis and Infrastructure Protection.

[2] The Planning and Partnerships Office (PPO) within IAIP assumed many of the responsibilities previously held by CIAO. The office's primary focus is to raise issues that cut across industry sectors and ensure a cohesive approach to achieving continuity in delivering critical infrastructure services.

[3] FedCIRC is the federal civilian government's trusted focal point for computer security incident reporting, providing assistance with incident prevention and response.

[4] 6 U.S.C. 121(b).

[5] 6 U.S.C. 143.

[6] 6 U.S.C. 144.

[7] 6 U.S.C. 145.

[8] As defined, any computer involved in interstate commerce or communications qualifies as a "protected computer."

[9] The text of the USA PATRIOT Act also expressly includes "cyber infrastructure, telecommunications infrastructure, and physical infrastructure" as critical infrastructure.

[10] 6 U.S.C. 133.

[11] 6 U.S.C. 186.

[12] 6 U.S.C. 185.

[13] 6 U.S.C. 188.

[14] 6 U.S.C. 188(b).

[15] 6 U.S.C. 187.

[16] 6 U.S.C. 187(c)(1).

[17] 6 U.S.C. 191.

[18] 6 U.S.C. 192.

[19] 6 U.S.C. 193.

[20] 6 U.S.C. 193(c)(1).

[21] Jurisdiction over a few matters is transferred from the INS to other agencies. For example, issues regarding unaccompanied alien children are transferred to the Office of Refugee Resettlement of the Department of Health and Human Services.

[22] 6 U.S.C. 295.

[23] 6 U.S.C. 442. The Act expressly permits the Secretary to reorganize the BTS Directorate so long as border control and immigration adjudication functions remain in separate organizational units. 6 U.S.C. 291(b). In a policy speech delivered in Miami on January 30, 2003, Secretary Ridge outlined the Department's amendment to its re-organization plan to merge the border investigative and enforcement functions of the Immigration and Naturalization Service (INS), U.S. Customs Service (USCS), and the Animal and Plant Health Inspection Service (APHIS) into the Bureau of Customs and Border Protection. *See* "DHS Announces Border Security Reorganization." Press Release, available at http://www.dhs.gov/dhspublic/display?content=422.

[24] EOIR remains a separate agency within the Department of Justice, under the authority of the Attorney General.

[25] *See* "ICE Announces Agency Reorganization Plan." Press Release, 16 May 2003. Available at http://www.dhs.gov/dhspublic/ display?content=722; "Homeland Bureau Consolidates Immigration and Customs Operations." *Government Executive Magazine.* Available at http://www.govexec.com/dailyfed/0503/051603sz1.htm

[26] 6 U.S.C. 271. While BTS is responsible for enforcement of our nation's immigration laws, the Bureau of Citizenship and Immigration Services is dedicated to providing efficient immigration services and easing the transition to American citizenship. The Director of Citizenship and Immigration Services reports directly to the Deputy Secretary of Homeland Security.

[27] *See* "This Is the BCIS." Available at http://www.immigration.gov/graphics/aboutus/thisisimm/index.htm.

[28] 6 U.S.C. 272.

[29] This section will take effect either when the president publishes notice in the Federal Register that Congress has received the memorandum of understanding between the Secretary and the Secretary of State governing implementation of this section or one year after the enactment of the Act, whichever comes first.

[30] 6 U.S.C. 238.

[31] 6 U.S.C. 312.

[32] 6 U.S.C. 314.

[33] 6 U.S.C. 318.

[34] 6 U.S.C. 319.

[35] 6 U.S.C. 318.

[36] 6 U.S.C. 312(7).

[37] 6 U.S.C. 143(1)(B).

[38] 6 U.S.C. 121(d)(5).

[39] 6 U.S.C. 162(b)(7).

[40] 6 U.S.C. 238.

Department of Homeland Security

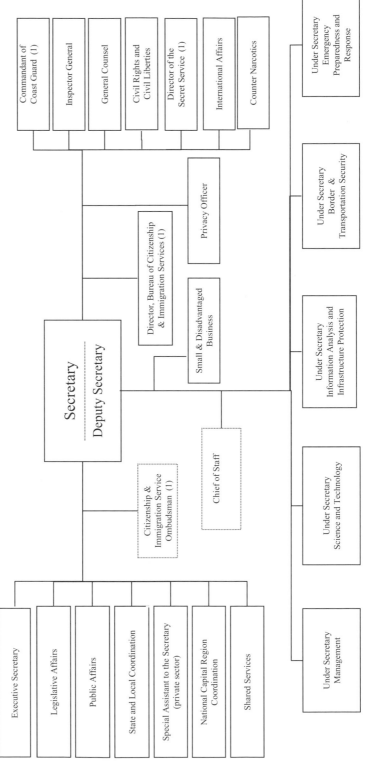

Index

C

Government Institutes Mini-Catalog

PC #	HOMELAND SECURITY TITLES	Pub Date	Price*
962	Homeland Security Law Handbook	2003	$89
844	Homeland Security Statutes, 2003 Edition	2003	$89
4810	Homeland Security Advisor, 1-year online subscription	2003	$1,995

PC #	ENVIRONMENTAL TITLES	Pub Date	Price*
812	Achieving Environmental Excellence	2003	$79
846	Clean Water Handbook, Third Edition	2003	$125
4300	EH&S Daily Federal Register Notification Service (e-mail)	2003	$150
4045	Environmental, Health & Safety CFRs on CD-ROM, single issue	2003	$450
955	Environmental Law Handbook, Seventeenth Edition	2003	$99
688	Environmental Health & Safety Dictionary, Seventh Edition	2000	$105
956	Environmental Statutes, 2003 Edition	2003	$125
958	Information Technology Solutions for EH&S Professionals	2003	$95
936	Managing Your Hazardous Wastes, Second Edition	2002	$89
841	Risk Management Planning Handbook, 2nd Edition	2002	$115

PC #	SAFETY and HEALTH TITLES	Pub Date	Price*
843	Emergency Preparedness for Facilities	2003	$125
814	Fundamentals of Occupational Safety & Health, Third Edition	2003	$79
838	Managing Chemical Safety	2002	$95
947	Safety Metrics	2003	$85

Government Institutes

4 Research Place, Suite 200 • Rockville, MD 20850-3226
Tel. (301) 921-2323 • FAX (301) 921-0264
Email: giinfo@govinst.com • www.govinst.com

Please call our customer service department at (301) 921-2323 for a free publications catalog.

CFRs now available online. Call (301) 921-2323 for info.

*All prices are subject to change; please call for current prices.

Government Institutes Order Form

4 Research Place, Suite 200 • Rockville, MD 20850-3226
Tel (301) 921-2323 • Fax (301) 921-0264
www.govinst.com • E-mail: giinfo@govinst.com

4 EASY WAYS TO ORDER

1. Tel: **(301) 921-2323**
Have your credit card ready when you call.

2. Fax: **(301) 921-0264**
Fax this completed order form with your company
purchase order or credit card information.

3. Mail: **Government Institutes**
ABSG Consulting Inc.
P.O. Box 915097
Dallas, TX 75391-5097 USA
Mail this completed order form with a check,
company purchase order, or credit card information.

4. Online: **Visit http://www.govinst.com**

PAYMENT OPTIONS

❏ **Check** *(payable in U.S. dollars to **ABSG Consulting Inc.**)*

❏ **Purchase Order** *(This order form must be attached to
your company P.O. <u>Note</u>: All International orders
must be prepaid.)*

❏ **Credit Card**

❏ ❏ ❏

Exp. ____ /____

Credit Card No. _____

Signature _____

(Federal I.D.# 13-2695912)

CUSTOMER INFORMATION

Ship To: (Please attach your purchase order)

Name: _____

GI Account # *(7 digits on mailing label):* _____

Company/Institution: _____

Address: _____
(Please supply street address for UPS shipping)
_____

City: _____ State/Province: _____

Zip/Postal Code: _____ Country: _____

Tel: ( ) _____

Fax: ( ) _____

E-mail Address: _____

Bill To: (if different from ship-to address)

Name: _____

Title/Position: _____

Company/Institution: _____

Address: _____
(Please supply street address for UPS shipping)
_____

City: _____ State/Province: _____

Zip/Postal Code: _____ Country: _____

Tel: ( ) _____

Fax: ( ) _____

E-mail Address: _____

Qty.	Product Code	Title	Price

30 Day Money-Back Guarantee
If you're not completely satisfied with any product, return it undamaged
within 30 days for a full and immediate refund on the price of the product.

Subtotal _____

Sales Tax (All U.S. local and state taxes apply; Canadian
orders must include 7% Goods and Service Tax)
_____

Shipping and Handling (see box below) _____

Total Payment Enclosed _____

SOURCE CODE: BP06

Shipping and Handling		
Within U.S:	1-4 products:	$6/product
	5 or more:	$4/product
Outside U.S:	Add $15 for each item	

ISBN 0-86587-962-1